Wissenschaftliche Untersuchungen
zum Neuen Testament · 2. Reihe

Herausgeber / Editor
Jörg Frey

Mitherausgeber / Associate Editors
Friedrich Avemarie · Judith Gundry-Volf
Martin Hengel · Otfried Hofius · Hans-Josef Klauck

220

Lars Kierspel

The Jews and the World in the Fourth Gospel

Parallelism, Function, and Context

Mohr Siebeck

Lars Kierspel, born 1972; 1998 Masters Degree from Freie Theologische Akademie in Gießen; 2006 Ph.D. from The Southern Baptist Theological Seminary in Louisville; Professor of New Testament at Trinity Bible College and Theological Seminary in Newburgh, Indiana.

ISBN 3-16-149069-X
ISBN-13 978-3-16-149069-9
ISSN 0340-9570 (Wissenschaftliche Untersuchungen zum Neuen Testament, 2. Reihe)

Die Deutsche Nationalbibliothek lists this publication in the Deutsche Nationalbibliographie; detailed bibliographic data is available in the Internet at *http://dnb.d-nb.de*.

The book was printed by Gulde-Druck in Tübingen on non-aging paper and bound by Buchbinderei Held in Rottenburg/N.

Printed in Germany.

With joyful praise
to my wife Laura.
Having you means
having God's favor
(Prov 18:22).

Preface

This book is an expanded form of my dissertation written in 2006 at The Southern Baptist Theological Seminary (Louisville, Kentucky) under the supervision of Dr. Mark A. Seifrid. Professor Udo Schnelle (Halle) did not only offer his service as the outside reader, but as a seasoned scholar he honored and encouraged a novice like me to publish this work. Though not a team-work in a narrow sense, its writing stands on the shoulders of many whom I owe gratitude. Hard to count is the number of scholars who have inspired, taught, challenged, and provoked me to further study and analysis mostly through their written works. How poor would my thinking be without the riches of Johannine scholarship that is fruitfully pursued beyond the boundaries of countries, continents, and denominations. The James P. Boyce Centennial Library and its helpful staff made it possible for me to gather this world of learning on my desk. Only decades of endless diligence are able to accumulate the treasures that I found here. The gracious support of my supervisor Dr. Mark Seifrid was a *sine qua non* for my thriving. John Simmons labored through the footnotes, caught many typos and offered valuable feedback. Tanja Mix patiently helped in matters of format. Special thanks are due to Professor Jörg Frey whose invitation for publication in the prestigious WUNT series is a great honor. As a first rank Johannine scholar and meticulous editor, he offered suggestions that earned my full attention. Finally, my wife Laura deserves my honest admiration. Not only did she willingly accept the burden of providing for us in general and for my studies in particular, but she offered her constant interest in the progress of my work and assistance in creating the indices. And if I sound less like the German foreigner that I am, it is because of her conscientious corrections with regard to English grammar and spelling. Endless praise be to God who has not just used all these people to bless my studies but also showered me with strength and joy during the long journey of research and writing.

Newburgh, Indiana, September 2006   Lars Kierspel

Table of Contents

The Fourth Gospel after the Holocaust

The past hundred years have been characterized as a "culture of death" or a "century of mega-death." State-sponsored genocides all across the globe have "claimed the lives of some 60 million people in the 20th century, 16 million of them since 1945."[1] This atrocious reality has led to a growing emphasis on the protection of human rights since the 1960s and to a sad new field of scientific study since the late 1970s: "Genocide Research."[2] Within this new awareness of global suffering through human hands, the history of violence from Christians as visible in the destruction of pagan religions and culture, crusades, witch-hunts, and inquisitions, their role in colonization and slavery, and particularly the persecution of Jewish people throughout church history occupies a place of major shame for the Church and critical interest for historians and theologians.[3] How was it possible, it is asked, that Christians developed a racial and religious hatred against Jews when the founder of their own faith was a Jew himself? More specifically, why was one out of two Jews in the last eight decades murdered in Europe, a continent rich in Christian heritage?[4] And finally,

---

[1] SMITH, "American Self-Interest," B6. A comprehensive attempt to describe all genocides of the twentieth century was undertaken by GELLATELY and KIERNAN, eds., *The Scepter of Genocide* (2003). After general reflections, the essays begin with "final solutions" against indigenous people under colonial rule (part II) and proceed with the era of the two World Wars (part III): the Armenian genocide in Turkey (1914–1915), the "great terror" in the Soviet Union (1937–38), the Holocaust (1941–1945), and in the post-1945 era (part IV): Indonesia (1965), Cambodia (1975–1979), Ethiopia, Rwanda (1994), Guatemala (1981 – 1983), former Yugoslavia (1991–1999). Strangely missing are the murder of two million Bengalis in Pakistan (1971) and Saddam Hussein's killing of about two-hundred thousand Kurdish people (1988). The number of human-instigated deaths in the twentieth century has to be nearly tripled, if we include the deaths of political dissidents under Communist rule (ca. sixty million in USSR and China) and babies in America that were aborted between 1973 and 2002 (ca. forty million).

[2] The *Journal of Genocide Research* is published since 1999 and edited by Henry R. Huttenbach.

[3] See DESCHNER, "Die unheilvollen Auswirkungen," 74-86. With regard to the history of Christian anti-Semitism, see FLANNERY (Catholic), *The Anguish of the Jews* (1964). CARROLL (Catholic), *Constantine's Sword* (2001). COHN-SHERBOCK (Jew), *The Crucified Jew* (1997). KEITH (Reformed), *Hated without a Cause?* (1997).

[4] BOROWSKY, "The Language of Religion," 8.

why did the extermination of European Jewry (Holocaust; also *Shoah*) occur in Germany, "the epicenter of 'Christian' Europe"[5] and a country with foundational significance for medieval, reformational and modern Christianity? This brings up the question if (and if so, to what extent) there is a link between these integrated institutions and traditions of German life and the causes of this diabolic genocide.[6] More than that, in light of a Christian anti-Judaism throughout the history of the Church,[7] the question has been raised if the Christian faith is inherently geared toward oppression of the Jews specifically, or if it was instrumentalized against its original intent and content.

It is this catalog of unsolved riddles which exposed German churches and theologians to the critical screening for anti-Semitic contents like every other sector of society since the Holocaust.[8] The Jewish-Christian

---

[5] RITTNER and ROTH, "Indifference to the Plight of the Jews During the Holocaust," 38.

[6] Just a few visible signs of compliance are, for example, pictures of Catholic clergy who give the Nazi salute, the formation of the centralized Protestant *German Church* under "Reichsbischof" Ludwig Müller, and the missing voice in defense of the Jews even in the "Barmen Confession" (1934) of the *Confessing Church* led by Martin Niemöller. Among theologians, Friedrich Delitzsch suggested already in 1902 to replace the Old Testament with tales of German heroes. Walter Grundmann argued in his *Jesus der Galiläer und das Judentum* (1940) that the ancestry of Jesus was Aryan, not Jewish. In 1945, Gerhard Kittel was dismissed from his teaching position, barred from ever entering Tübingen, and put into custody because of his support for the racist ideology of the national socialists (his *Die Judenfrage* was written in 1933, the year when Hitler seized power). See ERIKSEN, *Theologians under Hitler* (1985). MEEKS, "A Nazi New Testament Professor Reads His Bible," 513–44. Erich Sauer (*Das Morgenrot der Welterlösung*, 1937), an evangelical conservative theologian and the pillar of German dispensationalism at that time, saw in Hitler a divine instrument who would fulfill prophecy by bringing Jews back to their country, if necessary with force. He also adopted the common view of a Jewish conspiracy against the world and supported a German self-defense against this threat with reference to Noah's blessings (in Gen 9:25-27), which grant only spiritual blessings to the Semites, but world dominion to Japheth, the indo-German predecessor ("heilsgeschichtliches Rassenprogramm"). His views were not uncommon among conservative Christians. These are examples of a phenomenon that Alan T. Davies called the "nazification of Christianity." DAVIES, "The Aryan Christ," 569-79.

[7] Only a few works will be mentioned here. For the early church, see WILLIAMS, *Adversus Judaeos* (1935); SCHRECKENBERG, *Die christlichen Adversus-Judaeos-Texte* (1999). For the Middle Ages, see JOURNET, *The Church of the Word Incarnate* (1956); SYNAN, *The Popes and the Jews in the Middle Ages* (1965). For the time of the Reformation, see OBERMAN, *The Roots of Anti-Semitism in the Age of Renaissance and Reformation*, (1984). SPÄTH, *Luther und die Juden* (2001). For the modern era, see FLANNERY, *The Anguish of the Jews*, 145-267. COHN-SHERBOCK, *The Crucified Jew*, 113-221. KEITH, *Hated Without a Cause?*, 195-263.

[8] The discussion about the role of the Catholic Church in World War II is far from over. Passionate contributions fuel the debate with strong opinions on both sides. See, for

dialogue since World War II formed new paradigms in biblical studies that respond to these challenging questions by emphasizing the continuity between Judaism and Christianity. This begins with a new respect for the "value of the books of the Hebrew Scriptures in their own right, not merely as a backdrop for New Testament teaching."[9] In searching for the "historical Jesus," the so-called "Third Quest" is distinguished from earlier phases of research by "laying a clear emphasis and stress on the Jewishness of Jesus."[10] The "New Perspective" in Pauline studies focuses on the law as a positive element of the New Covenant.[11] Images of the

---

example, GOLDHAGEN as an accuser in *A Moral Reckoning* (2002). The conciliar document *Nostra Aetate* from 1965, on the other hand, does not confess any joint responsibility in the German genocide of the Jews. The statement is nevertheless regarded as the reason for a sea change in relationships between Catholics and Jews because it affirms that "the Jews remain very dear to God" and, with regard to Christ's crucifixion, we read that "neither all Jews indiscriminately at that time, nor Jews today, can be charged with the crimes committed during his passion." See *Vatican Council II*, 741. LÖW thoroughly documents the anti-Christian, especially anti-Catholic, politics of Hitler's government in *Die Schuld* (2002). The most important documentation about the role of the Protestant Church during WWII by Klaus Scholder is still unfinished. His two volumes end with the year 1934. SCHOLDER, *Die Kirchen und das Dritte Reich. Bd. 1: Vorgeschichte und Zeit der Illusionen 1918–1934, Bd. 2: Das Jahr der Ernüchterung 1934* (1977). His student Gerhard BESIER covered the following years until 1937 in *Die Kirchen und das Dritte Reich. Bd. 3.: Spaltungen und Abwehrkämpfe 1934–1937* (2001).

[9] PAWLIKOWSKI, "Accomplishments and Challenges," 30. German OT commentaries in the series Herders Theologischer Kommentar zum AT, edited since 1999 by the Catholic scholar Erich Zenger (Münster), are responding to the "rediscovery of the theological dignity of Judaism as the first address of the Hebrew Bible" in the last thirty years of ecumenical discourse. ZENGER, "Exegese des Alten Testaments," 357-58 (translation mine). They follow a "Christian/Jewish discourse-hermeneutic" with a theocentric (as opposed to christocentric) focus. Ibid., 359.

[10] See THEISSEN, MERZ, *The Historical Jesus*, 10. HOLMÉN, "The Jewishness of Jesus in the 'Third Quest'," 144. See his note 5 for a long list of literature between the end of the 1970s and 1997. Holmén continues to show that the 'Third Quest' is in a "state of turmoil" because it is "not the least clear what 'Jewishness' means." Ibid., 156, 154. Thus Jesus is portrayed by different scholars as an eschatological prophet (Sanders), a political revolutionary (Maccoby), a magician (M. Smith), a Hillelite Jew (Falk), someone with non-eschatological views (Borg), a Cynic philosopher (Crossan), a sage (Witherington), a social prophet (Horsley), or one with apocalyptic ideas (Rowland). Ibid., 154.

[11] Pawlikowski mentions scholars such as E. P. Sanders, James D. G. Dunn, Alan Segal, and Lloyd Gaston. He summarizes the new insight as follows, "In fact, some scholars are now persuaded that Paul likely favored the continuation of Torah practice among Jewish Christians. And should a Gentile Christian freely decide to undertake Torah observance there is nothing in Pauline teaching, as now interpreted, to suggest that such a person would be endangering their faith or salvation. Hence, the traditional contrast between Judaism as a religion of law and Christianity as a religion of

Pharisees[12] and of Judas,[13] both usually regarded as *the* representatives of Judaism in later Christianity, are thoroughly revised as well.

While most of these projects operate under the premise of preventing the misuse of Scripture, a strong tradition of so-called "post-Holocaust theology" emerged over the last fifty years which regards the New Testament itself as contaminated, first with supersessionism, and second with racial hatred against the Jews in general, the killers of Christ ("deicide").[14] The Jewish

---

freedom/grace is profoundly simplistic." PAWLIKOWSKI, "Accomplishments and Challenges," 32, 33.

[12] At least two large monographs about the understanding of Pharisees in the history of Jewish and Christian research were recently published: In his historical analysis of research about the Pharisees from 1860 to the beginning of WWII, Roland Deines explains a twofold change of paradigm in the last years. Theologically, the Pharisees are exonerated from accusations such as "legalistic" and "works-righteousness" (cf. E. P. Sanders). Historically, the Jewish history before AD 70 is re-evaluated. Today the emphasis lies on the pluralism and diversity of Judaisms in the first century AD (e.g., J. Neusner) whereas, Jewish and Christian scholars at the beginning of the twentieth century viewed early Judaism as normative and pharisaic (see Jewish works by Graetz, Kohler, Lauterbach, Montefiore, Abrahams, Baeck, Klausner, Buber). Montefiore speculates even that "five-sixth of the nation were pharisaic more or less, though where and how the limits ran it is hard to say." DEINES, *Die Pharisäer*, 367; cf. 9-11, 184, 313, 333, 371, 493, 495-96, 502. Deines himself supports the older paradigm by regarding pharisaism as a "Bewegung *im* Volk *für* das Volk, deren Rechtmäßigkeit von weitesten Teilen des Volkes auch *akzeptiert* wurde, wenn auch die Forderungen derselben nicht im gleichen Maße *praktiziert* wurden." Ibid., 512. Josephus certainly lends credence for this evaluation according to whom the Pharisees have influence over the "multitude" (πλῆθος; *A.J.* 13.288, 408; 18.17), "the nation" (ἔθνος, *A.J.* 13.401) and "the cities" (αἱ πόλεις, *A.J.* 18.11) and who could oppose the king (*A.J.* 17.41; cf. *B.J.* 1.112). If it is true that Pharisees represent the essence of Judaism before and after AD 70, then Jesus' denunciation of them as "hypocrites" could be understood as a qualification of second temple Judaism in general. So at least according to Brumlik's often quoted comment that a rejection of a theologically inspired Christian anti-Judaism is impossible without rehabilitating the Pharisees. BRUMLIK, *Der Anti-Alt*, 63. The second recent monograph about the Pharisees by Waubke opens with Brumlik's statement and supports the new paradigm of diversity within Judaism in contrast to Deines. WAUBKE, *Die Pharisäer*, 1-4. See also chap. 2 n. 19.

[13] Böttrich notices that the "jüngeren Arbeiten über Judas sind wesentlich von dem Bestreben einer Rehabilitierung bestimmt gewesen. Einen wichtigen Impuls hat dafür sicher auch der jüdisch-christliche Dialog der letzten Jahrzehnte vermittelt." BÖTTRICH, "Judas Iskarioth zwischen Historie und Legende," 54. He points to LIMBECK, "Das Judasbild im Neuen Testament," 37-101. Recently, KLASSEN, *Judas* (1996) exposed the traditional vilification of Judas by tracing popular images of this disciple to medieval legends that have little in common with the information we are given in the Gospels.

[14] Only a few works can be mentioned as landmarks in this tradition: Besides the contributions from Elie Wiesel, Richard Rubenstein, Eliezer Berkovits, and Emil Fackenheim, see especially ISAAC, *Jesus and Israel* (1971, orig. 1948) and SIMON, *Verus Israel* (1986, orig. 1948); RUETHER, *Faith and Fratricide* (1974). Ruether shifts gears in

historian Daniel Goldhagen, for example, counted recently about 450 anti-Jewish texts in the Gospels and Acts alone.[15] Thus, it is said that both claims provided a necessary (though not sufficient) condition, background, preparation and motivation for the Holocaust,[16] thus minimizing, if not eliminating, a crucial distinction between 'anti-Judaism' and 'anti-Semitism.'[17] As a consequence, the demand is put on Christian leaders,

---

the post-Holocaust debate and claims that anti-Judaism is the "left hand" of New Testament Christology. See further WILLIAMSON, *A Guest in the House of Israel* (1993); BECK, *Mature Christianity in the 21st Century* (1994); TOMSON, *'If this be from Heaven'* (2001). GAGER explains the beginnings of a post-Holocaust theology briefly in *The Origins of Antisemitism*, 13-23. In his long "Exkurs: Israel und die Kirche," Reventlow discusses many important declarations and documents about Christians, the New Testament, and the Holocaust, issued by various European and American churches. REVENTLOW, *Hauptprobleme der Biblischen Theologie im 20. Jahrhundert*, 67-124. Birte PETERSEN sketches the history and the questions of the post-Holocaust theology in *Theologie nach Auschwitz?* (2004). Other current contributors to this tradition include Samuel Sandmel, Paul M. Van Buren, Eugene J. Fisher, and George M. Smiga in the Anglo-Saxon world. Important German post-Holocaust theologians are, among others, Franz Mußner, Peter von der Osten-Sacken, Friedrich W. Marquardt, Berthold Klappert, Rolf Rendtorff, and Erich Zenger. A helpful annotated bibliography, listing biblical studies on this topic as well as ecclesiastical statements, theological, educational, and liturgical resources, is offered by BOYS and SMITH, "A Select, Annotated Bibliography on Jewish-Christian Relations," 600-20. For recent theological contributions, see GROHMANN, "Judentum und Christentum" 151-81; FISCHEL and ORTMANN, *The Holocaust and Its Religious Impact* (2004).

[15] GOLDHAGEN, *A Moral Reckoning*, 263-65.

[16] ROTH, "What does the Holocaust have to do with Christianity?," 6, 7. Roth links this claim with the demand of a "Christian re-identification after the Holocaust," subjecting Christian theology to an "'ideological critique'" which purges the Church from the "Christian 'teaching of contempt.'" Ibid., 9, 38, 40.

[17] The term 'anti-Semitism,' which was coined by the German journalist Wilhelm Marr the 1870s, refers to hatred against the Jews as a race, while 'anti-Judaism' rejects Judaism as a way to salvation but does not *necessarily* include violent hostility against Jews as a people. Many if not most Christians believe that Christianity is an exclusive religion. But they do not engage in persecuting those of other beliefs and to assume so would be utterly unjust. Maybe the "dividing line . . . is a fine one, as they are often intermingled." FLANNERY, *The Anguish of the Jews*, xiv. And although the term was coined late, the reality of (even genocidal) anti-Semitism certainly predates the 19th century and existed even before and beside the early Church (see, for example, Esth 3:8, 13; Add Esth 13:3-7; Jdt 10:19; 1 Macc 12:53; 13:6; 2 Macc 8:9; Tac., *His.* 5.5.1; Irenaeus, *Heresies* 1.24.2). But for the authors of the New Testament the dividing line between them and other groups were defined on *religious* terms. The contrast to anti-Semitism is dramatic because here we find the premise, in Nazi terminology, that 'die Religion ist einerlei - in der Rasse liegt die Schweinerei.' "Therefore, the anti-Jews seek Jewish conversion. The anti-Semites seek Jewish death. For them, nothing less will do since they view Jews as 'Ungeziefer,' vermin whose nature cannot change and whose 'crimes' are the consequence of racial characteristics." So FALK, *The Jew in Christian*

educators and theologians to liberate the Church and the Jewish-Christian dialogue from the fountain of oppression[18] by eliminating anti-Jewish texts from the New Testament (polemics); by understanding Jesus as a reformer within Judaism[19] and thus by reducing the "Christ of faith" to the Jesus of history, the "Jewish brother" who preached not himself but God; by purging Christianity from exclusive claims (Christology);[20] by revising the passion

---

Theology, 50. Unless we oversimplify causal connections and ignore evidence contrary to quick conclusions, we have to maintain a distinction between (polemic) disagreement of ideas and murderous hatred. See also the discussion in *Anti-Semitism and Early Christianity*, 128-30, 171.

[18] Williamson explains that "Post-Holocaust theologians share with other theologians concerned to liberate theology from its inherited ideologies an awareness that it is not just 'that scripture has been used to legitimate oppression (although this is a continuing problem), but that the Bible itself is both a product and a producer of oppression, that some of its content is oppressive' (Schneiders). We are concerned not only to retrieve the Christian tradition but also to submit it to a hermeneutic of suspicion, to de-ideologize it by disengaging it from the political, social, economic, and cultural injustices that it has been used to condone." WILLIAMSON, *A Guest in the House of Israel*, 15.

[19] Pawlikowski describes this understanding as a development away from the "Bultmannian perspective" which tried to "distance Jesus from his concrete ties to biblical and Second Temple Judaism so that he could emerge as a decidedly more 'universal' person." Scholars mentioned as architects of the new perspective about Jesus and Judaism are, among others, W. D. Davies, E. P. Sanders, Clemens Thoma, Cardinal Carlo Martini of Milan, James Charlesworth, Daniel Harrington, and Robin Scroggs. PAWLIKOWSKI, "Accomplishments and Challenges," 31.

[20] Borowitz made the following observation: "Nothing so divides Judaism and Christianity as the Christian doctrine of Christ." BOROWITZ, *Contemporary Christologies*, 1. Williamson and Allen describe four themes of Christian anti-Jewish preaching, among which is "the displacement/replacement theme, that might also be called the 'salvation through Jesus Christ alone' motif." WILLIAMSON and ALLEN, "Interpreting Difficult Texts," 40. Under the headline "The Post-Holocaust Critique of Christology" in his dissertation, Fuller discusses the works of Michael J. Cook, Hyam Maccoby, Eugene B. Borowitz, and Michael Wyschogrod. FULLER, "Contemporary Judaic Perceptions of Jesus," 154-214. For Thyen, an interpretation of John 14:6 as exclusivism is rooted in the ages of imperialism and hinders the unity of Jews and Christians, as desired and expressed by Jesus in his last words to his mother and the beloved disciple (19:25-27). Thyen thinks that John 14:6 wants to say only that the way to the Father is the way of martyrdom. THYEN, "Das Johannes-Evangelium als Literarisches Werk," 112, 130, 131. Franz Rosenzweig explained with regard to John 14:6 that Jews do not have to "come to the Father" because they are already there. Mayer follows Rosenzweig and rejects mission efforts to the Jews who began recently to resettle in Germany. MAYER, "'Ich bin der Weg, die Wahrheit und das Leben'," 183-95, esp. 194-95. Charlesworth calls John 14:6 an "exceptional embarrassment to Christians who are seeking a fruitful dialogue with persons of other religions, especially Jews." He argues that 14:6b is "redactional and misrepresents Jesus' purpose." CHARLESWORTH, "The Gospel of John," 259, 261. Koester turns the charge of exclusivism around by reasoning that "it would be exclusivistic to say that Jesus is the way for some but not all,

narratives which blame the Jews and exonerate Pilate;[21] and by maintaining the validity of God's covenant with Israel and therefore limiting the Christian mission effort to the Gentiles alone (ecclesiology). Some of these demands lead far away from traditional Christianity, and scholars of various backgrounds have responded critically.[22]

In this quest for new ways of relating the daughter church to the mother synagogue, the Fourth Gospel received more attention than any other book of

---

for it would mean that Jesus reveals God's love only for some but not for all." KOESTER, "Jesus as the Way to the Father in Johannine Theology (John 14,6)," 133.

[21] Sanders explains that Jesus was crucified because of legitimate concern about a riot in Jerusalem. Misunderstandings or theological differences between Jesus and Pharisees played no role. The Gospels' presentation of Pilate as someone who pleaded for Jesus and hesitated to crucify him stems from "Christian propaganda" that desires "to get along with Rome and to depict Jews as their real opponents." The real Pilate, as described by Philo and Josephus, regarded Jesus as "a religious fanatic whose fanaticism had become so extreme that it posed a threat to law and order." SANDERS, *The Historical Figure of Jesus*, 268-69, 273-74. Sanders downplays theological causes because he reduces the influence of the Pharisees and thus the importance of their *halakhah* for the nation. See DEINES, *Die Pharisäer*, 322. Paula Fredriksen explains that "viewing the matter [of Jesus' death sentence] as primarily between the priests and Jesus only increases the difficulty in seeing why Pilate would have executed him by crucifixion." FREDRIKSEN, *Jesus of Nazareth, King of the Jews*, 226. In her view, Pilate knew that Jesus posed "no first-order political threat," but the people who hailed him as king saw in him a messianic pretender. Thus Pilate chose crucifixion as a method of deterring the crowd and thus preventing a riot. Ibid., 254, 255. See also CROSSAN, *Who Killed Jesus?* (1995). Idem, *The Roots of Anti-Semitism in the Gospel Story of the Death of Jesus* (1995). PATTERSON, "The Dark Side of Pilate," 32-37, 47-48. Stegemann denies any direct or indirect Jewish influence on the crucifixion of Jesus. STEGEMANN, "Gab es eine jüdische Beteiligung an der Kreuzigung Jesu?," 3-24. For a critical discussion of Stegemann's thesis, see SÄNGER, "'Auf Betreiben'," 1-25. Noticing that the Talmud (see *b. Sanh.* 106a) and Maimonides' *Mishneh Torah* largely agree with the Gospels' passion accounts, the Jewish intellectual David Klinghoffer writes, "To say that Jewish leaders were instrumental in getting Jesus killed is *not* anti-Semitic. Otherwise we would have to call the medieval Jewish sage Moses Maimonides anti-Semitic and the rabbis of the Talmud as well." KLINGHOFFER, *Why the Jews Rejected Jesus*, 72-73.

[22] See especially EVANS and HAGNER, eds., *Anti-Semitism and Early Christianity* (1993). With regard to the Gospel of John, at least the following authors do not side with the view of post-Holocaust theology for various reasons (for literature see bibliography): Michaels, Leistner, Harrington, Segovia, Kysar, Kaufmann, D. M. Smith, Motyer, Rensberger, Wahlde, Dunn, de Jonge, de Boer, and Marrow. In critical response to Jules Isaác, the Catholic Gregory BAUM argued against the presence of anti-Judaism in the New Testament in his book *The Jews and the Gospel* (1961). Later, the same book was given a different title: *Is the New Testament Anti-Semitic?* (1965). After a while, Baum changed his mind, and we read in his foreword to Ruether's *Faith and Fratricide* (1974) that "the Church has produced an abiding contempt among Christians for Jews and all things Jewish, a contempt that aided Hitler's purposes." RUETHER, *Faith and Fratricide*, 7.

the New Testament. Its generalizing language about "the Jews," the Johannine way of applying texts and traditions of Judaism to Jesus (cf. 2:18-22, 4:21-23, 6:32),[23] the strong polemic in 8:44 ("You are of your father the devil")[24] and the peculiarities of the trial account have preoccupied many theologians not only in the context of a post-Holocaust theology. At the beginning of the twentieth century (in 1905) the American Rabbi, scholar, and one of the editors of *The Jewish Encyclopedia*, Kaufmann Kohler, understood the Fourth Gospel already as "a gospel of Christian love and Jew hatred."[25] In his commentary from 1908, Julius Wellhausen speaks of the Gospel's "deep hatred against the nation that crucified Jesus and persecuted his disciples."[26] In his *Studien zum vierten Evangelium* from 1936, Emanuel Hirsch traces the Gospel's sources back to, among others, a "strongly anti-Jewish gospel" X which the evangelist employed to create the "beautiful" idea of an opposition between Jews and Gentiles.[27] The *Expository Times* observed in 1938 that the Nazis used the Fourth Gospel as "a favourite text-book of anti-Jewish propaganda."[28] Even after WW II, Eldon Epp makes the bold statement in 1975 that

---

[23] See discussion and literature in Scholtissek, "Antijudaismus," 171-77.

[24] All Scripture quotations are taken from the New American Standard Version unless otherwise noted. Grant postulates that the New Testament is infected with pre-Christian anti-Semitism as a literary response of retaliation for the persecution and exclusion of believers from the Synagogue. The Gospel of John, particularly the polemic against the Jews in John 8:44, is the climax of this development. GRANT, *An Introduction to New Testament Thought*, 94. Vollenweider discusses three texts as examples of anti-Judaism in the New Testaments (1 Thess 2:14-16, Matt 27:20-26 and John 8:37-47) of which the latter qualifies as the strongest statement against the Jews ("die schärfsten Aussagen des Neuen Testaments über die Juden"). VOLLENWEIDER, "Antijudaismus im Neuen Testament," 44. Tomson comments with regard to John's diabolizing language in 8:44, "Put provocatively, *John 8 is the classical starting point for Christian hatred for the Jews*." TOMSON, '*If this be from Heaven*', 402 (italics his). For further discussion, see REIM, "Joh 8,44 – Gotteskinder / Teufelskinder," 619-24. FREEMAN, "The Function of Polemic in John 7 and 8" (1991). PEDERSEN, "Anti-Judaism in John's Gospel: John 8," 172-93. REINHARTZ, "John 8:31-59 from a Jewish Perspective," 213-27. HASITSCHKA, "Joh 8,44 im Kontext des Gesprächsverlaufes von Joh 8,21-59," 109-16.

[25] KOHLER, "New Testament," 9:251. The teachings of Jesus are summed up in the love-commandment, "and yet this teaching of love is combined with the most intense hatred of the kinsmen of Jesus." Ibid.

[26] WELLHAUSEN, *Das Evangelium Johannis*, 117 ("tiefe Hass gegen das Volk, das Jesum kreuzigte und seine Jünger verfolgte.")

[27] HIRSCH, *Studien*, 135. Hirsch says literally, "Es ist bei R[edaktor] hier auch etwas Schönes herausgekommen, ein Gegenbild von Griechen und Juden nach ihrem Verhältnis zu Jesus." Ibid., 97. He calls Wellhausen one of his formative influences. Ibid, iv, 134.

[28] EVELYN, "The Supra-Racial Gospel," 419. Windisch wrote in 1933, "Eine gewisse Vorliebe zeigen manche Feinde des Judentums für das Johannesevangelium, weil hier der Kampf des Christus ganz wesentlich als ein Kampf gegen die Juden geführt wird."

the Fourth Gospel, more than any other book in the canonical body of Christian writings, is responsible for the frequent anti-Semitic expressions by Christians during the past eighteen or nineteen centuries and particularly for the unfortunate and still existent characterization of the Jewish people by some Christians as "Christ-killers."[29]

An abundance of intellectual and financial resources has been invested into conferences and long research projects which looked at all the issues involved.[30] This study will attempt to understand and evaluate the discussion about the frequent term 'Ιουδαῖος in the Fourth Gospel. The

---

WINDISCH, "Das johanneische Christentum," 99. Windisch writes his article to show that, in contrast to contemporary anti-Semitism, the conflict with the Jews in the Fourth Gospel has nothing to do with race but with religion. Therefore, the Gospel's polemic (e.g., 8:44) is "completely useless" ("völlig unbrauchbar") for the political battles of the 1930s. Ibid., 105. In the midst of a "revival of anti-Semitism," Sikes writes in 1941 that, among all writings of the New Testament, "the Fourth Gospel is most often cited as proof that Christianity was itself originally anti-Semitic." SIKES, "The Anti-Semitism of the Fourth Gospel," 23. Sikes maintains that the evangelist "intends to attack not the Jewish race and culture but only the self-conscious national and religious community; that is, the *gesetzgetreu* Jews." Ibid., 24. In contrast to the Gospel of John, Paul's writings were often attacked for making Christianity Jewish. See the discussion about the "Reception of Paul during the Third Reich" in BELL, *The Irrevocable Call of God*, 355-61.

[29] EPP, "Anti-Semitism And the Popularity Of the Fourth Gospel In Christianity," 35. Leibig insists that the Fourth Gospel provides "a catalyst, a rationale, a theological base for future racial antipathy toward the Jewish people" and speaks of the Gospel's inherent "'anti-Semitic potential'." LEIBIG, "John and 'the Jews'," 227. The Jewish social scientist Brumlik thinks that the composers and redactors of the Gospel suffer from a severe case of paranoia which expresses itself in a persecution mania (because of 9:22; 12:42; etc.) and a proto-racist doctrine (in 8:43-47). BRUMLIK, "Johannes: Das judenfeindliche Evangelium," 103. Idem, "Johannes: Das Judenfeindliche Evangelium," in *Teufelskinder oder Heilsbringer*, 7, 9. Pippin talks about the "Christian hatred of Jews expressed in the Gospel of John. . . . the Gospel itself is anti-Jewish – the opening into a horrible abyss of persecution and genocide. . . . The naming and framing of the opposition in the Gospel of John is dangerous; religion, race, ethnicity and class intersect in 'the Jews'." PIPPIN, "'For Fear of the Jews'," 82.

[30] The book *Teufelskinder oder Heilsbringer – Die Juden im Johannes-Evangelium* (1990) is the result of a conference in Germany held in 1989 with regard to the topic "Das Johannes-Evangelium im christlich-jüdischen Dialog." A three year long research program from 1998 to 2001 was conducted at the Katholieke Universiteit Leuven (Belgium) and dealt with the "alleged anti-Judaism of the Gospel of John." It was concluded with an interdisciplinary academic seminar in the year 2000 in Leuven and the essays were collected in the book BIERINGER, POLLEFEYT, and VANDECASTEELE-VANNEUVILLE, eds., *Anti-Judaism and the Fourth Gospel* (2001). An American research project dealt with the question of "anti-Judaism and the Gospels," involving seventeen scholars and lasting from 1994 to 1997. The essays out of this endeavor were assembled in the volume FARMER, ed., *Anti-Judaism and the Gospels* (1999).

lexical form Ἰουδαῖος occurs seventy-one times in the Gospel in contrast to only five times in Matthew, seven times in Mark and five times in Luke[31] and is therefore particularly suspicious of polemic if not racist implications. Where the Synoptics single out the Jewish *leaders* as the perpetrators of Jesus' death, the Fourth Gospel speaks predominantly in this generalizing fashion, presenting the Jews as a homogeneous group.[32] It

---

[31] Matthew: 2:2; 27:11, 29, 37; 28:15. Mark: 1:5; 7:3; 15:2, 9, 12, 18, 26. Luke: 7:3; 23:3, 37, 38, 51. In the Gospel of John, Ἰουδαῖος is used 61x by the narrator, 4x by Jesus (4:22; 13:33; 18:20, 36), 2x by Pilate (18:39; 19:19), 2x by the Jews (19:21), 1x by the soldiers (19:3), 1x by the Samaritan woman (4:9).

[32] Many occurrences of Ἰουδαῖοι in John appear in material unique to this gospel, such as in the account about John the Baptist (1:19), the wedding in Cana (2:4), notes about Jewish customs and feasts (2:6, 13; 5:1; 6:4; 7:2; 19:40, 42 [cf. Luke 23:54]), the healing at the pool (5:10, 15-18), Jesus' appearance at the Feast of the Tabernacles (7:1, 2, 11, 13, 15, 35; 8:22, 31, 48, 52, 57), etc. In texts that have parallels in the Synoptics, John sometimes "adds" Ἰουδαῖοι (see 19:38 [cf. Matt 27:57]; 20:19 [cf. Luke 24:36]) or he "changes" terms: In the Synoptics Jesus defends his actions in the temple before οἱ ἀρχιερεῖς καὶ οἱ γραμματεῖς καὶ οἱ πρεσβύτεροι (Mark 11:27 par) but in John he is confronted by the Ἰουδαῖοι (2:18). In Luke, Pilate testifies to the innocence of Jesus πρὸς τοὺς ἀρχιερεῖς καὶ τοὺς ὄχλους (Luke 23:4), while in John he speaks πρὸς τοὺς Ἰουδαίους (John 18:38).

But the Synoptics are not free from generalizing language as well. In Crossan's reconstruction, Mark already created "both the open Passover amnesty, the shouting crowd, and its choice of Barabbas over Jesus." The "crowd" in Mark (15:8, 11, 15) then became "all the people" in Matthew (27:25) and finally "the Jews" in John (19:7). CROSSAN, "The Passion after the Holocaust," 176-79. In the Gospel of Matthew, John the Baptist preaches judgment against the Pharisees and Sadducees (Matt 3:7-10). But in the Gospel of Luke, the same message with exactly the same wording is addressed to the "crowds" (ὄχλοις, 3:7). Especially the speeches of Acts emphatically assert the people's responsibility for the death of Jesus (e.g., Acts 2:23, 36; 3:13-15; 10:39; 13:27-29). See the discussion by Weatherly who tries to argue that these texts (and also the meaning of Ἰουδαῖοι in Acts) suggest a limited "indictment to the people of Jerusalem only." WEATHERLY, *Jewish Responsibility for the Death of Jesus in Luke-Acts*, 83; see pp.82-90. Besides the woes against religious leaders, Haufe examines words of judgment against whole cities (Luke 10:13-15 and Matt 11:21-23; 13:34-35 and Matt 23:37-39) and sayings about all Israel (cf. "this generation" in Luke 7:31-35 and Matt 11:16-19; Luke 11:29-35 and Matt 12:38-42; Luke 11:49-51 and Matt 23:34-36; also Luke 13:28-29 and Matt 8:11-12). Haufe understands these statements as situational polemics from frustrated Christian missionaries and not as ideological anti-Judaism and evaluates, "Mit grundsätzlichem Antijudaismus hat die Haltung der Q-Gemeinde nichts zu tun." HAUFE, "Israel-Polemik in Q," 67. Furthermore, in Matthew "the multitude" (ὄχλος) is an active agent in the passion of Jesus (27:15, 20, 24) to such an extent that πᾶς ὁ λαὸς speaks a curse on itself, "His blood be on us and our children" (27:25). For a comparison of the Synoptic passion accounts, see SUHL, "Beobachtungen zu den Passionsgeschichten der synoptischen Evangelien," 321-77; with regard to Matthew, see 343-53. Suhl explains that a reading of the curse as grounds for anti-Semitism is "eine Perversion des von Matthäus Gemeinten" because the curse was already fulfilled in the destruction of Jeruis "the Jews" who were persecuting Jesus (5:16) and "the Jews" tried to kill him (5:18; 7:1; cf. 7:19, 20, 25; 11:53; 18:31). Since Abraham's descendants attempted to murder Jesus (8:37, 40), they have the devil as their father (8:44). On two occasions "the Jews" tried to stone Jesus (8:59; 10:31) and it was "the Jews" who "were grumbling about him" (6:41). People lived in "fear of the Jews" (7:13; 9:22; 19:38; 20:19) since they were threatened with the exclusion from the synagogue if they followed Jesus (9:22; 12:42; 16:2). Statements such as these explain George Smiga's response: "It is his use of 'the Jews' more than any other factor which has made John a prime candidate for the most overtly anti-Jewish account in the gospels."[33] Some modern English and German translations of the Fourth Gospel since the 1970s responded to this charge in three ways: the omission of the term altogether or the narrowing of the referent either to a small subgroup of "Jewish leaders / authorities" or to "Judeans.[34] Do these decisions improve our interpretation of the text or do

---

salem in AD 70 (ibid., 348). Not only do we find polemic directed against groups and Israel in the Synoptics, but John himself makes specific references to Pharisees (cf. 4:1; 7:47, 48; 8:13; 9:13, 15, 16, 40) or Pharisees and chief priests (7:32, 45; 11:47, 57; 18:3) as the perpetrators of Jesus' death. Thus the differences between John and the Synoptics are not clear-cut, and the data is complex.

[33] SMIGA, *Pain and Polemic*, 139-40. The Jewish scholar Reinhartz, daughter of Holocaust survivors, shared that when she read the Gospel of John for the first time, "Each Johannine usage of the term *Jew* felt like a slap in the face." REINHARTZ, "'Jews' and Jews in the Fourth Gospel," 213. Tomson reiterates that the "anti-Jewish attitude of the Gospel is clear from its indiscriminate designation of Jesus' enemies as 'the Jews'." TOMSON, *Presumed Guilty*, 110. All of part II in *Anti-Judaism and the Fourth Gospel* (2001) is reserved for the discussion of the Ἰουδαῖοι and presents five essays to this issue. Simon writes, "There is no shadow of anti-Semitism in St. Paul. . . . Anti-Jewish feeling is manifest in the Fourth Gospel, where the word *Jew* takes on a pejorative sense." SIMON, *Verus Israel*, 207. The Third Commission of the International Emergency Conference of Christians and Jews met 1947 in Seelisberg, Switzerland, and wrote the document "Ten Points of Seelisberg" in order to prevent Christians from using their own Scriptures against the Jewish people. Point no. 6 possibly alludes to a certain interpretation of the Gospel of John, "Avoid using the word 'Jews' in the exclusive sense of 'the enemies of Jesus,' and the words 'the enemies of Jesus' to designate the whole Jewish people." Quoted from the appendix of ISAAC, *Jesus and Israel*, 405.

[34] See Appendix 1 and 2 for a comparison of different English and German translations of Ἰουδαῖος. The three trends mentioned above are especially present in the GNT (1976), JNT (1989), CEV (1995), NLT (1996), NET (2000), the TNIV (2002), furthermore in the *Hoffnung für alle* (1996), *Gute Nachricht* (1997), *Münchener NT* (1998), and *Neues Leben* (2002). The committee of the CEV, which omits the term more than any other translation (34 times!), was influenced by the founder of the American Interfaith Institute (1982) and Jewish businessman Irvin J. Borowsky, who made it his mission to change the rendering of "the Jews" in future editions of the New Testament. See BOROWSKY, "The Language of Religion," 7-10. The same conclusion comes in the

they create a new "rewritten Bible" altogether? The question is if reference, meaning and function of Ἰουδαῖος in the Fourth Gospel actually *intend* to teach Christian hatred and condemnation of the Jews. To say that the Gospel has "anti-Semitic *potential*"[35] does not clarify the issue since communication is loaded with complexities and all disagreements, small or significant, can develop into hate and conflict. Our human mind is prone to distort and invent, to blow out of proportion, to blame and to create the rationale for its own wicked intent. Therefore, a text-oriented approach to the matter has to insist on finding subtle or obvious features *in the Gospel itself* that deserve the blame or merit vindication. It is our main contention that "the Jews" are paralleled throughout the Gospel with "the world" which makes humanity in general, including Gentiles, the main antagonist against Jesus and the disciples. This view renders a literalist reading and racist interpretation of "the Jews" as a grave mistake.

This study is structured as follows: Chapter 1 reviews five interpretations of the Ἰουδαῖοι in the Fourth Gospel, twelve dissertations to the topic, and concludes with methodical reflections for our own study. Chapter 2 discusses various nuances of the term "the Jews" in the Gospel in order to grasp its range of connotations. Chapter 3 describes various parallel positions of Ἰουδαῖοι and κόσμος in the Gospel (compositional, narratological, and conceptual) and exposes the tight link between both terms. Chapter 4 inquires about the function of this parallelism within the macro-structure and micro-structure of the Gospel. In chapter 5 we first evaluate three different proposals about the relationship between the Ἰουδαῖοι and κόσμος and then discuss the possible historical context which best fits the results of our textual analysis. Our study ends with a conclusion, two appendices, and a bibliography.

---

form of an exegetical and text-critical argument which regards "the Jews" in the Gospel as "pointless additions to the narratives" that go back to anti-Jewish contamination through scribal glosses. So O'NEILL, "The Jews in the Fourth Gospel," 58, 74. The HCSB (2000) and the ESV (2001) continue the traditional rendering with "the Jews" among modern translations. The rendering of Ἰουδαῖος with "Jewish" and few omissions such as those of JB in 9:22; 19:21, 42 seem to have stylistic rather than theological reasons (similarly also, for example, the NIV's omission of ὄχλος in Matt 14:23 and of γραμματεύς in Mark 12:32). All translations render the feminine adjective in 3:22 (τὴν Ἰουδαίαν γῆν) as "Judea." Therefore this instance does not relate to our question.

[35] CULPEPPER, "Anti-Judaism in the Fourth Gospel," 66, 67.

CHAPTER 1

History of Research and Method

This chapter first describes and discusses critically five proposals for the translation and interpretation of the Ἰουδαῖοι in the Gospel of John. We will then examine followed by reflections about our method.

1. Various Proposals for the Meaning of "the Jews"

The last twenty years have seen a host of studies that use a variety of methods for understanding reference and function of the term "the Jews."[1] We will review the proposals from the narrowest to the broadest ones.

1.1. Religious Authorities

Terry L. Schram observed in 1974 that "modern translators have no difficulty in deciding which English lexical item to use to represent *Ioudaios* in modern translations" by choosing "the Jews" as the proper English equivalent.[2] In his review of more recent research between 1983 and 1998, von Wahlde witnessed a significant change when he stated that "the majority of scholars have also concluded that the term refers exclusively to religious authorities,"[3] a new consensus displayed in various

---

[1] VON WAHLDE provides us with a detailed survey for the time between 1983 and 1998 in "'The Jews' in the Gospel of John," 30-55. He organizes the article by the methods that were employed: (1) Narrative Criticism (R. A. Culpepper; Gérald Caron; R. Kysar; S. Motyer); (2) Social Science Criticism (Malina/Rohrbaugh). (3) Psycho-logical Approach (W. Pratscher; S. Brown); (4) Traditional Historical Critical Approach (D. M. Smith; J. L. Martyn; M. Rissi); (5) Textual Criticism (J. C. O'Neill).
[2] SCHRAM, "The Use of ΙΟΥΔΑΙΟΣ in the Fourth Gospel," 31.
[3] VON WAHLDE, "'The Jews' in the Gospel of John," 44. Even von Wahlde himself thinks that not just some but all 71 occurrences of οἱ Ἰουδαῖοι refer to "religious authorities," the only exception being 6:41-52. Ibid., 39, 45. Commenting on 1:19, Tholuck maintained already in 1837, "οἱ Ἰουδαῖοι bei Johannes Bezeichnung der Volksrepräsentanten C. 5, 15. 7, 11." THOLUCK, *Commentar zum Evangelio Johannis*, 67. See also EVELYN, "The Supra-Racial Gospel," 421. In 1974, the Catholic Church issued the document "Guidelines on religious relations with the Jews" which explains, among other things, that "the formula 'the Jews' in St. John, sometimes according to the context

modern English and German Bible translations (e.g., GNT, NLT, CEV, NET, TNIV).[4] Several observations might have contributed to that change.

The first occurrence of οἱ Ἰουδαῖοι is found in 1:19, which says, "The Jews sent to him priests and Levites from Jerusalem to ask him 'Who are you?'" One wonders who else has the authority to commission those priests and Levites for this interrogation, if not Jewish religious authorities.[5] The same thought is entertained with regard to the

---

means 'the leaders of the Jews,' or 'the adversaries of Jesus,' terms which express better the thought of the evangelist and avoid appearing to arraign the Jewish people as such." *Vatican Council II*, 746 n. 1. Also HENGEL, *Die johanneische Frage*, 297. TSUCHIDO, "Is There Anti-Semitism in the Fourth Gospel?" 68, 71. BEASLEY-MURRAY, *John*, lxxxix, 62, 332 (but see also 270, 276). DUNN, "The Embarassment of History," 54. De Boer says with regard to John 8 that this term serves as an "acknowledgment of the claim on the part of Jewish authorities in the synagogue to be the authoritative arbiters of a genuinely Jewish identity." DE BOER, "The Depiction," 148, 142. The *Greek-English Lexicon* lists the following entries for Ἰουδαῖος, "1. as a real adj., 'Jewish.' 2. as a noun a) the Jew, b) the Jewess, c) the Jews, d) Jewish Christians, e) in John the Ἰουδαῖοι are the enemies of Jesus." BAUER, *A Greek-English Lexicon of the New Testament*, 379. In the new third edition, F. W. DANKER adds the following meaning for Ἰουδαῖος, "Those who are in opposition to Jesus, with special focus on hostility emanating from leaders in Jerusalem, center of Israelite belief and cult; there is no indication that John uses the term in the general ethnic sense suggested in modern use of the word 'Jew.'" In *BDAG*, 479.

[4] See Appendix 1 and 2 for a detailed comparison. *The Good News Translation* (formerly TEV 1966, 1976) renders the 71 occurrences of οἱ Ἰουδαῖοι in John as follows: 19x "Jewish authorities," always in texts with a negative meaning; 13x "Jews," only in texts with a positive or neutral meaning; a few times we find "Jewish" (3:1; 18:12; 19:40); also "Judea(ns)" (3:22; 11:19, 54). Surprisingly, the GNT omits the translation of the term in 33 instances or simply replaces it with "crowd" or "people," thereby eliminating any connection to a Jewish referent. We read for example, "So *they* began to persecute Jesus" (5:16) and "The *people* started grumbling about him" (6:41) and "Then the *people* again picked up stones to throw at him" (10:31), italics added. In John 8 a translation of Ἰουδαῖος is omitted 4 x so as to avoid any sense of demonizing the Jews (8:44) and Jews demonizing Jesus (8:48, 52). This phenomenon of simply omitting the term from nearly 50 percent of all occurrences is paralleled in the *New Living Translation* (1996). There, Ἰουδαῖος in John is rendered as follows: 1x "Judea," 4x "Jewish," 11x "Jew(s)," 26x "Jewish leaders," 29x the term is omitted or replaced with "they" or "people." Similarly again, the *Contemporary English Version* (CEV 1995) translates Ἰουδαῖος in John 1x "Judea," 1x "Jewish man," 3x "Jewish people," 4x "Jewish," 6x "Jewish leaders," 10x "Jews," 11x "leaders," and 34x omission or "they"/"people"/"crowd." The *Today's New International Version* (TNIV 2002) moderates this trend: 1x "Judean," 2x "leaders," 8x omitted (or "they"), 9x "Jewish," 14x "Jewish leaders," 37x "Jew(s)."

[5] Third Maccabees 1:8 displays a similar way of phrasing: "Since the Jews had sent some of their council and elders (τῶν δὲ Ἰουδαίων διαπεμψαμένων πρὸς αὐτὸν ἀπὸ τῆς γερουσίας καὶ τῶν πρεσβυτέρων) to greet him [Ptolemy], to bring him gifts of welcome, and to congratulate him on what had happened" (RSV). Josephus can also say that "the Jews" (*A.J.* 14.477; 15.407) and "the cities" (πόλεις, *B.J.* 1.242) sent embassadors.

interrogation mentioned in 2:18, 20[6] and the expulsion from the synagogue (9:22; 12:42; 16:2).[7]

The Gospel mentions Jews positively as those who believe Jesus (8:31), including the officers of the leaders (7:46) and leaders themselves (3:1). On the other side, the Pharisees and chief priests are singled out as the spearhead of the opposition: "No one of the rulers or Pharisees has believed in Him, has he? But this multitude which does not know the Law is accursed" (7:48-49). The Pharisees complain later that "the world has gone after Him!" (12:19). This seems to suggest that the religious leaders are the prime adversaries of Jesus and the masterminds of his death. It is they who express political fears about Jesus' popularity (11:45-48)[8] and who issued the command to seize Jesus wherever he showed up (11:57).

Sometimes the term "the Jews" is used interchangeably with "high priests" and "Pharisees." After John described how Judas led a group of Romans and "servants of the high priests and Pharisees" to Jesus (ἐκ τῶν ἀρχιερέων καὶ ἐκ τῶν Φαρισαίων ὑπηρέτας, 18:3), he calls the latter in 18:12 "servants of the Jews" (οἱ ὑπηρέται τῶν Ἰουδαίων), thus implying that "the Jews" are identified as high priests and Pharisees.[9] The parable of the Good Shepherd in 10:1-18 is addressed to the "Pharisees" (9:40) and continues the theme of judgment from 9:41. After Jesus finishes his comparison of good and bad leadership over the sheep, the author lets "the Jews" respond, thus equating the Φαρισαῖοι of 9:40 with the Ἰουδαῖοι of 10:19. Furthermore, in 11:47-50 Caiaphas addresses the "high priests and the Pharisees" in the Sanhedrin (11:47) about the man who should die for the nation. In 18:14 John brings this meeting back to the reader's memory by saying that Caiaphas had advised "the Jews" about the death of one man.

Elsewhere, Josephus is more specific when he cites a decree from officials in Pergamus which mentions that "the nation of the Jews, *and their high priest Hyrcanus*, sent as ambassadors" three men to the Romans (*A.J.* 14.248, italics added; cf. 14.305). While a Roman decree says that ambassadors were sent "by the people of the Jews" (ὑπὸ δήμου τοῦ Ἰουδαίων; *A.J.* 13.260), Josephus mentions beforehand that it was Hyrcanus the high priest who actually sent the ambassadors (13.259; also 14.185, 223, 228, 241, 304). This shows how "the Jews" can be used as a synecdoche for their leaders.

[6] OESTERREICHER, *The New Encounter between Christians and Jews*, 399-400.

[7] SMITH, "Judaism and the Gospel of John," 82.

[8] Tsuchido tries to argue against Stibbe that the Ἰουδαῖοι of 11:45-46 parallel the leaders implied in 11:53 and not the Ἰουδαῖοι of 11:54. He concludes that "the Jews" in 11:45 and 11:54 are "an elite and religious group in Jerusalem." TSUCHIDO, "Is There Anti-Semitism in the Fourth Gospel?," 68.

[9] This is the main thesis of the dissertation by LEISTNER, *Antijudaismus im Johannesevangelium?* (1974). See also BROWN, *The Gospel*, 1:LXXI. SCHNACKENBURG, *Das Johannesevangelium*, 3:284.

We read of Jews who "feared the Jews" (9:22; 19:38). Flannery
maintains that taking Ἰουδαῖοι as the totality of all Jewish people does not
make sense in these texts.[10] Sometimes John says that "the Jews"
persecuted Jesus (5:16) and are trying to kill him (5:18; 7:1). But in 7:20
"the multitude" (ὁ ὄχλος) responds to Jesus' question, "Why do you seek
to kill me?" with the words: "You have a demon. Who seeks to kill you?"
This further indicates that "the Jews" are not the same as "the multitude,"
the common Jewish people.[11]

Nevertheless, the last dialogue begins to indicate a problem for the
proposal to see religious leaders as the only referent for οἱ Ἰουδαῖοι. Why
does Jesus address the *crowd* with this question ("Why do you seek to kill
me"?) when only the *leaders* have such a plan? Maybe Jesus asked the
wrong people;[12] maybe the people did not respond honestly.[13] Or perhaps
there is a connection of some sort between the leaders and the people.
Freeman noticed that the charge of demon possession "is brought by the
crowds [7:20] and the 'believing' Jews [8:48, 52], but never by the
authorities"[14] and concludes against Culpepper that John "did not
distinguish clearly between the degrees of hostility the two groups [Jews
and crowds] manifested toward Jesus."[15] Just before Jesus engaged with
the crowd in Jerusalem, he said to his brothers, "The world cannot hate
you; but it hates me because I testify of it, that its deeds are evil" (7:7).
Nothing indicates here that "the world" refers merely to the leaders of the
Jews. In his interrogation before the high priest, Jesus explains that he
always taught in the synagogue and the temple where "all the Jews" gather
(πάντες οἱ Ἰουδαῖοι, 18:20). Tolmie rightly comments that in "this case, it
[the term 'the Jews'] does not refer to the authorities only."[16]

---

[10] So FLANNERY, *The Anguish of the Jews*, 30. Reinhartz also observes that in these
instances of expulsion Ἰουδαῖοι denotes "the feared rather than the fearful." But in her
eyes the nuance is not strong enough to avoid the generalizing sense of the term.
REINHARTZ, "'Jews' and Jews in the Fourth Gospel," 217-18. Josephus relates how
Herod feared "the multitude of the Jews" (πλήθους τῶν Ἰουδαίων, *B.J.* 7.300).

[11] But for Reinhartz, the term Ἰουδαῖοι in 5:16 is an example of "blurred distinctions
between the 'Jews' and the 'Jewish establishment.'" REINHARTZ, *The Word in the World*,
90 n. 51.

[12] This would be the natural conclusion of Bratcher's explanation which
acknowledges that Jesus speaks to "the crowd" but who explains the "you" in his
question as the authorities. BRATCHER, "'The Jews'," 405.

[13] Hakola explains that the "question 'Who is trying to kill you?' is not a sign of
ignorance but an attempt to deny that anyone seeks Jesus' life." HAKOLA, *Identity
Matters*, 132.

[14] FREEMAN, "The Function," 123.

[15] Ibid., 123 n. 63.

[16] TOLMIE, "The ΙΟΥΔΑΙΟΙ in the Fourth Gospel," 393.

Also, we read of a division among the crowd: some Jews believed Jesus and others did not (7:12, 40-44; 8:45-47; 9:18; 10:19, 25). In chapter six, it is the crowd (ὁ ὄχλος, 6:24) who hears the words about the bread from heaven. After Jesus finished his speech, "the Jews then complained about Him" (6:41).[17] A clear distinction between opposing leaders and affirming people seems to fail here.[18] The same is true in chapter 10. While we can equate "the Jews" from 10:19 with the Pharisees in 9:40 and with the bad *shepherds* of 10:8 ("thieves and robbers"),[19] we have to understand the Ἰουδαῖοι in 10:24 as the *sheep* who do not belong to Jesus because they do not listen to his voice (10:26-27).

After the resurrection of Lazarus, "many of the Jews" (Πολλοὶ οὖν ἐκ τῶν Ἰουδαίων) see what he did and believe (11:45). Then "some of them" (τινὲς δὲ ἐξ αὐτῶν) go to the Pharisees to tell them what Jesus had done (11:46). Again, the Jews seem distinct from the Pharisees.

Furthermore, it appears that John is not drawing absolute lines even between (superficial) believers and unbelievers. Those who believe (8:31) are said to desire the death of Jesus (8:37, 40) and thus to have the devil as their father who is a murderer from the beginning (8:44). In the same context, the affirmation of belief is completely negated when Jesus asks at the end, "If I speak the truth, why do you not believe me?" (8:46). The world that has gone after Jesus (12:19) is the same world that did not know him or receive him (1:10-11; cf. 2:23-25)!

One wonders also why the author did not make his intentions less ambiguous if he wanted to single out a specific group among the Jews. He does not hesitate to use titles and offices of Jewish leadership, especially Φαρισαῖος and ἀρχιερεύς.[20] He also specifies subgroups of the Jews such

---

[17] Von Wahlde, who sees a narrow view of "religious authorities" throughout the Gospel, notices with regard to 6:41, 52 a reference to common people. In an earlier article, Von Wahlde understood 6:41, 52 even as a redaction. VON WAHLDE, "The Johannine 'Jews'," 43-44.

[18] Pryor argues against von Wahlde for a connection between "the crowd" and "the Jews" in 7:15, 35; 10:31, 33. PRYOR, *John*, 183. Broer rightly asks "warum die Grenze zwischen Obrigkeit und Volk bei Johannes permanent verschwimmt" when the author employed Ἰουδαῖοι in order to refer to leaders only. BROER, "Die Juden," 339.

[19] Others maintain that Ἰουδαῖοι in 10:19 refers "not just to the Jewish leaders but more broadly to the people at large." KÖSTENBERGER, *John*, 308.

[20] The Φαρισαῖοι are mentioned 20 x (29xMatthew, 12xMark, 27xLuke) and the ἀρχιερεῖς 21 times (25xMatthew, 22xMark, 15xLuke). Other offices and titles of Jewish leaders found in the Gospel are the following: No mention is made of Σαδδουκαῖος (7xMatthew, 1xMark, 1xLuke), only 1x of ἱερεύς (1:19; 3xMatthew, 2xMark, 5xLuke), Λευίτης (1:19; 0xMatthew, 0xMark, 1xLuke), of γραμματεύς (8:3; 22xMatthew, 21xMark, 14xLuke), and of πρεσβύτερος (8:9; 12xMatthew, 7xMark, 5xLuke). And 7x we read of the ἄρχων (5xMatthew, 1xMark, 8xLuke). See already FISCHER, "Ueber den

as "the Jews of Jerusalem" (1:19; cf. 7:25) or "the high priests of the Jews" (19:21). Furthermore, Luke shows that vocabulary was available for referring to "Jewish leaders" without implying the involvement of the Jewish people as a whole. We read about the πρεσβύτεροι τῶν Ἰουδαίων (Luke 7:3; Acts 25:15), οἱ πρῶτοι τῶν Ἰουδαίων (Acts 25:2), and τοὺς ὄντας τῶν Ἰουδαίων πρώτους (Acts 28:17).[21] Not a few scholars observe the terms at hand and ask why John did not make use of expressions such as these if he wanted to point out Jewish *leaders* as the responsible executioners of Jesus.[22] In light of these linguistic options, the term "the Jews" seems rather *intentionally* unspecific.[23] Raymond E. Brown changed his interpretation over the years and thus adds to the criticism of the new consensus. In his commentary of 1966 he defended the meaning of "religious authorities."[24] But almost four decades later, he favors the religious (not ethnic) sense "for a large number of Johannine passages"[25] and asks "why John would use the designation 'the Jews,' which in itself

---

Ausdruck," 99. LÜTGERT, "Die Juden," 149. ASHTON, "The Identity," 57. LINGAD, *The Problems*, 118. BROWN, *An Introduction*, 164-65.

[21] Josephus calls the leaders of the Jews, for example, ἄρχων τῶν Ἰουδαίων (*A.J.* 11.13), ἡγεμόνες τῶν Ἰουδαίων (*A.J.* 11.89, 32), Ἰουδαῖοι καὶ ἡγεμόνες αὐτῶν (*A.J.* 11.101), πρεσβύτεροι τῶν Ἰουδαίων (*A.J.* 11.105), ὁ Ἰουδαίων ἀρχιερεύς (*A.J.* 11.333; 13.223; 14.139 [Strabo], 241 [Laodiceans]), ἀρχιερεύς τῶν Ἰουδαίων (*A.J.* 11.336; 12.1, 16, 39, 40; 13.45; 14.151 [Athenians], 191 [Julius Caesar], 196, 199, 200, 211, 212, 226, 306; *C. Ap.* 1.187), οἱ ἱερεῖς τῶν Ἰουδαίων (*C. Ap.* 1.188), στρατηγός τῶν Ἰουδαίων (*A.J.* 13.6), Οἱ ἐν τέλει τῶν Ἰουδαίων (*A.J.* 14.163, 271, 302; 17.160; 18.284; *B.J.* 1.243), οἱ πρῶτοι τῶν Ἰουδαίων (*A.J.* 14.165; 17.342; 20:1, 130), οἱ πρωτεύοντες τῶν Ἰουδαίων (*A.J.* 20.182), Ἰουδαίων οἱ δυνατοί (*B.J.* 1.31, 242; 2.287, 336), οἱ γνώριμοι τῶν Ἰουδαίων (*B.J.* 2.240, 243), Ἰουδαίων οἱ γεραιοί (*B.J.* 2.267).

[22] Granskou reminds that "the impression one gets in reading chaps. 7 to 10 and 18 to 19 is blurred. Sometimes when 'Jew' is alternated with 'Pharisee' or 'High Priest' the impression is created that these authorities are speaking for the people, not always against them or apart from them." GRANSKOU, "Anti-Judaism," 206. According to Boyarin, "the Jews" are not the leaders because the "text inscribes for us very clearly who the leaders are, as they have been throughout the Gospel, namely, the Chief Priests and the Pharisees." BOYARIN, "*Ioudaioi* in John," 238. See also LEIBIG, "John and 'the Jews'," 214.

[23] Leibig comments that to "concentrate all exegetical efforts upon determining the historical 'identity' of 'the Jews' in John is to disregard the Evangelist's intention." LEIBIG, "John and 'the Jews'," 215. Culpepper maintains against von Wahlde that "the amount of discussion generated by John's varied use of the designation shows that the gospel does not attempt to distinguish and separate these groups; all are called Ἰουδαῖοι." CULPEPPER, *Anatomy*, 126.

[24] BROWN, *The Gospel*, 1:LXXI.

[25] BROWN, *An Introduction*, 166.

has no implication of 'authorities,' if he was thinking only of the authorities."[26]

Finally, even a consistent rendering with "Jewish authorities" for all negative meanings of "the Jews" (see TEV, NLT, CEV, TNIV) does not necessarily avoid a negative impression about the Jews in the Gospel. A rigid distinction between leader and people is blurred by the fact that even a narrow referent "can have a far-reaching sense in the narrative world of a text" via the conceptual category of "corporate personality."[27] For Allen it is clear that "the Jews" do not denote "the Jewish community as a whole, but its leaders."[28] Yet, on the other hand, "their attitude to Jesus is not an individual one, it is representative of the community. They are as it were spokesmen of the Synagogue in its conflict with the Church."[29] Belser and Hahn understand the Ἰουδαῖοι sometimes as Jewish leaders from Judea who represent the unbelieving part of Judaism.[30] The Jewish scholar Geza Vermes affirms in the light of 11:47-50 that John is "symbolically placing the guilt of the entire Jewish people on the shoulders of their official religious spokesmen." But with that insight Vermes still states that "John's hatred of the Jews was fierce."[31] After several decades of intense debate since the 1980s, it becomes evident that interpreters and translators who regard the Ἰουδαῖοι as religious leaders are skating "on thin linguistic

---

[26] Ibid., 164. Moloney seems to think that von Wahlde changed his position from "religious authorities" to the "the Jews" with a religious meaning, just as Brown did. Ibid., 165 n. 39. But that is a misunderstanding of von Wahlde's expression "the authoritative position of the traditional Judaism." VON WAHLDE, "'The Jews' in the Gospel of John," 53. Earlier in the same article, von Wahlde makes his understanding of Ἰουδαῖοι clear when he says that he did "not find evidence for seeing 'the Jews' as referring to the common people any place except 6,41.52." Ibid., 39, also p. 45.

[27] BIERINGER, POLLEYFEYT, VANDECASTEELE-VANNEUVILLE, "Wrestling with Johannine Anti-Judaism," 16. See also Pryor, *John*, 183.

[28] ALLEN, "The Jewish Christian Church," 88.

[29] Ibid., 88.

[30] Belser discerns three meanings for Ἰουδαῖοι in John (nation of Jews; Judeans; high priests of Jerusalem) and conveniently limits all negative occurrences to the religious leaders of Jerusalem who are the "Repräsentanten des ungläubigen Judentums." BELSER, "Der Ausdruck οἱ Ἰουδαῖοι," 175, 195, 204, 210. Hahn insists, "Wenn an vielen Stellen des Johannesevangeliums bei der Verwendung von οἱ Ἰουδαῖοι die offiziellen Vertreter des Judentums gemeint sind, darf das natürlich nicht in dem Sinne verstanden werden, daß es nur um einzelne geht, vielmehr reden und handeln die Inhaber amtlicher Funktionen als Repräsentanten des Judentums schlechthin." HAHN, "'Die Juden'," 435.

[31] VERMES, *The Changing Faces of Jesus*, 34, also 21. Vermes wrote this book in remembrance of his parents, who both died in 1944 as "innocent victims of the evil and madness called anti-Semitism." Ibid., 5. Similar to Vermes, Haufe understands the woes against religious leaders in the Synoptics (cf. Luke 11 and Matt 23) as generalizing polemics. HAUFE, "Israel – Polemik in Q," 56-60.

ice."[32] They were neither able to refute serious criticism of their proposal nor avoid charges of changing the text.[33]

1.2. Inhabitants of Judea

Ἰουδαῖοι can have a geographical sense and denotes people from Judea in contrast to those from Galilee and Samaria.[34] We find this limited regional sense already in the LXX, so in 2 Kings 16:6 (NAS, NAB, RSV "men of Judah"), 1 Esdras 1:21; 2:17 (RSV) and Isa 19:17. A clear example in the Fourth Gospel is the feminine singular adjectival form of Ἰουδαῖος in 3:22, where old and new translations correctly render εἰς τὴν Ἰουδαίαν γῆν as "into the land of Judea" (NRSV "Judean countryside").

While various scholars regard "Judeans" as a possible reference for *some* occurrences of οἱ Ἰουδαῖοι,[35] only a few interpreters render most or

---

[32] So MOTYER, *Your Father*, 51.

[33] Caron summarizes his criticism as follows: "Lire ou discerner 'les autorités (juives)' chaque fois qu'interviennent les 'Juifs' dans cet évangile, c'est tout simplement changer le texte." CARON, *Qui sont les Juifs*, 47-48.

[34] In this case, Ἰουδαία denotes only a part of the country. See Josephus, *B.J.* 2.95-96, 247; 3.35-58; *A.J.* 13.50; 17.318-319. This means that a Ἰουδαῖος is an inhabitant of Judea who can be contrasted to Samaritans, Galileans, etc., as, for example, in *B.J.* 2.43 (parallel in *A.J.* 17.254). Hengel notes the different ways Luke uses Ἰουδαία, such as (1) for Judea and Samaria in contrast to Galilee (Luke 3:1; 23:6); (2) for the whole of Palestine (Luke 1:5; 7:17; 23:5; Acts 10:37); (3) but mostly for "the part of Palestine inhabited by Jews, apart from Samaria and Galilee, and even excluding Caesarea (Luke 4:44; 5:17; Acts 1:8; 9:31; 11:29; 12:19; 15:1; 20:10; 26:20; 28:21); (4) finally even for Judea apart from Jerusalem (Luke 6:17; Acts 1:8; 8:1). HENGEL, "The Geography of Palestine in Acts," 32.

[35] The New English Translation (2000), an online Bible, renders 10 times this way or similarly (3:22; 8:31, 48, 52, 57; 11:19 ["Jewish people of the region"], 54; 12:9, 11 ["Jewish people from Jerusalem"]; 19:20 ["Jewish residents of Jerusalem"]). Tillmann translates only in 3:25 with "Judäer." TILLMANN, *Das Johannesevangelium*, 101, also 8, 66-67. Brown sees the meaning "Judeans" in John 11-12, a special strata of material that was later inserted into the Gospel. BROWN, *The Gospel*, 1: LXXI. Years later Brown evaluates in the same way: "Overall I would judge that 7:1; 11:8, 54 are possible examples of the meaning Judeans, but there is no indisputable instance." BROWN, *An Introduction*, 163. Bratcher finds the meaning "Judeans" in 11:8, 19, 31, 33, 36, 45, 54; 12:9, 11; 19:20. BRATCHER, "'The Jews'," 409. See also ASHTON, "The Identity," 62. Carson finds a geographical reference to Judea in the expression τὸ πάσχα τῶν Ἰουδαίων (2:13) because "the Passover was celebrated in the temple *in Judea*, and the residents of Judea were called 'Jews' by both Galileans and diaspora Hebrews . . . ." CARSON, *The Gospel According to John*, 176. But "most commonly" Ἰουδαῖοι "refers to the Jewish leaders, especially those of Jerusalem and Judea." Ibid., 142. Siegert sees a geographical meaning in 11:36. SIEGERT, "Vermeintlicher Antijudaismus," 75-76. Compare also English translations of the LXX which vary in its translation of the term within one book. The NAS translates in 2 Kgs 16:6 with "Judeans" and in 25:25 with "the Jews." The RSV

all occurrences this way.[36] Malcolm Lowe's article from 1976 still presents the strongest arguments for such a reading. His opening discussion of the semantic history of the term concludes that during the New Testament period, Ἰουδαῖος had a religious meaning ("Jews") for Gentiles and Diaspora Jews, while it maintained a strict geographical sense ("Judean," "Israelite") for Jews within Palestine. He then applies the latter meaning to the occurrences in the Gospels which deal "exclusively with events in Palestine" and the former meaning to the occurrences in the rest of the New Testament which "largely concerns events in the Diaspora."[37] Furthermore, Ἰουδαία in the Gospel always refers to "Judea" in the strict geographical sense, excluding Samaria and Galilee (4:3, 47, 54; 7:1, 3; 11:7).[38] Thus the etymological connection between Ἰουδαῖοι and Ἰουδαία favors a geographical meaning, especially in 7:1 and 11:7-8. The phrase "feasts of the Ἰουδαῖοι" (2:13; 5:1; 7:2-3; 11:5) always occurs before an actual pilgrimage to Jerusalem, thus explaining to the reader the required journey to Judea. The only exception is 6:4, which Lowe understands as

---

translates Ἰουδαῖος in 1 Esdras as "the Judaeans" (1:21; 2:17) and as "the Jews" (2:18; 4:49, 50; 6:1).

[36] See LOWE, "Who Were the ΙΟΥΔΑΙΟΙ?," 101-30. Cuming explained already in 1948 that "'the Jews' . . . are not the Jewish nation as a whole. . . . it means Judaeans as opposed to Galileans. . . . 'the Jews' are dwellers in Jerusalem." CUMING, "The Jews," 292. See also PIETRANTONIO, "Los Ἰουδαῖοι," 39. SCHEIN, *Following the Way*, 63, 77, 91, 108, 109, 119, 121, etc. WEHRMANN follows Schein in "Der Weg und die Wiege," 106. See also GEYSER, "Israel in the fourth Gospel," 13-30, who relies on Lowe. SLOYAN, *John*, 4, 23, 33, 40, 48, 205-06. In his *Jewish New Testament* from 1989, David H. Stern translates 59 times as "Judeans" and follows Lowe's argument. See STERN, *Jewish New Testament Commentary*, 158-59. See also HAACKER, "Die neutestamentliche Wissenschaft," 86. HORSLEY, *Galilee*, 45. DUNN, "The Embarassment of History," 54. Malina and Rohrbaugh speak of "Judeans" throughout their commentary. MALINA, ROHRBAUGH, *Social-Science Commentary*, esp. 44-46. Brodie comments on 1:19, "The confrontation, therefore, may be described as being between John and the assembled Judeans." BRODIE, *The Gospel*, 148. PHILLIPS, *The Prologue*, 64, 71. A similar trend in translation has reached the shores of the Josephus research. The *Brill Josephus Project*, which works on a new translation and commentary of Josephus' works, led by Steve Mason as the general editor, changed the traditional translation of the title of Josephus' twenty volumes about the history of the Jews from "Jewish Antiquities" to "Judean Antiquities." In the second edition of his *Josephus and the New Testament*, Mason himself states without much explanation that the "Greek and Latin words for 'Jew' (*Ioudaios, Iudaeus*) simply mean 'Judean'." MASON, *Josephus*, 58, also 69, 92, 111. For a challenge of this translation see the forthcoming volume *Jewish Identity in the Greco-Roman World*, ed. J. Frey, D. R. Schwartz (Leiden: Brill, 2007).

[37] LOWE, "Who were the ΙΟΥΔΑΙΟΙ?," 107. Lowe repeats many times throughout his article that Ἰουδαῖοι in the sense of "Judeans" is the "ordinary Palestinian usage of the period." Ibid., 115, 118, 119, 125.

[38] Ibid., 112.

later redactional input. The expression "king of the Ἰουδαιῶν" is first used
by Pilate who supposed "Jesus to be a Judean upstart trying to seize power
in his procurate."[39] Again, Lowe explains the two previous references to
Ἰουδαῖοι in Capernaum / Galilee (6:41, 52) as the work of later
redaction.[40] The only exception to the narrow geographical sense occurs in
John 4:9, 22, which reflect the "*Samaritan* usage of the period."[41] Lowe
finishes by exposing this mistranslation of "the Jews" for Ἰουδαῖοι as a
"constant excuse for antisemitism whose further existence cannot be
permitted."[42]

While a rendering with "Judeans" prevents at first sight any
implications of race or religion and thus possibly avoids an anti-Semitic
reading of the Gospel, this proposal has found more criticism than
approval among scholars.[43] Various reasons might account for this
hesitation. Lowe's need to explain the occurrences in 6:41, 52 as
redactional input in order to maintain his thesis might be one of various
weaknesses.[44] Lowe also does not adequately discuss 2:6, which mentions
six stone waterpots that were being used not in Judea but *in Galilee* κατὰ
τὸν καθαρισμὸν τῶν Ἰουδαίων.[45] In this instance, if we want to consider a
narrow spatial connotation, it can be no more than an indicator for the
geographical origin of a custom of religious purification that was practiced
in all of Palestine, if not even by Jews in the Diaspora as well.[46] This
incident also shows how difficult it is at times to strictly separate a
geographical meaning of Ἰουδαῖοι from a religious one, especially if the
word is used in connection with religious beliefs, practices and titles as it

---

[39] Ibid., 119.

[40] Ibid., 120, also p. 116. So also CUMING, "The Jews," 292.

[41] LOWE, "Who were the ΙΟΥΔΑΙΟΙ?," 125.

[42] Ibid., 130.

[43] For critical evaluations, see WENGST, *Bedrängte Gemeinde*, 58-60. BROWN, *An Introduction*, 162-63.

[44] In Keener's view, the use of Ἰουδαῖοι in 6:41, 52 suggests "that John was aware of other associations of the term [other than 'Judeans'] which his readers might naturally infer as well." KEENER, *The Gospel of John*, 1:221. Lieu argues that the use of Ἰουδαῖοι in 6:41, 52 is "thus invalidating the translation 'Judaeans'." LIEU, "Temple and Synagogue in John," 65 n. 53. See also FREEMAN, "The Function," 130-31. MOTYER, *Your Father*, 49. LINGAD, *The Problems*, 116. Josephus provides parallels for the use of Ἰουδαῖοι as a reference to Jews in Galilee (*A.J.* 12.332; [cf. 18.23]; 20:43, 102, 118-124; *B.J.* 2.232-238; 3.229).

[45] See the criticism against "Judeans" because of John 2:6 by BOYARIN, "*Ioudaioi* in John," 234-35. Lowe briefly mentions 2:6 and 19:42 but imposes his overall solution on these texts without letting them influence his discussion of the meaning of the term. LOWE, "Who were the ΙΟΥΔΑΙΟΙ?," 117-18 n. 54.

[46] Similarly, Lowe does not discuss the burial custom of the Ἰουδαῖοι mentioned in 19:40. See also REINHARTZ, "'Jews' and Jews in the Fourth Gospel," 219.

is so often in the Gospel of John.[47] The Ἰουδαῖοι are "disciples of Moses" (9:28), a religious label that certainly applies to more than just the Judeans.[48] For this reason, David Stern, for example, who favors the meaning of "Judeans" in fifty-nine occurrences, nevertheless favors "the Jews" in twelve cases in his *Jewish New Testament* (1989).[49] Also, since Lowe agrees to the religious sense for Ἰουδαῖος in the context of the Diaspora and therefore in all NT writings but the Gospels, his thesis only works if we limit the provenance, purpose and intended audience of the Gospel of John to Jews of Palestine. While there are scholars who attempt such an endeavor, the typical provenance assigned to the Gospel is Asia Minor. Such a location requires us to read Ἰουδαῖοι in a large sense as "the Jews" which is why Reinhartz, for example, regards Lowe's thesis as irrelevant.[50] But even a Palestinian provenance does not automatically limit the reference to Judea. Ἰουδαῖοι can denote people from Palestine, including the regions of Idumea, Judea, Samaria, Perea, Galilee (geographic-ethnic sense).[51] Recently, Shaye Cohen has shown that the term Ἰουδαῖοι underwent a semantic shift as soon as the Maccabean period from an ethnic meaning to one that describes a common way of life and of worship.[52] Finally, even if we ignore all objections just mentioned, the

---

[47] See temple (2:13-25; cf. 18:20), purification (2:6; 3:25), religious feasts (2:13; 5:1; 6:4; 7:2; 11:55), the Sabbath (5:10), and the mentioning of Moses, Abraham, Jacob, and Isaiah. Freyne criticizes a rigid split into political and religious meaning and emphasizes the unifying power that the term Ἰουδαῖος exercised on Judeans, Samarian Yahweh-worshipers and the Judean *'am ha-'aretz*, "Thus, to restrict Ἰουδαῖος to a geographical-political meaning, without attending to the very definite associations of the term with worship in the Jerusalem temple and acceptance of the customs, rituals and practices associated with that worship, is to ignore the powerful impetus that religious belief and practice can give in transcending intolerable social and economic factors, which from a secular post-Marxist perspective may be judged as being thoroughly alienating." FREYNE, "Behind the Names," 127.

[48] See DE BOER, "The Depiction," 150-54.

[49] Stern renders as "the Jews" in the following texts: 2:6 ("Jewish"); 4:9 (2x), 22; 18:20, 33, 35, 39; 19:3, 19, 21 (2x).

[50] See REINHARTZ, "'Jews' and Jews in the Fourth Gospel," 218-19.

[51] Ἰουδαία can denote the whole country of Palestine. In this sense Tacitus can call Judea a "province" of which Galilee and Samaria are a part (*Annals* XXII, 54). See also Josephus' use of Ἰουδαῖοι in *A.J.* 17.253-254; 18.2; 20:43; *B.J.* 2.232. In Luke 1:5, Herod the Great is called "king of Judea" (βασιλέως τῆς Ἰουδαίας; also Josephus, *A.J.* 15.373, 409; *B.J.* 1.282).

[52] See COHEN, "Ἰουδαῖος τὸ γένος," 26-27. Idem, "Ioudaios: 'Judean' and 'Jew'," 1:211-20. In both essays, Cohen argues for the translation of Ἰουδαῖος as "Judaean" and not as "Jew" as do most (if not all) translations of Josephus, Susanna, and 1-2 Maccabees. His thesis is "that all occurrences of the terms *Ioudaios* and *Yehudi* before the end of the second century BCE mean not 'Jew' but 'Judean.' After the end of the

expression "the Judeans," though reducing the possibility for racial and religious connotations, does not eliminate awkward generalizations in statements such as "the Judeans were seeking . . . to kill him" (5:18) or the "Judeans took up stones again to stone him" (10:31). The translation is still too broad and imprecise, considering that the agent of the historical reality must have consisted of few individuals and bearing in mind that options for specification were readily at hand.[53] It is this generalization *in the context* which opens up even the word "Judeans" for allegorical inter- pretations with broader racial-religious and therefore hostile implica- tions.[54] Lowe himself cautiously considers such a possibility[55] which others before and after him embraced more boldly.[56]

1.3. Ethnic-Religious Term

The meaning of Ἰουδαῖοι can even be broader, including all followers of the Jewish religion, either Jews or Gentiles inside Palestine or outside of

---

second century BCE these terms may mean either 'Jew' or 'Judean,' depending on the context." COHEN, "Ioudaios: 'Judean' and 'Jew'," 211-12.

[53] See the comments in our previous discussion about the translation with "Jewish authorities."

[54] We point again to Geza Vermes who agrees to understand the referent for οἱ Ἰουδαῖοι as "the Jews, or at least the inhabitants of Judaea." But in his eyes, this still encourages the impression of profound hostility between Jesus and the Judeans. Vermes comments, "John's hatred of the Jews was fierce. I often wonder whether he could possibly have been Jewish himself." VERMES, *The Changing Faces of Jesus*, 21. Culpepper comments, "Even if *hoi Ioudaioi* once denoted 'the Judeans' or the Jewish authorities, the Gospel of John generalized and stereotyped those who rejected Jesus by its use of this term." CULPEPPER, "The Gospel of John," 284.

[55] Lowe agrees that the "author may have intended to convey an allegorical message too." LOWE, "Who Were The IOYΔAIOI?," 110.

[56] Similarly to Lowe and others, Westcott already suggested in his commentary from 1908 that Ἰουδαῖοι "is perhaps used exclusively of those who lived in the limited region of Judaea." Yet, he also finds a paradigmatic sense when he says that "from first to last they appear as the representatives of the narrow finality of Judaism (ii. 18, xix. 38). . . . 'The Jews' thus presented to a writer who looked back ... the aggregate of the people whose opinions were opposed in spirit to the work of Christ." WESTCOTT, *The Gospel*, 1:xvii; 2:284. Fortna explains that "Judea is a microcosm of humanity hostile to God's revelation." And later, "It is not the Jews or Judaism historically that is John's real concern, but the religion and people as symbols, types, of the universal human condition." FORTNA, "Theological Use," 92, 93. While Thyen agrees with Lowe that Judeans are the reference for Ἰουδαῖοι, he argues against Lowe that Judea is a province of high theological importance and that Judeans are the representatives of normative Judaism after the Jewish war. Since the regeneration of Judaism after the war happened under Judean-pharisaic leadership, "ist die 'falsche' Übersetzung 'die Juden' am Ende tatsächlich die allein richtige." THYEN, "'Das Heil kommt von den Juden'," 180.

it.[57] The use of ἰουδαΐζω for the conversion of Gentiles to Judaism (Esth 8:17; Gal 2:14; Josephus *B.J.* 2.454 [cf. *A.J.* 13.257-258; also 20:38-39]; Ignatius *Magn.* 10.3) and of Ἰουδαῖοι for Gentiles in Bel 28 and 2 Maccabees 9:17 (for Antiochus Epiphanes) illustrates that one can enter (and exit) the ethnic community of the Jews through the religious gate. Most traditional English translations render οἱ Ἰουδαῖοι simply as "the Jews," denoting a broad sense with nuances of race and religion.[58] In the LXX, the term is certainly used with an ethnic-religious meaning, describing Jews in Israel as well as those in exile as a monotheistic nation that abides by certain laws (Sabbath, circumcision) in contrast to polytheistic Gentiles. This use can be found in the mouth of Jews themselves[59] and in the mouth of Gentiles the term can be used either positively[60] or negatively.[61] The ethnic usage of Ἰουδαῖοι "as distinct from other ethnic groups" is the "normal usage in the Pauline writings and Acts,"[62] both texts which speak either directly to Gentiles or to Jews in the diaspora. In the Gospel of John, an ethnic sense seems obvious from contrasts drawn between Ἰουδαῖοι and Samaritans (4:22) and Ἰουδαῖοι and

---

[57] WILLIAMS discusses inscriptional evidence in "The Meaning and Function," 249-62. Also MIRANDA, "La Comunità Giudaica," 109-55.

[58] The standard English translations render all occurrences of Ἰουδαῖος as "Jews," some translate a few times as "Jewish" (such as in 2:6; 7:2; 18:2; 19:42). See AV, NKJ, ASV, NAS, NAB, RSV, NRSV. The new Holman Christian Standard Bible (HCSB, 2000) continues this way among recent translations.

[59] See, for example, Neh 2:16; 4:1; 5:1, 8, 17; 13:23; Esth 5:1; 6:14; 1 Macc 8:20. This is the prominent use of Ἰουδαῖος in the LXX where we find it 213 times, most often in Esther (44x) and 1-3 Maccabees (123x: 37x 1 Maccabees, 59x 2 Maccabees, 27x 3 Maccabees), books that tell stories of the Jewish race living under the oppressive rule of foreign nations, resulting in liberation and new feasts, the Purim feast in Esther (cf. Esth 9:24-32; 2 Macc 15:36), the feast of dedication in 1-2 Maccabees (1 Macc 4:52-59; 2 Macc 10:5-8; cf. John 10:22).

[60] See LXX Esth 6:7-8 (Cyrus); Add Esth 16:15, 19 (Artaxerxes), also 1 Esdr 6:8; 8:10 (governors of Syria and Phoenicia); 1 Macc 8:23, 25, 27, 29 (Romans, who call the Jews here "our friends and allies" [φίλους ἡμῶν τοὺς συμμάχους], 8:31).

[61] See Ezra 4:12 (Samaritans; see parallel in 1 Esdr 2:14, 17 [RSV 2:18, 22]); Neh 6:6 (Sanballat); Bel 28 (Babylonian king); 1 Macc 10:23 (Demetrius).

[62] BROWN, *An Introduction*, 161. BULTMANN, *The Gospel of John*, 86 n. 2. See the use of Ἰουδαῖοι in Acts for "the Jews" who live "among the Gentiles" (κατὰ τὰ ἔθνη, 21:21) and "throughout the world" (κατὰ τὴν οἰκουμένην, 24:5; see Josephus, *A.J.* 19.290; 2 Macc 3:12) such as in Syria (Damascus 9:22; Antioch 11:19), Phoenicia, Cyprus (11:19; cf. 13:4), Asia (see οἱ ἀπὸ τῆς Ἀσίας Ἰουδαῖοι in 21:27; 24:19; Pisidian Antioch 13:14, Iconium 14:1, Lystra 16:1-3, Pontus 18:2, Ephesus 19:10, Tarsus 21:39), Greece (Thessalonica 17:1; also 20:3), Italy (Rome 18:2) and Egypt (Alexandria 18:24). Paul indicates the ethnic sense of Ἰουδαῖοι by his frequent juxtaposition of the term with Ἕλλην (Rom 1:16; 2:9, 10; 3:9; 10:12; 1 Cor 1:22, 24; 10:32; 12:13; Gal 3:28; Col 3:11) or with ἔθνη (Rom 3:29; 9:24; 1 Cor 1:23; 2 Cor 11:24-26; Gal 2:14-15).

Romans (18:35).[63] A strong religious connotation appears where disciples of John the Baptist, most likely Jews themselves, are set in opposition to "the Jews" while they debate about purification (3:25). Further, the controversies around figures, institutions, customs and feasts of the Old Testament in the Fourth Gospel show that a religious meaning plays into the term.[64] Thus, even if Ἰουδαῖοι includes a geographical sense, the text does not permit a strict separation from ethnic-religious meanings. A close reading indicates nuances such as "religious leader" (in 1:19; 2:18; 18:12; etc.), "Jerusalemites" (in 11:19; 12:10, 11), or "the crowd" (6:41, 52). But the impression is unavoidable that these different circles are melted together into one homogenous group.

The broad sense of Ἰουδαῖοι suggests "a remoteness, of distance in space and time" between Jesus and the readers of the Gospel.[65] Explanations of Jewish customs and feasts (2:6, 13; 5:1; 6:4; 7:2; 19:31, 40, 42),[66] translations of Hebrew terms (1:38, 41, 42; 9:7; 20:16) as well as

---

[63] See GUTBROD, "Ἰσραήλ," 377. In Matt 10:5 Jesus makes a similar threefold *ethnic-religious (-geographical?)* distinction between Gentiles, Samaritans and Israel. Josephus reports about bitter hostilities between the Σαμαρίται and the Ἰουδαῖοι (including the Γαλιλαῖοι) which were carried out before the Ῥωμαῖοι (*A.J.* 20:118-136; see also 9.288-291; 11.341; 12.257-261). The Mishnah prohibits taking money from "Gentiles" and "Samaritans" (*m. Šeqal.* 1.5).

[64] See n. 43 on p. 26.

[65] See GUTBROD, "Ἰσραήλ," 377. Robertson comments on John 1:19, "John, writing in Ephesus near the close of the first century long after the destruction of Jerusalem, constantly uses the phrase 'the Jews' as descriptive of the people as distinct from the Gentile world and from the followers of Christ (at first Jews also)." ROBERTSON, *Word Pictures*, 5:18. See also TOWNSEND, "The Gospel of John," 80-81. Porsch explains that at least part of the reason why the author uses Ἰουδαῖοι has to do with the "weiten Abstand von den konkreten Ereignissen der Zeit Jesu. Differen-zierungen sind bedeutungslos geworden." F. PORSCH, "'Ihr habt den Teufel zum Vater'," 55. According to Hengel, the author's use of Ἰουδαῖοι expresses distance from Jews and Judaism. The conflict with them occurred maybe two or three decades earlier. HENGEL, *Die johanneische Frage*, 298. Besides the nuance of hostility, Ridderbos explains the frequent use of Ἰουδαῖοι in the Gospel of John with the non-Palestinian provenance of the Gospel, written for readers who "live at a great distance – in time, place, and mind – from the events in Palestine recounted in the gospel." RIDDERBOS, *The Gospel of John*, 62.

[66] Mark, who wrote his Gospel in distant Rome, parallels such a usage in 7:3, "For the Pharisees and all the Jews do not eat unless they carefully wash their hands, thus observing the traditions of the elders." John thus employs a language which makes sense for his audience, remotely similar to Americans who speak of "the Europeans," or Europeans who speak of "the Asians" or "the Africans." Once one sets foot on one of these continents, one start to distinguish immediately. It seems that spatial distance leads to simplified and very general categories.

the traditional identification of Ephesus as the provenance of the Gospel[67] support such a thesis. The spatial and temporal distance of the writer comes together with the "metaphoric" nature of writing. Baruch Halpern writes,

> History is not what happened. What happened, after all, was a sequential direction, velocity, and acceleration of particles. *History is our way of organizing particle configurations into perceptible fictional blocks, such as individuals, groups, and the environment*. . . . So like everything else human, and reliant on the *macroscopic perceptions of humans, all history is flawed, in the sense that it is all metaphoric*. . . . Historiography cannot – and should not – be infinitely detailed. All history is at best an abridgment – better or worse – of an originally fuller reality.[68]

The question is if the metaphoric nature of historiography explains the use of the Ἰουδαῖοι in the Fourth Gospel *exhaustively*. It is difficult to avoid a pejorative impression when reading phrases such as "*the Jews* persecuted Jesus" (5:16; cf. 2:20; 3:25; 5:10, 15, 18; 6:52 etc.).[69] A mere descriptive function may be in place where the author explains unfamiliar customs. But in other cases, "the Jews" are the opponents who hate Jesus, persecute him and try to kill him because he reinterprets the pillars of their religious identity in a way that is offensive to their own self-understanding (5:10, 16, 18; 6:41; 7:1, 13; etc.). Historiographical reasons are not sufficient to explain the intentional focus on large narrative blocks of people. Fischer explained therefore already in 1840 that the gentile Christian author of the Gospel wanted to contrast the unbelieving Jews *as a race* with Greeks who, according to 12:20, show the opposite desire for truth and faith.[70] In his commentary from 1933, Walter Bauer spoke about the Gospel's

---

[67] See our discussion about the Gospel's provenance in chapter 5 (5.4).

[68] HALPERN, *The First Historians*, xxxiii, 7 (italics added). When we read in 2 Sam 3:35 that "all the people (כָּל־הָעָם / πᾶς ὁ λαὸς) came to persuade David," we encounter an example of such a "macroscopic perspective" in which the whole ("all the people") stands in reality for a part. See also 2 Sam 11:1; 17:1, 13, 14, 24, 26; 18:17. Halpern speaks later of the "use of synekdoche" by the Deuteronomist. Ibid., 276. Third Macc 1:8 certainly falls into this category as well: "Since the Jews had sent some of their council and elders to greet him [Ptolemy], to bring him gifts of welcome, and to congratulate him on what had happened." The resemblance in wording to John 1:19 is striking.

[69] Gutbrod explains the descriptive and pejorative function and explains about the latter, "In all this the author is separated from the Jews by a deep cleft which is much greater than the historical and national remoteness of his readers." GUTBROD, "Ἰσραήλ," 379.

[70] See FISCHER, "Ueber den Ausdruck," 131-35. Fischer himself disqualifies the Gospel's verdict about the Jews as historically unreliable because "so entsetzlich borniert, wie sie bei Johannes erscheinen, können jüdische Schriftgelehrte und Volksobere nicht gewesen seyn. So ungläubig, wie hier die Nation im Ganzen dargestellt werden soll, war sie nicht." Ibid., 135, also 104.

"Antisemitismus" and the author's and his community's "Judenhaß" which led to the "schroffen Ablehnung des jüdischen Volkes wie seiner Religion" and the "harten Worte der Verdammung gegen die christenfeindlichen Juden."[71] Colwell stated explicitly in 1936, during Hitler's dictatorship, that the Fourth Gospel caters to an ancient form of anti-Semitism that is similar to the hatred of the Jew during the *Third Reich*![72] While this kind of language is avoided after the holocaust, the conclusion that "the Jews" in the Fourth Gospel are the "religious-national community" is not.[73] If this is a proper conclusion about the author's view of the Ἰουδαῖοι remains to be seen. The following study in this dissertation certainly points in a different direction.

1.4. Fellow Christians

A less followed explanation identifies "the Jews" in the Gospel of John with Jewish Christians.[74] As with the previous interpretations, some scholars are willing to view *some* occurrences of Ἰουδαῖοι as a reference to an inner-Christian conflict. The mentioning of the "Jews who had believed" (τοὺς πεπιστευκότας αὐτῷ Ἰουδαίους) in John 8:31 is the main support for this assumption, besides other texts such as 6:60-66, and 7:3-

---

[71] BAUER, *Das Johannesevangelium*, 243, 245, 248, also p. 31. Against Bauer, see TILLMANN, *Das Johannesevangelium*, 8.

[72] COLWELL, *John Defends the Gospel*, 41. He later writes that the first readers of the Gospel "were an anti-Semitic group, patriotic citizens of the Roman Empire." Ibid., 150, also p. 143. In his preface, Colwell acknowledges a "heavy debt" to Walter Bauer.

[73] See PANCARO, "The Relationship," 400-04. Pancaro views the language as a mirror of a conflict between Jewish Christians and the synagogue. According to Brown, the term Ἰουδαῖοι cannot be narrowed to "religious authorities" and reflects the conflict with "the Jews" during the Gospel's pre-literary phase when the church was expulsed from the synagogue. Brown offers the comment, "It would be incredible for a twentieth-century Christian to share or to justify the Johannine contention that 'the Jews' are the children of the devil, an affirmation which is placed on the lips of Jesus (8:44); but I cannot see how it helps contemporary Jewish-Christian relationships to disguise the fact that such an attitude once existed." BROWN, *The Community*, 41-42. Although he explains, if not defends, the Gospel's use of "the Jews" as the language of "disappointed love" ("enttäuschte Liebe") by a "threatened minority" of Jewish Christians ("bedrohte Minderheit"), Thyen calls "den schroffen Antijudaismus des vierten Evangeliums als die historisch verständliche, wenngleich in ihrer Maßlosigkeit bedauerliche Kehrseite seines unaufhebbaren . . . Judaismus." THYEN, "'Das Heil kommt von den Juden'," 183, also 168, 177.

[74] In a similar way with regard to the Synoptics, LaVerdiere interprets the "Pharisees of Jesus' story . . . as symbols for neo-Pharisees in the gentile communities addressed by Luke." LAVERDIERE, *Luke*, xlvii. Minear views Matthew's woes against the scribes and Pharisees in Matthew 23 as a warning for Christian scribes "of his own day against multiple forms of hypocrisy." MINEAR, "The Disciples," 36.

5.[75] But Rissi goes so far as to spread this possible meaning in John 8 to all occurrences of "the Jews" in the Gospel.[76] Richter divides the Gospel into three layers of redaction: the evangelist takes a "Grundschrift," in which Jewish Christians proclaimed Jesus as the prophet-Messiah, and reinterprets it into a Son-of-God Christology, mostly by adding the speeches of Jesus. "The Jews" represent the objections by Jewish-Christians which the evangelist projects back into the adversaries of Jesus.[77] For de Jonge, the evangelist's polemic aims at non-Johannine

---

[75] From a two-level perspective, Allen finds especially in Nathanael (1:44-51) and in the blind man who was healed (chap. 9) reflections of a "Jewish Christian Church, still faithful to the Law but acknowledging Jesus as Messiah." ALLEN, "The Jewish Christian Church," 92. Besides them, Allen sees the Gospel addressing problems with disciples of John the Baptist and "a current heresy of docetist type." Ibid., 92. Brown understands 6:60-66; 7:3-5; 10:12 and 8:31 as a reference to Jewish Christians and explains with regard to the latter text "that they are Jewish Christians who strongly resent the Johannine community because of its high Christology." BROWN, *The Community*, 77. Similar but distinct from them are the "crypto-Christians" (cf. 12:42-43) who "were afraid to confess their faith publicly less they be expelled from the synagogue." Ibid., 71. Though focused on the conflict between church and synagogue, even Martyn identifies "Christian Jews" with reference to 2:23-25; 11:46; 12:42; and 8:31-59. MARTYN, *History and Theology*, 159-63. Besides acknowledging the sense of "Judeans" (7:1) and "the Jerusalem officials, leaders, or authorities" (e.g., 9:22), Kaufman understands the use of Ἰουδαῖοι in 8:30-31; 5:16-47; 6:41, 52; 10:22-40 as a reflection of a "clash between the Johannine church and other Christian communities composed of Christian Jews who were still committed to observance of the Law." KAUFMAN, *The Beloved Disciple*, 57. Siegert identifies "the Jews" with Christians only with reference to John 8:30-59 since Jesus speaks πρὸς τοὺς πεπιστευκότας αὐτῷ Ἰουδαίους (8:31). SIEGERT, "Vermeintlicher Antijudaismus," 75-76. Besides strengthening Christians in their conflict with the synagogue, Shepherd speculates that it "may also be that the evangelist was concerned with an internal problem within the Church itself – a form of 'judaizing' from certain Christians." SHEPHERD, "The Jews," 106. Shepherd then lists examples of heresies that mix Jewish and Gnostic teachings, such as Cerinthus, possibly also the Nicolaitans of Rev 2:6, 15, the opponents mentioned in the Pastoral Epistles (Titus 1:10, 14; 1 Tim 1:4, 6-7; 4:4-14; 6:20; 2 Tim 2:18), and those attacked in the letters of Ignatius of Antioch. Ibid., 106-11. According to Rebell, Nicodemus represents (a) non-Christian Jews until 3:11 and (b) Christians from 3:12 on who need to be corrected for their overreliance on signs which neglects the emphasis on Christ's death and resurrection. REBELL, *Gemeinde als Gegenwelt*, 168-73, also 55-58, 203. Beside the use of midrashic techniques in John 6 and the contrast to major Jewish heroes (Jacob, Abraham, Moses), Tanzer finds in the characters of Nicodemus, Joseph of Arimathia, and the parents of the man born blind evidence for an audience that consisted of "closet Christian Jews" who were "straddling the fence between Judaism and Johannine Christian community." TANZER, "Salvation Is for the Jews," 300, 297. See also TOMSON, *Presumed Guilty*, 110-11.

[76] RISSI, "Die 'Juden'," 2099-141.

[77] According to Richter, a third redactor adds an anti-docetic layer to the Gospel. RICHTER, *Studien*, 356-57, 406-07. For a discussion and critique of Richter's proposal see BROWN, "Johannine Ecclesiology," 383-93.

Christians for two main reasons: First, the cause for breaches between Jesus and his opponents in John 5-12 is not the complete rejection of Jesus but only the denial of the unity between Father and Son. According to de Jonge, Jewish opponents would have brought up "completely different subjects, namely, whether Jesus was someone sent by God at all, or whether it was even possible for him to be the definitive agent of God's eschatological salvation." Second, the speeches of Jesus display "a certain amount of positive appreciation of Jesus," which would be inconceivable for non-Christian Jews.[78]

Altogether, the scope of the claim exceeds the available evidence. While the attributive participle τοὺς πεπιστευκότας αὐτῷ in 8:31 in itself could imply a reference to Jewish Christians in a two-level reading, this possible incident stands without any parallel and further support in the Gospel. Jesus' speech in John 5 displays a certain disconnection from Jewish charges,[79] but the subjects addressed are certainly hot buttons in a conflict between Jews and Christians. The clash over healing on a Sabbath day (5:1-23; 7:19-24; chap. 9) and the cleansing of the temple, the contrast between Moses and Jesus (1:17; 6:32) and the Abraham debate (chap. 8) touch on major tenets of the Jewish faith. Furthermore, the Synoptics parallel and thus validate the probability that the *Jewish* crowd responded to the ministry of Jesus not only with division (John 7:43; Matt 16:14-16; Luke 12:51-53) and rejection (John 6:60-66; Matt 13:15; Mark 6:3; Luke 6:11), but also with faith (John 11:45; 12:11; Matt 8:19; Mark 12:28-34; Luke 20:40). Rissi can uphold this view only by understanding the ἀποσυνάγωγος-texts (9:22; 12:42; 16:2) as interpolations of later redactors in the face of attacks from a militant Judaism.[80]

1.5. Religious Term without Empirical Reference

While the previous suggestions differed on the identity of the 'Ιουδαῖοι, they all understood "the Jews" as a reference to a real, existing group of people. Contrary to these views, Bultmann holds that "οἱ 'Ιουδαῖοι does not relate to the empirical state of the Jewish people, but to its very

---

[78] DE JONGE, "'The Jews'," 122-23. M. de Jonge analyses the function of the texts about the Messiah in the Gospel of John (7:27, 31, 41-42; 12:34) and concludes, against Meeks and Martyn's thesis of conflict between synagogue and church, that "Johannine Christology is developed not only in contrast with Jewish thinking but also with other Christological views." The Johannine community "tries to formulate its own standpoint over against christological discussions in the Church." M. DE JONGE, "Jewish Expectations," 264.

[79] See our discussion in chap. 4, pp. 78-79.

[80] RISSI, "'Die Juden'," 2133.

nature."[81] Bultmann is led to this conclusion because the Gospel contrasts "the Jews" many times with other Jews such as Jesus (see "your law" in 8:17), John the Baptist (1:19; 3:25), the blind man's parents (9:22), and the disciples (13:33). While he does recognize a historical reference to Jewish people in some cases (2:6, 13; 4:9, 22; etc.),[82] Bultmann understands these texts as glosses and views "the Jews" in general as "representatives of unbelief" and "of the unbelieving 'world' in general."[83] The Jewish religion serves as an example and "John makes clear through it how the human will to self-security distorts knowledge of God . . . . In so doing, John takes as his starting-point not the Jewish striving after 'righteousness' but the will-toward-life which is active in every religion."[84] On the other hand, when asked who exactly "the world" refers to, Bultmann tends to narrow κόσμος to empirical Jews and their rulers[85] who, at the time of the evangelist, excommunicated Christians from the synagogue.[86] There remains thus an odd tension between Bultmann's existential interpretation which diffuses an anti-Jewish reading of the Gospel, and an underlying historical reading which ties the language to a Jewish setting and conflict.[87]

---

[81] BULTMANN, *The Gospel of John*, 87. See also Fischer, "Natürlich sind nicht die empirischen Juden gemeint, sondern sie sind eine Metapher für die Ungläubigen überhaupt." FISCHER, "Der johanneische Christus," 251. More recently, Zumstein affirmed that "Dans le quatrième évangile, ce terme ['Ιουδαîοι], dans la grande majorité de ses occurrences, désigne non pas une appartenance ethnique ou nationale, mais des personnes qui, confrontées au Christ, ont choisi le camp de l'incrédulité." ZUMSTEIN, "Crise du Savoir," 173.

[82] BULTMANN, *The Gospel of John*, 86 n. 2, also 87 n. 1.

[83] Ibid., 86. Porsch explains it this way: "'Die Juden' bei Johannes sind also nicht die Juden in ihrer Gesamtheit und auch nicht das jüdische Volk. Mit diesem Ausdruck bezeichnet Joh die Gegner Jesu als 'die Repräsentanten der 'Welt' überhaupt, die Jesus den Glauben verweigert' (R. Bultmann)." PORSCH, "'Ihr habt den Teufel zum Vater'," 55.

[84] BULTMANN, *Theology of the New Testament*, 2:27.

[85] According to Bultmann, Pilate "by no means represents the world in the same way as the Jews and their ruler" whose "father is the devil, and who therefore are bent on murder and lying (8.44)." BULTMANN, *The Gospel of John*, 647, 656. See also chap. 5, p.113 n. 60. See our discussion of Bultmann's view on p. 127 n. 69.

[86] BULTMANN, *The Gospel of John*, 54-55, 555 n. 5.

[87] In the same odd way, Lincoln recently speaks of 'the Jews' as "representatives of the unbelieving world as a whole" but maintains an exclusively "intra-Jewish conflict" as the historical setting. LINCOLN, *The Gospel According to John*, 72. Bultmann's commentary culminates a development in Johannine scholarship which views the Fourth Gospel exclusively as a theological treatise and does not even ask for the specific historical context and purpose that triggered the composition of the text. Other scholars with this view include Holtzmann (1886), Heitmüller (1908), Bauer (1933), Kümmel

In addition to Bultmann's arguments, Grässer, points to the synonymity of the terms Ἰουδαῖος and κόσμος, which shows that whatever is said of "the Jews" applies also to "the world."[88] Furthermore, the other writing by the author of the Gospel, the First Letter of John, parallels the importance of κόσμος but does not have even one occurrence of Ἰουδαῖοι. Grässer concludes that, while Jewish hostility to the Johannine community at the time of the Gospel's composition certainly contributed to the polemic tone, these tensions are absorbed into a vertical dualism that is aimed against the threat of "wordliness" (disbelief, darkness, lying) in the church itself.[89] Although Ashton affirms many details and conclusions of Lowe's historical identification of the Ἰουδαῖοι with "Judeans," he nevertheless sees the need to distinguish between the (historical) *reference* of Ἰουδαῖοι and the term's *sense* (literary function) within the Gospel itself. It is the latter which convinces Ashton to side with Bultmann's reading of the "symbolic role" of the Judeans,[90] a function that others have called "theological,"[91] "salvation-historical,"[92] or "paradigmatic."[93] These differ-rent labels agree that the key to the interpretation of the term does not lie

---

(1973), Grässer (1973), Schnelle (1987), and Barrett (1990). See SCHMITHALS, *Johannesevangelium und Johannesbriefe*, 152-53.

[88] GRÄSSER, "Die Antijüdische Polemik," 88.

[89] Ibid., 90.

[90] ASHTON, "The Identity," 57. Smith speaks of the Jews as "symbols of human rejection of God's revelation in Jesus." SMITH, *Theology of the Gospel of John*, 56. Léon-Dufour explains that in John, "the word ['the Jews'] generally ceases to have an ethnic meaning, in order that it might designate a category of unbelievers." LÉON-DUFOUR, *Dictionary of the New Testament*, 249. See also PRYOR, *John*, 184. DE BOER, "The Depiction," 146 n. 23. WOODBRIDGE, "'The World'," 8 n. 11.

[91] LIEU, "Anti-Judaism," 112. Similarly, Davies explains that "the 'Jews' exemplify the world's rejection of Jesus (5.10, 18; 8.48, 52; 10.10, 31, 33, 39; 11.54; 18.35; 19.12, 15)." Thus, Ἰουδαῖοι is not so much a historical reference to actual people. Rather, the "theological structure, made clear in the Prologue, is obscuring the full dimensions of the historical reality." DAVIES, *Rhetoric and Reference*, 290.

[92] Köstenberger suggests that "the thrust of John's use of the term 'the Jews' is not ethnic, it is salvation-historical. What John is seeking to forestall is Jewish presumption upon their religious heritage." KÖSTENBERGER, *Encountering John*, 248. He then seems to adopt Stephen Motyer's proposal when he understands the function of this reference not in terms of John's hostility to the Jews, but in terms of "an effort at Jewish evangelism" (249). See also KÖSTENBERGER, "John," *NDBT*, 280, 282.

[93] KUHLI, "'Ιουδαῖος,'" in *EDNT*, 3:196. Grässer speaks of a "*Paradigma* also für die Offenbarung als Krisis." GRÄSSER, "Die Antijüdische Polemik," 89. See also GRELOT, *Les Juifs*, 186. Grelot uses other terms, saying that the Jews are a "parable" of humanity, that they "personify" or "represent" the world. Ibid., 190. According to Busse, 'the Jews' are "fictional eine für das Verständnis des Evangeliums wichtige Diskurs- bzw. Identifikationsfigur des Autors" and serve as the "Anti-Paradigma zum Paradigma 'der Erwählten.'" BUSSE, *Das Johannesevangelium*, 303-04.

in the question about the historical referent but in the literary significance of "the Jews" within the Gospel.[94]

On the other hand, Bultmann's concession to an empirical meaning for the Ἰουδαῖοι in at least *some* texts and Grässer's recognition of Jewish hostility at the time of the Gospel's composition indicate that the element of historical reference in the language of the Gospel cannot be dismissed categorically. At least in 4:9 (dialogue with the Samaritan woman), 4:22 ("salvation is of the Jews"), in descriptions of Jewish customs (2:6, 13; 3:1; 5:1; 6:4; etc.), in the designation of Jesus as 'king of the Jews' (18:33, 39; 19:3, 19, 21) and in Pilate's mouth (18:35) the term "the Jews" is not a mere symbol or paradigm for "the world" but refers to one unique people group.[95] By calling them Abraham's children (8:33, 37), the Jews are recognized as the historical people of God with a national identity (11:49-51).[96] Furthermore, there are many disputes between Jesus and "the Jews" which relate to particularly *Jewish* points of contention (Sabbath, Moses, origin of the Messiah).[97] And can one understand the term ἀποσυνάγωγος

---

[94] Culpepper regards "the Jews" as representatives of unbelief because "'the Johannine use' of the term has no nationalistic meaning since it distinguishes 'Jews' from others of the same national, religious, cultural group and designates a group with a constant, unchanging hostility toward Jesus." CULPEPPER, *Anatomy*, 126. See Schnelle, "Schlüssel zur Interpretation der Ἰουδαῖοι ist nicht die geschichtliche Rückfrage [so Martyn, Wengst] sondern die literarische Bedeutung der Juden innerhalb des Evangeliums." SCHNELLE, "Die Juden im Johannesevangelium," 255. Frey speaks of the use of Ἰουδαῖοι as a "dramatisches Stilmittel." FREY, "Das Bild," 42. Idem, "Heiden – Griechen – Gotteskinder," 235-37. For references to German and Anglo-American support of this thesis, see NICKLAS, *Ablösung und Verstrickung*, 19 n. 19.

[95] Nothomb rejects the idea of equating "the Jews" with "humanity" and points to John 4:22 as his argument, "Ce que Jésus a dit en Jean 4, 22 signifierait-il au fond 'le salut vient des hommes'? C'est absurde!" NOTHOMB, "Nouveau Regard," 69. On the other side, Nothomb neglects to investigate the parallelism between κόσμος and Ἰουδαῖοι in the Gospel.

[96] RUCKSTUHL, *Die literarische Einheitlichkeit*, 176.

[97] NICKLAS, *Ablösung und Verstrickung*, 19-20. Nicklas mentions the following critics of Bultmann: "In diesem Zusammenhang sei v.a. auf die Kritik des Ansatzes durch Sandmel (Anti-Semitism, 117f.) verwiesen. Die Ansicht, dass der *spezifische* Unglaube der joh 'Juden' nicht einfach mit dem der Welt gleichzusetzen sei, betonen auch Hahn (Heil, 80), Harvey (True Israel, 93: Joh auch in Auseinan-dersetzung mit 'real Jews and Judaism') und Smiga (Pain, 171). Auch Goppelt (Christentum, 258f.) kritisiert Bultmann dahingehend, dass der Unglaube, den die 'Juden' im JohEv Jesus entgegenbringen, als spezifisch jüdischer Unglaube anzusehen sei." Ibid., 19 n. 20. Caron criticizes that Bultmann "ignore finalement le rôle très particulier que cet évangile attribue à ceux que nous avons appelés les Juifs johanniques." CARON, *Qui sont les Juifs*, 45; also 167, 282.

merely as a symbolical chiffre without a reference to historical hostilities between synagogue and church?[98]

Thus, instead of giving up the historical element in the Gospel at large as well as in particular terms, we have to seek a solution that reconciles functional *and* referential aspects, theological and historical facets. If the Jews are representatives of the world, then they do so without ceasing to be identifiable as Jews.[99] And if ethnic Jews are the referent to Ἰουδαῖοι, then the metaphorical use does not automatically exclude an anti-Semitic motif.[100] Like Bultmann, Fischer regards Ἰουδαῖοι as a metaphor for the unbelieving world. But as such, the term *enhances* the anti-Jewish polemic, just as the parallels of the usage in anti-Jewish Gnostic literature.[101] Brown regards the Gospel's language of Jews who "fear the Jews" as part of the

---

[98] Frey insists against Grässer that the reading of "the Jews" as a mere cipher for unbelief is "in der Tat eine Verkürzung, die nur noch die 'symbolische' bzw. theologische Lektüreebene wahrnimmt, nicht mehr die geschichtlich-konkreten Umstände, d.h. die Gegnerschaft der einflußreichen Synagoge." FREY, "Das Bild," 50 n. 104. Although Busse regards "the Jews" as a fictional category and views them as a paradigm for unbelief, he cannot avoid a polemic connotation in the term that refers back to bitter experiences of expulsion from the synagogue. BUSSE, *Das Johannesevangelium*, 313.

[99] Goppelt's words suggest this solution when he says that the "Jude wird für J in umfassender Weise zum Repräsentanten der Welt, ohne aufzuhören, Jude im eigentlichen Sinn zu sein." GOPPELT, *Christentum und Judentum*, 255. While Dahl rejects charges of anti-Semitism because the Jews represent the world (so with Bultmann), he also concedes that it "is, however, equally important that *the Jews* are those who represent the world. . . . that the world's enmity and opposition to God gets its concentrated expression through the Jews" (italics his). DAHL, "The Johannine Church," 152, also 157-58.

[100] Motyer argues that "even if 'the Jews' are symbols of something else, we must still ask, 'which Jews?'. A derived symbolic *reference* feeds on a primary *sense*, as Rosemary Ruether has acutely seen in objecting that this symbolic interpretation of 'the Jews' does not absolve the fourth evangelist of anti-Judaism . . . ." MOTYER, *Your Father*, 50 (italics his).

[101] Fischer explains, "Gewiß hat es auch in der werdenden frühkatholischen Kirche eine scharfe Judenpolemik gegeben. Aber daß sie bis zur Metapher 'Juden' für: ungläubige Welt *gesteigert* wurde, ist nur vereinzelt zu finden. Für die Gnosis, sofern sie die *antijüdische* Wendung vollzogen hat, ist die Metapher dagegen selbstverständlich und kann unter der Voraussetzung, daß der Demiurg mit dem Gott der Juden identifiziert wird, sogar im System begründet sein. Der Demiurg ist es, der sich freventlich gegen die obere Welt erhebt mit den Worten: 'Ich bin Gott und außer mir ist keiner.' Dieser Gott wählte sich sein eigenes Volk, das ihm besonders treu ergeben ist: 'Jaldabaoth erwählte Abraham und machte dessen Nachkommen zu Juden' (Iren. *Adv. Haer.* 30.10). Weniger scharf, aber ebenso deutlich heißt es im Philippus-Evangelium: 'Wer den Herrn nicht empfangen hat, ist noch ein Hebräer' (EvPhil 46)." FISCHER, "Der johanneische Christus," 251-52 (italics added). For parallels to Gnostic anti-Judaism, see Bauer with reference to Mandean (Ginza 12.5) and Manichean literature in *Das Johannesevangelium*, 31.

historical conflict with the synagogue. Those who were expulsed "no longer considered themselves Jews despite the fact that many were of Jewish ancestry."[102] For Pratscher, Bultmann divorces theology from history and misses to ask for the genesis of the author's generalizing way of speech.[103] In his eyes, "the world" is a *theological* term which interprets a reality that is rooted in *historical* experiences of Jewish violence. Pratscher himself employs psychological models of collective projection which explain the hostile language as the result of objective pressures by Jews and subjective failures by Christians.[104] In the end, he cannot avoid the conclusion that the Gospel's language is improper, does not relate to reality and is devoid of differentiation and responsible theological speech.[105]

1.6. Conclusion

These five interpretations of Ἰουδαῖοι do not exhaust the contributions to the discussion. In a recent essay, Moloney resists identifying the Ἰουδαῖοι and simply insists that the unbelieving Jews "are not the only Jews in the story" and that "there were ethnic Jews on both sides of this divide."[106] More frequently, we find various combinations of the meanings introduced above. Some scholars mix, for example, a religious and a geographical meaning (law-abiding Jews in Judea)[107] or define "the Jews" even more

---

[102] BROWN, *The Community*, 41.

[103] Pratscher criticizes that Bultmann's view "erklärt aber nicht ausreichend die Genese dieser Redeweise. Es hat nur eine Seite dieser Genese im Blick, die spezifisch johanneischen Theologumena." PRATSCHER, "Die Juden," 180.

[104] Ibid., 182-83.

[105] Ibid., 184. Recently, Pratscher repeated his interpretation and defended a psychological approach to the New Testament in "Tiefenpsychologische Erwägungen," 277-90, esp. 282-85.

[106] MOLONEY, *The Gospel of John*, 40-41. Somewhat exaggerated, and therefore unconvincing, sounds Moloney's claim that "the repeated use of the expression 'the Jews' in a negative sense has *nothing* to do with national, political, or religious affiliation. It has *everything* to do with the definitive rejection of Jesus as the revelation of God." Ibid., 40 (italics his). Was Jesus not rejected because of religious differences that even included national and political implications? Already two sentences later Moloney reveals the false dichotomy in his claim: "The world 'behind' the story that produced this hostile group consisted of ethnically Jewish people, fiercely committed to the reestablishment of Jewish life and religious practice after the devastation of the Jewish War (66-73 C.E.), especially the loss of the temple and the city of Jerusalem. They necessarily came into conflict with the Johannine Christians." Ibid., 40. Jewish life and religious practice led "necessarily" to conflict with the Jesus of John!

[107] Lütgert understands "the Jews" as a religious (not a national) term, describing that part of Israel which abides by the law. Among those are also "judaizing people from Galilee," as the occurrences of Ἰουδαῖοι in John 2:6; 6:41, 52 suggest. LÜTGERT, "Die

narrowly as religious authorities around Jerusalem.[108] But, as the specific definitions discussed earlier (authorities, Judeans), these identifications are so precise that they emerge only after a detailed comparison of very subtle nuances of the term in *some* of the occurrences. Besides the question whether such analytical efforts could be expected by the first readers,[109] it is not comprehensible why the author missed to name these particular groups when the language for them is readily available.[110]

Our discussion has shown that a broader definition for Ἰουδαῖοι (ethnic-religious term, religious term) fits the context better than very precise proposals (authorities, Judeans). It leads to the frightening question if the author, for whatever historical and / or psychological reasons, carried with him a notion of anti-Semitism.

2. Review of Previous Studies

Between 1972 and 2005, over ten dissertations and monographs were written about the Jews in the Gospel of John, using a variety of methods to approach our topic.[111] Their different conclusions demonstrate again the absence of a consensus and the pluralism of methods employed in the field. Few of the works support the mainstream views outlined above, many offer new and idiosyncratic results that merit their separate discussion. We will discuss them as we did the previous interpretations, but now with special focus on method and specific texts selected for examination. This should help to identify and define our own approach in this study.

Juden," 152. According to Boyarin, the Ἰουδαῖοι denotes "the particularist and purity-oriented community in and around Jerusalem" from which others such as Galileans and Samaritans were excluded. BOYARIN, "*Ioudaioi* in John," 235. Motyer indicates the weakness of this interpretation when he regards the Ἰουδαῖοι as 'the religious of Judea' "except the handful of places where it has a purely ethnic force, particularly in the phrase 'King of the Jews'." MOTYER, *Your Father*, 213.

[108] We mentioned Belser earlier. See now also GÜTING, "Kritik an den Judäern," 158-201, esp. 172-77.

[109] Belser himself acknowledges at the end that his proposal sounds strange because it demands a reader with a lot of analytical power and attention to detail. BELSER, "Der Ausdruck οἱ Ἰουδαῖοι," 222.

[110] Josephus, for example, can speak about the οἱ Ἱεροσολύμοι Ἰουδαῖοι (*A.J.* 17.293; 19.1; *B.J.* 7.431) or the οἱ ἐν τῇ Ἀλεξανδρείᾳ Ἰουδαῖοι (*A.J.* 13.77; *B.J.* 2.499; *C. Ap.* 2.7)

[111] This is not an exhaustive count. Balfour's dissertation does not discuss the Ἰουδαῖοι in the Gospel and addresses a different question. BALFOUR, "Is John's Gospel Anti-semitic? With Special Reference to its Use of the Old Testament" (Ph.D. thesis, University of Nottingham, 1995).

2.1. Diachronic Approaches

In their attempt to understand the use of the Ἰουδαῖοι, some scholars focus on an inner-Jewish conflict after AD 70 as the suggested *historical context* of the Gospel. The textual analysis is therefore limited to those chapters and verses that provide the most evidence for this contextual reconstruction. The methods chosen include the use of rabbinic literature (Bowman), the use of Jewish pseudepigrapha (Motyer), socio-rhetorical criticism (Hendricks), and source criticism (White, Grelot, Lingad).

2.1.1. Rabbinic Literature: Bowman (1975)

Bowman opens with a chapter on "Akiba, Text, Canon and Exegesis" in which he outlines the literalist approach to the Torah by Rabbi Akiba, the "most significant contemporary teacher in Judaism," and his possible influence on an early revision of Targum Onkelos (*memra*).[112] He identifies the unspecified "feast of the Jews" in John 5:1 as the Purim feast mentioned in the book of Esther which, together with the feast of Hanukkah (see 10:22), told the story of deliverance "and fostered national pride."[113] According to Bowman, John's Gospel responds to the book of Esther which was incorporated into the Hebrew canon by the scholar and messianist Rabbi Akiba after the Synod in Jamnia between 80 and 90 AD. In times of trouble with Rome, John suggests a universalist and pacifist solution against Esther's and the Sadducean establishment's ("the Jews") "nationalist and retaliatory" answer.[114] Various parallels are mentioned to strengthen the reading of the Gospel as an antithesis to the book of Esther, such as the deaths of Haman and Jesus (ch. 6; both died in the month of Nisan), the six meals mentioned in each of the books, the love between Jesus and Lazarus analogue to that between Esther and Mordechai (ch. 9) and the parallels between Judas / the Jews and Haman (ch. 11).

As a Semitist, Bowman draws heavily from sources of rabbinic literature, all of which date later than the Fourth Gospel (Midrash, Mishnah, Talmud) except maybe the Targumim.[115] Unfortunately, he does

---

[112] BOWMAN, *The Fourth Gospel and the Jews: A Study in R. Akiba, Esther and the Gospel of John*, viii.

[113] Ibid., 42.

[114] Ibid., viii, 41, 142.

[115] The index to references counts nine pages with references to the Targumim and rabbinical literature compared with eight pages of references to Old Testament literature. There is no index for non-Jewish literature. According to Evans, the rabbinic literature was completed and edited at the following dates: Mishnah 200–220 C.E., Tosefta 220–230 C.E., Palestinian Talmud 400–425 C.E., Babylonian Talmud 500–550 C.E.; *Mekilta*, the earliest tannaic midrash, 4th century. EVANS, *Ancient Texts*, 216-46. When discussing the date of the Targumim, Evans agrees with McNamara and against Fitzmyer that they

not offer any methodological justification or qualification for such a liberal use of much younger material.[116] The Mishnah contains the earliest rabbinic traditions and it was written ca. 200 A.D.[117] Furthermore, Bowman's view of Rabbi Akiba as "the most significant contemporary teacher in Judaism" is challenged by the current emphasis on the complexity of Judaism[118] and on the late development of rabbinic orthodoxy after the Bar Kokba revolt in 132-135 AD.[119] As Meeks observes, most of the parallels drawn between Esther and the Gospel seem "nothing more than free association."[120] The frequent use of 'Ιουδαῖοι in Esther (44 times) is the most striking parallel to John, but here 1 Maccabees (37 times) and 2 Maccabees (59 times) certainly do not lag behind. When evaluating his textual analysis, we observe that Bowman centers most discussion on John 9-13 and 18-19, thus largely excluding, among others, the prologue and the farewell discourse from his considerations. There is much to learn from Bowman's monograph, but it hardly serves as an answer to the identity and role of the Jews in the Gospel of John.

2.1.2. Second Temple Judaism: Motyer (1997), Fuglseth (2005)

After specifying in chapter 1 a "holistic approach" which moves from the general to the particular, i.e., "from *context* to *co-text*, and finally to the

---

"do preserve *some* tradition that dates to, and possibly before, the time of the NT." Ibid., 186 (italics added). Note the careful qualification!

[116] See also the criticism of FREY, *BZ* 46 (2002): 137-38, against Wengst' commentary with regard to the use of the Rabbinica. Similarly, SALMON, *Journal of Law & Religion* 17 (2002): 425, criticizes Alan Watson in a review of his book *Jesus and the Jews: The Pharisaic Tradition in John* (1995) for basing much of his major thesis on the use of the Mishnah. See also MOTYER, *Your Father*, 75-76 (in response to J. L. Martyn's use of the Rabbinica) and POPKES, *Die Theologie der Liebe Gottes*, 68. In their compilation of background material to the Gospels, Bock and Herrick recently expressed the necessary caution when they write, "If care needs to be exercised in using the Mishnah, even more care is called for in appealing to the Talmud because of the late dates of these sources." BOCK, HERRICK, *Jesus in Context*, 22, also 14. In an unfinished multi-volume project, Instone-Brewer recently began to apply 13 levels of probability to rabbinic material that possibly predates AD 70. See INSTONE-BREWER, *Traditions of the Rabbis*, esp. 39-40.

[117] For this reason, Rabbi Burton L. Visotzky suggests to regard rabbinic parallels to the Fourth Gospel as part of the Gospel's history of interpretation, much like Patristic commentators such as John Chrysostom or Jerome. VISOTZKY, "Methodological Considerations," 95-101.

[118] This complexity is evident, for example, in ideologies as opposite as nationalism (e.g., Sibylline Oracles, book 5) and universalism (e.g., Testament of Abraham). See MOTYER, *Your Father*, 75-76.

[119] See MOTYER, *Your Father*, 75.

[120] See the review by MEEKS, *Interpretation* 31 (Oct. 1977): 422.

text on which our interest focuses,"[121] Motyer discovers seven 'points of sensitivity' which link the Fourth Gospel with first-century Judaism (ch. 2), such as the Temple and the Festivals, the law, revelation and apocalyptic, the creation of faith, the signs, some aspects of Johannine language and argumentation, and 'the Jews.' Following Lütgert (1914), Bornhäuser (1928) and others, Motyer understands the Ἰουδαῖοι as the temple- and Torah-oriented *"Pharisees* in the period before 70, . . . and the *sages of Yavneh* [Palestine] and their followers in the period after 70" which Jews in the diaspora "generally would have recognized . . . as something distinct within this overall spectrum" of first century Judaism.[122] After delving into the Jewish pseudepigrapha for exploring various Jewish reactions to the destruction of the temple as the historical context for the Gospel (ch. 3) and further defining techniques of narrative criticism (ch. 4), Motyer centers his textual analysis first on John 5-12 (ch. 5) and then on 7:1-8:59 (ch. 6) and 8:31-59 (ch. 7). Although admitting that the Gospel is in one way "strongly inimical to the Yavneh programme,"[123] he regards the statement in 8:44, "You are of your father, the devil," as part of a *prophetic* appeal[124] to those and other Jews with an *evangelistic* purpose that enables "the Gospel to be *Good News* in the environment of late first-century Judaism."[125] The Gospel's rejection of the cult has to be seen as a response to the calamity of the temple destruction that is also echoed by the authors of 4 Ezra and 2 Baruch.

The Norwegian scholar Sigvald Fuglseth published a comparative study about the behavior to outsiders in the writings of John, Philo, and Qumran and his conclusion resembles that of Motyer. The designation of Jesus' body as a temple (John 2:21) as well as the new definition of worship apart from geographical location "in spirit and truth" (4:24) reveal a 'tense' but not a 'high-tension' situation with Judaism.[126] While the pejorative use of Ἰουδαῖοι reflects "conflict with a local synagogue,"[127] the reference to Jesus' body as a temple is not explicitly linked to a replacement theme but

---

[121] MOTYER, *Your Father the Devil? A New Approach to John and "the Jews."*, 32.

[122] Ibid., 54, 55, also 153-54. Elsewhere, Motyer identifies the Ἰουδαῖοι as the "Judea-based, Torah-loyal adherents of the Yavneh-ideals, the direct heirs of pre-70 Pharisaism." Ibid., 213.

[123] Ibid., 213.

[124] Motyer compares John 8 especially with Hosea, and John 8:44 (devil) with Hosea 11:2 (Baal). Ibid., 146-48.

[125] Ibid., 74-75. The author of Gospel is a "Jew speaking to Jew, in just the same way as the authors of 4 Ezra and 2 Baruch" address a post-temple Judaism. Ibid., 212.

[126] FUGLSETH, *Johannine Sectarianism in Perspecitve*, 248-4985. On a scale between rejection and acceptance, Fuglseth finds the Gospel more on the side of "critical acceptance" with regard to Judaism. Ibid, 176.

[127] Ibid, 351, 76, 314-17.

seems to address the desire for worship after the destruction of the temple in AD 70.[128] Philo and the Qumran literature show how a temple-critical attitude can use Jerusalem's physical temple as a metaphor for reason (λογισμός, *Virt.* 88), the mind (διάνοια, *Praem.* 123), the soul (ψυχή, *Somn.* 1.215), the κόσμος (*Spec.* 1:66) or the dissenting religious community (1QS 8) *without* completely loosing loyalty to the cult in general and to Judaism as such.[129]

Motyer's and Fuglseth's historical studies avoid Bowman's short-comings by relying not on the Rabbinica but on the literature of Second Temple Judaism and by recognizing Judaism's diversity in the first century AD. While operating with a different Sitz im Leben (evangelism; local conflict with synagogue), both scholars find that the writings of Second temple Judaism provide a context in which the Gospel's view on matters of Jewish identity appear less tense than often assumed (Fuglseth) or even to be good news (Motyer). The problem is that John's frequent pejorative use of 'the Jews' *distinguishes* him from these contemporary writings and give parallel concepts often a much more polemical context and connotation.[130] Furthermore, it does not seem warranted to limit the search for 'points of sensitivity' between text and historical context to first-century Judaism at the exclusion of hellenism and the Roman empire. Motyer asserts this point more than he argues for it and finds only a Jewish context because that is all he is searching for. He ignores the *religionsgeschichtliche* complexity of the text which is evident today more than ever before in scholarship.[131] Fuglseth does discuss the references to 'the world,' the Samaritans, the Ἕλληνές, etc. and concludes that all of these people groups belong to the "general addressees" of the Gospel, be they in Palestine or in the Greco-Roman diaspora.[132] But Fuglseth limits his analysis of parallels to Jewish writings only (Philo and Qumran) without asking the question how Gentiles would understand the term Ἰουδαῖοι.[133] The view of

---

[128] Ibid, 185, 295.

[129] Ibid., 201-40. Alexandrian Jews, including Philo himself, observed the Law by their pilgrimage to the temple and payment of the temple tax (*Spec.* 1:77-78; *Prov.* 2:64).

[130] Fuglseth admits this difference when he writes, "Philo does not, on the other hand, use the notion of Ἰουδαῖος in a similar negative way as in Jn 8." Ibid., 314.

[131] In support of a postulated "wide consensus" for reading the Fourth Gospel in a Jewish context, Motyer merely offers a reference to an article by J.A.T. Robinson from 1959. In the next sentence, he also refers to Günter Reim, Frédéric Manns and J.C. Thomas who utilize the rabbinica. Ibid., 35. But later Motyer himself rightly disqualifies such material because of its younger age. Ibid., 75-76. We elaborate on the Gospel's *religionsgeschichtliche* complexity in chapter 3 (1.1.3).

[132] Ibid., 318, see 287-319.

[133] Fuglseth pursues more the question of Johannine sectarianism than that of anti-Judaism in the Fourth Gospel.

exclusively Jewish readers is more directly challenged by the translations of common Aramaic words into Greek terms, such as Ῥαββί (1:38; 20:16) and Μεσσίας (1:41; 4:25) which seem to serve as an aid for Gentiles. Being most likely written towards the end of the first century, the Gospel has *also* been preached to the Gentiles and the text shows ample evidence of their presence in and around the Johannine community (e.g., 7:35; 12:20; 4:42; 21:18-19).[134] The question then becomes what happens if the pages of the Gospel hit the eyes of the gentile reader. The solid distinction which Motyer makes between a religious sense of Ἰουδαῖοι and an ethnic one is at least blurred by his own concession that the term does have an ethnic meaning as, for example, in the title 'King of the Jews' (18:20, 33, 35; 19:3, 19, 21).[135] And it is rather unlikely that Gentiles would have distinguished between Palestinian-based Yavneh-Jews and diaspora Jews and considered the Gospel as part of a debate within the family.[136] If for them the various Judaisms are not already united by race than at least so by religious concerns such as Sabbath, circumcision, Abraham, Moses, etc.[137] Finally, Motyer's limited focus on John 5-12 in general and on 8:31-59 in particular as well as Fuglseth's focus on John 2 and 4 exclude the prologue and the farewell discourse from any interpretive influence on their conclusions. The term κόσμος (or 'world') is hardly discussed and not indexed at the end of both works.

2.1.3. Socio-Rhetorical Criticism: Hendricks (1995)

In a first lengthy chapter, Obery M. Hendricks introduces his "new perspective" on the issue by describing a socio-rhetorical approach (leaning on

---

[134] In this regard, Motyer resembles J. L. Martyn who neglects to include the Gentiles in his historical reflections about the Gospel's *Sitz im Leben*. See our discussion in chapter 5 (2.1.2.).

[135] MOTYER, *Your Father*, 213.

[136] This issue touches on the debate about the existence of one normative Judaism during the time of Jesus. Michael Maher summarizes the three current points of view. Until the 1950s most scholars held that there was one normative/orthodox Judaism. The discovery of the Dead Sea Scrolls triggered the view of many different Judaisms (Morton Smith, Jacob Neusner). Martin Hengel and Roland Deines suggest a *via media*: There was one complex Judaism, united on the outside against the foreign rule of Rome, but divided on the inside into various groups and sects. MAHER, "Knowing the Tree by Its Roots," 1-28.

[137] But even from an insider perspective, the diaspora Jews might not have made that distinction when reading the Gospel. They were understood even by Gentiles as Abraham's children (cf. Josephus, *A.J.* 14.255) and surely would have taken sides with the Ἰουδαῖοι's claim "We are Abraham's seed" in John 8:33. When Motyer himself uses the *Testament of Abraham* to illustrate a thought parallel to the Gospel, he uses literature from the *diaspora* in Egypt and not from Yavneh-Jews in Palestine. Ibid., 203.

Vernon Robbins) that leans especially on John 7:52 ("You are not also from Galilee, are you?") in order to postulate a *literary Ioudaioi-Galilaioi* opposition which stems from a *historical* class conflict in first century Palestine between urban elites and rural peasants.[138] He then analyzes the point of view of the "Galilaioi (chap. 2; 7:52; 2:13; 7:14; 10:22; 1:11, 12-13, 19; 4:45; 1:47; 6:4-5; 10:11; 11:1; 4:21; 3:10-11) and the "Ioudaioi" (chap. 3; 8:33; 7:15, 49; 19:15; 4:21; 12:4-6; 18:3; 4:22c; 1:46; 6:41; 7:3) and offers in his conclusion (chap. 4), among others, that 'Ιουδαῖοι is best translated with 'the party of Judas' or 'Jerusalem priestly aristocracy.'[139]

While many interpreters acknowledge a topographical symbolism of "Galilee" in John 2-4 as the "land of acceptance, refuge, and belief in Jesus" in contrast to Judea as "the land of rejection, hostility, and disbelief,"[140] Hendrick's postulate blows the biblical evidence out of proportion. Not only is there unbelief in Galilee (6:36)[141] and faith in Judea (9:38; 12:11), which compromises a categorical opposition between (literary and historical) 'Galileans' and 'Jews.' But the Γαλιλαῖοι are mentioned only once in the Gospel (4:45; Γαλιλαία 18 times). To use this occurrence and the text in 7:52 as the basis for reconstructing the "social location" of the author and his community is too thin of a textual foundation for the historical reconstruction. And if, contrary to Hendricks, the provenance of the Gospel is metropolitan Ephesus and not an agrarian part of Syro-Palestine, it becomes a challenge to understand how a rural ideology can serve urban Christians. Hendrick's thesis presupposes Lowe's rendering of 'Ιουδαῖοι as 'inhabitants of Judea' and suffers thus from the weaknesses we mentioned in our discussion of this interpretation (see 1.2). His paradigm also does not consider values in the Gospel that run counter to the morals one would expect of a peasant society, such as altruism (13:34; 15:12, 17), egalitarian traits (4:27), the sacrifice of safety (12:25; 15:18) and the creation of fictive kinship (1:12; 19:26-27).[142]

---

[138] HENDRICKS, "A Discourse of Domination: A Socio-Rhetorical Study of the Use of IOUDAIOS in the Fourth Gospel," (1995).

[139] Ibid., 241, 251.

[140] BASSLER, "The Galileans," 250, with reference to Meeks, Olsson, Fortna, Merino, and Scobie.

[141] Hirsch argues further that Jesus' escape beyond the Jordan (10:40) shows that Galilee was no place of refuge for him, not to speak of faith and support. HIRSCH, *Studien*, 139.

[142] According to Moreland, these morals are found in Q and contradict values of peasants. MORELAND, "The Galilean response," 37-48.

2.1.4. Literary Criticism

In the tradition of Raymond Brown's multiple stage theory, various scholars ascribe different nuances of 'the Jews' to different sources or redactions.

2.1.4.1. White (1972), Tomson (2001)

After a survey of literature (ch. 2) and a review of the term "Jews" in ancient literature (ch. 3), Martin White analyzes in chapter 4 the meaning of 'Ἰουδαῖοι in the whole Gospel and observes not only different but even contradictory usages of "the Jews" (positive and negative, believing and unbelieving). He therefore describes the Gospel as a "patchwork" that is "put together from varying sources in the Johannine communities without any attempt to unify the material in either language or theology."[143] Similarly, Peter Tomson notices various connotations of 'Ἰουδαῖοι and understands them as the result of "patchwork editing of received material."[144] The prologue, the farewell discourse, and chapter 21 have no influence on the understanding of "the Jews" because they belong "to a later stratum" in which the Gospel was "re-edited in a non-Jewish speech situation."[145]

2.1.4.2. Grelot (1995)

Pierre Grelot begins his study by briefly reviewing the occurrences of 'Ἰουδαῖοι in biblical and non-biblical literature, including the Gospel of John (part 1). Grelot concludes the study of the latter by rejecting the geographic meaning "Judeans" and insisting that the text demands the "sens national et religieux."[146] Part 2 analyzes the "situation historique des textes" (part 2) and finds multiple stages in the composition of the book. Grelot infers that the final edition of the Gospel "reflète l'opposition entre chrétiens et Juifs"[147] and responds to the 18. benediction against the minim by Rabbi Gamaliel II.[148] In part 3, Grelot studies the Gospel as a mirror of this controversy between Jews and Christians (see purification, Sabbath, temple; etc.) and defends the text by saying that, besides other points, it is not a polemic attack against the Jews nor an apologetic defense of the

---

[143] WHITE, "The Identity and Function of Jews and Related Terms in the Fourth Gospel," 58, 336.

[144] TOMSON, "'Jews' in the Gospel of John," 198.

[145] Ibid., 192, also 201-03.

[146] GRELOT, *Les Juifs dans l'évangile selon Jean: Enquête historique et réflexion théologique*, 47.

[147] Ibid., 121. It is the time when the "Judaisme rabbinique se constituait." Ibid., 166; also 178-82 ("L'évangéliste devant le Judaisme Rabbinique").

[148] Ibid., 95-96. Strange enough, Grelot does not mention J. Louis Martyn at all.

church but "une confession de foi."[149] Nevertheless, after seven chapters of discussion, the question if the Gospel is anti-Semitic is still in the air for Grelot. He finally refutes this charge in chapter 8 with reference to (1) the Jewishness of Jesus (e.g., 4:22; 7:47; 6:42; etc.), (2) to the "purely religious" and personal nature of the disagreement with Rabbinic Judaism,[150] and (3) to the "valeur paradigmatique" of the Jews via the use of the term κόσμος which indicates that "le monde entier est impliqué dans cette opposition à Jésus."[151]

It is stunning that Grelot finds no reason to refute the charges of anti-Semitism until the last fifteen pages of his monograph. In the context of a conflict with the synagogue, a broad lexical meaning for Ἰουδαῖοι creates a violent rhetorical counter-attack and not simply a confession. According to Grelot's study, the Gospel's use of κόσμος is the strongest indication that the author does not stigmatize the Jews as the murderers of Christ but treats them as part of an opposition to Jesus and the church that is global in scope. Yet, contrary to the Gospel where κόσμος appears on the first page, Grelot reserves the discussion for the end and can afford to discuss "the Jews" in the Gospel's history and theology in complete separation from the term "the world." The reason for this dichotomy is not apparent, but we may speculate that his understanding of the Gospel's composition in multiple stages accounts for the separate interpretation of distinct redactional layers. It remains to be seen if there are not literary connections between Ἰουδαῖοι and κόσμος which *require* to interpret one in light of the other.

2.1.4.3. Lingad (2001)

Similar to Grelot, but with a different arrangement, Celestino Lingad employs Brown's multiple stage theory to understand different meanings of 'the Jews.' After an elaborate introduction to "Jewish Christians" (ch. 1), Lingad traces the early history of the Johannine Community by dividing the composition of the Gospel into an early, middle, and late period (ch. 2). He distinguishes between "the Jews" as non-Christian outsiders in the middle period of the Gospel's composition and "the Jews" as Jewish Christians in the third and final stage (cf. 2:23-25; 3:1-21; 6:2-4;

---

[149] Ibid., 156.

[150] Grelot explains that "le reproche est purement religieux" and that, in contrast to Paul (cf. Rom 9-11), it is the "*l'aspect individuel du problème*" which the author of the Fourth Gospel is interested in. Ibid., 179, 180 (italics his).

[151] Ibid., 185. Grelot also sees, for example, all of humanity addressed in 16:9 where the paraclete will "convict the world" because "they do not believe in me."

7:5; 8:31).[152] Using a socio-historical method, Lingad explains that the use of 'Ιουδαῖοι in the middle period was due to a conflict not with Jews as a race or nation but with early rabbinic Judaism as the most influential *part* of Jewish religion.[153] The replacement of 'Ιουδαῖοι with κόσμος is noted with regard to the farewell discourse, but Lingad observes with reference to 16:2 that the denotations of both terms "are not distinct."[154]

Lingad's view of the use of 'Ιουδαῖοι in the middle period basically repeats J. L. Martyn's famous thesis and finds a more refined form in the work of Stephen Motyer which we discussed and criticized above. Finally, Lingad's equation of 'the world' with 'the Jews' is challenged, for example, by Grelot's discussion of κόσμος as a term larger than 'Ιουδαῖοι, a matter that invites for further study.

While not unparalleled in the current debate,[155] the confident attempt of White, Grelot, Lingad, and others to distinguish various sources or redactional stages in the Gospel in the tradition of Bultmann and Brown stands in contrast to much of modern Johannine scholarship. For one reason, the Gospel's *stylistic unity* convinced even older scholars such as Segovia and Ashton, who formerly employed source-criticism, to adopt a more coherent view of the Gospel's text.[156] Without denying that the Gospel might have had a history of gradual growth, the confidence of going behind the text in order to find individual sources or multiple editions has largely eroded. Most modern discussions about "the Jews" in John use text-immanent tools of *narrative criticism* for their analysis. They demonstrate the fundamental shift in Johannine studies from diachronic to synchronic studies which focus their attention on the final form of the text.[157] Secondly, the Gospel's *theological complexity* often challenges the

---

[152] See chapter 2 in LINGAD, *The Problems of Jewish Christians in the Johannine Community* (2001).

[153] They are "those who, after the debacle of AD 70, had succeeded once again in gathering the reins of power into their own hands." Ibid., 123-24.

[154] Ibid., 122. Chapter 3 and 4 of Lingad's work continue to trace the history of the Johannine community beyond the Gospel (Epistles in ch. 3; second century in ch. 4) and chapter 5 studies selected texts of John 2-8 as a mirror of problems with Jewish Christians.

[155] See, for example, EHRMAN, *The New Testament*, 163-73. See also our discussion in chapter 5 (2.1.2) of J. L. Martyn and his reliance on Fortna's source criticism.

[156] See the discussion in KEENER, *The Gospel of John*, 37-39. BEASLEY-MURRAY, *John*, xxxviii-xlii.

[157] Schnelle speaks of a "grundlegenden Wende" which is evident from four commentaries that were all published in 1998 and which show heavy influence of synchronic analysis (Wilckens, Moloney, Schenke, Schnelle). SCHNELLE, "Ein neuer Blick," 21. See Frey's discussion of the earlier works by Thyen, Schenke, Neugebauer, and Reinhartz, who do not categorically reject literary criticism but start their work with the premise of

reader to hold together two concepts that are set in seeming opposition to each other, such as Jesus' humanity (1:14) and divinity (1:1), equality between the Son and the Father (10:30) and the Son's subordination (14:28), God's love (3:16; cf. 1 John 4:10) and the Gospel's dualism (Joh 8:44-47; cf. 1 Joh 3-7-10), present (5:25) and futurist (5:28) eschatology. Barrett rehearses some of these antitheses (including Judaism and anti-Judaism) and refuses to understand them as the product of an author/redactor who was simply "too careless and too stupid to notice an actual incompatibility."[158] Instead of perceiving them as "unharmonized tendencies of different sources," Barrett speaks of the "dialectic of Christian truth" which finds parallels in the Old Testament and Judaism as well.[159] A more cautious and self-critical approach will seek to understand the function of seemingly incoherent concepts as part of the gospel's communicative goal and literary symphony.[160]

2.2. Synchronic Approaches

Distinct from the preceding works, the following dissertations take more interest in the text itself than in the reconstruction of the Gospel's historical background or genesis. While assumptions about a historical context are not rejected *per se*, they are subordinated under text-immanent tools of analysis.

2.2.1. Linguistic Method: Schram (1974)

In part I of his dissertation, Terry Schram offers some "linguistic insights" in which he basically explains his synchronic approach that focuses on "*Ioudaios* within the lexical structure of the book, not the historicity of the

---

textual coherence. FREY, *Die johanneische Eschatologie. Band I*, 298-330. Besides the essays by Boer (1980), Philips (1983) and Wuellner (1981), Staley traces the origin of narrative criticism in the Fourth Gospel back to monographs by Olsson, *Structure and Meaning in the Fourth Gospel* (1974) and Culpepper, *Anatomy of the Fourth Gospel* (1983). Staley, *Print's First Kiss*, 10-19. Hallbäck mentions the works of Culpepper (1983), Kermode (1987), Staley (1988), and Stibbe (1992) as instrumental for English scholarship. See HALLBÄCK, "The Gospel of John as Literature," 31-46. According to Moloney, Robert Kysar "was perhaps first to break ground with a narrative approach to this Gospel" in his *John's Story of Jesus* (1984). MOLONEY, *The Gospel of John*, 194 n. 5. In 1991, Johannes Beutler spoke of literary criticism as a "new branch of international criticism of the New Testament, which originated predominantly in the United States of America." BEUTLER, "Response," 191.

[158] BARRETT, *The Gospel of John and Judaism*, 73.

[159] Ibid., 72, 75.

[160] POPKES, *Die Theologie der Liebe Gottes*, 60.

book."[161] Part II analyzes all occurrences of Ἰουδαῖος in the gospel. After the function and the structure of an "episode" is established, the linguistic criteria of manifestation, distribution, feature and reference are applied to the word Ἰουδαῖος within that sense unit. Chapters 4-6 present the analysis of the whole gospel. While the term denotes various *historical* referents such as Pharisees, Jewish people as a nation, people of Galilee, etc.,[162] the author uses "the Jews" for a *theological* purpose, namely "to introduce Jesus and further the argument that he is the Messiah."[163] Chapter seven relates the single word and episodes to the whole gospel and specifies at least three observations. A) Schram comments that Jesus' life and death is not understood as the result of a struggle between him and his opponents but that his death "is his own doing."[164] Their active contribution to the crucifixion of Jesus is part of the proposition which Jesus gives to the Samaritan woman: "Salvation is from the Jews."[165] Furthermore, Jesus' strong words of judgment (e.g., 12:49, 50) are "no harsher than words recorded about the people of Israel in the Law and the prophets."[166] B) The gospel contrasts the response of the Ἰουδαῖοι to the signs and words of Jesus and with that of the disciples (μαθητής occurs 78 times in John).[167] This is underlined with general observations (disciples believe Jesus, Jews do not) and specific comparisons (see proximity of both terms in 8:31, 9:27-29) which show that the author uses Ἰουδαῖοι as a theological chiffre for unbelief. C) The extensive use of κόσμος in the gospel provides "a more general background" to Jesus actions in Judea and Galilee and the Jewish response.[168] In their disbelief and contribution to Jesus' death, the Jews "represent the world," a typical relationship that is found already in Jeremiah 9:25, 26.[169] According to Schram, the Roman mockery of Jesus

---

[161] SCHRAM, "The Use of ΙΟΥΔΑΙΟΣ in the Fourth Gospel: An Application of some Linguistic Insights to a New Testament Problem," 46.

[162] He observes that the word denotes various specific referents in the real world, such as Pharisees, Jewish people as a nation, people of Galilee, etc. SCHRAM, "The Use of ΙΟΥΔΑΙΟΣ," 63, 69, 71, 81, etc.

[163] Ibid., 69. For example, Jesus' cleansing of the temple and the mysterious words about rebuilding it in three days do not constitute an intended attack on Judaism. The Jews' inability to understand Jesus' enigmatic statement has the readers' full sympathy, and so does the quest for a sign, justified by the demands of Deut 18:21, 22:20 (ibid., 68-69; cf. 137). Instead, the evangelist uses the response of the Jews "as part of his own message to the reader," which is focused on the identity of Jesus. Ibid., 63, 69, 116, etc.

[164] Ibid., 132; also p. 208.

[165] Ibid., 139.

[166] Ibid., 141.

[167] Ibid., 136ff.

[168] Ibid., 143.

[169] Ibid., 143; also p. 210.

in 18:33 and 19:3 is the only examples of possible anti-Semitism in the
gospel: "If there is an 'anti-Semitic' use of *Ioudaios* in the Fourth Gospel,
it is probably here in the reported speech of the non-Jewish participants in
the action."[170]

Schram's linguistic analysis regards the single word Ἰουδαῖοι as the
bottom item of a lexical hierarchy in which higher orders of texts
(discourse, episode, statement, kernel) influence the meaning of single
words. This approach helpfully avoids excessive attention to details and
places language into the context of the whole narrative and its purpose. Yet
the most important question remains unanswered: Why did the author use
the generic Ἰουδαῖοι when, as the immediate context of a single
occurrence shows, the actual referent is obviously much more limited?
More precise terms such as "Pharisees" or "Jewish leaders" would not
have ruined the function of the episode to establish the identity of Jesus.
Schram's analysis (part II) focuses exclusively on the occurrences of
Ἰουδαῖοι which limits the study mostly to the narratives of the gospel and
underemphasizes the speeches with their frequent use of κόσμος. Schram's
explanation of the superordinate, co-ordinate or subordiante "semantic
hierarchical relation" between terms such as *Ioudaios, anthropos,*
samarites, romaios, ethnos, helene, pharisaios, archierus, ochlos, archon
is very helpful.[171] But the lack of *kosmos* in this discussion marks a crucial
omission. Thus, Schram's linguistic approach provides indispensable
insights into the mechanics of language but proves to be insufficient to
capture the gospels' complex dynamics between narrative and speech.

2.2.2. Narrative Criticism: Caron (1997)

Gérald Caron begins with a review of different views and notes that various
historical interpretations of the Ἰουδαῖοι (authorities, unbelieving Judaism,
Judeans) simply change the text and are thus unacceptable.[172] The symbolical
interpretation (Bultmann, Schram, Culpepper) ignores the particularity which
the term "the Jews" adds to the gospel and dismisses without warrant their
specific responsibility for the death of Jesus in the passion account.[173] Caron
then outlines a literary approach which reads the gospel as a coherent textual
artifact and not as a window into a history of Jesus or of the Johannine
community.[174] His study asks how the author "fabricates" his characters,[175]
how he introduces them, how he lets them speak and act and meet in relations

---

[170] Ibid., 119; also p.21.
[171] Ibid., 22-23.
[172] CARON, *Qui sont les Juifs de l'Évangile de Jean?*, 22-34, 42-44.
[173] Ibid., 45-46.
[174] Ibid., 52.
[175] Ibid., 53 ("fabrique ses personnages").

to other actors. Caron then investigates John 5 (ch. 2) and 8 (ch. 3). He notices that the confrontations between Jesus and "the Jews" happen always in a *religious* context of feasts in Jerusalem, with the exception of those in chapter six.[176] The points of disagreement surround subjects such as the temple (John 2), the Sabbath, the law and blasphemy (John 5). Furthermore, the relationship of "the Jews" to other people in a pericope shows that the term denotes various kinds of people, such as the crowd, Pharisees, chief priests, chief priests and Pharisees.[177] Thus, the Ἰουδαῖοι refer neither to the Jewish *people* or to the Jewish *race* in general[178] nor to the Pharisees or any other particular group.[179] Instead, they represent a certain type of Judaism, namely the "'pseudo-Judaisme' officiel de Jérusalem."[180] Moreover, Caron observes that in 8:23 κόσμος is used to define the Ἰουδαῖοι and not the other way round. The Jews are not considered as an example of the world (so Bultmann) but "the world" is an "attitude" of darkness (1:4-5) and sin (1:29), a quality and character trait which defines "the Jews."[181] In a final chapter (ch. 4), Caron places his previous interpretation into a larger context. He observes that judgment and condemnation do not have the last word in the gospel. Jesus speaks about the "greater works" that the father will show him "that you may marvel" (5:20). The "greater works" refer, according to Caron, to the elevation of Jesus at the cross, a moment of glorification at which the Jews will know the true identity of Jesus (8:28) and at which Jesus will draw all people to himself (12:32; also 3:16).[182] Caron calls his exegetical analysis a "beginning" ("debut") which needs to be followed by reflections about the text's "responsibility" for the scandalous history of Christian anti-Semitism The gospel's apparent anti-Jewish rhetoric and its deformed image of Judaism is one of the "principal causes" for the incomprehension and the hatred of the Jewish people in the last two thousand years of Christianity.[183]

Caron's literary approach is a welcome attempt to let the text speak for itself rather than give precedence to historical reconstructions that begin with too many vague assumptions. However, choosing John 5 and 8 for analysis is selective and excludes the gospel's macrostructure at the expense of important insights. Furthermore, the most unique contribution

---

[176] Ibid., 69-70.
[177] Ibid., 172.
[178] Ibid., 68, 261.
[179] Ibid., 172.
[180] Ibid., 285. Idem, "Exploring a religious dimension,"165, 167.
[181] CARON, *Qui sont les Juifs*, 166-67, 177, 283.
[182] Ibid., 120-121, 197, 285-286, 289.
[183] Ibid., 291-92.

of Caron's thesis is also the most vulnerable. His *abstract* definitions for Ἰουδαῖοι as "Judaism" and for κόσμος as an "attitude" of darkness and sin stand at the extreme end of a narrative approach and totally dispense with any referential aspect of the terms. If one would continue on this avenue, then there is no reason to refrain from understanding other characters as mere concepts as well (e.g., Jesus; the disciples). While the confusion about the identity of the Ἰουδαῖοι is regrettable, the gospel's historical and biographic features (e.g., 19:35; 1 John 1:1-3) do not allow one to solve the problem by taking the history out of the story. The actions require a *personal* agent. The "Jews" who try to kill Jesus (5:18) and the "world" which hates the disciples (15:18) are not metaphysical ideas but concrete opponents of flesh and blood. If the gospel cannot withstand the charges of anti-Semitism without de-historicizing its terminology, then it cannot withstand them at all.

2.2.3. Reader-Response Criticism: Nicklas (2001)

Tobias Nicklas analyzes six texts (John 1:19-28; 1:29-34; 1:35-51; 3:1-21; 5:1-18; 9:1-41) and studies each with regard to text-critical issues; the structure of the pericope and structural matters; the characterization of individuals and groups through actions and words; and tensions, doublets, and gaps which open the text for multiple readings and invite the active participation of the reader in the process of interpretation. Nicklas refuses to identify the Ἰουδαῖοι with any particular group (Judeans; leaders) because they are portrayed in a very general fashion without particular attributes.[184] There are no "neutral" portrayals of "the Jews" because as characters of a narrative world the reader consumes the whole text and fills the meaning of a term used in one sentence with connotations picked up from another occurrence.[185] Nicklas finds that the Jews are depicted unfairly throughout the gospel and become victims of the author's irony.[186]

---

[184] NICKLAS, *Ablösung und Verstrickung: "Juden" und Jüngergestalten als Charaktere der erzählten Welt des Johannesevangeliums und ihre Wirkung auf den impliziten Leser*, 282, 285, 364.

[185] Thus, the Jews in the first occurrence in 1:19 do not know who John the Baptist is and are ignorant of the information given before. Ibid., 393. Nicodemus in 3:1 is mysterious and ambivalent and his marginal position between two groups misses a clear positive portrayal. Ibid., 393. The expression "the feast of the Jews" (5:1) is not simply neutral but creates a distance between the reader and the character. Ibid., 292, 393.

[186] With regard to the Jews' protest against Jesus' healing on the Sabbath in John 9, for example, Nicklas points to Deut 13 (false prophets) and Exod 7 (miracles by Egyptian magicians) as legitimate reasons for protest against Jesus' attempt to legitimize his claims with miracles. Ibid., 373-74. Nicklas explains that the Johannine perspective is

But this language *originates* in inner-Jewish polemic which Nicklas distinguishes from its *history of interpretation* during which Gentiles used the text for attacking Jews.[187] On the other hand, Nicklas can say that the negative presentation of "the Jews" does not serve a polemic purpose but is employed as a negative foil to convince the reader about the claims of Jesus as the Son of God and to follow the examples of the disciples (see also Schram).[188] At the end of his book, Nicklas explains the terrible anti-Jewish and anti-semitic effects of the gospel by a) a reading of the gospel in bits and pieces disconnected from its inner-Jewish context, b) by the claim of the gospel writer to correspond to historical realities and to present the truth about "the world" and c) by the reader who applies the author's view about characters in the narrative to real groups in present life.[189]

Nicklas' book is rich in detail and discussion and displays elaborate text-critical work as well as interaction with secondary literature. The texts that were chosen for analysis certainly surprise when compared with other contributions to the discussion. Nicklas tries to disprove any 'neutral' sense of Ἰουδαῖοι and attempts to show that even the first uses of Ἰουδαῖοι are loaded with ideological criticism. The prologue certainly guides the reader to perceive "the Jews" as early as in 1:19 as part of the "world" who "did not know him" (1:10) and as "his own" who "did not receive him" (1:11). Yet, there is no reason to negate the positive meaning of Ἰουδαῖοι in Jesus' dialogue with the Samaritan (4:9, 22) or even in the discourse with the Roman procurator (18:33 f.). Thus Nicklas' selection of texts supports his thesis without giving sufficient room for examples that would balance it. As with the previous dissertations, the selectivity of the study impedes the guidance given through the gospel's context. Only scant attention is given to the term κόσμος.[190] Yet, Nicklas' second text, 1:29-34, begins with the statement that Jesus is the "lamb of God who takes away the sin of the world" (1:29). How does this universal perspective fit together with the particular emphasis on the Jews and how would it influence his speculation about an inner-Jewish conflict? Another un-

---

"genausowenig nachweisbar wie die der Pharisäer" (ibid., 384) and that the narrator wants "dem Leser seine Sicht 'überstülpen'" (ibid., 386). See also pp. 389, 406.

[187] Ibid., 71-72, 407.

[188] Ibid., 401. Similarly, Burridge argues in his discussion of "the Jews" that the "gospel of John is not '*anti-*' any racial or national grouping; but, having been wounded in conflict, it pleads with the reader to make a decision 'for' Jesus the Messiah." BURRIDGE, *Four Gospels*, 153.

[189] NICKLAS, *Ablösung und Verstrickung*, 407-409.

[190] He only mentions at one place that the "Jews" are comparable to but not identical with the "world." Ibid, 392.

resolved question has to do with the gospel's narrative and historical character. On the one side the term "the Jews" points to a historical inner-Jewish conflict, but on the other hand it serves as a mere 'character' and 'negative foil' for a Christological and adhortative purpose. Where and how exactly do these two lines of argument meet in Nicklas' model? Can they both be true to the same extent? Does one have prominence over the other? Finally, Nicklas' does not make a strong distinction between original intent (not anti-Jewish) and history of interpretation (anti-Jewish) which allows him to ask if not some elements of the texts are responsible for violence done to Jews.[191] Does Nicklas follow here a more radical model of reader-response criticism which locates meaning in the event of reading rather than in the content of the text?[192]

2.2.4. Ancient Theories of Drama: Diefenbach (2002)

Early on in his introduction, Manfred Diefenbach explains that he seeks to disprove a negative interpretation of the Jews in the Fourth Gospel with the help of ancient theories of drama.[193] Modern literary approaches, which are based on 20th century theories and classifications, are anachronistic when applied to writings that were written 1900 years earlier.[194] Therefore antique theories about analyzing dramas provide us with better criteria to analyze tragedies, such as Aristoteles' (384-322 B.C.) *Poetics* and Horace's (65-68 B.C.) *Ars Poetica*.[195] The hellenization of Palestine since Alexander the Great brought also Greek theories of drama into the Jewish culture as the example of Ezechiel's "Exagoge" (2nd cent. B.C.)

---

[191] He writes, "Wenn auch die Zeitbedingtheit der Aussagen des JohEv diese mit großer Wahrscheinlichkeit *in ihrer ursprünglichen Intention* als nicht antijüdisch oder gar antisemitisch im heutigen Sinne bezeichnen lässt, so stellt sich doch die Frage, ob der Text nicht trotzdem Anhaltspunkte gibt, die manchen Aspekt seiner *Wirkungsgeschichte* erklären lassen." Ibid., 72.

[192] Nicklas' use of reader-response criticism is evident from his other writings as well. In an article about John 3:22-4:3, Nicklas emphasizes how the text's doublets, tensions, and gaps open it for various interpretations that require the reader's active participation in the creation of meaning. See NICKLAS, "Literarkritik und Leserrezeption," esp. 191-92. And in an article about John 21:11 (the 153 fish), Nicklas tries to demonstrate how a reader-oriented model of interpretation can serve to explain a text's history of interpretation ("Rezeptionsgeschichte"). NICKLAS, "'153 große Fische'," esp. 386-87.

[193] DIEFENBACH, *Der Konflikt Jesu mit den 'Juden': Ein Versuch zur Lösung der johanneischen Antijudaismus-Diskussion mit Hilfe des antiken Handlungsverständnisses*, 9.

[194] Ibid., 62. He refers to Vladimir J. Propp 1928, A. J. Greimas 1966; J. Barr 1961, C. Bremond, E. Güttgemanns, D. O. Via 1970, W. Harnisch 1985. Ibid., 21-23.

[195] Ibid., 32, 39-40.

demonstrates.[196] The most important methodological implications center on what Diefenbach calls the "Primat der Handlung," meaning that the question of "what" and the "why" of an action has priority before the question of "who" actually does something.[197] With this concept in mind, Diefenbach first reviews the whole gospel (3.1.) except the prologue, the farewell discourse and chapter 21. He then pays special attention to the actions of the Ἰουδαῖοι (3.2.) in relation to groups (Pharisees, high priests, crowd, servants) and individuals (Caiaphas, Hannas, Nicodemus, etc.). He concludes that the author does not condemn the Jews as people but their behavior. As such, they embody the group of all those that do not believe in Jesus.[198]

Diefenbach is not alone in emphasizing the behavior of the Jews versus their identity.[199] And the comparison between ancient forms of drama and the Gospel of John also finds a repeated echo in Johannine scholarship.[200] But similar to Bultman and Caron, Diefenbach depletes the term Ἰουδαῖοι of any referential aspect. The decisive matter has to do with the genre of the text. The question is if *some* dramatic features in the gospel justify in using complete ancient theories of drama as the hermeneutical key for its interpretation. Asking the same question about the gospel's genre, Burridge's results "place the Fourth Gospel clearly in the same genre as

---

[196] Ibid., 48-49.

[197] Ibid., 59, 61, 68, 214, 216.

[198] Ibid., 269-70. He explains that "nicht 'die Juden' als Kollektiv generell im vierten Evangelium verurteilt werden; vielmehr sind damit all jene gemeint, die sich aus freien Stücken heraus gegen den Glauben an Jesus Christus entscheiden und lossagen." Ibid., 265.

[199] Similarly, de Boer explains with regard to John 8:44 that it is not Jews who are diabolical, "rather, their murderous behavior is diabolical . . . John 8:44 claims that the devil is the father not of 'the Jews' as such but of their behavior." DE BOER, "The Depiction," 147-148. Tolmie also points out the behavior of "the Jews" rather than their identity. He explains the blurring of distinctions between "the Jews" and the Pharisees (1:19-28; 9:1-10:21), "the Jews" and the crowd (6:1-59) and "the Jews" and the authorities (18:1-19:42) as an indication that "what is important is not *who* they are, but what they *do* in the narrative world." TOLMIE, "The ΙΟΥΔΑΙΟΙ in the Fourth Gospel," 395.

[200] There are many scholars who find within the narrative of the Gospel resemblances to elements of drama. See SCHNACKENBURG *Das Johannesevangelium*, 2:12 ("Regiebemerkungen"), 24 (6:14 is a "Chorschluß"). ASHTON, "The Identity," 58. SCHENKE, "Joh 7-10: Eine dramatische Szene," 187. BRODIE, *The Gospel*, 171. KEENER, *The Gospel of John*, 1:217. Only a few scholars connect the whole Gospel with a narrow definition of drama as a play written solely for performance on the stage in a theater. So, for example, BOWEN, "The Fourth Gospel as Dramatic Material," 296. KEMPER, "Zur literarischen Gestalt des Johannesevangeliums," 254-58. See also our note in chapter 4 on John's prologue as a hermeneutical key with similarity to openings in Greek tragedies.

the synoptic gospels, namely βίοι."[201] Dealing more with the text itself, the explanations of Jewish customs (2:6; 19:31, 40), the mentioning of Jewish feasts (2:13; 5:1; 6:4; 7:2; 19:42) and the importance of the Jewish religion (law; purification; Moses; Abraham) strongly indicate that the Ἰουδαῖοι are understood as a historical people with a specific ethnic-religious identity. Finally, Diefenbach criticizes that modern literary theories narrowly focus on the actions of a narrative and neglect the element of speech.[202] He counts that thirteen of the gospel's twenty-one chapters are speeches, which amounts to ca. 65 percent.[203] Yet, in his own analysis Diefenbach excludes the largest speech from his analysis, the farewell discourse (John 13-17), and disregards the prologue whose concepts connect predominantly with those of the discourses. It shows that the interpretive focus on the gospel's actions ignores the dialogues as one of the most outstanding features of the gospel and does not do justice to its idiosyncratic design.

2.2.5. Mixed Methods: Hakola (2005)

A recent Finnish dissertation by Raimo Hakola challenges two major assumptions in modern Johannine scholarship: In his eyes (1) the theory of a violent conflict between Johannine Christians and Jews behind the Gospel is as unfounded as (2) a recent unqualified acceptance of the Gospel's Jewishness.[204] In contrast to Martyn's thesis of a two-level drama, historical analysis (chap. 2) shows that a *theological* disagreement about "basic matters of Jewish identity" (Sabbath, circumcision, Moses, etc.) led to "the break between some early Christians and other Jews," not a violent conflict.[205] Hakola's investigation of texts from the first half of the Gospel (chaps. 3-6: John 2:13-22; 4:20-24; 5:1-18; 7:19-24; 5:37-47; 6:26-59; 8:31-59) demonstrates John's ambivalent relationship to and detachment from Jewishness. The distance is even so large that the Johannine Jesus calls the Jews "children of the devil" (8:44) and thus lays "some seeds for later development of Christian anti-Judaism."[206] The Gospel argues this way because the Johannine Christians merely "*felt* themselves to be persecuted in a world governed by Jews,"[207] which led

---

[201] BURRIDGE, *What are the Gospels?*, 232 (213-32).

[202] DIEFENBACH, *Der Konflikt Jesu*, 24-25.

[203] Ibid., 56-57.

[204] HAKOLA, *Identity Matters: John, the Jews and Jewishness*, 4.

[205] Ibid., 86.

[206] Ibid., 211, also 208, 238-39. Hakola speaks earlier of the "dark side" of the Gospel. Ibid., 39.

[207] Ibid., 77 (italics added). Hakola does not think that the Johannine Christians were really persecuted. He understands the language of persecution in the Gospel as part of a "symbolic universe" which developed from traditions of *earlier* Christian experiences.

them to "adopting a non-Jewish identity."[208] Hakola interprets the κόσμος-language as part of the Gospel's "symbolic universe" in which empirical animosities are interpreted in terms of a cosmic battle.[209] Such "apocalyptic polemic" finds parallels in the Qumran community (1 QS)[210] and functioned as a "warning against seeking contacts with any Jews who did not belong to the community."[211]

Hakola's mixed methodology does not contend with textual analysis but wrestles with Martyn's thesis and speculates about the historical cause for the writing of the gospel. He is certainly right that currently Johannine scholars tend to overemphasize Jewish features of the Gospel (and a Jewish religious-historical background) while sometimes softening the polemical tone of the text and its ties to the Greco-Roman world.[212] But we might understand this trend as a needed correction of a previous generation of interpreters who were all too willing to cut out 4:22 as a gloss and view Jesus as the Son of God who either stood above nationality (idealism) or was of Aryan descent (nationalism).[213] A balanced synthesis should try to bring anti-Jewish and pro-Jewish statements and features together. While Hakola affirms the Gospel's "paradoxical" and "ambivalent portrayal of Jewishness," [214] his selection of texts for analysis that describe conflict with the Jews (within John 2–8) as well as his conclusion reduce the complexity by postulating a one-sided negative image of the Jews. Motyer and Fuglseth (see above) would point out that parallels between the Fourth Gospel and the literature of Second temple Judaism temper if not correct the modern reader's impression of anti-Judaism. But more importantly, Hakola excludes from his radar screen rather neutral and positive

---

Ibid., 77-78. Similarly, Kysar reads the expulsion texts with a 'hermeneutic of suspicion' and explains that the "Jewish Christians *may have felt* the leaders of their synagogue had kicked them out of the community. . . . What we can know from these three passages is little more than that some Christians and Jews separated themselves from one another in some way and for some reason. I suggest the obvious, namely, that the text of the gospel presents readers with only one side of a story to which there most assuredly is another side." KYSAR, "The Expulsion from the Synagogue," 240 (italics his).

[208] HAKOLA, *Identity Matters*, 226.

[209] See his discussion on pp. 197-210. Hakola finds He can say that the Jews "symbolize the unbelieving world." Ibid., 8 (with regard to 1:9-11 and 15:18-25), also 185.

[210] Ibid., 198, also 203 (parallel to 2 Cor 6:4-7:1).

[211] Ibid., 186.

[212] See, for example, our discussion about "The Gospel's *religionsgeschichtliche* complexity" in chapter 3 (1.1.3.) and our excursus in chapter 4 about the Jewish feasts mentioned in the Gospel.

[213] See our discussion "Jesus is a Jew and Salvation is from the Jews (John 4:9, 22)" in chapter 2 with the excursus "Jesus as a Galilean Gentile?"

[214] HAKOLA, *Identity Matters*, 237.

connotations of the 'Ιουδαῖοι,[215] such as the positive portrayal of believing Jews in John 11-12, the love of God for the rejecting world (3:16), and the Son's mission for salvation (1:29; 3:17; 4:42; 12:47; 6:33, 51; 8:12; 9:5; 14:31; 17:23) that is to be continued by the church (17:18-23; 13:35; 15:27). In his recent *Theologie der Liebe Gottes* (2005), Popkes takes all these different trajectories into account and offers a more balanced theological synthesis. He points out, among others, that the Gospel's missionary emphasis stands in *contrast* to the Qumran community where followers are taught "to hate all the Children of Darkness" (1 QS 1.9-10; also 1 QH 6.10-11.25-27; 7.18-19; etc.).[216] While the Qumran community knows about the "sons of light" moving to the darkness (1QS 3:21-22), expressions for the reversed direction, such as "coming to the light" (John 3:20-21) and "the light of the world" (8:12; 9:5), are absent from the Dead Sea Scrolls.[217] While the 'light'-terminology functions here to strengthen the *boundaries* of the community, the Fourth Gospel employs it for the service of a distinct Christological *and soteriological* purpose. In summary, the challenge for a synchronic approach remains to grasp the details of *various* trajectories in the Gospel as parts of one coherent message.

---

[215] See our discussion in chapter 2.

[216] POPKES, *Die Theologie der Liebe Gottes*, 155-56; translation taken from WISE, ABEGG, COOK, *The Dead Sea Scrolls*, 127. This is a stronger statement than that of Fitzmyer's negative observation that "such [Qumran's] hatred is not found in the teaching of Jesus recorded in the Johannine writings . . ." FITZMYER, "Qumran literature," 125. Harrington completely overlooks the Gospel's soteriological emphasis when he, in his response to Fitzmyer, places the Gospel's negative language about 'the world' and 'the Jews' in the same camp with Qumran's dualism. Harrington, "Response," 137. More balanced, Zumstein observes that "despite its hostility and its unbelief, [the world] remains the place of necessary witness." ZUMSTEIN, "The Farewell Discourse," 472. Commenting on the term κόσμος in the Prologue, Phillips speaks of the Gospel's "mission-oriented antilanguage." PHILLIPS, *The Prologue*, 185. Josephus confirms the evidence from the Dead Sea Scrolls when he explains that part of the Essenes' code of conduct is to 'forever hate the unrighteous' (μισήσειν δ' ἀεὶ τοὺς ἀδίκους; *B.J.* 2.139). Ancient literature contains frequent and explicit hate-language. According to Philo, Germans "deserve to be hated" (ἄξιον μισεῖν) because they rebel against the natural rhythm of the tide's ebb and flow (*Somn.* 2.121-122). Tacitus calls the Jews a "race detested by the gods" (*Hist.* 5.3). Such language and ideas are not only absent in the Fourth Gospel but God's love and the Church's mission to the dark world is explicitly affirmed.

[217] FITZMYER, "Qumran literature," 123-24.

2.2.6. *Macrostructure: Schnelle (1999), Zumstein (2000)*

Udo Schnelle's contribution does not come in the form of a dissertation but of a relatively short essay of fourteen pages.[218] We include it in our review because his approach is not only innovative, but it allows for important observations that go mostly unnoticed in Johannine scholarship. Schnelle issued elsewhere a rare but important warning when he said that the "focus on the pre-history of the text leads to a neglect of the Gospel's macro-structure."[219] It is this strength of studying the Gospel's literary design *as a whole* which gives Schnelle's analysis its unique place among the contributions to the debate. He begins with a semantic study of Ἰουδαῖοι that recognizes eight different ways of using the term. Among those, only a third of all occurrences have a negative connotation of conflict.[220] In a second step, Schnelle asks for the term's "pragmatische Funktion" and notices that it is unevenly distributed in the Gospel, with neutral, positive, or no occurrences in John 1-4, 12-17, and negative occurrences largely concentrated in John 5-11 and 18-20. The shift in meaning is understood as a "dramaturgisches Element" according to which 'the Jews' are first introduced (chs. 1-4) before the conflict escalates (chs. 5-11) and finds its climax in the passion account (chs. 18-20).[221] After focusing on 4:22b and 8:44 as two texts that represent the Gospel's complex theology of 'the Jews',[222] Schnelle finally defines the relationship between Jesus the Jew and the Jews in the Gospel as a "dramatische Erzählung von Glauben und vom Unglauben."[223] In contrast to Bultmann who draws a line between believers and Jews, Schnelle points out that 'the Jews' are found on both sides. Finally, Schnelle discusses the Gospel's analogy between the Ἰουδαῖοι and the κόσμος. He observes that 'the world,' just as 'the Jews,' appears with neutral, positive, and negative connotations. Bultmann's interpretation of 'the Jews' as representatives of the 'unbelieving world' does not capture this diversity of the term's meanings. After observing the dominance of κόσμος in John 14-17, the chapters which allude "am

---

[218] SCHNELLE, "Die Juden im Johannesevangelium," 217-30.

[219] SCHNELLE, "Ein neuer Blick," 22.

[220] SCHNELLE, "Die Juden im Johannesevangelium," 218-19.

[221] Ibid., 220.

[222] According to Schnelle, the first statement, "salvation is from the Jews," constitutes a "fundamental and positive assertion without any restrictions" and "makes it impossible to speak of a johannine 'Anti-judaism'." Ibid., 221, 222. The second statement, "You are of your father, the devil," does not demonize 'the Jews' categorically as satanic in their essence. Rather, the pronoun ὑμεῖς singles out those among the Jews who were led by a foreign power (Satan) to kill Jesus. Ibid., 223.

[223] Ibid., 225.

intensivsten auf die Situation der textexternen Gemeinde,"[224] Schnelle
suggests the following interpretation:

> The function of the Ἰουδαῖοι on the text-internal level of the life of Jesus is taken
> over in the farewell discourse by the cosmos for the text-external audience. In
> positive and negative ways, the Johannine church experiences from the world
> whatever Jesus experienced from the Jews. The parallelism between the Ἰουδαῖοι and
> the cosmos is thus explained by the evangelist's intention to combine the phenomena
> of faith and unbelief on the text-internal level of Jesus' life with those in the
> Johannine church and the world on the text-external level. In this way the church is
> supposed to understand that she is now experiencing in both positive and negative
> ways the same things Jesus did.[225]

Despite its brevity, Schnelle's essay stands out by its dual attention to the
semantic details of the terms Ἰουδαῖοι and κόσμος as well to their *macro-
structural* position and parallelism in the Gospel. When taken together,
both observations exploit the strengths of a synchronic approach that
avoids the narrow focus of the previous synchronic studies and precludes
diachronical reconstructions that are based on textual bits and pieces. The
results of this approach are highly relevant for our topic. With regard to the
historical audience, the telling silence of 'the Jews' in the farewell
discourse and the dominance of 'the world' therein suggest that the
Johannine communities do not face opposition from the Ἰουδαῖοι but from
the κόσμος as a body of people that is larger than the Jews.

Schnelle's macrostructural approach stands, with few exceptions, alone
in Johannine scholarship and is largely unknown or often ignored. In the
volume *Anti-Judaism and the Fourth Gospel* (2001), it is only Jean
Zumstein's essay which draws especially on the farewell discourse in order
to understand "how the Johannine school formulated in a deliberate
fashion the identity of the Christian faith for the time after Easter."[226] He
observes that the Ἰουδαῖοι are "totally absent in chapters 13:31-16:33"
which "has an important consequence. Christian identity is no longer
formed in polemical opposition to the Jews, but in opposition to another
group, the κόσμος."[227] Zumstein observes the same with regard to the
prologue, the "hermeneutical framework in which the story is to be read,"
and notices that while "Israel is not passed over in silence," it is not a
conflict with Judaism but the rejection of "the entire κόσμος" that forms
part of the drama with the logos.[228] Finally, in the epilogue (John 21) "all

---

[224] Ibid., 225.

[225] Ibid, 228 (translation mine).

[226] ZUMSTEIN, "The Farewell Discourse," 462, see 461-78.

[227] Ibid, 463-64.

[228] Ibid., 473-74.

polemic against Judaism has disappeared" as well and the conflict, carried out on the literary level between the beloved disciple and Peter, is that between the Johannine school and the mainstream church.[229] Beside Zumstein, Jörg Frey has picked up Schnelle's solution and elaborated further on the historical circumstances of the text-external audience.[230] Outside of continental scholarship, these macro-structural considerations seem to be overlooked. Our study will elaborate on and expand beyond the observations of Schnelle and Zumstein and thereby strengthen their thesis that the Gospel's dualism does not target one ethnic race but is broadened to a universal scope. The Jews receive a *subordinate* function in the Gospel's narratological design which challenges not only frequent charges of the author's alleged anti-Judaism but confronts the paradigm of a church-synagogue conflict that has dominated Johannine scholarship in the last forty years since Martyn's *History and Theology in the Fourth Gospel* (1968).

3. Reflections on Method

In assessing these studies, the following methodological criteria are employed in this book: First, questions about the historical context of the Gospel should be placed *after* comprehensive textual analysis. Too often, assumptions about the *Sitz im Leben* of the text blur its analysis and minimize space for important observations (Grelot, Motyer, Lingad, Hakola). And it is no surprise that the narrow focus on single chapters or pericopes result in historical reconstructions that limit the Gospel's scope to particular conflicts with Jews while neglecting the universal emphasis.

Second, the use of narrative criticism *per se* did not maximize the agreement among scholars about the meaning and function of the Ἰουδαῖοι in the Gospel. The only feature that unites them is the negative evaluation of the Gospel's pre-literary history for the meaning of the text.[231] My contention is that the major strength of synchronic analysis, namely the consideration of the text as a *whole*, is hardly ever exploited for this topic.

---

[229] Ibid, 476-77.

[230] FREY, "Das Bild 'der Juden' im Johannesevangelium und die Geschichte der johanneischen Gemeinde," 33-53. For further description of Frey's proposal see our discussion in chapter 5, "Attempts about a Likely Scenario."

[231] What is true for synchronic studies of "the Jews" in the Gospel of John also applies to synchronic approaches to the Gospel in general. There is little common ground except the focus on the final form of the text and the exclusion of historical questions concerning its genesis. See the discussion by HALDIMANN, WEDER, "Aus der Literatur zum Johannesevangelium 1985-1994," 76.

Yet Schnelle and Zumstein have begun to demonstrate the heuristic value
of including the prologue, the farewell discourse, and chapter 21 into a
comprehensive study of 'the Jews' in the Gospel. While the term Ἰουδαῖοι
is absent in these texts, κόσμος takes its place and creates thus a parallelism
between 'the Jews' and 'the world' that is understood as a literary strategy
either in opposition to an anti-Jewish reading of the Gospel (Schnelle,
Zumstein) or in support of it (Caron, Hakola). Methodologically, this
parallelism challenges the dominant selective focus on a single word
(Ἰουδαῖοι) in single paragraphs with rather unsatisfying attempts of
redeeming the Gospel from charges of anti-Semitism (e.g., Caron, Nicklas,
Diefenbach).[232] Diefenbach, for example, criticizes modern literary
theories because they focus narrowly on the actions of a narrative and
neglect the element of speech.[233] Yet his own analysis, as well as that of
most scholars described above, does not improve the situation. Ironically,
when the narrative approach is used this way it repeats the same mistakes
of those methods that it sought to overcome. Long points to the drawbacks
of traditional form criticism and historical criticism which have "tended to
focus primarily, if not exclusively, on the smaller units, with far too little
attention being given to the larger."[234] He then emphasizes (with Robert
Bergen) the discourse principles according to which "each successively
higher level of textual organization influences all of the lower levels of
which it is composed. Language is organized from the top down." With
regard to the Jews in the Gospel of John, Schram pointed out with Pike
already in 1974 that meaning "has its locus not in the individual bits and
pieces of the total structure, but within the language structure as a
whole."[235] The term "Jews" is only one of these bits and pieces that needs
to be interpreted as such. Schram speaks of the importance to observe the
texts "semantic hierarchical relation" according to which words are
"arranged in hierarchies as subordinate to, co-ordinate with, and

---

[232] Ashton said it well when he observed in 1985 that "writers on the role of the Jews
in the Gospel mostly ignore this problem [the identification of Ἰουδαῖοι and κόσμος] is I
suppose to be explained by the fact that if the locus of one's enquiry is a word or an
expression, one tends to leave out of consideration passages where the word or
expression in question is not employed. Which, at least in this instance, is surely a matter
of regret." ASHTON, "The Identity," 67. When asking about the significance of the
farewell discourse for the meaning of the Ἰουδαῖοι, Zumstein makes a similar
observation in 2000 when he writes that in "our opinion, the question has not yet been
addressed in its true depth if one either limits oneself to analyzing the term Jew . . . or if
one concentrates on a particular passage that may be positive or problematic." ZUMSTEIN,
"The Farewell Discourse," 462.

[233] DIEFENBACH, *Der Konflikt*, 24-25.

[234] LONG, *The Art of Biblical History*, 46-47.

[235] SCHRAM, "The Use of ΙΟΥΔΑΙΟΣ," 41

superordinate to other lexical items in terms."[236] Unfortunately, levels *super*ordinate to "the Jews" do not receive the same attention in Schram's work as *sub*ordinate ones. Thus this dissertation seeks to fill a lacuna by operating with a synchronic approach that includes narratives as well as speeches, and by favoring a sequential reading that is sensitive to the literary structure and narrative strategies of the Gospel as a whole. While we do not exclude categorically that the text might show signs of redactional activity, the strong evidence of literary unity suggests taking the existing form as the starting point[237] and underlines that parts of the text may only be interpreted properly in light of the whole.[238]

Third, after the textual work has been given due space and consideration, our attention will turn to the context of the Gospel as well (chap. 6). As much as narrative criticism provided needed correctives for overconfident constructs of the text's pre-literary history, it would be superficial to limit analysis to the surface of the text itself. After all, no

---

[236] Ibid., 22.

[237] Following previous studies by Schweizer, Jeremias, and Menoud, Eugen Ruckstuhl observed fifty features of style in the Gospel (e.g., τότε οὖν, ἵνα-epexegeticum, etc.) which run across all divisions postulated by Bultmann (evangelist, redactor, speech-source, sign-source) and thus demonstrate the literary unity of all twenty-one chapters with the exception of 7:53-8:11. See the lists in RUCKSTUHL, *Die literarische Einheitlichkeit*, 203-05 and 208-209, 213-14. Ruckstuhl summarizes, "Die Liste zeigt ganz eindeutig die Unrichtigkeit der literarkritischen Aufstellungen und Scheidungen B(ultmann)s." Ibid., 215, also 218-19. For reactions to Ruckstuhl's study see VAN BELLE, *The Signs Source*, 368. Especially German studies continue to use diachronic methods which divide the text into layers of "Grundschrift," redaction, and evangelist. See with regard to John 3 and John 4 LINK, *„Was redest du mit ihr?"*; SCHMIDL, *Jesus und Nikodemus*, esp. 19-24 (criticism of Ruckstuhl).

[238] Stibbe assumes the use of a variety of oral and written sources behind the Fourth Gospel. Yet, out of all these, the author created a "literary whole" and, as a "story-teller," he "created a point of view and plot which were his own contribution." STIBBE, *John as Storyteller*, 31. See Haldimann's important methodological reflections about the "Redaktor als kongenialer neuer Autor." HALDIMANN, *Rekonstruktion und Entfaltung*, 34-39. He points out that the redactor "hat nicht einfach einen schon bestehenden Text erweitert oder partiell ergänzt, sondern er hat ihn grundsätzlich überarbeitet und daraus ein eigenständiges neues Werk geschaffen." Ibid., 34. He concludes with Thyen that "die redaktionellen Passagen nur als Teil des Gesamttextes interpretiert werden dürfen" and that "sich der Sinn eines Textes stets nur aus dem *Zusammenspiel aller Bausteine des Textes* ergibt, dass das Einzelne also nur vom Ganzen her seinen Ort und seine Funktion erhält." Ibid., 36-37, 38 (italics his). Philo noticed long ago that "no artist ever makes the whole for the sake of the part, but rather makes the part for the sake of the whole" (*Somn.* 2.116) and concludes elsewhere that the whole is greater and superior than the part (*Spec.* 1.229; *Aet.* 1.22, 50). This philosophical axiom lends itself well for hermeneutical reflections. It follows for our context that a term, a sentence, a paragraph, or even a chapter is not properly understood until we have grasped its position and significance within the whole book.

one can deny that the text owes its existence to a real author or authors
who wrote at a certain place and time for readers of flesh and blood which
lived under specific circumstances in the first century AD. Whether these
conditions are of central or subordinate importance for the meaning of the
text cannot be decided a priori but has to be investigated. The term
"authorial audience" describes a trend in current Gospel studies which is
exploring avenues to connect the narrative with extra-narrative realities. It
refuses to be content with an abstract "theology of John" or with a one-
dimensional "implied reader" and seeks instead "to locate the interaction
of text and reader in a particular socio-historical context."[239] In line with
such efforts, we will attempt to incarnate the first readers of the Gospel of
John by locating the language of κόσμος and Ἰουδαῖοι in a particular
situation.

---

[239] CARTER, HEIL, *Matthew's Parables*, 11. See YAMASAKI, *John the Baptist*. With
regard to the Gospel of John, see TILBORG, *Reading John*, 3. SALIER, *The Rhetorical
Impact*, esp. 5-15.

CHAPTER 2

Neutral and Positive Connotations of "the Jews"

The previous discussion might give the impression that the Fourth Gospel uses the term 'Jews' always in a negative sense. The following observations show that this is not true. There are neutral and positive connotations that should not be overlooked.

1. Neutral Connotations of Ἰουδαῖοι

In parenthetical remarks, Ἰουδαῖοι is used simply for the description of Jewish customs and an institution to aid non-Jewish readers or at least readers who are not from Palestine (2:6, 13; 5:1; 6:4; 7:2; 11:55; 19:40, 42; maybe 19:31). The term once denotes the geographic area of Judea (3:22). As a partitive genitive it specifies a subgroup among "the Jews," such as in 3:1 (ἄρχων τῶν Ἰουδαίων), 18:12 (οἱ ὑπηρέται τῶν Ἰουδαίων) and 19:21 (οἱ ἀρχιερεῖς τῶν Ἰουδαίων). The Jews are amazed about Jesus' learning (7:15). Their misunderstanding of Jesus' words about "going away" (7:35; 8:22) is not inherent to their characterization since the disciple Thomas is equally unable to make sense of this saying (14:5). Jesus' historical reminiscences in 13:33 and 18:20 seem as devoid of a pejorative sense as single usages in the passion account (18:14; 19:20). Beside these rather neutral connotations in the term, Ἰουδαῖοι is also used with positive meanings which we will discuss in the following.

2. Jesus is a Jew and Salvation is from the Jews (John 4:9, 22)

Probably the most philo-Semitic statements of the whole New Testament are found in the Gospel of John. Jesus is not merely a supernatural divine figure but the Samaritan woman calls him "a Jew" (4:9) and Pilate recognizes him as such as well ("your people" in 18:35). The presentation of Jesus going up to Jerusalem for a "feast of the Jews" (5:1) indirectly testifies to his Jewishness[1] as does his designation of the Jewish temple as "My Father's house" (2:16). Jesus himself maintains that, in contrast to the Samaritans, "we (ἡμεῖς) worship that which we know, for salvation is from the Jews" (4:22, ἡ σωτηρία ἐκ τῶν Ἰουδαίων ἐστίν). Different from the "we" of Christian confession in 1:14, 16 and 3:11, Jesus uses ἡμεῖς here in order to identify himself with the Jews as the people of God.[2] The universal "salvation" comes "from the Jews" because they are the people who received God's promises[3] which are fulfilled through "Jesus of Nazareth, the son of Joseph" (1:45b) who is not only the "Son of God" (1:34) and the "savior of the world" (4:42) but also a Jew (4:9), a "Rabbi" (1:38, 49; 3:2; 4:31; 6:25; 9:2; 11:8), the "Messiah" (1:41; 4:25) and the king of Israel (1:49) as foretold by Moses and the prophets (1:45; cf. 1:23; 6:45; 7:38; 12:13, 15, 38, 40-41; 13:18; 15:25; 19:24, 26-27).[4] Jesus praises Nathanael as "a true Israelite" (1:47) and addresses Nicodemus as a "teacher of Israel" (3:10), thus valuing "Israel" as a name of honor and respect. We conclude, against Käsemann's opinion that John is guilty of a naïve docetism, that Jesus' heavenly descent is nowhere stressed at the cost of his earthly origin. Rather, the depiction of his Jewish origin is an application of the concept of incarnation (1:14).[5] In an article written in the midst of Hitler's rage in 1941, Sikes points out these Jewish traits of Jesus in the Gospel of John and exposes the erroneous views of scholars in his time who suggest otherwise![6] The affirmations of the Jewish origin stand in stark contrast to the beliefs of Hitler and Nazi theologians who attempted to argue for Jesus' Aryan descent.

---

[1] See LÜTGERT, "Die Juden," 151. SÖDING, "'Was kann aus Nazareth schon Gutes kommen?'," 22.

[2] So most commentators. See LÜCKE, *Commentar*, 1:529. Meyer against Hilgenfeld (1863) in MEYER, *Kritisch-Exegetisches Handbuch*, 198. KEIL, *Commentar*, 195. PLUMMER, *The Gospel*, 120. HOLTZMANN, *Evangelium*, 104. SCHNACKENBURG, *Das Johannesevangelium*, 1:470. MOLONEY, *The Gospel of John*, 132. BEASLEY-MURRAY, *John*, 62. KÖSTENBERGER, *John*, 154.

[3] In discussing 4:22, Keil points to Abraham (Gen 12:1-3). KEIL, *Commentar*, 196. Haacker observes that, meeting at the well of "father Jacob" (4:12), Jesus reminds the Samaritan woman of Jacob's blessing in Gen 49:8-12 according to which the ruler over the nations will come from Judah. See HAACKER, "Gottesdienst ohne Gotteserkenntnis," 120-22. Calvin refers to Isa 2:3. CALVIN, *The Gospel*, 1:99. And Lindars thinks of Isaiah 9, 11, 45:8, 17, etc. LINDARS, *The Gospel of John*, 188-89.

[4] This connection between the Old Testament and Christ was rejected by the modern scholarship of Adolf von Harnack, Julius Wellhausen, and Friedrich Delitzsch, who attempted to purge the New Testament from Jewish influences and Scriptures!

[5] SÖDING, "'Was kann aus Nazareth schon Gutes kommen?'," 39.

[6] SIKES, "The Anti-Semitism of the Fourth Gospel," 25-26. Sikes explicitly opposes Ernest C. Colwell, *John Defends the Gospel* (1936).

Excursus: Jesus as a Galilean Gentile?

The dialectic philosophy of history of the 19th century, which analyzed history in movements from thesis to antithesis and synthesis (G. F. Hegel, 1792-1860), did not exhaust itself in intellectual speculations but was fueled by a growing romantic nationalism that expressed itself in a "racial dichotomy between Occident and Orient."[7] The inferior nature of oriental eastern culture was understood as diametrically opposite to the dynamic, capable and colonizing world of the west. The Tübingen School under F. C. Baur (1792-1860) adopted these secular categories and brought about a "racialization of biblical scholarship" according to which the Judaism of the East (thesis) stands opposed to the Protestant Christianity of the West (antithesis), with Roman Catholicism as the compromise (synthesis).[8] Later on, when Albert Schweitzer looks back in 1906 on the past forty years of German *Leben-Jesu Forschung*, he has to summarize that "an die Stelle des liberalen Jesus ist der germanische getreten."[9] Jesus has been popularized since the 1860s by reducing the Gospel's imperatives and world-negating claims (*Weltverneinung*) over the individual in order to avoid conflict with current cultural ideas and a principle of world-affirmation (*Weltbejahung*).[10] Within this conceptual climate of growing racial antithesis and German nationalism, Johann Gottlieb Fichte (1762–1814) makes the statement that the Fourth Gospel does not only cast doubt on the Jewish origin of Jesus but also denies that Judaism ever was the true religion.[11] In his infamous 1902 address "Babel und Bibel" before the German Oriental Society in Berlin, Friedrich Delitzsch, a leading German Semitist and historian of his time, proposed among others that "Jesus was of Babylonian descent. Jesus himself was not Jewish, but Babylonian and probably in part Aryan, since the Aryan Babylonians had settled Samaria and Galilee!"[12] Delitzsch argued that Jesus was a Jewish proselyte rather than a Jew. The American Baptist scholar Ernest Colwell argued in 1934 regarding the Johannine Jesus that he "is not a Jew in

---

[7] KELLEY, *Racializing Jesus: Race, Ideology and the Formation of Modern Biblical Scholarship*, 65.

[8] Ibid., 64. All of chapter 3 of Kelley's book (pp. 64-88) discusses "Jesus and the Myth of the West. Tübingen and the construction of early Christianity." Kelley sees the Tübinger influence continued in the work of scholars such as Bruno Bauer, *Die Judenfrage* (1843) and Ernst Renan, *Vie de Jésus* (1863) who posed the Semitic race as the antithesis of the Aryans. Ibid., 85. This dialectic philosophy of history influenced the dominant form of higher biblical criticism, represented by Wellhausen and Baur, according to which priestly, legal and institutional texts in Old and New Testament reflect late and degenerate traditions. Despite James Barr's protest, the anti-Jewish as well as anti-Catholic bent in this European Protestant tradition is obvious. See KRAUSE, BEAL, "Higher Critics on Late Texts," 18-26. HALPERN, *The First Historian*, 27. BRUEGGEMANN, *Theology*, 1. DEINES, *Die Pharisäer*, 41-42. BARR, *The Concept of Biblical Theology*, 299. Though not without weaknesses, see also FENSKE, *Wie Jesus zum "Arier" wurde*, esp. 1-14.

[9] SCHWEITZER, *Von Reimarus zu Wrede*, 306. Schweitzer points to Gustav Frenssen, *Hilligenlei* (1905) and Herrmann von Soden, *Die wichtigen Fragen im Leben Jesu* (1904) as examples of a germanic Jesus.

[10] Ibid., 398. Schweitzer points here to P. W. Schmidt, Bousset, Jülicher, Weinel, Wernle and their student Frenssen.

[11] See BELL, *The Irrevocable Call of God*, 356-57. With regard to Johann G. Herder, *Von Gottes Sohn, der Welt Heiland* (1797), see BUSSE, *Das Johannesevangelium*, 304.

[12] ARNOLD, WEISBERG, "Babel und Bibel und Bias," 37.

this gospel but a divine being above the classification of nationality."[13] In his *Das Wesen des Christentums* from 1939, the respected Systematic theologian Emanuel Hirsch explained that the inhabitants of Galilee between the 8th and 1st century B.C. were gentiles and even after that time only 10 percent of Jews lived there. Not only was Jesus' teaching marked by a "'wholly un-Jewish style'," but as a Galilean he even "stemmed from non-Jewish blood."[14] The Gospel of John, often misunderstood when reduced to its Christology for dogmatic interests, was written by a gentile Christian who made use of anti-Jewish sources and cast his text into the form of a Greek tragedy.[15] Hirsch published a *Volks*edition of the Gospel of John and cut out Jesus' statement in 4:22 as the later redaction of a Jewish Christian.[16] Grundmann argued for a mostly gentile Galilee and for Jesus' Aryan descent in *Jesus der Galiläer und das Judentum* (1940).[17] Similarly, Adolf Hitler's table-talk from 1941 reveals that he thought of Galilee, the home of Jesus, as a Roman colony, settled mostly by Roman soldiers. Jesus was not a Jew but the son of a prostitute and a Roman soldier who spoke out against Jewish capitalism before Paul distorted his teachings with his own emphasis on eternal life and universalism.[18] Whether knowingly or unknowingly, it is ironic that Hitler relies here on ancient *Jewish* sources from the third century and later which "speculate on Jesus' illegitimate origin from a man called Panthera (possibly a corruption of the word *parthenos*, 'virgin,' to the common Roman soldier's name Pantera)."[19] The question of Galilee's ethnic make-up stands again in the midst of vivid scholarly interest. Many Bible dictionaries speak

---

[13] COLWELL, "The Fourth Gospel and the Struggle for Respectability," 298. Idem, *John Defends the Gospel*, 39-49. So also WINDISCH, "Das johanneische Christentum," 148-49. BAUER, *Das Johannesevangelium*, 31. And after WW II see GRÄSSER, "Die Antijüdische Polemik," 80. BRATCHER, "'The Jews'," 402.

[14] Summary of ERICKSEN, *Theologians Under Hitler*, 164 (see 120-97). Hirsch, who wrote his *Habilitationsschrift* about J. G. Fichte and gives much credit to F. C. Baur and Wellhausen for his own views on the Gospel (*Studien*, IV), also makes use of the Jewish legends about Jesus as the "Son of Panther" to corroborate his thesis.

[15] See FREY, *Die johanneische Eschatologie*, 3:59-62. Hirsch's two volumes are the popular translation and explanation *Das vierte Evangelium in seiner ursprünglichen Gestalt verdeutscht und erklärt* (1936) and the scholarly support of his views in *Studien zum vierten Evangelium* (1936).

[16] HIRSCH, *Studien*, 189.

[17] HESCHEL, "Reading Jesus as a Nazi," 27-41, esp. 28-36.

[18] LÖW, *Die Schuld*, 118.

[19] BOCKMUEHL, *This Jesus*, 33. Bockmuehl refers to *Acts of Pilate* 2.3; Origen, *Cels.* 1.28, 32, 69; Epiphanius, *Pan.* 78.7; also *t. Hul.* 2.22-23 ["Jesus ben Pantera"]; *b. Sabb.* 43a (Baraita); *y. Abod. Zar.* 2.2, 40d73ff.; *y. Sabb.* 4.4, 14d70ff. Ibid., 191 n. 22. Hirsch and Grundmann employed the same Jewish legends. See VAN BELLE, "'Salvation is from the Jews'," 372. See also the discussion in MEIER, *A Marginal Jew*, 96, 107. HENGEL, *The Four Gospels*, 200, 321. The accusation that Jesus was born as a result of "fornication" (πορνεία) is expressed implicitly already in John 8:41. Chilton maintains today that Jesus was a *mamzer*, a "child born of a prohibited sexual union." CHILTON, *Rabbi*, 13 (3-22). Ziffer offered a slight emendation, substituting the *yodh* in פנדירא with a *waw* and reading "Pandora" which reminds of the mythological figure that brought a multitude of plagues upon the world. According to *Sanhedrin* 107b, Jesus (the *Ben Pandora*) "practiced magic and led astray and deceived Israel," thus, in Ziffer's words, "making Israel and the rest of mankind miserable in the eyes of the author." ZIFFER, "Two Epithets," 357.

of a "Gentile majority in Galilee."[20] Since Hengel's influential study *Judentum und Hellenismus* (1969), the conventional view of a Hellenized Judaism in Palestine might lend some credibility to the notion of a Gentile Galilee.[21] This understanding is elsewhere used to support the hypothesis of Jesus as a Cynic philosopher (F. G. Downing, B. Mack, L. Vaage).[22] And because of the association with Philip (a Greek name), 'Galilee' in John 1:43 (and 2:1) is interpreted as a topographical symbol for the "wide world of the Gentiles" even among modern Johannine scholars.[23] But there are important voices that warn, at least from a historical point of view, not to exaggerate the Greco-Roman impact on the Galilee of Jesus' time which differs from the dramatic shifts in the second century after the arrival of a large Roman garrison. According to Reed, the material culture of the first century-strata at Galilean sites is marked by Jewish stone vessels, *miqwaoth*, the absence of pork bones and the practice of secondary burial customs, all in contrast to the surrounding regions of Syro-Phoenicia, Iturea, and the Decapolis.[24] Freyne provides a summary and evaluation of the current discussion of Galilee and its inhabitants' ethnic identity and judges that the "case for a pagan Galilee is poorly supported by the literary evidence and receives no support whatsoever from the archaeological explorations."[25]

Consequently, statements such as 4:22 were simply taken out of editions of the Fourth Gospel during the *Third Reich*.[26] Puzzled by a positive statement about the Jews in a text that seems to convey a mostly hostile attitude towards them otherwise, scholars have found their own ways of neutralizing the impact of 4:22. Doubts about the proper fit of 4:22 within the context of the Gospel were raised at least since Ernest Renan's *Vie de Jésus* (1863).[27] But according to Hahn, it was Walter Bauer who strongly

---

[20] So the article about "Galilee" in the *Interpreter's Dictionary of the Bible* (1962), quoted by CHANCEY, *The Myth of a Gentile Galilee*, 1. He finds the same view in many other Bible dictionaries written between the 1960s and 1990s. Ibid., note 2.

[21] In a recent update, Hengel sees his main thesis confirmed by new archaeological discoveries, excavations, inscriptions, coins, and texts. HENGEL, "Judaism and Hellenism Revisited," 6-37.

[22] Hans Dieter Betz critically examines this hypothesis and notes, among others, that the connection between Jesus and cynic philosophy was not made until the Renaissance. BETZ, "Jesus and the Cynics: Survey and Analysis of a Hypothesis," 32-56. Downing does emphasize, though, that Jesus "remains no less a Jew than does Philo or Josephus" etc. even upon finding Cynic elements from the Greek tradition in Jesus' words. DOWNING, "The Jewish Cynic Jesus," 198. Hans Dieter Betz critically examines this hypothesis and notes, among others, that the connection between Jesus and cynic philosophy was not made until the Renaissance. BETZ, "Jesus and the Cynics: Survey and Analysis of a Hypothesis," 32-56.

[23] BRODIE, *The Gospel*, 172, 165.

[24] REED, "Galilean Archaeology and the Historical Jesus," esp. 117-19.

[25] FREYNE, "Galilee and Judea," 26. See also AVIAM, "First century Jewish Galilee," 7-27. SHAKED and AVSHALOM-GORNI, "Jewish Settlement," 28-36. CHANCEY, *The Myth of a Gentile Galilee* (2002). Idem, *Greco-Roman Culture and the Galilee of Jesus* (2005).

[26] See HAACKER, "Gottesdienst ohne Gotteserkenntnis," 110 n. 2.

[27] For a survey of research related to 4:22 see VAN BELLE, "'Salvation is from the Jews'," 371-81. Wellhausen raises doubts about 4:22-24 ("Im Einzelnen gibt namentlich

argued in 1912 that John 4:22 is a gloss which was added later to the Gospel text.[28] The Gospel's "Antisemitismus" and the author's and his community's "Judenhaß"[29] as visible in the negative use of Ἰουδαῖοι are incompatible with a positive statement such as 4:22. Realizing that Bauer is later able to accept a host of "contradictions and problems" as part of the text without explaining them as later insertions,[30] one has to wonder about the coherence of Bauer's literary-critical judgments. And if the Ἰουδαῖοι-language is not motivated by the author's racism, as we expect to show, then Bauer's major reason for cutting out 4:22 is unwarranted.[31] Most commentators do accept the verse as an expression of the author's

---

4,22-24 zu Bedenken Anlaß"), but he still interprets the pronoun ἡμεῖς as Jesus and the Jews. WELLHAUSEN, *Das Evangelium Johannis*, 23.

[28] HAHN, "'Das Heil kommt von den Juden'," 68. But according to Thyen, Kreyenbühl (*Das Evangelium der Wahrheit II*) called 4:22 already in 1905 "eine der abgeschmacktesten und unmöglichsten Glossen . . . die jemals einen Text nicht nur entstellt, sondern in sein gerades Gegenteil verkehrt haben." THYEN, "'Das Heil kommt von den Juden'," 169 n. 30. So also BULTMANN, *Das Evangelium des Johannes*, 130, 139 n. 6. BECKER, *Das Evangelium*, 207-08. Bauer explains that the ὑμεῖς in v.22 includes the Jewish worshippers who stand opposite of the ἡμεῖς which refers to the Christians as the true believers. After identifying the Jews with the "you" of the opposite religion, he then concludes, "Dann aber ist die Begründung 22b schlechthin unverständlich. Dass die Christen in klarem Bewusstsein dessen, um was es sich handelt, ihren Gottesdienst pflegen, kann seinen Anlass unmöglich darin haben, dass das Heil von den Juden stammt. Die σωτηρία nimmt auch gar nicht von ihnen seinen Ausgang, sondern von der Sendung des himmlischen σωτήρ τοῦ κόσμου (v. 42)." BAUER, *Das Johannesevangelium*, 70. Bauer held a different view in the first edition of his commentary from 1912 in which we read: "Die Verehrung Gottes als Vater schliesst im Grunde jede Bindung an eine bestimmte Stätte aus. Trotzdem die Juden noch keineswegs so weit sind, wird ihnen von Joh doch 22 ein gewisser Vorrang eingeräumt." See HAHN, "'Das Heil kommt von den Juden'," 68 n. 2.

[29] See our reference to Bauer in chapter 2 as a proponent of Ἰουδαῖοι as an "ethnic-religious" term.

[30] Among the "zahlreichen Widersprüche und sonstigen Schwierigkeiten," Bauer counts statements that no one accepts his message (1:5, 10; 3:11, 12, 32), yet everybody runs to him (3:26, 29f.); Jesus does not judge the world (3:17; 8:15; 12:47) and yet he does it (5:22); Jesus told his disciples everything (15:15), yet he cannot tell them much (16:12). BAUER, *Das Johannesevangelium*, 252.

[31] Hendricks has a rather idiosyncratic way of interpreting 4:22. According to him, the verse is misunderstood when taken literally. John's "assessment of the *Ioudaioi* in the *Galilaios* stream of discourse is deeply hostile" which renders 4:22 as "an example of Johannine irony" or "subaltern sarcasm," thus "signifying the direct opposite of its wording." HENDRICKS, "A Discourse of Domination," 210. We have discussed the problems of Hendricks' assumption about a social conflict between rural *Galilaioi* and urban *Ioudaioi* earlier (see chapter 2). As with Bauer, his interpretation of 4:22 fails if we can show that the Ἰουδαῖοι do not occupy the place of singular antagonists that he assigns to them.

salvation-historical consciousness and understand the apparent tension to, for example, 8:44 as part of the dialectic understanding of Christian truth that penetrates the whole Gospel.[32]

Apart from 4:22, the contention that John presents "Jesus no longer as a Jew" finds support even among modern scholars. Manns concludes this way because he thinks that Jesus distances himself from the Jews when he talks about "your law" (8:17; 10:34) or "their law" (15:25).[33] No matter how one evaluates Jesus' view of the Law,[34] the most this observation can do is to separate Jesus from loyalty to the Torah. But it certainly is no reason to deny the Gospel's positive affirmation of Jesus' racial ties to the Jews.[35]

3. Jesus is the King of the Jews (18:33, 39; 19:3, 19, 21)

Jesus is crucified as "King of the Jews," a title that was first employed by Pilate in his interrogation of Jesus (18:33) and in dialogue with the Jews (18:39). The Roman soldiers then used it mockingly (19:3) and the Jewish chief priests rejected it as a valid title (19:21). Nevertheless Pilate has it written against their will as an inscription on the cross (19:19). But the theme of Jesus' kingship pervades not only the whole passion account. Jesus was hailed earlier as "King of Israel" (βασιλεὺς τοῦ Ἰσραήλ) by Nathanael (1:49) and, in conjunction with a quotation by Psalm 118:25, by the crowd upon entering Jerusalem (12:13). In contrast to these Jewish interlocutors, it is only natural to find Gentiles like Pilate using Ἰουδαῖοι (cf. also 4:9) where Jews employ the honorific term Ἰσραήλ.[36] Similarly,

---

[32] According to Hahn, the following scholars consider 4:22 as an integral part of the text: Holtzmann, Schlatter, Zahn, Strathmann, Goppelt, Barrett, Cullmann, Haacker, Schnackenburg, Hoskyns, Morris, Lindars, Bernard. HAHN, "'Das Heil kommt von den Juden'," 68-70.

[33] MANNS, *John and Jamnia*, 30.

[34] For the discussion, see PANCARO, *The Law in the Fourth Gospel* (1975). LINDEMANN, "Moses und Jesus Christus," 309-34. See also the many essays in parts B ("Heilige Schrift") and C ("Heilsinstitutionen") in *Israel und seine Heilstraditionen im Johannesevangelium*, 91-364 and the essays by LOADER, "Jesus and the Law in Joh," 135-54 and MENKEN, "Observations on the Significance of the Old Testament in the Fourth Gospel," 155-75.

[35] See SIKES, "The Anti-Semitism of the Fourth Gospel," 24.

[36] In the Synoptics, it is also only the Roman governor and his soldiers who employ the title "king of the Jews" (Matt 27:11, 29, 37; Mark 15:2, 9, 18, 26; Luke 23:3, 37, 38). For a parallel see the gentile μάγοι who come to Judea and ask for the βασιλεὺς τῶν Ἰουδαίων (Matt 2:2). The ὃν λέγετε in Mark 15:12 is text-critically uncertain. But if we have to assume that Pilate learned about Jesus' kingship from the Jews, which is a likely assumption (see Luke 23:2), we may speculate that he heard them calling Jesus βασιλεὺς

we find in Matthew and Mark's passion account that the Roman soldiers mock Jesus as βασιλεύς τῶν 'Ιουδαίων (Matt 27:29; Mark 15:18) while the Jewish chief priests ridicule him as βασιλεύς 'Ισραήλ (Matt 27:42; Mark 15:32).[37] Beyond mere judicial duty or curiosity, Pilate's question "Are *you* are the king of the Jews?" (18:33) might include at least a sense of doubt and incredulity if not of ridicule and sarcasm (cf. 19:3).[38] It is a moment of utter irony, a literary device often used in the gospel,[39] that the title mentioned in Pilate's question does indeed make a true statement, although in a way that the governor does not realize. For in the passion narrative and beyond, Jesus is presented in a subtle way as a royal superior to the Jews as well as to the governor. He affirms explicitly that he is a "king" (βασιλεύς, 18:37) who has a "kingdom" (ἡ βασιλεία, 18:36) and "servants" (ὑπηρέται, 18:36). While the soldiers mean to ridicule Jesus by giving him a crown of thorns, the purple robe and by paying homage to him as "king of the Jews," they actually enthrone him as secret prophets of truth.[40] In a similarly veiled fashion, the 'elevation' of Jesus on the cross (cf. 3:14) turns out to be the enthronement in disguise.[41] But more than that, far from being a victim, Jesus remains sovereign even in his own

---

τοῦ 'Ισραήλ as in John 1:49; 12:13, and that he as a Gentile changed it into βασιλεὺς τῶν 'Ιουδαίων. Gutbrod points out that in the passion narrative 'Ιουδαῖοι occurs "on the lips of non-Jews." GUTBROD, "'Ισραήλ," 377.

[37] See also HAHN, "'Das Heil kommt von den Juden'," 77. Unlike the chief priests in the Gospels of Matthew and Mark, the "rulers" (οἱ ἄρχοντες) in Luke do not ridicule Jesus with the title "king of the Jews" but say instead (23:35): "He saved others; let Him save Himself if this is the Christ of God, His Chosen One" (ὁ χριστὸς τοῦ θεοῦ ὁ ἐκλεκτός).

[38] The emphatic position of σύ in the question (σὺ εἶ ὁ βασιλεὺς τῶν 'Ιουδαίων, 18:33; see also 3:10) is worth translating as such because it brings out the sense of surprise, skepticism, or even scorn in Pilate's attitude towards Jesus as if to say "how can someone like you claim to be a king of the Jews?" None of the standard English translations follow the Greek word-order and therefore loose the implication. The German revised Elberfelder translation marks the emphasis on the personal pronoun by printing it in italics: "Bist *du* der König der Juden?"

[39] Brown helpfully explains the use of irony in the Fourth Gospel as follows: "The opponents of Jesus are given to making statements about him that are derogatory, sarcastic, incredulous, or, at least, inadequate in the sense they intend. However, by way of irony these statements are often true or more meaningful in a sense they do not realize. The evangelist simply presents such statements and leaves them unanswered (or answered with eloquent silence), for he is certain that his believing readers will see the deeper truth. Good examples are iv 12, vii 35, 42, viii 22, xi 50." BROWN, *The Gospel*, 1:CXXXVI. One could easily add 4:25, 8:53, and 12:19 to the list. For a comprehensive study of the use of irony in the Gospel of John see DUKE, *Irony in the Fourth Gospel* (1983).

[40] TILBORG, *Reading John*, 214.

[41] VAN DER WATT, *Family of the King*, 379. NICKLAS, "'153 große Fische'," 385.

arrest and trial. Jesus initiates the conversation (18:4).[42] He speaks the powerful words ἐγώ εἰμι, which make his opponents fall to the ground (18:5, 6). The dialogue in 18:28-19:16 shows that Jesus is the judge, not Pilate.[43] The last words of Jesus, "It is finished" (19:30), sound more like a cry of victory and accomplishment than of despair. And the title on the cross, Ἰησοῦς ὁ Ναζωραῖος ὁ βασιλεὺς τῶν Ἰουδαίων, was written in Hebrew, Latin and Greek (19:19-20), thus "revealing how John turns the charge into a world-wide proclamation of enthronement."[44]

Jesus does not reject the royal title but defines it in ways contrary to Jewish and Roman expectation. Neither is his kingdom from this world (18:36) as Jewish-messianic hopes imagine (cf. 6:15; 12:13), nor is his authority limited to Israel or to the Jews as Pilate's words imply ("king of *the Jews*" in 18:33, 39; see 17:2; 13:3). With these modifications in mind, the reader perceives the designation "king of the Jews" with a positive meaning and connotation in the microcosm of Jesus' life as a Jew as well as in the narrative design of the Passion account for it enhances the sense of tragedy already known from the prologue (1:10-11), namely that a legitimate king is rejected by his own people.

Contrary to this understanding, Pancaro insists that the two royal titles differ in meaning[45] and that "Jesus is not the King of the Jews, he is the King of Israel."[46] While Ἰουδαῖοι stands here for the "religious-national community" and the title for a "national-political Messiah," Ἰσραήλ is a honorific title for the theocratic people which refers in the Gospel (in 1:31, 49; 3:10; 12:13) to Jewish Christians who are "born again of water and spirit"[47] as the "particularly instructive" occurrence in connection with Nathanael, the "genuine Israelite" (1:48) shows.[48] The title "King of the Jews," on the other hand, has a negative ring to it because it is found

---

[42] Morris explains that Jesus "is not 'arrested' at all. He has the initiative and he gives himself up" MORRIS, *The Gospel According to John*, 658.

[43] For further comments about this "Rollentausch" see chapter 4, "Pilate as an agent of the world."

[44] So BROWN, *The Gospel*, 2:919. ALLEN, "The Jewish Christian Church," 88. NICKLAS, "'153 große Fische'," 385.

[45] He presented his thoughts in two articles: PANCARO, "'People of God'," 114-29. Idem, "The Relationship of the Church," 396-405. See also STEGEMANN and STEGEMANN, "König Israels, nicht König der Juden?," 41-56, who nevertheless concede that the title of their essay might be a "überscharfe Pointierung" because terms in the Gospel of John often have a variety of nuances and "selten so eindeutig sind, wie dies eine Antithese, wie wir sie aufgestellt haben suggeriert." Ibid., 41-42.

[46] PANCARO, "The Relationship," 400.

[47] PANCARO, "'People of God'," 125.

[48] Ibid., 123. In the second article, Pancaro calls John 1:49 again "particularly enlightening." PANCARO, "The Relationship," 398.

"exclusively in the Passion narrative and the whole point of its use there is
to show that Jesus is not King of the Jews" since the Jews are not 'of the
truth' but presented instead as enemies of Jesus.[49] Pancaro rests the weight
of his argument on another pair of terms that differ in meaning. In his
view, the sense of λαός in 11:50 is influenced by the Septuagint and, as a
technical term, signifies the "theocratic people" while ἔθνος in the same
sentence refers, "against the usage of the LXX and the NT," to the "civil
organization of the Jews."[50] Since λαός "is no longer coextensive with 'the
Jewish nation'," Pancaro assumes that Ἰσραήλ, a term "closely related" to
λαός,[51] cannot refer to the Jewish nation as well and is therefore different
from Ἰουδαῖοι. He concludes with the proposition that the author's choice
of λαός and Ἰσραήλ presents the idea that "the Church is the new Israel"[52]
which contributes thus to the Gospel's ecclesiology.

In a critical response to Pancaro's articles, John Painter points out that
"there is no necessary clear-cut distinction between λαός and ἔθνος,"
neither in the Septuagint nor in the New Testament (e.g., Rev 10:11).[53]
Furthermore, while Painter acknowledges a difference in meaning between
Ἰουδαῖοι and Ἰσραήλ, he sees merely a shift in *nuance* which has to do
with the location of the speaker: "The language of Palestinian Judaism is
Israel, Israelite,' while Gentiles and Jews of the dispersion speak of the
Jews. Both descriptions express national and religious allegiance, but in
Palestine the political implications were much stronger."[54] Consequently,
he confirms our observation that the use of Ἰουδαῖοι in the title "king of
the Jews" is due to the non-Jewish ethnicity of the speaker (Pilate).[55] Even
the title "king of Israel" has "nationalistic and 'this wordly' political
implications" which require modification in the eyes of the Gospel's
author.[56] And, we may add, the term Ἰουδαῖοι in the Gospel has theocratic

---

[49] PANCARO, "The Relationship," 400.

[50] PANCARO, "'People of God'," 121.

[51] Ibid., 123.

[52] PANCARO, "The Relationship," 405.

[53] PAINTER, "The Church and Israel," 105.

[54] Ibid., 108. Hahn also explains that the use of Ἰουδαῖοι in the Gospel of John presupposes a diaspora context. HAHN, "'Das Heil kommt von den Juden'," 77, 81.

[55] Josephus corroborates the lexical option of using the titles 'king of the Jews' and 'king of Israel' largely synonymously. In his *Antiquities*, written ca. AD 75, he can call David 'king of the Hebrews' (βασιλεὺς ὑπὸ τῶν Ἑβραίων, *A.J.* 7.71), 'king of the Jews' (ὁ δὲ τῶν Ἰουδαίων βασιλεύς, *A.J.* 7.72; also *B.J.* 6.439), and 'king of Israel' (βασιλεὺς τῶν Ἰσραηλιτῶν, *A.J.* 7.76) in the same context without indicating a difference even in nuance.

[56] PAINTER, "The Church and Israel," 109. The use of 'king of Israel' in Pss. Sol. 17.42 confirms a Davidic-messianic idea with national-political implications. See STEGEMANN and STEGEMANN, "König Israels, nicht König der Juden?," 46, 49-50.

implications because otherwise Jesus could not say that "salvation is from the Jews" (4:22).

We conclude that the title "king of the Jews" does not carry any negative content that is either inherent in the term Ἰουδαῖοι itself or supported by an alleged rejection of Jesus' kingship in the passion account or by the parallel to the title "king of Israel."[57] Rather, the title reveals Jesus' royal office in a concealed manner contrary to the apparent context of accusation, trial, and death.[58]

Pancaro's thesis also fails to convince with regard to his interpretation of "Israel" in 1:31 and 3:10. When John the Baptist says that he came baptizing in order that Jesus "might be manifested to Israel" (1:31), Pancaro argues that he was "not sent to reveal Jesus to the Jews, but to Israel; to those Jews who, like Nathanael, were willing to accept the 'truth' when presented with it." But to say that John the Baptist only baptized Jews that later became Christians runs counter to any historical probability (see the formation of μαθηταὶ Ἰωάννου in contrast to Jesus' disciples [Matt 9:14; John 1:35] and the need for admonition such as John 3:30) and to the Gospel's attempt of responding to followers of John the Baptist after Easter who saw in him "the light" (1:8) and "the Messiah" (1:20). And when Jesus calls Nicodemus "the teacher of Israel," Pancaro finds therein "much irony" and speculates on Jesus' thoughts as follows: "You claim to be the authorized teacher of Israel, yet you do not understand what I am teaching you. You are not worthy of the name 'the teacher of Israel.' You are merely a teacher of the Jews.'" PANCARO, "The Relationship," 399. The irony lies with the word "teacher" and not with the term "Israel," as the second half of the sentence shows ("do not understand these things?"). Thus, without denying theological overtones, the term "Israel" in 1:31 and 3:10 carries an ethnic-religious sense as does the term "Jews." The Stegemanns miss to discuss the use of "Israel" in 1:31 and 3:10 altogether.

[57] Both titles teach positively about the kingship of Christ. Thyen comments, "Nur als 'König der Juden' . . . ist Jesus der 'König Israels' (1,49) und 'Heiland der Welt' (4,42)." THYEN, "'Das Heil kommt von den Juden'," 179. Geyser observes that "this gospel begins and ends with a kingdom statement: the confession by a guileless Israelite, 'You are the King of Israel' and Pilate's *titulus* on the cross, *Iesus Nazarenus Rex Iudaeorum.*" GEYSER, "Israel in the fourth Gospel," 13.

[58] Moloney briefly rehearses the Pancaro-Painter debate as well and sides with Painter's philological analysis regarding the meaning of Ἰσραήλ, λαός, and ἔθνος as a reference to the "religious national community of the Jews." MOLONEY, *The Gospel of John*, 24. He adds, however, that a more "more contextual and narrative reading of the use of 'Israel' and 'Israelite'" also corrects Painter by finding in 1:31; 3:10 and 1:47 a meaning for "Israel" which defines those who "receive the revelation of God that takes place in and through Jesus." Ibid., 28. Thus, Moloney takes a third position between Pancaro and Painter. For a positive interpretation of the title "king of the Jews" see also SÖDING, "'Was kann aus Nazareth schon Gutes kommen?'," 37. VAN DER WATT, *Family of the King*, 376-81.

4. Jews Believe in Jesus

Not a few but "many Jews" (11:45; 12:11) believed in Jesus as the Messiah and became his disciples, including leaders such as Joseph of Arimathea (19:38) and probably also Nicodemus (19:39). One can delegate these texts to a different redactional level, as Ashton did with regard to 11:19, 31, 36, 45 and 12:9, 11[59] and as Hirsch did with regard to 12:42-43.[60] But it is simply contrary to the evidence when Reinhartz claims that the term Ἰουδαῖος in the Gospel of John "is never used of a figure who is a believer."[61]

There are also "many in the crowd" who believed (7:31). The schism among the Jews concerning the identity of Jesus further testifies that some Jews accepted the claims of Jesus (10:19-21; cf. 9:16). While the immediate context suggests that some people's faith was only temporary or superficial (cf. 2:23-25; 8:30-31; 12:45), it would be a false generalization to expand that qualification to all expressions of faith in the Gospel.

5. Conclusion

Altogether, Ἰουδαῖος is used with positive, neutral and negative meanings. The term does not qualify the Jews unanimously as a *massa damnata*.[62]

21x neutral use: 2:6, 13; 3:1, 22; 4:9b; 5:1; 6:4; 7:2, 15, 22, 35; 8:22; 10:19; 11:55; 13:33; 18:12, 14, 20; 19:20, 21, 40, 42

16x positive use: 4:9a, 22; 10:19; 11:19, 31, 33, 36, 45; 12:9, 11; 18:33, 39; 19:3, 19, 21 (2x)

34x negative use: 1:19; 2:18, 20; 3:25; 5:10, 15, 16, 18; 6:41, 52; 7:1, 11, 13; 8:31, 48, 52, 57; 9:18, 22 (2x); 10:24, 31, 33; 11:8, 54; 18:31, 35, 36, 38; 19:7, 12, 14, 38; 20:19

We are left with a little less than half of occurrences of Ἰουδαῖοι that do not show any apparently positive or neutral qualifications.[63] The challenge

---

[59] See ASHTON, "The Identity," 62.

[60] Hirsch calls the testimony of Jewish faith in the context of God's wrath about the Jews in 12:37-41 (quoting Isa 6:10) "undenkbar" and delegates these verses to the work of the redactor. HIRSCH, *Studien*, 98.

[61] REINHARTZ, "'Jews' and Jews in the Fourth Gospel," 220.

[62] So already Grässer against the older scholarship of Wellhausen (*Das Evangelium Johannis*, 117), Heitmüller, and Overbeck. GRÄSSER, "Die Antijüdische Polemik," 77. See also WIEFEL, "Die Scheidung von Gemeinde und Welt," 224. HAHN, "'Die Juden'," 431, 433. ONUKI, *Gemeinde und Welt*, 35. REBELL, *Gemeinde als Gegenwelt*, 100. SCHNELLE, *Antidoketische Christologie*, 46.

remains to interpret positive and negative usages as part of one text that conveys a coherent theology. Rather than eliminating 'the Jews' with a positive meaning as a gloss[64] or postulating that the Gospel is a clumsy patchwork of different sources,[65] a synchronic approach will seek to understand how one element modifies the reading of the other.

---

[63] Grässer counts 33 polemic references to "the Jews." GRÄSSER, "Die Antijüdische Polemik," 76. Wengst suggests 40 negative occurrences because some neutral or positive usages receive a negative connotation in the context (so 8:31, 48-59; 10:19, 24, 31; 1:19 and 4:1-3). WENGST, *Bedrängte Gemeinde*, 55 n.2. Nothomb counts 39 pejorative occurrences of Ἰουδαῖοι. NOTHOMB, "Nouveau Regard sur 'les Juifs' de Jean," 66. See also LINCOLN, *The Gospel According to John*, 71. Frey and Schnelle regard only about one third of the occurrences as polemic, which is a little bit too low. FREY, "Das Bild," 37. SCHNELLE, "Die Juden im Johannesevangelium," 219.

[64] See our discussion of 4:22 above.

[65] So Martin C. White (1972) and Peter Tomson (2001) whom we mentioned in chapter 1 (2.1.4.1.).

CHAPTER 3

The Parallelism between "the Jews" and "the World"

Culpepper rejects all current efforts to neutralize ("Judeans") or narrow ("Jewish authorities") the reference of οἱ Ἰουδαῖοι and states that "the Gospel of John generalized and stereotyped those who rejected Jesus by its use of this term."[1] Our review in chapter 2 agrees with such a verdict. Although one can discern various nuances from a close reading of the text (geographical, ethnic, religious), it seems that the author used the plural οἱ Ἰουδαῖοι in an all-inclusive way to steer *away* from distinctions. Against current trends in translations, there is no probable evidence for limiting the reference to "religious authorities" or to "Judeans."

Does that mean that an honest reading of John faces an anti-Semitic theology? Our observations in chapter 3 have shown that such a static view of "the Jews" destroys the Johannine dialectic that penetrates the whole work.[2] We shall argue further that, for various reasons, such a broad meaning of οἱ Ἰουδαῖοι is misunderstood if interpreted as an expression of racial hostility. The key to understanding the meaning and function of "the Jews" is the parallelism between κόσμος and Ἰουδαῖος throughout the Gospel. The word κόσμος is used even more often in John (78 times) than the word Ἰουδαῖος (71 times), and with the exception of chaps. 2, 5, 19-20, "world" appears in every chapter. John relates κόσμος to Ἰουδαῖος in at least two different ways which will be called in the following "compositional" and "narratological parallelism." There are also a few conceptual parallels worth mentioning. In the next two chapters, we will first attempt to describe and then to explore this arrangement.

---

[1] CULPEPPER, "Anti-Judaism in the Fourth Gospel," 66.

[2] Hengel warns, "Es besteht hier die große Gefahr, daß mit einer einseitig-tendenziösen Deutung [of Ἰουδαῖοι] die typische johanneische Dialektik zerstört wird, die das ganze Werk durchzieht." HENGEL, "Die Schriftauslegung des 4. Evangeliums," 261-62.

1. Compositional Parallelism (Macrostructure)

Despite disagreement about details, the Gospel of John is often divided into two main parts which both end with a summary statement (12:37-50; 20:30-31) and which are enclosed by a prologue (1:1-18) and an epilogue (21): part 1 could be called "Jesus leaves the Father and goes to the world" (1:19-12:50), and part 2, "Jesus leaves the world and goes to the Father (13-20)."[3] The following table displays the distribution of κόσμος and Ἰουδαῖοι throughout the divisions of the Gospel:

John		κόσμος	Ἰουδαῖοι	Point of view	
1a		4x	0x	Universal	
	1b-12	28x	46x		Local
13-17		40x	1x	Universal	
	18-20	5x	24x		Local
21		1x	0x		

What becomes evident is that κόσμος, though not absent from the first twelve chapters, dominates the prologue and the farewell discourse (13-17), while Ἰουδαῖος is, with the exception of 13:33, exclusively confined to the first main part and the Passion narrative. Thus, speaking with regard to the macro-structure of the Gospel, both major parts *begin* with a strong emphasis on the κόσμος (prologue, farewell discourse) that is then *followed* by the Ἰουδαῖοι in the narratives (chaps. 1b-12, Passion). We will turn our attention specifically to the meaning of κόσμος within the prologue and the farewell discourse in order to understand contributions of both sections as openings to the Gospel's main parts.

1.1. The Prologue (John 1:1-18)

John's prologue has preoccupied scholars with such a number of questions[4] that we cannot aim to cover any of them comprehensively.[5] But some

---

[3] Barrett reminds us that the "structure of the gospel is simple in outline, complicated in detail." BARRETT, *The Gospel*, 11. Other suggestions for the headlines of the two main sections are, for example, "Jesus in the world" (part 1) and "his return to the Father" (part 2). So FEINE, BEHM, and KÜMMEL, *Introduction to the New Testament*, 137. C. H. Dodd called the first part "Book of Signs" and the second one "Book of the Passion." See THOMPSON, "John, Gospel of," 373-74. So also BERGER, *Bibelkunde*, 303.

[4] The following are some of the most frequently addressed issues with regard to the prologue: There are *historical* questions about the prologue's composition (sources, evangelist, redactor; prologue written after the Gospel?) and its religion-historical background (Genesis, Philo's *logos*, the *memra* of the Targumim, Gnostic sources, Heraclitus, Stoic philosophy). *Textual* questions deal with genre (hymn, confession),

reasoned assumptions relevant to our discussion need to be addressed before we proceed.

1.1.1. *Structure and train of thought*

The question of the prologue's compositional unity and structure has been answered either negatively with numerous attempts to split these eighteen verses into various layers of sources and redaction[6] or, on the other hand, by proposals of elaborate chiasms that go to the opposite extreme.[7] Both

---

style (poetry, prose), structure, center/climax (suggestions are vv. 12b, 14, 14a, 14b, 18), the point of incarnation (*logos asarkos / ensarkos* already in v. 5 or not before v. 14?), and matters of dispute in individual verses (punctuation in vv. 3-4; are vv. 16-18 part of John the Baptist's speech in v. 15? etc.). Then, there is the important question of the prologue's *literary* connection to the Gospel. Needless to say, all issues are interrelated and the answer of one affects that of the other.

[5] Some important contributions to the study of the prologue are the following (in chronological order): HARNACK, "Über das Verhältnis des Prologs des vierten Evangeliums zum ganzen Werk," 189-231. KÄSEMANN, "Aufbau und Anliegen des johanneischen Prologs," 2:155-80. HAENCHEN, "Probleme des Johanneischen 'Prologs'," 114-43. ROBINSON, "The Relation of the Prologue to the Gospel of St. John," 120-29. BORGEN, "Observations on the Targumic Character of the Prologue of John," 288-95. HOOKER, "The Johannine Prologue and the Messianic Secret," 40-58. CULPEPPER, "The Pivot of John's Prologue," 1-31. HOFRICHTER, *Im Anfang war der „Johannesprolog"* (1986). MILLER, *Salvation-History in the Prologue of John* (1989). THEOBALD, *Die Fleischwerdung des Logos* (1988). CARTER, "The Prologue and John's Gospel," 35-58. HARRIS, *Prologue and Gospel* (1994). SCHOLTISSEK, "Relecture und réécriture," 1-29. BOYARIN, "The Gospel of the Memra," 243-84. PATTERSON, "The Prologue to the Fourth Gospel," 325-32. SEGOVIA, "John 1:1-18 as Entrée into Johannine Reality," 33-64. REED, "How Semitic Was John?," 709-26. LIOY, *The Search for Ultimate Reality* (2005). PHILLIPS, *The Prologue of the Fourth Gospel: A Sequential Reading* (2006). For a bibliography that covers literature about John's prologue between the years 1800 to 1988, see THEOBALD, *Die Fleischwerdung*, 498-514.

[6] Numerous are the attempts to find a *Vorlage* of an original (non-)Christian hymn or confession in the prologue, which the evangelist then worked over before it was supplemented by a final editor. Miller compares seventeen proposals of which none equals the other! MILLER, *Salvation-History*, 6. For a thorough argument about the prologue's literary unity, see RUCKSTUHL, *Die literarische Einheitlichkeit*, 63-97.

[7] Culpepper, who learned from the proposals of Lund (1931) and Boismard (1953), suggests the following chiasm: A (1-2), B (3), C (4-5), D (6-8), E (9-10), F (11), G (12a), H (12b), G' (12c), F' (13), E' (14), D' (15), C' (16), B' (17), A' (18). CULPEPPER, "The Pivot," 9-17. But just as in Boismard's model, B (3) and B' (17) do not correspond well. Verse 3 has stronger verbal (δι' αὐτοῦ ἐγένετο) and thematic (creation; cf. πάντα and κόσμος) ties to v. 10. Culpepper can only strengthen the assumed parallelism by pointing to the strengths of other parallels in his chiastic arrangement, i.e., by cumulative evidence. Ibid., 11. Similarly, Culpepper himself acknowledges that C (4-5) and C' (16) are not obvious parallels and he calls attention to conceptual rather than verbal similarities. Pryor's evaluation seems valid when he says that Culpepper's model "is too

ways are paralyzed by the individualistic nature of the reconstruction and by catalogs of criteria that please a modern sense of order but seem alien to the text. We suggest a moderate chiasm that uses key-terms to indicate structure but also leaves lots of room for variety in style and "asymmetries."[8] Peder Borgen[9] observed the following inverted parallelism:

1-2 ὁ λόγος, θεὸς
3 πάντα δι' αὐτοῦ ἐγένετο
4-5 τὸ φῶς
6-9 τὸ φῶς
10-13 ὁ κόσμος δι' αὐτοῦ ἐγένετο
14-18 ὁ λόγος, θεὸς

While Borgen attempts to present the first five verses as a basic exposition of Genesis 1:1-5 with targumic character, we contend with his observation that verses 1-5 are something of a "basic exposition"[10] that is elaborated on in verses 6-18 which apply terms and phrases "to the event of the appearance of Jesus Christ."[11] The Gospel's opening mentions Christ's preexistent relation to God (1-2), his relation to creation (3a-b) and his incarnation and ministry to humankind (3c-5),[12] and the following verses

---

precise." PRYOR, "Jesus and Israel," 202. Köstenberger's recent proposal (A [1-5], B [6-8], C [9-14], B' [15], A' [16-18]) favors a thematic parallelism but ignores the key terms as a structural principle: he cuts off v. 9 from the group of lines that are connected by the key term φῶς and ignores the parallels between vv. 3 (πάντα δι' αὐτοῦ ἐγένετο) and 10 (πάντα δι' αὐτοῦ ἐγένετο) and between vv. 1-2 (ὁ λόγος, θεὸς) and 14-18 (ὁ λόγος, θεὸς). KÖSTENBERGER, *John*, 21.

[8] Miller is puzzled by "asymmetries" such as the "overlapping references to the incarnation at vss. 9, 10, and 14 (and, we will argue later, at vs. 4a), the switch from the third to the first person at vs. 14, and irregular rhythms and groupings of lines at vss. 8-14, 16-18." MILLER, *Salvation-History*, 6.

[9] BORGEN, "Observations," 291. The most striking deviation from other proposed chiasms is the disappearance of the parallelism between vv. 6-8 and v. 15, the texts that speak about John the Baptist. But the prologue's strong Christological emphasis and John the Baptist's subordinate significance in comparison legitimates the preeminence of λόγος and φως as structural markers of the text.

[10] Scholtissek calls John 1:1-5 a "prologue in the prologue." SCHOLTISSEK, "Relecture und réécriture," 11.

[11] BORGEN, "Observations," 292.

[12] Miller made a good but often neglected case for the incarnational reading of vv. 3b-4. In this view, ὃ γέγονεν in v. 3c begins a new sentence (so P75ᶜ C D L Wˢ 050* *pc; lectio difficilor*! See the Greek text of Nestle-Aland since the 26ᵗʰ edition; also NRS, NAB, NJB, CEV) and does not refer back to the created things (πάντα) in v. 3a, as the changes of tense (γέγονεν instead of ἐγένετο) and preposition (ἐν αὐτῷ instead of δι' αὐτοῦ) indicate, but to the incarnation. Miller translates the phrase ὃ γέγονεν ἐν αὐτῷ

(6-18) are a "statement and restatement of the same message."[13] Each section transitions smoothly into the other: verses 4-5 mention "the light" that becomes the dominating term for verses 6-9. Verse 9 places κόσμος at the end of the sentence, the key term which immediately reappears in the statements that follow (vv.10-13). Verses 12 to 13 describe the believers' response which is then reflected in the personal pronoun "us" and "we" in verses 14-16. And verses 17-18 ("Moses," "Jesus Christ," ἐξηγήσατο) transition into the first scene that takes the reader out of the meta-narrative and into the story of "Jews," "priests," "Levites" and "Jerusalem" (1:19).[14] The general train of thought is characterized by what Segovia calls "a pattern of progression by concretization" in which the focus narrows from one subsection to the other: First we see the λόγος relating to God (1-2), then to creation (3), then to humanity (4-13), and finally to the children of God (14-16) before the author concludes with verses 17-18.[15] If we extend

---

ζωὴ ἦν as "What has appeared in him was Life." MILLER, *Salvation-History*, 109. For γίνομαι in the sense of "to come," "to happen," "to appear" (and not in the sense of "to become" as if created), see also 6:25, 12:30, 14:22 and the only parallel in the New Testament for ὃ γέγονεν in Mark 5:33. The change of the verbs' tenses in vv. 1-5 and the progression of thought therein imply a salvation-historical concept which Miller verbalizes this way: the Logos is presented in "his pre-existent relation to God [vv. 1-2, ἦν], his creative relation to the cosmos [vv. 3, ἐγένετο], his incarnate saving relation to men [vv. 3b-4, γέγονεν], and – from John's standpoint – his present and continuing victorious relation to evil [v. 5, φαίνει]." Ibid., 15. Other proponents of this view are, for example, Origen, Hilary, Ambrose, and, among modern scholars, Lacan, Vawter, Lamarche, and Schlatter. Ibid., 77. See also Theodor Zahn and A. Loisy, mentioned in BULTMANN, *The Gospel of John*, 16 n. 2. Furthermore, THYEN, " 'Das Heil kommt von den Juden'," 170. ONUKI, *Gemeinde und Welt*, 42. MOLONEY, *The Gospel of John*, 36. PHILLIPS, *The Prologue*, 162-64.

[13] MOLONEY, *The Gospel of John*, 34. ` calls an author's repetition and restatement of his own words within the same work 'réécriture' (synchronic), while a quotation or restatement of another person's words from another work is called 'relecture' (diachronic). SCHOLTISSEK, "Relecture und réécriture," 5-9; with regard to the prologue, see 9-13.

[14] Harris explains vv. 17-18 correctly as a "bridging summary . . . between the prologue and the Gospel." HARRIS, *Prologue and Gospel*, 90.

[15] SEGOVIA, "John 1:1-18," 38. Segovia offers the following structure: (A) The Word and God (1:1-2); (B) The Word and the World (1:3-17) with subsections: (1) The Word and Creation (1:3); (2) The Word and Humanity (1:4-13); (3) The Word and the Children of God (1:14-17); (C) The Word and God (1:18). Ibid., 60-61. There is some similarity with Theobald's proposal who regards 1:1-13 as a view from *without* (proclamation of the logos' universal significance) and 1:14-18 as a view from *within* (confession of believers). Both parts are held together by parallels (vv. 6-8, 15), similar techniques (reflections on previous statements) and the inclusio (v.1-2, 18). THEOBALD, *Die Fleischwerdung*, 206-07. Harnack already observed this movement from the general to the concrete in John 1:1-5. HARNACK, "Ueber das Verhältnis des Prologs," 218. See also KÄSEMANN, "Aufbau und Anliegen," 160.

the prologue to verse 51, regarding 1:19-51 as "Introduction, Part 2," then we observe a progress of concretization from Jesus as θεός (1:1) to Jesus as υἱὸς τοῦ ἀνθρώπου (1:51) with a combination of divinity and humanity in the titles Ἰησοῦς Χριστός (1:17) and μονογενὴς θεός (1:18) positioned as a bridge between both parts.

1.1.2. The universal opening

The synoptic Gospels lead the reader immediately into the world of the Old Testament and of first-century Judaism as the specifically Jewish setting of Jesus' life. Matthew opens with a Jewish genealogy (Matt 1:1-17), Mark begins with a quote from "Isaiah the prophet" (Mark 1:2-3), and after his preface, Luke locates his first narrative about the priest Zechariah "in the time of Herod king of Judea" (Luke 1:5). Thus, from the beginning the reader finds himself in the land of Palestine and in the religion of Judaism. Compared with that, John's opening is noticeable for its absence of particular circumstances, and even the end of the prologue does not arrive at the level of specificity as the Synoptics do. The author omits Old Testament prophecies and the circumstances of Jesus' birth. The main antagonists of the later narrative, the Jews, are completely absent, and only in verse 17, close to the beginning of the actual story, do we find an explicit reference to the Law and Moses as pillars of Judaism. Verses 6 and 15 mention John, but in contrast to the Synoptics (see Matt 3:1; Mark 1:4; Luke 1:13), the author strips John of particulars such as his title ("the Baptist," "prophet") and his place of ministry (in the desert), and presents him instead simply as a human (ἄνθρωπος 1:6) whom God sent as a witness.[16] The text does not describe Jesus as the Jew from Galilee but as "the word," as "God," and "light that became flesh." Instead of specific names and places, we find generic terms that can refer to any place (κόσμος in 1:9, 10a) and any people (πᾶς 1:7; πᾶς ἄνθρωπος 1:9; ὅσοι 1:12; τοῖς πιστεύουσιν 1:12; ἡμῖν 1:14; ἡμεῖς 1:16). The term κόσμος appears four times in 1:9-10:

1:9 Ἦν τὸ φῶς τὸ ἀληθινόν, ὃ φωτίζει πάντα ἄνθρωπον,
    ἐρχόμενον εἰς τὸν κόσμον.
10 ἐν τῷ κόσμῳ ἦν,

---

[16] Abbott notices about John the Baptist in the Fourth Gospel as well, "His [the author's] desire to subordinate the individuality of John the Baptist to his instrumentality in testifying to Christ will also explain why he is silent about 'Herod Antipas' and his brother 'Philip'." ABBOTT, *Johannine Vocabulary*, 156. Ebrard misses the point when he sees John the Baptist in John 1:8 as an "israelitische Prophet" whom the author employs to portray the "Gegensatz des *gesetzlichen* und *evang.* Standpunktes." EBRARD, *Wissenschaftliche Kritik*, 141 n. 3.

καὶ ὁ κόσμος δι᾽ αὐτοῦ ἐγένετο,
καὶ ὁ κόσμος αὐτὸν οὐκ ἔγνω.
11 εἰς τὰ ἴδια ἦλθεν,
καὶ οἱ ἴδιοι αὐτὸν οὐ παρέλαβον.

These verses are part of the exposition about the relationship between the λόγος and humanity (1:4-13) and deal specifically with the rejection of the word. Previoiusly, we have mentioned that this negative response was put in rather abstract philosophical terms: the darkness did not manage to understand / overcome the light (1:5). The text now specifies the darkness as "the world" (1:10) and "his own" (1:11).

Verse 9 expresses the past and ongoing revelation of the light in the world. The key-term φῶς connects the sentence with verses 4-8 and parallels it in thought with verse 5: where the latter simply mentions that the light shines into the "darkness," the former concretizes and identifies darkness with "every man" (πάντα ἄνθρωπον). Both verses contain a present tense for "shining" (φαίνει, φωτίζει) and a past tense verb (οὐ κατέλαβεν, ἦν). We can best understand the use of both tenses in one sentence when they refer to the activity of the incarnated λόγος (revealing, speaking, saving, judging, convicting, comforting, commanding) and its past rejection which both continue in this world until today.[17] The parallels between verses 5 and 9 then also imply that the incarnational reading of verse 9 strengthens the case for the same reading in verse 5 so that verses 5-9 (and vv. 10-13, even vv. 3c-4) are not talking about metaphysical realities before Jesus' appearance in human history but about his ministry and rejection on earth.[18] If we take with most modern commentators

---

[17] So already HARNACK, "Ueber das Verhältnis des Prologs," 219, 220; also BULTMANN, Das Evangelium des Johannes, 26, 32-33. KÄSEMANN, "Aufbau und Anliegen," 81.

[18] In contrast to that view, the majority of commentators from the patristics until the early nineteenth century relate 1:1-13 to the pre-existent λόγος and only with 1:14 does the incarnation come into focus. See THEOBALD, Die Fleischwerdung, 13 n. 27. Dodd still regards 1:1-13 as "celebrating the divine transcendence and the creation of the universe and of man through the eternal light immanent in the whole (ἐν τῷ κόσμῳ ἦν)." DODD, "The Prologue to the Fourth Gospel," 17. For Haenchen, the preexistent λόγος ἄσαρκος in vv. 1-13 operates similarly to the wisdom myths of Sir 24 and 1 Enoch 42, and only from v. 14 on does the λόγος ἔνσαρκος appear. HAENCHEN, "Probleme des johanneischen 'Prologs'," 130. See also LINDARS, The Gospel of John, 90. But Sir 24 (and 1 Enoch 42) can hardly serve as a background since here Wisdom is "established in Zion" and took root "in an honored people," i.e., in Israel (24:10, 12) in contrast to all other people or nations (24:6), whereas in John's prologue the λόγος is universally rejected. See the discussion in PRYOR, "Jesus and Israel," 204-07. Meeks sees the Wisdom myth as a parallel to John 1:10-11 (esp. 1 Enoch 42). But he also recognizes the contrast, namely where the myths add the acceptance of Wisdom "finally in Israel,

ἐρχόμενον εἰς τὸν κόσμον as a statement about the light and not about "every man," then κόσμος denotes the "place of inhabitation,"[19] although the various meanings of the term often overlap. As Jesus himself says later in the Gospel, he is the "light of the world" (φῶς τοῦ κόσμου, 8:12; 9:5; 11:9; 12:46), κόσμος standing here for fallen humanity in general.

Excursus: The Translation of John 1:9

The Greek text of John 1:9 can be understood differently: Ἦν τὸ φῶς τὸ ἀληθινόν, ὃ φωτίζει πάντα ἄνθρωπον, ἐρχόμενον εἰς τὸν κόσμον. The word ἐρχόμενον in v. 9 can be understood as an attributive participle (then accusative masculine) that further describes πάντα ἄνθρωπον, "That was the true Light, which lighteth every man that cometh into the world" (AV; cf. NKJ, ASV; so the older exegesis). Arguments in support of this translation might be the location of ἐρχόμενον immediately adjacent to ἄνθρωπον as well as parallels in Rabbinic literature in which "those that come into the world" is another expression for "humans" (Mekh Ex 18,12; Pesiq 172b; LevR 31).[20] But unless this rendering is an emphatic statement (cf. 6:14; 16:21), ἄνθρωπον seems superfluous or the wording contains even the strange possible notion that there are men that exist without coming into the world. Furthermore, the Rabbinic parallels differ by using the expression "those that come into the world" as the object or subject of the sentence and not as an attribute to "men" or "humans." Bultmann is willing to understand ἄνθρωπον as a commenting gloss of the translator from the Aramaic original in order to explain its position right beside ἐρχόμενον εἰς τὸν κόσμον.[21] On the other hand, we can read the participle ἐρχόμενον as part of a periphrastic construction (with ἦν) that describes the incarnation of τὸ φῶς, "There was the true light which, coming into the world, enlightens every man" (NAS; cf. also NAB, NIV, NJB, RSV, NRS, CEV, ESV, NLT, HCSB, NET). While there are instances in John where the finite verb and the participle stand closely together (3:24; 13:5, 23; 19:11, 19, 20, 41), both are often separated by two (1:28), three (10:40; 18:25), four (3:23), six (1:9), seven (5:5), or even eight (18:18) words, just as this reading of the sentence implies. Furthermore, the phrase of "light that comes into the world" would not be unique to the prologue, but finds parallels in the Gospel (3:19; 12:46; cf. 9:5) and thus reflects the author's style. Finally, read this way, the sentence creates a bridge to verse 10, which dwells on the incarnational presence of the light in the world. In short, there are good reasons why most modern commentators favor this reading.[22]

---

through the revelation at Sinai." MEEKS, "Man From Heaven," 61. See also BRANT, *Dialogue and Drama*, 19. Brown interprets 1:10-12 with Büchsel, Bauer, Harnack and Käsemann as "the Word incarnate" and argues convincingly against Westcott, Bernard, Boismard and Schnackenburg, who regard these verses as the "activity of the divine word in the OT period." BROWN, *The Gospel*, 1:28-30.

[19] *BDAG*, 561.

[20] See STRACK, BILLERBECK, *Das Evangelium*, 2:358.

[21] BULTMANN, *Das Evangelium des Johannes*, 32 n. 6.

[22] BEASLEY-MURRAY, *John*, 1. KEENER, *The Gospel of John*, 1:394-95. KÖSTENBERGER, *John*, 34. See also RUCKSTUHL, *Die literarische Einheitlichkeit*, 75-76. PRYOR, "Jesus and Israel," 203-04. Schnelle leaves the question undecided. SCHNELLE, *Das Evangelium nach Johannes*, 37. After weighing four different grammatical options

The two antitheses in verse 10-11 elaborate on the response to the universal activity of the λόγος. Verse 10 picks up the statement of creation from verse 3 and, according to the general development in the prologue of "progression by concretization," narrows the πάντα, "all things," to κόσμος, "humankind."[23] Although Jesus created (and enlightened, v. 9) all men, they did not "know Him," a soteriological expression (e.g., 17:3) that includes cognitive (6:69; 7:26-27) and ethical aspects (7:17; 1 John 2:3).

Depending on how we understand οἱ ἴδιοι in the following sentence, verse 11 either repeats the antithesis of verse 10 in different words (synonymous parallelism) or continues the idea of rejection by narrowing the focus from the world to Israel (synthetical parallelism). Pryor's main argument for the latter option is that τὰ ἴδια mostly means "home/homeland" in the LXX and the New Testament, not "property/possession,"[24] and thus refers to Israel as the home of Jesus. The οἱ ἴδιοι would then refer to Israelites as his countrymen. The thought in verses 10-11 progresses then from the culpability of humanity in general (including Gentiles) to that of Israel in particular.[25] On the other hand, if we consider the previous context, which intentionally *abstains* from specific identifications and prefaces the narrative with general notions of creation and humanity,[26] then we read verse 11 as part of the prologue's universal thrust without any hint to Israel in particular.[27] The terms τὰ ἴδια and οἱ ἴδιοι denote men who are "his own" since they belong to the λόγος

---

of 1:9, Phillips even asks, "Do we have yet another example of deliberate ambiguity in the text?" PHILLIPS, *The Prologue*, 181.

[23] Schnackenburg comments, "Der κόσμος in V 10 ist die Welt als Wohnraum der Menschen und geht dann in die Bedeutung 'Menschenwelt' (= Menschheit) selbst über. . . . 'Er war in der Welt', den Menschen nahe und erreichbar, so daß sie sich an ihn zu ihrem Heile halten konnten." SCHNACKENBURG, *Das Johannesevangelium*, 1:231.

[24] PRYOR, "Jesus and Israel," 208-09. Pryor argues that this reading has the benefit of saving the gospel from charges of being "naively docetic" since it "acknowledges the Jewish heritage of the human Jesus." Ibid., 217.

[25] GRELOT, *Les Juifs*, 191. SEGOVIA, "John 1:1-18," 44-45. Segovia makes the important observation that "despite the distinction introduced, it is clear that rejection – and, indeed, the same kind of rejection – is associated with both the 'world' and 'his own'." Ibid., 45. Brown also argues with regard to 1:11 for a "narrowing down of the activity of the Word to Israel." BROWN, *The Gospel*, 1:30. Pryor himself even reduces the meaning of "the world" in verse 10 to "the world of the Jews" in which the historical rejection happened. PRYOR, "Jesus and Israel," 218. See also our discussion in chap. 6.

[26] Creation in 1:3 and 1:10a, the generic ἀνθρώπων in 1:4 and πάντα ἄνθρωπον in 1:9.

[27] This interpretation is further strengthened when we consider the similarity between prologue and the speeches of Jesus which refrain from particulars and contend with universal notions as well. For details, see chap. 5. Also ONUKI, *Gemeinde und Welt*, 107.

as their creator.[28] They also stand parallel to κόσμος in verse 10 and make the contradiction more explicit that those who owe their existence to the creator reject him as their savior.[29] While verse 10 emphasizes the quantity of rejection (the whole world), verse 11 exposes the quality of the response as deeply ironic.[30]

1.1.3. *The Gospel's religionsgeschichtliche complexity*

A focus on the *Jewish* religious-historical background sometimes mitigates the universal thrust of the prologue.[31] But this option deserves as much

---

[28] BULTMANN, *The Gospel of John*, 56. Schnackenburg explains that the true home of the logos is with God (1:1b). SCHNACKENBURG, *Das Johannesevangelium*, 1:235, 236. See also 3:240-41. Hoskyn comments, "There is, however, no final distinction between Israel and the world, between Jew and Greek. As the creation of God, all men are His property (Isa. lxvi. 1); and Jesus was in the world, not merely in Israel. This double reference to the whole earth and to Israel as God's possession has also its parallel in Exod. xix. 5." HOSKYNS, *The Fourth Gospel*, 146. Similarly Bonney, "Since Jesus historically did appear to the Jews, they appear to be the most likely referent. The cosmological scope of the prologue, however, tells the reader that for John the Jews represent humanity in general." BONNEY, *Caused to Believe*, 51.

[29] Maybe another argument in favor of identifying τὰ ἴδια and οἱ ἴδιοι with κόσμος is the following: The speeches of Jesus, which continue the style of the prologue in the body of the Gospel, use ἔρχομαι and εἰς always and only in connection with κόσμος, just as in 1:9 (3:19; 9:39; 12:46; 16:28; 18:37; cf. also 6:14; 11:27). Nowhere does Jesus speak of a special mission to Israel but, in contrast to the Gospel of Matthew (Matt 10:6, 23; 15:24), his coming, speaking, judging and saving is always done to "the world." Thus, the style of using ἔρχομαι plus εἰς favors reading τὰ ἴδια and οἱ ἴδιοι as a parallel to κόσμος in verse 9. A reference to Israel would be a statement without any parallel in the Gospel.

[30] For the understanding of ἴδιος in v. 11 as parallel in meaning to κόσμος in v. 10 see BULTMANN, *The Gospel of John*, 56. KÄSEMANN, "Aufbau und Anliegen," 161. SCHNACKENBURG, *Das Johannesevangelium*, 1:236. He also refers in n. 5 to other scholars with this view: Thomas Aquinas, Loisy, Bauer, Schlatter, Wikenhauser. Furthermore, see QUIÉVREUX, "'Les Juifs'," 256-57. Miller explains, "Here we have a similar narrowing from τὰ ἴδια, which we take to designate the whole created order, to οἱ ἴδιοι, which we take to designate the sphere of humanity." MILLER, *Salvation-History*, 75. Harris argues, "For in view of the state of universal non-comprehension depicted in 1.1-5 'his own' could well be humankind, who are part of the created order referred to in 1.1-4. In that case the believers are Christians, but without any suggestion that they are a 'new Israel' or people of God in direct succession to the Jews." HARRIS, *Prologue and Gospel*, 23, also p. 62. Gnilka explains, "Die Juden werden zu den Repräsentanten dieser Entscheidung, treten somit aus der heilsgeschichtlichen Rolle Israels heraus, so wie die Seinen, die das Wort nicht aufnahmen (1,11) nicht die Juden, sondern schlechthin die Menschen sind." GNILKA, *Johannesevangelium*, 9.

[31] Hakola observes that in "the 30's 'almost everything in the New Testament was suffused with a Greek light' (W. D. Davies), whereas today everything is seen in a Jewish light." HAKOLA, *Identity Matters*, 22, also 6-7. Parsenios confirms this

suspicion as rigid contrasts between Hellenism and Judaism. The conceptual overlap between Wisdom literature and Gnosticism, for example, reveals the proximity of two traditions that were formerly divided into early Jewish and late Hellenistic writings.[32] Furthermore, the second volume of the *Neuer Wettstein* (2001) presents multiple intertextual links of the Gospel to Greco-Roman literature that stand completely independent of any Jewish influence. The editors needed no less than 850 pages to collect parallels from Jewish, Greek, and Hellenistic literature to the Fourth Gospel! With regard to John 1:1-18, we find ca. 90 citations from Jewish literature (Proverbs, Sirach, Philo, Josephus, Wisdom of Solomon) and ca. 120 quotations from authors and writings such as Homer, Hesiod, Orphic literature, Isis Aretalogies, Greek Magic Papyri, Heraclitus, Aeschylus, Sophocles, Euripides, Plato, Aristotle, Xenophon, Cleanthes, Aratus, Menander, Aristophanes, Lucretius, Sallust, Virgil, Horace, Ovid, Seneca, Plutarch, Cicero, Epictetus, Porphyry, Philostratus, Appian, Diogenes Laertius, Lucian, and Plotinus.[33] These writers lived

---

observation when he remarks with regard to modern Johannine scholarship, "Current trends place the Gospel of John against the backdrop of the Dead Sea Scrolls and other contemporary Judaisms, rather than against the broader Greco-Roman world." PARSENIOS, *Departure and Consolation*, 1. Beside a few Christian authors and merely two Greco-Roman sources (Plutarch and Cicero with regard to John 19:17-30), Bock and Herrick, for example, cite only Jewish sources as parallels to the Gospel of John. BOCK and HERRICK, *Jesus in Context*, 208-252. They themselves refer to their work as a "'poor man's Strack-Billerbeck'." Ibid., 15. Parsenios himself makes a statement against the trend when he suggests that non-Jewish genres such as the literary symposium and "the exit to death in ancient drama and certain aspects of ancient consolation literature" influenced the composition of the farewell discourse as well. Ibid., 6.

[32] Since its publication in 1973, the treatise "Trimorphic Protennoia" of the Nag Hammadi library, for example, has triggered a vivid discussion. The many parallels to John's prologue led to the assumption that it belongs either to the Gospel's history of interpretation (Janssen, McL. Wilson, Helderman, Perkins, Yamauchi, Hofrichter) or that it represents an independent Logos-tradition which illuminates the influence on John and which depends, together with John's prologue, on Jewish wisdom traditions (C. Colpe, C. A. Evans, J. M. Robinson, Theobald). Schlatter observed already the "gnostische Gärung" within Palestinian Judaism (so also Kittel and Goppelt). See SCHULZ, *Komposition und Herkunft*, 165. THEOBALD, *Die Fleischwerdung*, 483-86. Besides the Gospel of Thomas, Patterson affirms Mandaean and Sethian texts from Nag Hammadi as "Jewish traditions of speculative theology" and "heterodox Judaism" to which the evangelist was attracted when writing his Gospel. PATTERSON, "The Prologue to the Fourth Gospel," 329, 331. Smith discusses theories that consider a Christian, Iranian, Platonic, Hermetic, pagan, and Jewish origin of Gnosticism and decides for the latter. SMITH II, *No Longer Jews*, 18-43.

[33] *Neuer Wettstein*, 1-77. For a much shorter collection of parallels to the Gospel of John in general and to the prologue in particular, in English translation and accompanied by helpful comments, see *Hellenistic Commentary*, 238-308, 238-47.

between 800 BC and AD 300 and include Greek and Roman poets, philosophers, historians, orators, politicians, and dramatists. Their diversity just with regard to the first eighteen verses of the Gospel illustrates the futility of trying to reduce the multitude of parallels to one single stream of Jewish influence or to put the burden of proof on those scholars who postulate parallels to non-Jewish literature. In his recent review about the history of research from the second to the twentieth century with regard to the Gospel's history-of-religion background, Jörg Frey concludes by noticing the *"Komplexität des religionsgeschichtlichen Hintergrundes,"* which leads him to propose an "eclectic" approach that avoids claims of dependence on only one tradition and contends for describing analogies rather than postulating genealogies.[34] One cannot avoid the impression that the language of the prologue is intentionally open to all kinds of traditions and requires the knowledge of both Jewish and Hellenistic bodies of literature in order to be understood. The author chooses terms and concepts that are immediately available to Jewish and Greek readers alike. Words such as Ἐν ἀρχῇ (1:1), ὁ λόγος (1:1), or ἐσκήνωσεν (1:14) remind the reader familiar with the LXX of the opening words of the book of Genesis, [35] of "the word of the Lord" in the Old Testament, of Wisdom literature (Prov 8; Sir 24), Philo, or maybe even of the "memra" in the Targumim.[36] But Greco-Roman traditions are familiar

---

[34] FREY, "Auf der Suche," 31 (italics his), 33, 35. Frey summarizes, "Die alte Alternative zwischen 'jüdischen' und einer 'hellenistischen' oder gar 'gnostischen' Erklärung kann nach Auffassung der meisten Ausleger als nicht mehr angemessen gelten." Ibid., 31. See also Phillips' search, explicitly not for *sources* but for *echoes* of John's term and concept of λόγος in literature contemporary to the Fourth Gospel. PHILLIPS, *The Prologue*, 73.

[35] See LIOY, *The Search for Ultimate Reality*, esp. 81-94 where he discusses the "Intertextuality between the Genesis and Johannine Prologues." Reed even translates John 1:1 as "In the beginning was the Torah." REED, "How Semitic Was John?" 723.

[36] Boyarin postulates connections between John's Logos-Christology and the Memra of the Targum. BOYARIN, "The Gospel of the Memra," 243-84. But Keener contradicts, "The case for this is questionable, however. To what extent does the Memra represent a personified concept or, still more relevant, a hypostatization, and to what extent is the Memra merely a figurative expression, a verbal buffer, not distinct from God?" KEENER, *The Gospel of John*, 1:349. See also the "Exkurs über den Memra Jahves" with a negative conclusion in STRACK and BILLERBECK, *Das Evangelium*, 2:302-33. Keener suggests instead that "the Fourth Gospel presents the Logos of its prologue as Torah" due to playing on the link between Wisdom and Torah in rabbinical sources. KEENER, *The Gospel of John*, 1:359-60. Phillips maintains against McNamara and Craig Evans that the alleged parallels in the Targumim "can be understood as being qualities of God rather than of a second divine being." PHILLIPS, *The Prologue*, 133, see 131-36.

as well with expressions such as ἐν ἀρχῇ (1:1),[37] λόγος,[38] φῶς and σκοτία,[39] τέκνα θεοῦ,[40] or ἐξηγήσατο.[41] Phillips' conclusion from his recent extensive study concerning the intertextual links of the term λόγος to Hellenistic (Heraclitus, Stoics, Gnostic/Hermetic material), Hellenistic-Jewish (Philo), and Jewish literature (Hebrew Bible, Wisdom literature, Targumim, Dead Sea Scrolls) applies well to the other key-terms of the prologue: "The point is not that λόγος picks up one tradition, but rather that it points to an ambiguous amalgam of different traditions. The breadth of the discussion shows that the author has chosen to use a word understood at many levels."[42] Similar evaluations permeate Johannine scholarship and should warn against postulating a narrow stream of influence on the language of the Gospel.[43]

---

[37] Anaxagoras of Clazomena (496-428 BCE) writes, "In the beginning everything was chaotic; but reason [νοῦς] divided and ordered it." (In Plutarch, *Moralia*, "Placita Philosophorum" 1.3.) See *Hellenistic Commentary*, 239. Classen comments on John 1:1, "It reminds the reader either of *Genesis* 1,1 (cf. A. Rahlfs [ed.], Septuaginta [see n.4], I 1), of a mythological tale (cf. Kritias frg. 25 Diels Kranz), a fable or the beginning of the narrative part in a speech." CLASSEN, *Rhetorical Criticism*, 91. He explains with regard to the statement about creation in 1:3, "At the beginning John states that everything came into being through God (1:3) – a statement which both Jews and Greeks could readily accept." Ibid., 94. See also PHILLIPS, *The Prologue*, 146-50.

[38] See PHILLIPS, *The Prologue*, 73-141. Dodd sees an allusion to the Torah at least in v. 17 ("grace and truth" was used of Torah) but does not exclude non-Jewish overtones in the term λόγος as well. DODD, *The Interpretation of the Fourth Gospel*, 295. Justin Martyr is thus able to speak of Jesus' pre-existent presence as λόγος among the Greeks (*1 Apol.* 5, 22, 46; *2 Apol.*8, 10, 13) as well as among the Jews (*1 Apol.* 59, 64).

[39] Classen again, "John gives this metaphor special prominence at the beginning of his gospel because it is known to the Jews from the Bible and to the Greeks from their poets and philosophers." CLASSEN, *Rhetorical Criticism*, 96. He discusses in an essay how light and darkness are used as a metaphor in early Greek philosophy in the limited realm of religion and myth (especially Parmenides). CLASSEN, "Licht und Dunkel in der frühgriechischen Philosophie," 131-73. Beasley-Murray comments on 8:12 ("I am the light of the world"), "That would have been quite comprehensible to readers of the Fourth Gospel, reared in the faiths of the Hellenistic world, for the thought of God as Light and his messengers as bringers of light to the world was familiar (see Dodd, *Interpretation*, 201-8; Odeberg, 286-92; Bultmann, 40-44, 342-433)." BEASLEY-MURRAY, *John*, 128.

[40] See Hengel's section about parallels to the Son-of-God title in Greek and Hellenistic literature. HENGEL, *The Son of God*, 23-41.

[41] With regard to the Jewish usage of ἐξηγήσατο, Barrett reminds one of Sir 43:31. Lindars points out that the Hellenistic culture also used the term in a technical sense "for the declaration of divine secrets by an oracle or priest . . ." Quoted in PHILLIPS, *The Prologue*, 218-19.

[42] PHILLIPS, *The Prologue*, 138, also 224, 226-27.

[43] Schnelle explains that no single history-of-religions background caused the use of λόγος in the prologue and describes influences such as the Old Testament, Heraclitus of

1.2. The Farewell Discourse (John 13-17)

The elements of the compositional parallelism are the prologue and the first half of the Gospel on the one hand, and the farewell discourse and the

---

Ephesus, Stoic philosophy, Wisdom traditions, and Philo. SCHNELLE, *Antidoketische Christologie*, 234-35. According to Lamarche, the prologue has universal relevance because 1:1-9 is addressed to Gentiles and 1:14-18 to Jews. LAMARCHE, "Le Prologue de Jean," 497-537, esp. 512-14. Longenecker thinks that the author used λόγος in the prologue as a "terminological bridge" between Jewish and Greek thinking. LONGENECKER, *The Christology of Early Jewish Christianity*, 147. Vouga mentions the influences of Hermetic literature, Philo, Qumran, Mandaean literature, Odes of Solomon, and Nag Hammadi literature and explains, "Il serait vain de chercher une dépendance littéraire ou idéologique . . . *à l'exclusion des autres.*" VOUGA, *Le cadre historique*, 13 (italics his). Earlier affirmation of Jewish and non-Jewish influences on the logos-theology came from scholars such as C. H. Dodd, G. Kittel, E. K. John, G. Lindeskog, and S. Schulz. See the discussion in SCHULZ, *Komposition und Herkunft*, 44-48. We concur with McRae's thoughts, "Since the age of the Fourth Gospel was the age of Roman Hellenism, characterized in many respects by a kind of religious universalism or syncretism, is it not possible that the Fourth Evangelist may have tried deliberately to incorporate a diversity of backgrounds into the one gospel message precisely to emphasize the universality of Jesus?" MACRAE, "The Fourth Gospel and Religionsgeschichte," 15. Brodie pictures the Gospel of John as an "encyclopedic synthesis" and affirms "the view, held by Bultmann and others, that, however deep John's Jewish roots, he was in dialogue with the Hellenistic world, in other words, with the world at large." BRODIE, *The Quest for the Origin*, 30-31. With regard to the Jewish and Hellenistic influence, Tilborg speaks of the "marvelous mixture which makes John's Gospel so fascinating." TILBORG, *Reading John*, 3. After discussing various assumptions about Hellenistic (Philo, Gnosticism, Hermetic Literature, Mandaism) and Jewish (Old Testament, Rabbinic Judaism, Qumran, Samaritan Religion) traditions as the background to John's Gospel, Beasley-Murray concludes, "From the foregoing review it is evident that the religious relations of the Fourth Gospel are complex. The links traceable between the Gospel and diverse Hellenistic and Semitic traditions make it implausible to settle for any one of them to the exclusion of the rest." BEASLEY-MURRAY, *John*, lxv; also p. 6. With regard to the categories used in the prologue, Beasley-Murray says, "The remarkable feature of this presentation is that it employs categories universally known, possessing universal appeal, which would attract and have attracted alike Jews, Christians and pagans, Hellenists and Orientals in their varied cultures, followers of ancient and modern religions, philosophers and people of more humble status who were yet seekers after God." Ibid., 5. Similarly, Moloney recently stated that "the Fourth Gospel cannot be conveniently situated in any one cultural milieu . . . It is Greek and Jewish, and its language, background, and theological point of view would resonate within a number of worldviews. It looks back to the foundational story of Jesus of Nazareth, but tells it in a way that addressed the religious and cultural maelstrom of Asia Minor at the end of the first century." MOLONEY, *The Gospel of John*, 6. See also BURRIDGE, *What Are The Gospels?*, 214, 228. POPKES, *Die Theologie der Liebe Gottes*, 64-71.

account about Jesus' passion and resurrection on the other.[44] After the prologue (1:1-18), the Gospel enters the account of Jesus' public ministry in which the conflict with the Jews stands at the heart of the plot development (chaps. 1:19-12:50). This is not the least indicated by the use of the term Ἰουδαῖοι (47 times) against which the word κόσμος takes at least a numerical backseat (29 times). In the next literary unit, the "farewell discourse" (chaps. 13-17),[45] Jesus addresses his own immediate and distant future as well as that of his disciples. A simplified overview reveals the following alternation of predictions and prescriptions, framed by a preamble (13:1-17) and a prayer (17:1-26):

13:1-17	Preamble: Jesus washes feet and prescribes to do the same
13:18-30	Prediction of Judas' betrayal
13:31-33	Prediction of his going
13:34-35	Prescription to love one another
13:36-38	Prediction of Peter's denial and martyrdom
14:1-4	Prediction of Jesus' going, parousia, preparation of rooms

---

[44] The farewell discourse continues to be the object of many studies, especially in German scholar-ship. The following works are some of the major contributions since the 1980s: CARSON, *The Farewell Discourse* (1980). PAINTER, "The Farewell Discourses and the History of Johannine Christianity," 525-43. WINTER, *Das Vermächtnis Jesu und die Abschiedsreden der Väter* (1994). DETTWILER, *Die Gegenwart des Erhöhten* (1995). NEUGEBAUER, *Die eschatologischen Aussagen in den johanneischen Abschiedsreden* (1995). TOLMIE, *Jesus' Farewell to the Disciples* (1995). HOEGEN-ROHLS, *Der nachösterliche Johannes* (1996). DIETZFELBINGER, *Der Abschied des Kommenden* (1997). MOLONEY, "The Function of John 13-17," 43-65. BROUWER, *The Literary Development of John 13-17* (2000). HALDIMANN, *Rekonstruktion und Entfaltung* (2000). KELLUM, *The Unity of the Farewell Discourse* (2004). WEIDEMANN, *Der Tod Jesu im Johannesevangelium* (2004).

[45] What we regard as one literary unit is frequently divided into at least three different speeches, as it is indicated by the transitions from 14:31 to 15:1 and from 16:33 to 17:1. Often chaps. 15-16 are also divided into two or three speeches. See the discussion of different positions in HALDIMANN, *Rekonstruktion und Entfaltung*, 94-122. Whether these transitions indicate various layers of composition and redaction or are to be explained on inner-textual grounds continues to be a matter of heavy dispute. The coherence of the farewell discourse as a whole is nevertheless apparent as elements of *inclusio* in chapters 13 and 17 ("hour" in 13:1; 17:1; theme of "authority" in 13:3; 17:2; believers are "sent," see 13:20 [πέμπω] and 17:18 [ἀποστέλλω]; "glory" in 13:31-32; 17:1, 4-5) and frequent repetitions between chaps. 13/14 and 15/16 demonstrate. See the table in BROWN, *The Gospel*, 2:589-593. PAINTER, "The Farewell Discourses," 529-30. MOLONEY, "The Function of John 13-17," 58-61. NEUGEBAUER, *Die eschatologischen Aussagen*, 93-96. This observation compels even diachronic models of composition (see Brown, Dettwiler, Becker, Winter, Thyen) to consider the redactor as a creative author who did not merely expand or complement existing traditions but reworked them in such a way that he created a new and independent piece of literature. See SCHNELLE, *Das Evangelium nach Johannes*, 237-38. HALDIMANN, *Rekonstruktion und Entfaltung*, 29-42.

14:5-14   Prediction that the disciples will do "greater things"
14:15-31 Prediction of Jesus' going, resurrection, the Paraclete
15:1-17   Prescription to abide in Jesus and love one another
15:18-16:4 Prediction of hate and persecution of the disciples
16:5-15   Prediction of Jesus' going and Paraclete's coming
16:16-28 Prediction of Jesus' leaving, coming again, grief and joy
16:29-33 Prediction of the scattering of the disciples
17:1-26   Prayer: Jesus prays for himself and his disciples

While John 13-14 predict events that are mostly fulfilled in the following passion of Jesus (chaps. 18-19), the prescriptions therein as well as John 15-17 assume a time after Easter in which perseverance is made difficult by persecution.

Excursus: The Sitz im Leben of John 13/14 and 15-17

In Neugebauer's view, John 13-14 speak about the "einmalig level" of the historical Jesus (betrayal and denial of Judas, death and resurrection, martyrs of the first generation; see 14:25) while chaps. 15-17 refer to the "contemporary level" of the Johannine church (expulsion from the synagogue, persecution of the church, schism, delay of parousia; see 16:4b).[46] He lists the following differences between chaps. 13/14 and 15/16: (1) The next indicator after 13:31 about the situation of the narrative is found in 18:1, which connects well with 14:31. (2) Differences between 13/14 and 15/16: There are six dialogues of named disciples in 13/14, only one question of an unnamed disciple in 15/16 (16:17f). The content of the questions in 13/14 relates to Jesus' revelations in the Gospel, in 16 to the delay of the parousia. (3) Indicators about the situation in the statements of Jesus: In 14:25 Jesus is still present with the disciples, in contrast to 16:4. Predictions in 13:19 (betrayal of Judas) and 14:29 (going to the Father) are fulfilled in chapters 18-21, whereas commentaries in 16:1, 4 point to a situation beyond the gospel (expulsion from the synagogue, persecution). 13:34-35 speaks about the "*new* commandment*," whereas 15:12-13 only mentions "commandment," just as in 1 John (3:11, 23; 2 John 5). In 14:16, 26 it is the Father who sends the Paraclete, while in 15:26 and 16:7 it is the Son. In 14:30 the ruler of the world "comes" while in 15/16 he is already judged (16:11) and the world is already overcome (16:33). In 14:31 Jesus *acts* (present) as the father told him; in 15:10 he said that he has *kept* (past) the commandments. In 14:31 conversion is still a goal for the world, while in 15:18, 24 the world has already seen and hated him (past). The frequent use of the perfect tense in 15/16 gives the impression that the events mentioned have already happened.[47] Earlier, Neugebauer discussed the similarities between chaps. 15/16 and 1 John.[48] While his observations support this difference in time-reference, the distinctions are not absolute. The commandment to love one another (13:34-35) and Jesus' preceding example of washing feet (13:3-17) have imperative force beyond the immediate situation. The hint to Peter's martyrdom in 13:37-38 points far beyond Easter. The invitation to "ask anything in my name" in 14:13-14 presupposes that Jesus already rose and ascended. And the

---

[46] NEUGEBAUER, *Die eschatologischen Aussagen*, 143.
[47] Ibid., 141-45.
[48] Ibid., 111-17.

coming of the Paraclete is still a promise for the future in 15:26 and 16:7-14, although the "contemporary" level would require that the Paraclete is already present (see also 16:28). And we have not yet even discussed the overlap in 14 and 16.[49] We concur, therefore, with Köstenberger, who rightly sees that the "underlying assumption" of all of John 13-17 "is that Jesus has been exalted."[50]

1.2.1. The universal content.

The theme of conflict and contrast between believers and unbelievers permeates both major parts of the Gospel. But in John 13-17 it is not the Jews who constitute the group of antagonists, as they did in the previous twelve chapters. Instead, Ἰουδαῖοι occurs in the farewell discourse only once (13:33) and there is no other reference to any particular Jewish sect, institution, belief or behavior except the expulsion from the synagogue in 16:2 and the fulfillment of Scripture (13:18; 15:25; 16:12). On the other hand, κόσμος increases numerically throughout the discourse and culminates in chapter 17 with eighteen occurrences.[51] While the interlocutors *narrow* from the crowd, the Pharisees and the Jews in the first twelve chapters to the ones that are "his own" (13:1; see 13:14, 16, 33, 34), such as Peter (13:6-9, 23, 36), the beloved disciple (13:23-25), Philip (14:8), Judas (14:22), and some unnamed disciples (16:17-18, 29-30), the scope of opposition *broadens* to a universal extent.

A few times the author uses κόσμος to designate a place of human habitation as opposed to heaven and the Father from which the Son of Man descended (13:1; 16:28; 17:5, 11, 13, 24; cf. 3:13; 6:33). But the term stands mostly for non-believers who stand opposite to three different persons: Jesus, the Paraclete, and the disciples. The world cannot receive the Paraclete (14:17) who will convict of sin, righteousness, and judgment (16:8). In contrast to the disciples, the world will not see Jesus anymore once he departs (14:19). The world gives a peace that is different from that of Jesus (14:27). The world is a place of trouble (θλῖψις) that Jesus has overcome (16:33). It does not know God (17:25) and Jesus does not pray for it (17:9). The world hates the disciples just as it hated Jesus (15:18-19; 17:14). What causes grief for the believers is reason to rejoice for the

---

[49] See SCHNACKENBURG, *Das Johannesevangelium*, 3:102. DETTWILER, *Die Gegenwart des Erhöhten*, 296-99.

[50] KÖSTENBERGER, *John*, 397.

[51] Chapter 12 uses κόσμος two times, chap. 14 six times, chap. 15 six times, chap. 16 eight times, and chap. 17 eighteen times. See appendix 2. As we will see in the next section, throughout the Gospel Ἰουδαῖοι occurs mostly in the narrative, while κόσμος is mostly used in the speech of Jesus. Since the farewell discourse consists predominantly of Jesus' words, the absence of Ἰουδαῖοι is due to the absence of narrative, and the exclusive presence of κόσμος comes with the discourse basically as a monologue of Jesus.

world (16:10). The world is headed by the "ruler of the world" (ὁ ἄρχων τοῦ κόσμου) who will be cast out (12:31), who has nothing in Jesus (14:30) and who has been judged (16:11). The antithetical tone of the farewell discourse is accompanied by a strong emphasis on mission to the world in which Jesus sends the disciples (13:16, 20; 17:18) in order to make his identity known through their witness (15:27) and their love in unity (13:35; 17:20, 21, 23).[52]

2. Narratological Parallelism (Microstructure)

The parallelism between the Jews and the World extends beyond what we mentioned so far. Besides the macrostructural symmetry, we will now look at the distribution of both terms in the microstructure of the Gospel. The following table displays the speaking roles in the Gospel:[53]

	Ἰουδαῖος	κόσμος
Jesus (speech)	4	64
Narrator	59	7
Jews	3	6
Gentiles	5	1
Total	71	78

There is an astonishing numerical balance between Ἰουδαῖος and κόσμος. Not only do they appear with a similar frequency in the Gospel (71 and 78 times), but their two main users employ each of them with the same percentage: 82 percent of all occurrences of κόσμος appear in the mouth of Jesus (64 times) and the narrator employs 83 percent of all occurrences of Ἰουδαῖος (59 times). He limits his use of κόσμος to the prologue (1:9-10) and to another three times in the second half (13:1 [2x]; 21:25).[54] Jesus uses Ἰουδαῖος only four times, namely in the following texts:

---

[52] We refrain from detailed exegesis of single propositions and contend with this general summary since the main concern lies with macro-structural observations.

[53] See again appendix 2 for a more detailed table.

[54] Here we assume that the five occurrences of κόσμος in 3:16-19 are perceived by the reader as part of Jesus' speech and not as the narrator's voice, even though a technical analysis of style might conclude otherwise. Our simple numerical comparison corrects an impression expressed by Reinhartz, who finds the "cosmological tale" more "in the words of the narrator rather than on the lips of the Johannine Jesus or any other character in this gospel." REINHARTZ, *The Word in the World*, 44.

4:22 we worship that which we know, for salvation is from the Jews.

13:33 and as I said to the Jews, I now say to you also, ...

18:20 I always taught in synagogues, and in the temple, where all the Jews come together.

18:36 . . . If my kingdom were of this world, then my servants would be fighting, that I might not be delivered up to the Jews.

In the first instance, as we have noted, Jesus makes the most philo-Semitic statement in the whole Gospel, if not the whole New Testament (4:22). Two of his other usages display a neutral meaning (13:33; 18:20) while 18:36 might have a negative connotation.

The terms "the Jews" and "the world" differ *so precisely* with regard to their roles (narrator and protagonist) and genres (narrative and speech) that we are justified to speak of an intentional "narratological parallelism." It is worth describing this phenomenon in more detail.

2.1. Overview of the Narratological Parallelism

While the compositional symmetry operates within the Gospel's macrostructure, the narratological parallelism works on the level of the Gospel's microstructure. Single pericopes that include narration as well as speech, and which contain the narrator's voice as well as Jesus' words, display a consistent interchange between Ἰουδαῖοι and κόσμος. This includes specifically the following texts: 2:1-25; 3:1-21; 4:1-42; 5:1-47; 6:25-59; 7:1-24; 8:12-30; 9:1-41; 10:1-41; 12:20-36; 12:37-50; also 18:19-24, 28-40. The focus is naturally on the first part of the Gospel and on the Passion since the distribution of Ἰουδαῖοι concentrates on these sections.[55] We will briefly look at some pericopes in more detail and discuss the relevant phenomenon. A table for each text displays the spreading of Ἰουδαῖος and κόσμος with regard to narrative and speech (italics). Often the genre shifts within one verse, especially when a narrative introduction precedes direct speech, e.g., "He came to Jesus at night and said, ..." (3:2a; cf. 4:9). For the sake of simplification, we count these narrative introductions as part of the speech unless they introduce the Ἰουδαῖοι (as in 5:10; 6:41; 7:15; 8:22). Dialogues in which speakers alternate also appear simply as one element of "speech" (e.g., 3:2-21; 9:24-41). Our comments focus then on the parallelism of both terms and other related matters of formal design.

---

[55] John 1 displays what we called the "compositional" parallelism (cf. 1:10 and 1:19) and can be omitted at this point.

2.1.1. John 2:1-11

1-3		Narrative	--
	4	*Speech*	--
5-6		Narrative	Ἰουδαῖος (6)
		Speech	--
9		Narrative	--
	10	*Speech*	--
11		Narrative	--

Several people fill the stage in this scene about the miraculous change of water into wine: Jesus, the disciples, Jesus' mother, the servants, the headwaiter and the bridegroom. Although "the Jews" are not present as a people group, the term Ἰουδαῖοι appears in the narrator's comment about the "purification of the Jews" (2:6) in order to explain the presence of six large stone vessels at the wedding. The normal assumption would be that those present at the wedding are therefore "Jews" who live in Cana in Galilee. Jesus addresses his mother with the vocative γύναι (v. 4) and the servants with imperatives (γεμίσατε v. 7; ἀντλήσατε, φέρετε v. 8). His language communicates in the situation at hand and contains neither κόσμος nor Ἰουδαῖοι.

2.1.2. John 2:12-25

12-15		Narrative	Ἰουδαῖος (13)
	16	*Speech*	--
17-18		Narrative	Ἰουδαῖος (18)
	19	*Speech*	--
20a		Narrative	Ἰουδαῖος (20)
	20b	*Speech*	--
21-25		Narrative	--

The narrator carefully situates the report about the cleansing of the temple in time and space. Jesus went up to Jerusalem, to the temple courts when the "Passover of the Jews" (τὸ πάσχα τῶν Ἰουδαίων, v. 13) was near. As in 2:6, Ἰουδαῖοι is employed here for the description of a religious custom. The narrator uses this term another two times to identify the interlocutors of Jesus (2:18, 20; see 1:19). Jesus himself addresses the Jews again with imperatives (ἄρατε, μὴ ποιεῖτε, v. 16; λύσατε, v. 19; see 2:7-8) but does not name them any further. A gnomic tone finishes the account about the first Passover. While some people in Jerusalem believed in Jesus because of his miracles, Jesus himself did not trust them because he knew "all" (πάντας) and he was aware what was in a "man" (ἐν τῷ ἀνθρώπῳ).[56]

2.1.3. John 3:1-21

1		Narrative	Ἰουδαῖος (1)
2-21		*Speech*	κόσμος (16, 17, 19)

The narrator introduces Nicodemus in 3:1 as the "ruler of the Jews" (ἄρχων τῶν Ἰουδαίων) who comes to Jesus to speak to him. Attention to the personal pronouns employed reveals that the following dialogue is not only one between two individuals but between two groups of people. Nicodemus opens with the statement, "Rabbi, *we* know (οἴδαμεν) that You have come from God as a teacher; . . . ." (3:2). In all of his three answers (3:3, 5-8, 10-21), Jesus begins with words directed specifically to Nicodemus as an individual (3:3 [σοι], 7a [σοι], 10 [σύ], 11a [σοι]). But in verse 7 he starts with the singular "you" (σοι) and changes into the plural, "You [ὑμᾶς] must be born again" (also verses 11, 12).[57] It becomes clear to the reader that Nicodemus, the "ruler of the Jews" (3:1) and "teacher of Israel" (3:10), represents not just his own questions and doubts but those of others as well.[58]

Verses 13-21 leave the language of personal dialogue between Jewish individuals and groups behind and formulate a creedal summary in which God is the subject, the "only begotten Son" the agent and the world the object of redemptive as well as punitive action (κόσμος in 3:16, 17, 19). Thus, generally speaking, 3:1-21 develops from a personal dialogue between Jesus and a Jewish leader (3:1-8) to a monologue about the Son and the world (3:13-21) with a transitional we-you (pl.)-dialogue in between (3:7-12). The scope widens gradually from individuals to groups

---

[56] See FORTNA, "Theological Use of Locale in the Fourth Gospel," 92-93. When Colwell interprets 2:23-25 with regard to Jews only, he completely misses the existential turn of the text and tries to find evidence for his theory that the Gospel attempts to appear anti-Jewish and pro-Gentile. COLWELL, *John Defends the Gospel*, 43-44.

[57] See similarly also the second plural "you" (ὑμεῖς) in Jesus' address to the Samaritan woman (4:20, 22) and to the royal official (4:48).

[58] As Nicodemus in 3:2, Jesus shifts from the singular into the plural as well: "Truly, truly, I (λέγω) say to you, we speak (λαλοῦμεν) that which we know, ..." (3:11). Similarly, he uses the first person plural also in the dialogue with the Samaritan woman, "we (ἡμεῖς) worship that which we know (οἴδαμεν)" (4:22; also in 9:4). While here the pronoun explicitly refers to the Jews as an ethnic-religious body in contrast to the Samaritans ("salvation is from the Jews," 4:22), the "we" in 3:11 might refer either to Jesus and God or to the Jesus-community. Keener suggests the former and Moloney the latter. KEENER, *The Gospel of John*, 1:558. MOLONEY, *John*, 94.

to "the world," a surprising development considering the narrative introduction of the interlocutor (3:1) and the Jewish color of the discourse up until verse 14.[59]

2.1.4. John 4:1-41

1-6		Narrative	--
	7	*Speech*	--
8		Narrative	--
	9a	*Speech*	Ἰουδαῖος (9a)
9b		Narrative	Ἰουδαῖος (9b)
	10-42	*Speech*	Ἰουδαῖος (22)
			κόσμος (42)

With regard to our question, the encounter between Jesus and the Samaritan woman is remarkable for the following reason: besides the narrator, four other speakers in the Gospel use Ἰουδαῖοι, the Samaritan woman being the first one in 4:9a.[60] Jesus just asked her for a drink and she responds with astonishment, "How is it that You, being a Jew, ask me for a drink since I am a Samaritan woman?" And the narrator adds an explanatory note, "For Jews have no dealings with Samaritans."[61] The contrast with "Samaritans" clearly reveals the ethnic meaning of Ἰουδαῖοι in this text. In his various answers, Jesus addresses her neither by name nor as a "Samaritan."[62] He first uses imperatives and singular pronouns (δός, v. 7; ᾔδεις, σοι, v. 10), and then switches in 4:13-14 to gnomic language: πᾶς

---

[59] Moloney expresses that surprise when he states with regard to 3:16-21, "A universal element enters Jesus' words *despite* the strongly Jewish context of the encounter with Nicodemus that prefaces this brief discourse." MOLONEY, *John*, 96 (italics added). Kvalbein explains, "Nicodemus . . . represents the Jews (v.10) that again represent the *kosmos*. The author invites Nicodemus/the Jews/the world to listen to the voice of the Spirit and believe in God's beloved Son, whom God *sent* to the world (17) and *gave* for the world (16) . . . ." KVALBEIN, "The Kingdom of God," 225.

[60] Besides the narrator (59 times), Ἰουδαῖοι is used by the Samaritan woman (4:9, 20), Jesus (4:22; 13:33; 18:20, 36), the Jews (11:8; 19:21, 21), Pilate (18:33, 35, 39), and the soldiers (19:3). For a comparison between the Samaritan woman and Pilate, see WEIDEMANN, *Der Tod Jesu*, 322-24.

[61] For the origin of the Samaritans, see 2 Kgs 17:24-34; Josephus, *A.J.* 9.14.3. For the opposition between "the Jews" and "the Samaritans," see Ezra 4:1-5; Josephus, *A.J.* 18.2.2; 20.6.1-3; Sir 50:25-26; mShebith 8.10; mShekalim 1.5; mGittin 1.5; mBerakoth 8.8.

[62] The NIV translates Jesus' words in 4:22 as "You *Samaritans* worship what you do not know." But the term "Samaritans" is added to the Greek for the English reader who otherwise cannot recognize that the pronoun "you" in the same verse is plural (ὑμεῖς). For the same reason, "Jews" is added in 4:20.

with conditional participle (πᾶς ὁ πίνων) and a conditional clause (ὃς δ' ἂν πίῃ). After Jesus asks for her husband (4:16-18), the dialogue turns to the center of worship. As before in 3:7, the pronouns now turn from singular into plural. The woman explains, "Our fathers (οἱ πατέρες ἡμῶν) worshiped in this mountain, and you (ὑμεῖς) say that in Jerusalem is the place where men ought to worship" (4:20). Jesus responds on the "we-you" level when he answers, "You (ὑμεῖς) worship that which you do not know; we (ἡμεῖς) worship that which we know, for salvation is from the Jews" (4:22). Jesus uses Ἰουδαῖοι only four times in the Gospel, the first time being here in 4:22 (also 13:33; 18:20, 36).

After the woman goes back to her home, she tells her village about Jesus. Then they meet Jesus themselves and, as a result, many believe (4:41) and confess him as σωτήρ τοῦ κόσμου, "Savior of the world" (4:42). This is the third time that κόσμος appears in the Gospel (after 1:9-10, 29) and again it comes in an emphatic statement uttered here as the climactic confession that summarizes the content of Jesus' theology about worship as it was unfolded in the dialogue with the Samaritan woman.

2.1.5. John 5:1-47

1-5		Narrative	Ἰουδαῖος (1)
	6-8	*Speech*	--
9-10a		Narrative	Ἰουδαῖος (10)
	10b-14	*Speech*	--
15-16		Narrative	Ἰουδαῖος (15, 16)
	17	*Speech*	--
18		Narrative	Ἰουδαῖος (18)
	19-47	*Speech*	--

The account about the healing of the invalid at the pool near Jerusalem on a Sabbath (5:1-9) turns into a dialogue between the healed man and the Jews (5:9-15) and then to a dialogue between the Jews and Jesus (5:16-18) which leads into a long monologue (5:19-47). Besides identifying a "feast of the Jews" (ἑορτὴ τῶν Ἰουδαίων) as the occasion for Jesus' journey to Jerusalem (5:1), the narrator uses Ἰουδαῖοι another four times to name the interlocutors of the healed man (5:10, 15) as well as those of Jesus (5:16, 18). Jesus' words to the sick person respond to the situation at hand, "Do you wish to get well?" (5:6); "Arise, take up your pallet, and walk" (5:8); "Do not sin anymore" (5:14). But Jesus' answer to the Jews is amazingly disconnected from their accusation of breaking the Sabbath. While later

Jesus does engage in a specific argument to refute the charge (7:21-24),[63] here he merely offers general claims and conclusions. The claim is that God is his Father and that he gave him authority over life and death (5:19-22). The conclusion is that "all (πάντες)" should honor the Son in the same way they honor the Father (5:23). Jesus does not use κόσμος in this context but maintains typical gnomic language (ὁ μὴ τιμῶν, verse 23; ὁ τὸν λόγον μου ἀκούων, verse 24; πάντες οἱ ἐν τοῖς μνημείοις, verse 28; οἱ τὰ ἀγαθὰ ποιήσαντες, verse 29) and the undefined second person plural "you" during the whole monologue (see ὑμῖν in 5:19, 24, 25, 38; ὑμεῖς in 5:20, 33, 34, 35, 38, 39, 44, 45). The "Scriptures" and "Moses" are mentioned as part of his defense (5:39, 45), but it is never spelled out how exactly they serve as evidence. Consequently, the question of the Sabbath is not the focus of the story but appears instead "as a means to assert Jesus' close relationship to his Father"[64] and to demonstrate the hostile response to such a claim.

2.1.6. John 6:25-59

After Jesus fed the five thousand people (6:1-15) and walked on the Sea of Galilee (6:16-24), he enters the synagogue in Capernaum and begins a dialogue about the "bread that comes down from heaven" (6:25-59; cf. 6:33, 38, 41, 42, 50, 51, 58).

25		Narrative	-- (ὁ ὄχλος, 24)
	26-40	*Speech*	κόσμος (33)
41a		Narrative	Ἰουδαῖος (41)
	41b-51	*Speech*	κόσμος (51)
52		Narrative	Ἰουδαῖος (52)
	53-58	*Speech*	--
59		Narrative	--

The narrator describes those who listen first with the personal pronoun αὐτοῖς (6:26) which refers back to "the crowd" that followed Jesus because of the miraculous meal (ὄχλος in 6:2, 5, 22, 24). They reveal their Jewish descent when they call the Israelites "our fathers" who "ate the manna in the wilderness" (6:31; Exod 16). The narrator switches the term in verses 41 and 52 and calls the interlocutors now "the Jews" (οἱ

---

[63] In the Synoptics, Jesus refutes the charge of breaking the Sabbath with examples of David and priests doing the same (Matt 12:3-5; Mark 2:25-26; Luke 6:3-4), with a comparison between animals and people (Matt 12:11-12; Luke 13:15-16), and with a sharp rhetorical question ("Is it lawful on the Sabbath to do good or to do harm, to save a life or to kill?" Mark 6:3).

[64] HAKOLA, *Identity Matters*, 120. Later, Hakola reiterates, "In John 5 the Sabbath is not a main issue, but the controversy soon focuses solely on Jesus' person." Ibid., 142.

Ἰουδαῖοι). Although Jesus engages the specific reference to Israel's provision with manna in the desert (6:32, 49, 58), he does not address the people in front of him either as "crowd"[65] or "Jews." Instead, besides the use of personal pronouns (ὑμῖν in vv. 26, 27, 32, 36, 53) and unspecific gnomic language (ὁ ἐρχόμενος πρός ἐμέ v. 35,[66] πᾶν v. 37, τις v. 46, etc.), Jesus tells those whom the narrator identifies as *Jews* that he is the Bread of God that gives life to "the *world*" (6:33, 51).

2.1.7. John 7:1-24

Jesus stays in Galilee and avoids Judea because, as the narrator explains, "the Jews were seeking to kill him" (7:1).

1-2		Narrative	Ἰουδαῖος (1, 2)
	3-4	*Speech*	κόσμος (4)
5		Narrative	--
	6-8	*Speech*	κόσμος (7)
9-15a		Narrative	Ἰουδαῖος (11, 13, 15)
	15b-24	*Speech*	--

Jesus stays in Galilee and avoids Judea because, as the narrator explains, "the Jews were seeking to kill him" (7:1). But as is typical for the speeches of Jesus throughout the Gospel (cf. 3:19-20; 15:18, 19, 23, 24, 25), not "the Jews" but "the world" is the subject which rejects him, "The world cannot hate you; but it hates Me because I testify of it, that its deeds are evil" (7:7). We read earlier of the Jews' attempt to persecute and kill Jesus because of his healing on a Sabbath (5:16, 18). That Jesus refers in 7:7 to this violent rejection is clear from 7:23. Thus, although the narrative frame clearly points to Ἰουδαῖοι as the antagonists, Jesus points to the κόσμος in his words. The following succession of discourse and narrative maintains this distinction (7:9-24). While Jesus does address matters of Jewish religion in 7:19, 21-24 (Moses, circumcision, patriarchs, Sabbath), only the narrator uses the term Ἰουδαῖοι (7:11, 13, 15, 35).

2.1.8. John 8:12-59

It is worth mapping the long dialogue in 8:12-59 the way we did below, for it shows the *consistency* with which the narrator assigns κόσμος to the

---

[65] The term ὄχλος occurs 20x in the Gospel of John, 2x in direct speech: the Pharisees call the crowd "accursed" because they do not know the Law (7:49) and Jesus mentions the people in his prayer before resurrecting Lazarus (11:42).

[66] There is only one parallel to this phrase in the Synoptics: πᾶς ὁ ἐρχόμενος πρός με (Luke 6:47).

speech of Jesus and Ἰουδαῖοι to the narrative even over a long stretch of text with frequent changes of the speaking roles.

	12-19	*Speech*	κόσμος (12)
20		Narrative	--
	21	*Speech*	--
22a		Narrative	Ἰουδαῖος (22a)
	22b-26	*Speech*	κόσμος (23, 23, 26)
27		Narrative	--
	28-29	*Speech*	--
30-31a		Narrative	Ἰουδαῖος (31a)
	31b-32	*Speech*	--
33		Narrative	--
	34-38	*Speech*	--
39a		Narrative	--
	39b-41a	*Speech*	--
41b		Narrative	--
	42-47	*Speech*	--
48		Narrative	Ἰουδαῖος (48)
	49-51	*Speech*	--
52-53		Narrative	Ἰουδαῖος (52)
	54-56	*Speech*	--
57		Narrative	Ἰουδαῖος (57)
	58	*Speech*	--
59		Narrative	--

After the text-critically dubious pericope of the adulteress (7:53-8:11), verse 12 simply resumes Jesus' words with Πάλιν οὖν αὐτοῖς ἐλάλησεν ὁ Ἰησοῦς λέγων· ἐγώ εἰμι τὸ φῶς τοῦ κόσμου. Jesus is still in Jerusalem during the Feast of the Tabernacles (7:2) and teaching in the temple courts (8:20). Since the beginning of the feast the narrator has involved the Pharisees more and more as specific opponents of Jesus (7:32, 45-49) and, presupposing the same setting for John 7 and 8, he can simply allude to them with the personal pronoun αὐτοῖς (also v. 21, 23). They appear explicitly one more time (οἱ Φαρισαῖοι, 8:13) before the narrator switches from one designation to the other and calls the interlocutors "the Jews" (v. 22). In fact, he keeps using Ἰουδαῖοι throughout the dialogue (v. 31, 48, 52, 57) and does not return to "the Pharisees" until the beginning of the interrogation of the blind man who was healed (9:13). In contrast to these specific designations, Jesus opens the dialogue by calling himself "the light of *the world*" (φῶς τοῦ κόσμου in 8:12; also 9:5; 11:9; 12:46). In the verses that follow he employs the Jewish law for his defense (8:17; see

Deut 17:6), discusses Abraham's significance (8:33-41, 56-58) and calls his interlocutors even "Abraham's children" (8:37, 56). But Jesus describes the origin of his listeners in terms of a vertical dualism: they are "from below . . . from this world" (ὑμεῖς ἐκ τῶν κάτω ἐστέ . . . ἐκ τούτου τοῦ κόσμου, 8:23) while he is "from above" (ἐγὼ ἐκ τῶν ἄνω).[67] Furthermore, while talking to Jews and discussing Jewish matters, Jesus explains that "the things which I heard from him these I speak to *the world*" (8:26; also 18:20). Again we recognize the consistent absence of Ἰουδαῖοι and the use of κόσμος and pronouns (ὑμεῖς in v. 14, 15, 23, etc.; ὑμετέρῳ in v. 17) instead. The gravity of the dispute culminates in the famous statement, "You belong to your father, the devil" (8:44). Jesus does not say that the devil is the father of the Jews. In contrast to, for example, the Gnostic near-contemporary Saturnius, who taught at Antioch during Hadrian's reign (AD 117-138) that "Christ came to destroy the God of the Jews" (Irenaeus, *Haer*. 1.24.2), the author of the Fourth Gospel addresses his judgment in terms that resist the definition of one ethnic group as the special agent of Satan. This observation is confirmed by a statement in the same discourse which expresses an important rule in gnomic language, "Truly, truly, I say to you, everyone who commits sin (πᾶς ὁ ποιῶν τὴν ἁμαρτίαν) is the slave of sin" (8:34).[68]

2.1.9. John 9:1-41

1		Narrative	--
	2-5	*Speech*	κόσμος (5, 5)
6-7		Narrative	--
	8-12	*Speech*	--
13-14		Narrative	--
	15-17	*Speech*	--
18		Narrative	Ἰουδαῖος (18)
	19-21	*Speech*	--
22-23		Narrative	Ἰουδαῖος (22, 22)
	24-41	*Speech*	κόσμος (39)

---

[67] The prepositional phrase ἐκ τοῦ κόσμου, used in 8:23 for the first time in the Gospel, is employed in two different ways: It denotes the *physical* realm of existence out of which Jesus ascended to heaven (13:1) and in which he left the disciples (17:15). But more often the emphasis lies on the *metaphysical* quality of the space and the people which stand opposite to the origin of Jesus (8:23b; 17:14, 16), his disciples (15:19, 17:6, 14, 16; see also 1:12-13; 3:3-8), and his βασιλεία (18:36).

[68] See QUIÉVREUX, "'Les Juifs'," 259-60.

In the pericope about the healing of the man born blind, Jesus appears at the beginning and at the end. His answer to the disciples' question about the blind man's condition culminates in the mission statement, "While I am in the world, I am the light of the world" (9:5; see 8:12). After the healing (9:6-7), the author structures the following events into four scenes in which the miracle is discussed by various parties. The narrator designates them explicitly as the "neighbors" (9:8-12; γείτονες in v. 18), the "Pharisees" (9:13-17; Φαρισαῖοι in vv.13, 15, 16), the "Jews" and the "parents" (9:18-23; Ἰουδαῖοι in vv. 18, 22; γονεῖς in v. 18), and again the Pharisees (9:24-34), now simply included into the form of the verb (e.g., ἐφώνησαν in v. 24). As the particle οὖν in 9:18 indicates (temporal, "still"), the Jews who interrogate the parents (9:18-23) are the Pharisees who cross-examined the blind man before (9:13-17).[69] We recognize this particular interchange of terms from our discussion of the previous text (8:12-30). The narrator clarifies that the final dialogue (9:39-41) occurs between Jesus and the "Pharisees" (9:40). But while Jesus pronounces the guilt of his immediate interlocutors (9:41), he does so in the familiar axiomatic and nameless terms that could apply to anyone, "For judgment I came into this world, that those who do not see may see; and that those who see may become blind" (9:39).[70] The *narrator* in the Gospel of John often names the areas into which Jesus went, such as "Judea" (3:22), "Galilee" (4:45), or "Jerusalem" (12:12).[71] But as here in 9:39, *Jesus* always speaks about his coming "into the world" (εἰς τὸν κόσμον; also 3:19; 12:46; 16:28; 18:37).[72] We find this language in the prologue (1:9) and in the mouth of other speakers as well.[73]

---

[69] Beasley-Murray observes similarly, "The 'Pharisees' of vv 13, 15, 16 have now become 'the Jews.' This reflects the Evangelist's own terminology, and not least his tendency to vary his terms (cf. a comparable exchange of the two names in 7:13, 32, 47; 8:13, 22, 48, 57)." BEASLEY-MURRAY, *John*, 157.

[70] The contrast to Jesus' speech in Matthew is particularly striking since there the theme of blindness is applied specifically to the scribes and Pharisees (Matt 15:14; 23:16, 26).

[71] See the narrator's use of ἔρχομαι together with εἰς τὴν Ἰουδαίαν γῆν (3:22), εἰς πόλιν τῆς Σαμαρείας λεγομένην Συχὰρ (4:5), εἰς τὴν Γαλιλαίαν (4:45), εἰς τὴν Κανὰ τῆς Γαλιλαίας (4:46), εἰς τὴν κώμην (11:30, Βηθανία, see v. 1), εἰς Βηθανίαν (12:1), εἰς Ἱεροσόλυμα (12:12).

[72] The same is observed by MENKEN, "Die Redaktion des Zitates aus Sach 9,9," 203.

[73] After feeding five thousand people, the Galileans say that Jesus is "the Prophet who is to come into the world" (6:14). And Martha calls Jesus "the Christ, the Son of God, even he who comes into the world" (11:27). "The world" appears in the Synoptics as the stage of the *future* global mission of the disciples (Matt 5:14; 26:13; 28:19-20; Luke 24:47) whereas it designates the stage and object of Jesus' ministry in the Gospel of John. This does not deny the presence and importance of Gentiles in the Synoptics: In the Gospel of Matthew, for example, there are four Gentiles in Jesus' genealogy (1:2-16,

2.1.10. John 10:1-21, 22-38

	1-5	Speech	--
6		Narrative	--
	7-18	Speech	--
19		Narrative	Ἰουδαῖος (19)
	20-21	Speech	--
22-24a		Narrative	Ἰουδαῖος (24a)
	24b-30	Speech	--
31		Narrative	Ἰουδαῖος (31)
	32-33a	Speech	--
33b		Narrative	Ἰουδαῖος (33a)
	33c-38	Speech	κόσμος (36)

The beginning of a new chapter in 10:1 seems like an arbitrary divide[74] since the "Pharisees" from 9:40 continue to be the addressees of the allegory (παροιμία in 10:6) of the Good Shepherd (10:1-18). The narrator indicates that the response to the allegory comes from "the Jews" (10:19), thus alternating again between φαρισαῖοι and Ἰουδαῖοι (see 8:12-30; 9:13-23). Jesus' relatively long speech is remarkably devoid of any personal address to his immediate interlocutors, apart from the pronoun within the two solemn preludes Ἀμὴν ἀμὴν λέγω ὑμῖν in 10:1 and 10:7. While it seems natural to set forth the allegory itself in such a fashion (10:1-5), Jesus' following explanation and expansion (10:7-18) includes a pictorial manner of speech ("gate for sheep," "thieves and robbers," "good shepherd," "hireling") without applying it to his listeners. The author apparently expects the reader to make the connections himself or herself.

While 10:22 introduces a new time and place, the narrator continues to use "the Jews" as the interlocutors of Jesus, carefully interspersing them in every one of his narrative parts between those of Jesus' speech (10:24, 31, 33). Jesus picks up the sheep-metaphor in an address that is emphatically

---

Ruth, Rahab, Bathsheba, Tamar); Gentiles are the first to come to baby Jesus and honor him as king (2:1-14, story of the Magi); Jesus' ministry happens not only in Judea but also in "Galilee of the Gentiles" (4:15, quote from Isa 9:1); etc.

[74] The expression Ἀμὴν ἀμὴν λέγω, used in 10:1, always occurs either as an answer to a previous question, statement or action (3:3, 5; 5:19; 6:26, 32, 53; 8:34, 58; 21:18) or within Jesus' speech (1:51; 3:11; 5:24, 25; 6:47; 8:51; 10:7; 12:24; 13:16, 20, 38; 14:12; 16:20, 23). Only in 13:21 may we find Ἀμὴν ἀμὴν λέγω at the beginning of a new statement, but even here we are given a narrative introduction first. Thus, chapter 9 "flows into chap. 10 without a break" and "the hostile actions of the Pharisees provide the context for the parabolic discourse of the Shepherd and the Sheep." BEASLEY-MURRAY, *John*, 148. For various views on the connection between John 9 and 10 see REINHARTZ, *The Word in the World*, 63-65.

personal, "you (ὑμεῖς) do not believe because you are not of my sheep" (10:26). After an attempt to stone him for blasphemy ("I and the Father are one," 10:30), Jesus answers with a quotation from "your law" (Ps 82:6) and uses it for a *qal wahomer* argument: if mere humans were called "gods" in the Scripture, how much more is he "whom the Father . . . sent into the world" (10:36; also 3:17; 17:18)[75] justified in his way of speech? Jesus' use of κόσμος stands in striking contrast to the narrator's detailed references in 10:22 to a specific place (Jerusalem, temple), a specific time (winter) and occasion (Feast of Dedication), and a particular group of people (Jews, 10:33).

2.1.11. John 12:20-36

20-22		Narrative	--
	23-28	*Speech*	κόσμος (25)
29		Narrative	--
	30-32	*Speech*	κόσμος (31, 31)
33		Narrative	--
	34-36a	*Speech*	--
36b		Narrative	--

The narrator pictures Jesus in his last days and dialogues before Passover as being surrounded by a many people, whether it be in Bethany at the house of Mary and Martha (ὄχλος πολὺς, 12:9) or on his way to Jerusalem (12:12, 17, 18, 29, 34). In fact, six out of twenty occurrences of ὄχλος in the Gospel of John appear in this narrative prelude to the passion alone, thus indicating the public nature of (cf. 18:20) and large attraction to Jesus' life and teaching (many believers are mentioned in 12:11, 12-15, 18-19). The Pharisees even exclaim in frustration, "the world has gone after him" (12:19). Jesus uses this large audience to announce and interpret his death as a moment of glory for him (12:23, 28-29) and a time of judgment for "this world" and for "the prince of this world" (ὁ ἄρχων τοῦ κόσμου, 12:31; also 14:30; 16:11).

2.1.12. John 12:37-50

37-43		Narrative	--
	44-50	*Speech*	κόσμος (46, 47)

---

[75] Jesus can say that he was "sent into the world" by the Father, but also that he "came into the world."

12:37-50 forms the conclusion of the first main section in the Gospel (chaps.1-12) which unfolds the life and ministry of Jesus and peoples' responses to it. The conclusion clearly divides into two parts: First, the narrator himself describes and evaluates two negative reactions to the message of Jesus (37-43):

>   (1) No faith (12:37-41)
>   a) Statement (v. 37)
>   b) Evaluation: fulfillment of Isa 53:1; 6:10 (v. 38-41)
>   (2) Faith without confession (12:42-43)
>   a) Statement (v. 42)
>   b) Evaluation (v. 43)

He does not mention the term Ἰουδαῖος, but quotations from Isaiah 53:1 and 6:10 (God hardened the listeners), the naming of the "Pharisees" who began to put people "out of the synagogue" (ἀποσυνάγωγοι, 12:42) and the dominant use of the aorist indicative to describe actions of the past[76] show that the focus is nevertheless on the Jewish setting of Jesus' life.

The second part of the conclusion consists of Jesus' own summarizing words (12:44-50) which form "a sort of epilogue" that matches the prologue.[77] The speech has three parts:

>   Content (vv. 44-45) and consequences (v. 46) of faith
>   Content and consequences of rejection (vv. 47-48)
>   Reason (causal ὅτι) for salvation and judgment (vv. 49-50)

In contrast to the narrator's summary, specifically Jewish terms do not appear. Instead we find the generalizing style so typical for the words of Jesus: substantival participles (vv. 44, 45, 46, 48), κόσμος (vv. 46, 47), πᾶς (v. 46), αὐτός (vv. 47, 48), τίς (v. 47), purpose-statements with ἵνα (vv. 46, 47), third conditional statements to describe general rules (v. 47), dominance of the present tense indicative.[78] The *Leitwort* that connects both sections of the conclusion is the verb πιστεύω. But while the narrator always uses this verb in the past tense (impf. ind. v. 37; aorist ind. vv. 38, 42; inf. to ἠδύναντο v. 39), Jesus uses this verb twice as a substantival participle (vv. 44, 46) and in the present tense (v. 44), suggesting the

---

[76] In his conclusion (12:37-43), the narrator uses mostly the aorist tense (10x indicative, 5x other moods), 3 times imperfect, 2 times perfect (1x indicative, 1x participle) and 1 time future.

[77] KÖSTENBERGER, *John*, 393.

[78] In the speech of Jesus, the present tense dominates (8x indicative, 6x participle), the aorist occurs only 4x in the indicative (plus 3x participle, 7x subjunctive), and the perfect 4 times.

relevance of his words for the reader. Thus, the conclusion seems to develop from the description and evaluation of past Jewish responses (12:37-43) to a last invitation and warning for those for whom the Gospel was written (12:44-50).

2.1.13. John 18:19-40

19		Narrative	--
	20-23	Speech	κόσμος (20), Ἰουδαῖος (20)
24		Narrative	--
	25-26	Speech	--
27-28		Narrative	--
	29-31b	Speech	--
31a, 32		Narrative	Ἰουδαῖος (31a)
	33-38a	Speech	Ἰουδαῖος (33, 35, 36)
			κόσμος (36, 37)

After the long absence of "the Jews" in the farewell discourse (chaps. 13-17), they reappear forcefully twenty-two times (30 percent of the total 71 times) in the passion account (chaps. 18-19). While direct speech in the Gospel contains Ἰουδαῖοι altogether twelve times,[79] eight of these occurrences are found in chapters 18 and 19, mostly in form of the title "King of the Jews" in the mouth of Pilate (18:33, 39), the soldiers (19:3) and the Chief priests (19:21).[80] Jesus employs the term twice. He says in the hearing before the high priest Annas, "I have spoken (λελάληκα) openly to the world. I always taught (ἐδίδαξα) in the synagogue and in the temple where all the Jews come together; and I spoke nothing in secret" (18:20). Jesus stated earlier, while standing in the temple and talking to Jews, that he speaks to the world (λαλῶ, 8:26, see 8:20).[81] But only the narrator mentioned before 18:20 that Jesus "taught," namely in Capernaum's synagogue (6:59) and in the temple (7:14, 28; 8:2, 20). In fact, Jesus uses συναγωγή and ἱερόν only here in the gospel.[82] Thus, although he employed the term Ἰουδαῖοι before (4:22, 13:33), Jesus' statement in 18:20 uniquely *combines* his typical use of κόσμος with the narrator's style of naming Jewish people (the Jews) and places (synagogue, temple) as the particular context of his ministry. The specificity of the language does not only

---

[79] See 4:9, 22; 11:8; 13:33; 18:20, 33, 35, 36, 39; 19:3, 21.

[80] Furthermore, Pilate responds to a question of Jesus with the condescending statement, "I am not a Jew, am I?" (18:35).

[81] In 13:33, Jesus says that he "talked" (εἶπον) to the Jews.

[82] The term συναγωγή occurs 2 times in the gospel (6:59; 18:20) and ἱερός 11 times (2:14, 15; 5:14; 7:14, 28; 8:2, 20, 59; 10:23; 11:56; 18:20).

match the Synoptic parallels (Matt 26:55; Mark 14:49; Luke 22:53), but as a retrospective and non-theological summary it captures well the concrete nature of Jesus' public appearance on earth. It is the first part of 18:20, "I have spoken openly to the *world* (τῷ κόσμῳ, italics added)," which not only juxtaposes κόσμος and Ἰουδαῖοι in one verse in the mouth of one speaker for the first time in the Gospel, but which seems to indicate that the ministry of Jesus transcends the originally Jewish context.[83]

Finally, in his trial before Pilate, the governor asks, "Are you the king of the Jews?" (18:33) and Jesus answers that his kingdom "is not of this world" (οὐκ ἔστιν ἐκ τοῦ κόσμου τούτου), otherwise he would not have been "delivered up to the Jews" (18:36). While formally κόσμος and Ἰουδαῖοι appear in one verse as in 18:20, "the world" takes on the meaning of "realm"[84] and does not constitute a direct semantic parallel to "the Jews." Both terms are nevertheless related. Jesus' answer implies that to be the king of the Jews would mean to have a kingdom "of this world," a human reign on earth which rules with the fist as opposed to the "kingdom of God" from above (see βασιλεία τοῦ θεοῦ in 3:3, 5) which shows its glory in overcoming disease and death.

Jesus finishes Pilate's first interrogation with the mission statement, "For this I have been born, and for this I have come into the world, to bear witness to the truth" (18:37). The reader is already familiar with Jesus' language of "coming into the world" (3:19; 9:39; 12:46; 16:28; also 1:9; 6:14; 11:27). But now, uttering them inside the Praetorium and in the face of a *Roman* official (cf. 18:28, 33), the narrative frame actually supports a meaning of κόσμος that is larger than the previous Jewish setting.

3. Conceptual Parallelism

After describing macrostructural and narratological parallels between Ἰουδαῖοι and κόσμος, we finally have to consider briefly some terms and concepts which the author applies to the Jews and to the world alike. Though not immediately obvious, these parallels nevertheless emerge from a close reading of the text.

A verbal parallel relates to the kind of antagonism. As the Jews "persecuted" Jesus (ἐδίωκον οἱ Ἰουδαῖοι, in 5:16), so the world "will persecute" the disciples (διώξουσιν in 15:20, κόσμος six times in verses 18-19). While in previous parallels "the Jews" and "the world" appeared as

---

[83] Bultmann comments: Jesus' λελάληκα τῷ κόσμῳ shows that "Judaism represents the 'world.'" BULTMANN, *The Gospel of John*, 646.

[84] See the adverb of *place* ἐντεῦθεν in the parallel expression in 18:36b.

agents within the life of Jesus (compositional and narratological parallelism), the verbs in these verses refer to the same activity performed at different times (past and future) to different people (Jesus and disciples).

Jesus creates a conceptual parallelism when he speaks of the transcendent antagonist. Once he says to the Jews (8:31, 37), "You are of your father, the devil" (8:44). But three times we also hear from him that the devil is "the ruler of the world" (12:31; 14:30; 16:11).

Westcott interprets "his own" in 1:11 as Israel's rejection of the Messiah. He then argues that the same response appears in the past tense with regard to the "world" in 3:19.[85]

There are also parallels between Nicodemus and Pilate who engage in the Gospel's first and last dialogue between individuals and Jesus[86] and who represent the Jews and the world as religious and political leaders. Both misunderstand the nature of Jesus' kingdom. And, as Köstenberger noticed, in "both cases, their conversation with Jesus ends on an abrupt note with an exasperated question on their part."[87] Nicodemus asks, "How can these things be?" (3:9) and Pilate poses the question, "What is truth?" (18:38). A positive correspondence can also be seen between Caiaphas and Pilate.[88] The Jewish highpriest testifies to the need and efficiency of Jesus' death "for the people" (11:50) while the Roman judge witnesses Jesus' innocence (19:6). Thus two authorities of two different people groups are added to the list of witnesses for the Son of God in the Fourth Gospel.

Lastly, both terms are used with neutral, positive, and negative nuances. We described these different colors of Ἰουδαῖοι in chapter 2. The 'world' has a rather neutral meaning when it describes the realm of human existence (1:10a; 17:24; 21:25). It is recognized in the Gospel as created and loved by God (1:10b; 3:16), as the subject of God's and Christ's mission (1:29; 3:17; 4:42; 6:33; etc.) and consisting of people that follow Jesus (12:19). On the other hand, it is clear from the beginning that the κόσμος "did not know him" (1:10c), even hates Jesus (7:7) and the disciples (15:18) and cannot receive the Spirit of truth (14:17). It thus

---

[85] Westcott explains, "The message of the Gospel had already been proclaimed in such a way to Jew and Gentile that a judgment could be pronounced upon the general character of its acceptance." WESTCOTT, *The Gospel*, 1:lxxvii. Porsch writes about the same texts, "Die Welt lehnt Jesus ab (1,10; 3,19) und haßt ihn (7,7). Sie kann Gott nicht erkennen (17,25) und ist unfähig, den 'Geist der Wahrheit' zu empfangen (14,17). Weil Jesus und die Jünger 'nicht aus der Welt' sind (8,23; 15,19; 17,14.16), werden sie von der Welt gehaßt (15,18f.; 17,14; vgl. 16,20.33). Was hier von 'der Welt' gesagt wird, gilt in gleicher Weise von den ungläubigen Juden, den Gegnern Jesu." PORSCH, "'Ihr habt den Teufel zum Vater'," 55.

[86] Jörg Frey drew my attention to this observation in an email from January 27, 2006.

[87] KÖSTENBERGER, "'What is Truth?'," 51.

[88] Thanks again to Jörg Frey for sharing this parallel with me.

differs from the disciples (14:19; 17:9, 16) and stands under divine judgment (12:31). After observing these parallel nuances, Schnelle rightly concludes that "die Analogien zwischen den Ἰουδαῖοι und dem Kosmos liegen auf der Hand."[89]

4. Summary

This chapter described the various ways in which the author of the Fourth Gospel parallels the expressions Ἰουδαῖοι and κόσμος throughout his writing. First, both terms alternate in the Gospel's macrostructure in the form of an a-b-a-b pattern (compositional parallelism). Second, the author assigned the terms precisely to the differing roles of narrator and protagonist and to the genres of narrative and speech (narratological parallelism). Third, one can find occasional conceptual parallels between "Jews" and "the world" in matters of terms, concepts, people, and nuance (5:16 and 15:20; 8:44 and 12:31; 14:30; 16:11; Nicodemus and Pilate).

---

[89] SCHNELLE, "Die Juden im Johannesevangelium," 228.

CHAPTER 4

The Function of "the World"
in Relation to "the Jews"

What is the purpose of this compositional, narratological and conceptual parallelism? Why does the Gospel's macrostructure alternate between universal and local perspectives? Why does the narratological design ascribe most of the κόσμος-language to Jesus, who spoke to the Jews, and most of the Ἰουδαῖοι-language to the narrator? And for what reason is there an apparent correspondence between the Jews and Jesus on the one hand, and the world and the disciples on the other?

Unfortunately, the few discussions about the parallelism between Ἰουδαῖοι and κόσμος in the vast landscape of Johannine scholarship stand in opposite proportion to its magnitude and importance in the Gospel itself.[1] Even more frequently, one term is analyzed without discussing any connections to the other at all.[2] With regard to older scholarship, this omission is certainly due to the influence of form-criticism and literary criticism. The focus on the smallest unit of oral tradition or on separate literary and pre-literary sources systematically excludes macro-structural considerations such as the links between prologue and Gospel or discourse

---

[1] Bultmann's view of the Jews as representatives of the world is the only interpretation that understands the meaning of the Ἰουδαῖοι in dependence of the κόσμος. Apart from a few pages here and there, none of the dissertations discussed in chapter 1 provide any substantial discussion of the term κόσμος. Bratcher makes a promising start when he observes at the outset of his article, "In order to better understand the meaning of 'the Jews' in the Gospel of John, we must first look at the use and meaning of 'the world' in this Gospel." Unfortunately, the following analysis about "the world" does not shape his understanding of "the Jews" in *any* way for the rest of his study. BRATCHER, "'The Jews'," 401.

[2] Culpepper does recognize that the Jews have "representative value" and he makes a brief reference to "the world." CULPEPPER, *Anatomy*, 128, 130. But the connection between both terms is so underrated that he does not mention it at all in a later article. Idem, "The Gospel of John," 273-88. Geyser does not see the appearance of κόσμος in the mouth of Jesus and merely observes that "except for the conversation with the Samaritan woman, Jesus on the other hand never uses Ἰουδαῖοι." GEYSER, "Israel in the fourth Gospel," 18. On the other hand, Baumbach investigates the use of "the world," but he does not relate it anywhere to "the Jews." BAUMBACH, "Gemeinde und Welt," 121-36. So also CASSEM, "A Grammatical and Contextual Inventory," 81-91.

and narrative.[3] Our history of research in chapter 1 has shown that, apart from Schnelle's and Zumstein's studies, even more recent narrative approaches do not remedy the situation (see Schram, Caron, Nicklas, Diefenbach, Hakola, etc.). This blind spot in Johannine scholarship is not a negligible omission but a deplorable situation when we consider its significance for the question of anti-Judaism. Granskou expresses a rare insight when he states the relevance of the parallelism:

> What does this association between 'world' and 'the Jews' mean for the understanding of the question of anti-Judaism? The association could cut both ways. It could spread the hostility toward Jesus out beyond the Jews, thereby diluting the gospel's anti-Judaism. Or it could heighten the anti-Judaism by suggesting that the quintessence of the world's unbelief can be seen in Judaism.[4]

Depending on how we understand the connection between "the Jews" and "the world," the anti-Jewish reading of the Gospel is either heightened or diluted.[5] The next two chapters seek to find out which of the two options is truer to the text.

1. The Function of the Compositional Parallelism

We have noticed already the a-b-a-b pattern in the Gospel's macrostructure. The Gospel opens with a universal point of view (chap. 1a) and zooms then to a local level of reality in order to present details in the life of Jesus (chaps. 1b-12). After the Messiah enters Jerusalem, "the hour" of the son's glorification finally comes (cf. 12:23, 27; 13:1; 17:1).[6] Jesus finishes his ministry and turns exclusively to the training of his disciples and the preparation for his departure. The particulars of his own history disappear behind the universal language of Jesus' address (chaps. 13-17) before the passion narrative resumes with the details of his trial and crucifixion (chaps. 18-19). What is the purpose of prefacing both major divisions of the Gospel (chaps. 1b-12; 13-20) with discourses that are largely universal in outlook (chaps. 1a; 13-17)?

---

[3] See our discussion of a literary critical approach by White, Tomson, Grelot, and Lingad in chapter 1 (2.1.4).

[4] GRANSKOU, "Anti-Judaism," 204-05. Similarly ZUMSTEIN, "The Farewell Discourse," 464.

[5] Wengst overlooks that the parallelism between both terms can be interpreted in two ways when he argues against Brown's reading of "the world" as Gentiles in John 13-17 simply because such an understanding would contradict the parallelism between "the Jews" and "the world." WENGST, *Bedrängte Gemeinde*, 58 n. 7.

[6] See the repeated announcements of "the hour" in 2:4; 4:21, 23; 5:25, 28; 7:30; 8:20.

1.1.   The Function of the Prologue for the Gospel

Does it matter if the reader skips the first eighteen verses and begins his reading immediately with 1:19 "And this is the witness of John, when the Jews sent to him priests and Levites from Jerusalem to ask him, 'Who are you?'"? Although *historical* and *exegetical* matters have preoccupied most analytic energies with regard to the prologue, a synchronic method must give equal importance to the question about its *functional* significance for the whole gospel. A form critical study of narrative beginnings in ancient literature offers three types of openings:[7] (1) The *preface* (Greek *prooimium*, Latin *exordium*) states the purpose of the writing as Luke does in Luke 1:1-4. (2) The *dramatic prologue*, used in Greek and Roman drama, provide, according to Aristotle (*Rhetoric* 3.14.1/6), a

> paving [of] the way for what follows [by giving] a sample of the subject, in order that the hearers may know beforehand what it is about, and that the mind may not be kept in suspense, for that which is undefined leads astray; so then he who puts the beginning, so to say, into the hearer's hand enables him, if he holds fast to it, to follow the story.

The audience thus receives privileged information that is hidden from the characters in the play and that, "especially in comedy, is important for developing the motif of irony."[8] This has been a suitable model for understanding the openings of the Gospels of Luke (after the preface), Mark (after 1:1) and John.[9] (3) The last major category of ancient narrative beginnings is the *incipit* which consists of a less formalistic brief phrase as exemplified in the Gospels of Mark (1:1) and Thomas, or the σίλλυβος / *tituli* that were later attached to the canonical Gospels.[10]

Johannine scholarship offers three main answers: the Gospel of John opens with either (1) an introduction, or (2) a summary, or even (3) a hermeneutical key to the narrative. In the following, we will briefly discuss each proposal.

---

[7] SMITH, "Narrative Beginnings in Ancient Literature and Theory," 1-9. All articles in volume 52 of *Semeia* (1991) deal with the topic of "How Gospels begin."

[8] Ibid., 4.

[9] For an extensive discussion and affirmative evaluation of the Prologue as a *prooimion* in Aristotle's sense with irony as a means of persuasion see PHILLIPS, *The Prologue*, 39-45, 51-54.

[10] Ibid., 4-6. As a fourth type of beginning, Smith mentions the 'virtual preface' which Lucian finds in narratives that simply begin with the story. There is no example of such a beginning in the New Testament.

1.1.1. Introduction

The first answer emphasizes discontinuity between prologue and Gospel and suggests that the opening either serves to introduce Hellenistic readers (Harnack, Dodd) or was composed after the body of the Gospel in response to a docetic misunderstanding as discussed in 1 John (Robinson, Brown).

In his 1892 article, Adolf von Harnack observed that the body of the Gospel never comes back to the idea of the λόγος expressed in 1:1, but that instead it speaks specifically of "the Son," the "Son of Man," or "the Son of God."[11] Thus the logos-Christology is not the key to the Gospel,[12] but it picks up the Hellenistic reader who is familiar with the concept of the λόγος (cf. Philo) and develops this unspecific notion of "the word" by concretizing it throughout the verses[13] until the author finally substitutes it with the historical person of "Jesus Christ," the "only begotten" (v.18).[14] Verse 18 then constitutes the climax of the prologue and the headline of the following narrative. Secondly, the λόγος-idea indirectly fights those proto-Gnostic ideas that are directly confronted in the first letter of John.[15]

---

[11] HARNACK, "Über das Verhältnis des Prologs," 194-208, 224.

[12] Ibid., 226-27.

[13] Ibid., 219.

[14] Ibid., 214-15, 224-25. Dodd explains similarly, "The Logos-doctrine is placed first, because, addressing a public nurtured in the higher religion of Hellenism, the writer wishes to offer the Logos-idea as the appropriate approach, for them, to the central purport of the Gospel, through which he may lead them to the historical actuality of the story, rooted as it is in Jewish tradition." DODD, *The Interpretation of the Fourth Gospel*, 296. Recently, Phillips also observes the progression from λόγος to Jesus. We read that "by the end of the Prologue, the characteristics and associations of λόγος are so bound up with Jesus that the word does not appear again in the Gospel in the same sense. . . . In the beginning, there is λόγος, but in the end there is only Jesus." PHILLIPS, *The Prologue*, 224. He regards the prologue as a "lower, more accessible threshold" than those of the Synoptics. Ibid., 15. While the polemic against the "Judeans" reflects a worsening "domestic dispute," the prologue's "evangelistic focus" was created for readers "who have a Hellenistic worldview." Ibid., 64, 71, 227. Contrary to Harnack, Phillips views the prologue not merely as a *transition* to the actual text of the Gospel but (with Genette, *Paratext*, 1997) as a *transaction* which helps "to get the book read properly" and to "encourage the reader to interpret those contents correctly." Ibid., 5. Despite his premise, Phillips misses to ask how the prologue influences the interpretation of the dispute with the Ἰουδαῖοι.

[15] HARNACK, "Über das Verhältnis des Prologs," 193 n. 1, 217, 223. Dodd explains similarly, "The Logos-doctrine is placed first, because, addressing a public nurtured in the higher religion of Hellenism, the writer wishes to offer the Logos-idea as the appropriate approach, for them, to the central purport of the Gospel, through which he may lead them to the historical actuality of the story, rooted as it is in Jewish tradition." DODD, *The Interpretation of the Fourth Gospel*, 296.

John A. T. Robinson thought of the order of the Johannine writings in this way: (1) The body of the Gospel, (2) the Epistles, (3) the Gospel's epilogue and prologue.[16] The main reason for disconnecting the prologue from the Gospel stems again from the observation that John uses λόγος as a title for Jesus only in 1:1 and that the Gospel uses key-terms in the expression "the word became flesh" in 1:14 differently.[17] On the other hand, the notion of the Son of Man who descends from heaven (3:13) does not appear in the prologue, just as the title "Christ, the Son of God" (20:31) is absent from the first eighteen verses.

Harnack and Robinson are certainly right when they observe the singularity of some titles and concepts in the prologue. What is indeed absent in later chapters is the mediatorial role of the λόγος for the creation of the world (1:3, 10b), λόγος as a title for Jesus (1:1, 14; see Rev 19:14; Wis 18:15), the statement of incarnation (1:14) and the word "grace" (χάρις only in 1:14, 16, 17). But a comparison with the prologues of the other Gospels shows that, at least according to ancient conventions of writing, the language of a book's opening does not have to match exactly the following narrative in order to serve the whole Gospel.[18] The infancy narrative in the Gospel of Luke alone contains over thirty hapax legomena, terms that are not used anywhere later in the book (or in the New Testament)![19] A closer look at *Christological titles* reveals the unique position of the Gospels' openings as well. For example, the title Ἰησοῦς

---

[16] ROBINSON, "The Relation of the Prologue," 120-29. He is followed by MILLER, *Salvation-History*, 4. See also BROWN, *The Gospel*, 1:i-xii, LXIX, CXXXII. Idem, *An Introduction*, 129. Michael Theobald concludes his monograph with a similar thesis: First, the body of Gospel was composed with a Son-of-man Christology. Members of the Johannine church misused this Christology for a dualistic view of Jesus according to which the son of Joseph was given the *pneuma* of Christ after his baptism (cf. conflict in 1 John). The prologue was then written as a polemic response which corrects the heresy by prefacing the Gospel with the prologue and its emphasis on the preexistence (1:1-5) and incarnation (1:14-18) of the logos. See THEOBALD, *Die Fleischwerdung*, 490-91.

[17] ROBINSON, "The Relation of the Prologue," 123.

[18] The following analysis was inspired by Hooker who observed the similarity between the prologues of Mark, John, Luke, and Matthew in general but without spelling out the details, as we do here. HOOKER, "The Johannine Prologue," 42-43, 51-52. Gibbs offers some intriguing insights that nevertheless do not overlap with our observations. GIBBS, "Mark 1, 1-15," 154-88.

[19] The terms are the following: ἐπειδήπερ (1:1), ἀνατάσσομαι (1:1), διήγησις (1:1), αὐτόπτης (1:2), ἱερατεύω (1:8), θυμιάω (1:9), σίκερα (1:15), διανεύω (1:22), περικρύβω (1:24), ὄνειδος (1:25), διαταράσσω (1:29), συγγενίς (1:36), γῆρας (1:36), ἀναφωνέω (1:42), περίοικος (1:58), ἐννεύω (1:62), πινακίδιον (1:63), περιοικέω (1:65), ἀνάδειξις (1:80), Αὔγουστος (2:1), Κυρήνιος (2:2), ἔγκυος (2:5), ἀγραυλέω (2:8), τρυγών (2:24), νοσσός (2:24), ἐθίζω (2:27), ἀγκάλη (2:28), Ἄννα (2:36), Φανουήλ (2:36), παρθενία (2:36), ἀνθωμολογέομαι (2:38), συνοδία (2:44), συγγενής (2:44).

Χριστός is completely absent from the gospels of Matthew and Mark except for their prologues (Matt 1:1, 18; Mark 1:1). Matthew also fills his opening narratives with titles for Jesus such as υἱός 'Αβραάμ (1:1), 'Εμμανουήλ (1:23), and ἡγούμενος (2:6, from Micah 5:2), designations that never return later in the text. On the other hand, the expression υἱὸς τοῦ θεοῦ does not occur in Matthew until 4:3. The genealogy in Matthew 1 "serves to establish Jesus' messianic prerequisites by demonstrating that both his ancestry and activity" fulfill major elements of God's promise to David in 2 Samuel 7.[20] Furthermore, Matthew 1-2 and 28 form a thematic inclusio as both the beginning and the end give particular attention to the Gentiles. Luke's beginning employs titles such as σωτήρ (2:11; see 2:30; 3:6), χριστὸς κύριος (2:11), χριστός κυρίου (2:26), and φῶς (2:32) that remain without parallel in the rest of the book. The first two chapters serve as a Gospel "in nuce" which conditions the reader to understand the subsequent narrative (chapters 3-24) along the Christological and eschatological lines outlined in the beginning.[21] Mark's opening fifteen verses provide the reader with keys to the identity of Jesus without which the reader would be as caught up in the "messianic secret" as the people, the disciples, and the religious leaders in the Gospel.[22] On the other hand, the title υἱὸς τοῦ ἀνθρώπου appears in the body of all four Gospels but not in their prologues (first in Matt 8:20; Mark 2:10; Luke 5:24; John 1:51). What we find then is that the Gospels open with Christological statements that are stronger and richer than any other single expression in the rest of their works. Even if we regard Robinson's *observation* as valid, his *conclusion* remains premature unless we are bold enough to postulate that the prologues of all four Gospels do not belong originally to the body of the text. Instead, we suggest that the differences between prologue and Gospel in form and content do not point to independent composition but lead to the question of why John and the Synoptics preface their narratives with ideas that reach Christological heights unsurpassed in the following chapters.

---

[20] NOVAKOVIC, *Messiah, the Healer of the Sick*, 11. See also NINEHAM, "The Genealogy in St. Matthew's Gospel," 433. WAETJEN, "The Genealogy as the Key," 205-30. Scott speaks of Matthew's opening as an "ideological orientation to the rest of the Gospel." SCOTT, "The Birth of the Reader," 83.

[21] See MÄRZ, "Die theologische Interpretation," 137-38 n. 15 and 16. He explains that the opening chapters draw an ideal picture concerning the reception of the Messiah, which serves as a measuring rod for everything that occurs later.

[22] In Mark 1:1-13 we find titles for Christ ("Jesus Christ, the Son of God," 1:1), prophecy fulfilled (Isa 40:3), John the Baptist's witness to the one coming after him (1:7) and God's voice during Jesus' baptism ("You are my Son," 1:11). HOOKER, "The Johannine Prologue," 42-43.

1.1.2. Summary

The view opposite to that of Harnack and Robinson emphasizes the continuity in language and concept between prologue and Gospel.[23] While there are five words which do not appear in the Gospel outside of the prologue,[24] a concordant analysis quickly reveals that many key terms are repeated in later chapters:

ζωή	1:4; 3:15, 16, 36; 4:14, 36; 5:24, 26, 29, 39, 40; 6:27, 33, 35, etc.
φῶς	1:4, 5, 7, 8, 8, 9; 3:19, 19, 20, 20, 21; 5:35; 8:12, 12; 9:5; 11:9, etc.
σκοτία	1:5; 6:17; 8:12; 12:35, 46; 20:1
μαρτυρία	1:7, 19; 3:11, 32, 33; 5:31, 32, 34, 36; 8:13, 14, 17; 19:35; 21:24
μαρτυρέω	1:7, 8, 15, 32, 34; 2:25; 3:11, 26, 28, 32; 4:39, 44; 5:31,32, etc.
πιστεύω	1:7, 12, 50; 2:11, 22, 23, 24; 3:12, 15, 16, 18, 36; 4:21, 39, 41, etc.
σάρξ	1:13, 14; 3:6; 6:51, 52, 53, 54, 55, 56, 63; 8:15; 17:2
ἀλήθεια	1:14, 17; 3:21; 4:23, 24; 5:33; 8:32, 40, 44, 45, 46; 14:6, 17; etc.
γεννάω	1:13; 3:3, 4, 5, 6, 7, 8; 8:41; 9:2, 19, 20, 32, 34; 16:21; 18:37
Μωϋσῆς	1:17, 45; 3:14; 5:45, 46; 6:32; 7:19, 22, 22, 23; 8:5; 9:28, 29
νόμος	1:17, 45; 7:19, 23, 49, 51; 8:5, 17; 10:34; 12:34; 15:25; 18:31; etc.

Beyond terms that are loaded with meaning, the prologue also displays the author's style with regard to less significant vocabulary.[25] With the key terms comes a continuity of concepts as Robinson himself has shown.[26]

---

[23] Hoskyns emphasizes the summarizing content of the prologue, "So the preface to the Fourth Gospel . . . is both an introduction and a conclusion of the whole work. In it the themes of the gospel are set forth and summed up." HOSKYNS, *The Fourth Gospel*, 140. Käsemann points to the Catholic scholar Belser (1903) for a similar view. KÄSEMANN, "Aufbau und Anliegen," 2:156.

[24] They are λόγος (1:1, 14), σκηνοῦν (1:14), χάρις (1:14, 16, 17), πλήρης (1:14) and ἐξηγεῖσθαι (1:18). See SCHULZ, *Komposition und Herkunft*, 11.

[25] Morgenthaler lists 73 terms that are of special preference, "Vorzugswörter," in the whole Gospel of John. MORGENTHALER, *Statistik*, 182. He discusses them on p. 52. Other words deserve to be added to this collection such as ἀληθινός, δόξα, μαρτυρέω, μαρτυρία, σημεῖον and φῶς. The following 21 of the Gospel's Vorzugswörter" are found in 1:1-18 (total of 252 words): ἀλήθεια, ἀλλά, γεννάω, γινώσκω, δίδωμι, εἰμί, ἐκ, ἐκεῖνος, ἔρχομαι, ζωή, Ἰησοῦς, ἵνα, κόσμος, λαμβάνω, ὁράω, ὅτι, οὐ, οὐδείς, πατήρ, περί, πιστεύω. There is a similar amount of 24 "Vorzugswörter" in 1:19-34, a text of comparable length (total 272 words). Thus, the prologue contains an average amount of typical Johannine language. Apart from matters of vocabulary, there are also typical characteristics of Johannine *style* in the prologue: ἵνα-epexegeticum (1:7, 8), ἐκεῖνος (1:8, 18), οὐκ . . . ἀλλ' ἵνα (1:8), σκοτία instead of σκότος (1:5), μαρτυρέω περί τινος (1:7, 8), πιστεύειν εἰς τινα (1:12c). See SCHULZ, *Komposition und Herkunft*, 11.

[26] So ROBINSON, "The Relation of the Prologue," 122. See also the table in KÖSTENBERGER, *John*, 586. A discussion of terminological and thematic links between prologue and Gospel can be found in HOFRICHTER, *Im Anfang war der „Johannesprolog"*, 83-105.

John the Baptist should be in the following list since he is also mentioned later (1:19-34; 3:22-36; 10:40-42).

	Prologue	Gospel
The pre-existence of the Logos or Son	1.1f.	17.5
In him was life	1.4	5.26
Life is light	1.4	8.12
Light rejected by darkness	1.5	3.19
Yet not quenched by it	1.5	12.35
Light coming into the world	1.9	3.19; 12.46
Christ not received by his own	1.11	4.44
Being born of God and not of flesh	1.13	3.6; 8.41f.
Seeing his glory	1.14	12.41
The only begotten Son	1.14, 18	3.16
Truth in Jesus Christ	1.17	14.6
No one has seen God, except the one who comes from God's side	1.18	6.46

Besides key terms and concepts, at least five themes of the prologue are repeated throughout the Gospel:[27] First, the origin of Jesus, the logos, as a pre-existent being with God (1:1-4) finds parallels, for example, in statements where Jesus claims to come from and go to the one who had sent him (7:16, 17, 34) and in the language of descend-ascend (3:13, 31; 6:62; 8:14; cf. 13:3; 16:28; 17:4-5). Second, Jesus' role as the revealer of God (image of "light," logos "dwelling") reappears in confessions of Jesus as the "light of the world" (8:12; 9:5; 11:9; 12:46) and as the one who has seen God and can therefore witness (μαρτυρέω) authoritatively about the truth (18:37) of God (3:32; 5:31; cf. 5:37; 6:46; 8:38), about himself (5:31; 8:13, 14, 18), and about the world whose deeds are evil (7:7). Third, the two responses to the λόγος (negative: 1:10b, 11b and positive: 1:12-13, 14c) accompany the reader in the discourses (3:15-18, 32-33, 36; 5:24; 6:40; 11:26; 16:2; 20:31) as well as in the narratives (1:35-49; 3:32-33; 4:39-42; 9:22; 12:42). Fourth, Jesus is described in relationship to other significant figures such as John the Baptist (1:6-8, 15, 19-23, 3:23-36) and Moses (1:17; 3:14; 5:45-47; 6:32; etc.).[28] Finally, while the proposition about the incarnation (1:14) is absent in later chapters, the (anti-docetic) emphasis of Jesus' humanity is readily available in statements that show him to have "flesh" (see σάρξ in 6:51, 52, 53, 54, 55, 56, 63), to be tired

---

[27] See CARTER, "The Prologue," 37-40. Carter mentions the first four themes. The fifth one is added here.

[28] See also Jesus' relationship to Jacob (4:12) and to Abraham (8:58).

(4:6), troubled (11:33, 38), weeping (11:38), fearful (13:21), thirsty (19:28) and bleeding (19:34).[29] Apart from the title υἱὸς [τοῦ] ἀνθρώπου, many people call Jesus ἄνθρωπος many times which implies his recognizable earthly existence.[30] The five themes further establish that "the Prologue's content is tightly interwoven with the central focus and claims of the gospel concerning Jesus, the revealer of God."[31]

1.1.3. Hermeneutical key

Many scholars maintain that the function of the prologue is not sufficiently understood when grasped merely as an introduction or a summary of what follows. Rather, they view both elements of continuity and discontinuity with the following text as a preparation on how to understand the Gospel as a whole,[32] maybe formally similarly to the opening in Greek tragedies.[33]

---

[29] In a recent study about Jesus' emotions in the Fourth Gospel, Voorwinde observes that "of the fifty-nine specific references to the emotions of Jesus in the canonical Gospels no less than twenty-eight are found in the Gospel of John." VOORWINDE, *Jesus' Emotions in the Fourth Gospel*, 3. See his Appendix 5 for a comprehensive list of Jesus' emotions. Reinhartz holds that the incarnation "is implied in Johannine descriptions of Jesus as the bread of life (6:48) and the true light (1:9; cf. 8:12), which has descended from heaven (6:51) and come into the world (1:9). The incarnation would seem to be the corollary of the Father's decision to send his Son into the world." REINHARTZ, *The Word in the World*, 81.

[30] Jesus is called ἄνθρωπος by the Samaritan woman (4:29), the Jews (5:12; 10:33), Jesus himself (8:40), the high priests and Pharisees (9:16; 11:47, 50; 18:14), the maid (18:17), and Pilate (18:29; 19:5).

[31] CARTER, "The Prologue," 42. Hooker would add at least a sixth topic. She maintains that the "theme of the λόγος . . . is recognizable in the disputes about the activity of Jesus interpreted as that of God himself (v. 17f.; x. 30-9)." HOOKER, "The Johannine Prologue," 45-46. Bultmann defends already against Harnack that "the 'Logos doctrine' of the prologue gives expression to the idea of revelation which dominates the whole Gospel." BULTMANN, *The Gospel of John*, 13 n. 1. Likewise, Gundry attempts to show "that a Christology of the Word pervades the whole of John's Gospel much more than has been recognized before." GUNDRY, "How the Word in John's Prologue," 325.

[32] Schnelle explains that the prologue "das Verständnis des Evangeliums vorbereitet und zugleich wesentlich bestimmt." SCHNELLE, *Antidoketische Christologie*, 232. Gibbs summarizes with regard to the prologues of all four Gospels that, among others, they provide "the setting or frame of reference in terms of which the whole of each gospel is to be understood." GIBBS, "Mark 1, 1-15," 154. Phillips calls the beginning of a text a 'threshold' at which the reader's impressions of the text are "crucial for what follows, since they will set the tone in which the reader will view the rest of the narrative." PHILLIPS, *The Prologue*, 3.

[33] The prologue reminds Hooker of "some Greek plays." HOOKER, "The Johannine Prologue," 51. Harris considers John 1:1-18 as "functioning like the prologue to a religious drama, with the foreannouncing of the past events, the present situation and the final outcome as being within the preordained will of God, and with the introduction in

Our comparison of the prologues of Matthew, Mark, Luke and John certainly supports such a view. Depending on the decision about what constitutes the climax in the prologue, some point to *specific* statements as lenses through which the narrative has to be read. If the train of thought culminates in 1:14, then the reader focuses on the Gospel's Christology.[34] Dodd explains that "The Word became flesh, and we beheld His glory"

> is written (by implication) over each of the episodes of which the story is composed. . . . When he relates the healing of the blind or the feeding of the hungry multitude, still more when he relates the passion, death and resurrection of Christ, he wishes us to overhear the implication: in this *action* and in *that* it was the eternal λόγος that became flesh.[35]

If 1:12b constitutes the high point of the prologue, then the reader might be prepared for an ecclesiological thesis in which the church as "the children of God" has replaced Israel as the elected body of God's favor.[36] But a decision between either Christology or ecclesiology seems arbitrary considering the presence of both themes in the Gospel and their theological interdependence. Instead, Hooker understands the whole prologue as the key that enables the reader to answer the question of Jesus' origin, which "is obscure to many of the main actors in the drama."[37] While the signs and discourses convince few and leave "men bewildered instead of enlightened,"[38] it is the privileged knowledge about the prologue's titles and descriptions that make the following chapters comprehensible. The

---

advance of principal figures as chief characters." HARRIS, *Prologue and Gospel*, 25. She does not think of exact parallels to the genre of Greek drama but only "that the evangelist could be writing with a convention of this kind somewhere in the background." Ibid., 38. Brant calls attention to the resemblance between the prologue of John's Gospel and those of Euripides in dramas such as *Hecubas*, *Iphignia among the Taurians*, *Bacchae*, and *Heracles*. BRANT, *Dialogue and Drama*, 17-19. PHILLIPS, *The Prologue*, 7, 223. See also our comments to Diefenbach in chapter 1.

[34] Thyen regards the prologue in general and 1:14 in particular as an instruction to the reader about how to read the whole Gospel, "Denn wie das Vorzeichen vor der Klammer die Wertigkeit des Ganzen bestimmt, so scheint mir der Prolog die Anweisung an den Leser zu enthalten, wie das ganze Evangelium gelesen und verstanden sein will." THYEN, "Aus der Literatur," 223.

[35] DODD, "The Prologue," 9, 10. Similarly, Reinhartz refers back to the prologue in order to identify the "sheepfold" in 10:1, 16. REINHARTZ, *The Word in the World*, 76.

[36] CULPEPPER, "The Pivot," 2.

[37] HOOKER, "The Johannine Prologue," 45.

[38] Ibid., 50. Brant elucidates that without the prologue, "the audience of the gospel would enter the action without orientation and be left to respond to Jesus' signs and assertions with the same bewilderment shown by characters within the gospel," and refers to Hooker in n. 9. BRANT, *Dialogue and Drama*, 18. See also REINHARTZ, *The Word in the World*, 45. PHILLIPS, *The Prologue*, 7.

narrator briefly comments on the first miracle in Cana that Jesus "manifested His glory" (δόξαν, 2:11). This note would be unintelligible without knowing since 1:14 about Jesus' preexistent "glory" as the λόγος and the μονογενής παρὰ πατρός.[39] While sympathizing with Nicodemus' confusion (3:4), the reader has known since 1:13 that the verb "to be born" does not refer to a physical experience but to a spiritual one.[40] When the Jews hear about Jesus healing the invalid on a Sabbath (5:1-15), they think of him as a mere miracle-worker who violates the law and who falsely claims equality with God by calling him "my Father" (5:17-18). But the reader has known since 1:1 that Jesus is not simply a healer, but θεός himself.[41] While the Jews are outraged that Jesus denies the importance of their physical descent from Abraham (8:39-47), the reader is aware since reading 1:11-13 that spiritual kinship with God does not depend on blood-relations or human will.[42] Thus the prologue reveals the mystery of Jesus' origin and of his mission;[43] it inaugurates the reader into an omniscient perspective and prepares him to stand above the confusion that puzzles the Jews and the disciples alike.

If the prologue functions as a necessary preparation for the right understanding of the Gospel itself, then it also makes a crucial contribution

---

[39] See FISCHER, "Ueber den Ausdruck," 127.

[40] Meeks explains that "the dialogue [with Nicodemus] is opaque" and requires "special prior information" in order to be understood. MEEKS, "Man From Heaven," 57.

[41] Nicklas argues that the train of thought in John 5 only makes sense on the basis of Christological statements such as those in the prologue. Since the prologue's Christology is simply declared without any reasons given in support of it, Nicklas concludes against Stephen Motyer that the Gospel does not try to evangelize Jews, but wants to edify Christians. NICKLAS, *Ablösung und Verstrickung*, 305. Similarly, Schnackenburg maintained forty years earlier against van Unnik and J. A. T. Robinson that the Gospel was written for believers because it would hardly be intelligible for outsiders. SCHNACKENBURG, "Die Messiasfrage im Johannesevangelium," 262. It is interesting in this regard when Harris points out that the reference to the γραφαί as support for Jesus' claims (5:39) is "by no means clear." HARRIS, *Prologue and Gospel*, 81. Bonney explains, "Having this knowledge [of the prologue], the reader will find him or herself in a position to comprehend Jesus' actions that is not shared by the characters Jesus encounters throughout the narrative. . . . The reader knows that when Jesus speaks, he is not merely a king (1:49) or potential messiah (4:29). . . . He is the incarnate *logos*. When the characters in the gospel, both Jesus' opponents and his disciples, do not understand Jesus' references to his place of origin (3:12-14; 6:38-42; 7:35-36; 8:14, 21-22; 14:2-5), the reader does." BONNEY, *Caused to Believe*, 50. See also HAKOLA, *Identity Matters*, 126.

[42] See HOOKER, "The Johannine Prologue," 47. GRÄSSER, "Die Antijüdische Polemik," 82.

[43] Caron says it this way: "Quel que soit le rôle ou la fonction que l'on attribue au Prologue, celui-ci dévoile au lecteur le mystère profond de l'identité et de la mission de Jésus Christ." CARON, *Qui sont les Juifs*, 58. He refers to Hooker's article in footnote 5.

to the interpretation of the Ἰουδαῖοι. For it is then highly significant that the author does not begin his account with a particular conflict between Jesus and the Jews, but between "the word" and "the world." Just as knowledge about Jesus' pre-existence shapes the reader's perception of the Christological disputes, so the universal opening of the Gospel, and especially the extension of the conflict in 1:10 to all of humanity, prohibits the reader from understanding the antagonism in the narrative at a local and ethnic level. Instead, from the beginning in 1:19 the author crafts the Jews not only as a specific ethnic-religious entity, but as part of a whole, as one concretization of that which happens everywhere among all people.[44] Right from the start, the reader knows that disbelief is a universal phenomenon and not the stigma of one particular group.[45]

We conclude that the prologue does not serve merely as an opening or as a summary but, in the words of Reinhartz, "as *the reader's guide* to the cosmological tale as it comes to expression throughout the body of the gospel narrative."[46] This significance of the opening indicates the importance of a sequential reading that follows the linear development of the text. The narrator indicates such a need at other places as well. The discernible structuring of the Gospel into prologue (1:1-18, 19-51), body of the text, and epilogue (chap. 21), and the two divisions, the "book of signs" (chaps. 1-12) and the "book of glory" (chaps. 13-21), indicate that the author expects the reader to follow this sequence.[47] Within part one, the plot develops from a positive notion of Jesus as the Savior of the world

---

[44] We agree thus that, under the influence of the prologue, the occurrence of Ἰουδαῖοι in 1:19 cannot retain a neutral or positive connotation. So already FISCHER, "Ueber den Ausdruck," 108. Güting concedes the negative meaning for "the Jews" in 1:19 when read after the prologue, but he rejects it on literary-critical grounds. GÜTING, "Kritik an den Judäern," 178.

[45] We agree with Schnelle when he explains, "Die Ablehnung der Offenbarung ist ja keineswegs auf die *Ioudaioi* begrenzt, wie bereits der Prolog deutlich zeigt: 'Er war in der Welt, und die Welt ist durch ihn geworden, aber die Welt erkannte ihn nicht' (Joh 1,10). Der Unglaube ist wie der Glaube ein universales Phänomen und nicht auf bestimmte Menschengruppen zu beschränken." SCHNELLE, "Die Juden im Johannesevangelium," 224. Harris understands similarly, "The background indicated is one of cosmic conflict which embraces all humankind. The results of appropriating the heavenly gifts are universal, but since they originate from God who is the God of the Jews, the conflict has to be set out in terms which allow for the development of the theme, not only of the ignorance and culpability of humankind in general, but also of the Jews who worship him." HARRIS, *Prologue and Gospel*, 16. Salier expresses as well, "While the detail of the story that follows in the body of the Gospel is located very much in the specific story of the encounter of Jesus with his people, the universal implications are never far away as a result of this expansive opening." SALIER, *The Rhetorical Impact*, 13, also 46.

[46] REINHARTZ, *The Word in the World*, 16 (italics added).

[47] For a richer description of the Gospel's plot see CULPEPPER, *Anatomy*, 89-97.

(chaps. 1-4) to his rejection by the world (chaps. 5-10), and within the latter from "rising opposition" (chaps. 5-7) to "radical confrontation" (chaps. 8-10).[48] Only a sequential reading is able to catch the dramatic element of growing intensity. Furthermore, John 4:54 speaks of "the second sign" and thus presupposes that the reader noticed the "first sign" in 2:1-11. Similarly, 21:14 mentions the "third time" that Jesus appeared to his disciples after he raised from the dead, expecting that the reader took notice of the first two appearances in 20:19 and 20:26. Jesus refers to the Jews' inquiry of John the Baptist in 5:33 which was reported before in 1:19. Jesus' healing on a Sabbath in chapter 5 is presupposed and alluded to in the dispute of chapter 7 (cf. 7:23). Jesus announces his death (in 13:18) *before* it happens (in chap. 19) so that the prediction can strengthen the disciples' faith *after* the fulfillment (13:19; 14:29). There are other instances of prophecy and fulfillment within the Gospel that further underline the importance of a linear movement through the text.[49] The analepsis in 7:50 and 19:39, pointing back to Nicodemus' "earlier" (τὸ πρῶτον) meeting with Jesus in John 3, only makes sense when the Gospel is read progressively. A parenthetical remark about the beloved disciple in 21:20 further identifies him as "the one who had leaned back against Jesus at the supper and had said, 'Lord, who is going to betray you'," an occurrence described earlier in 13:24-25. These and other explicit hints reveal a sequential reading of the story as an intentional and *necessary* requirement for a proper understanding of the text. We may thus formulate a rule for responsible reading with a paraphrase from John 10:8-10: 'He who does not enter the Gospel through the prologue but by some other way is a robber who kills context and steals meaning.'[50]

---

[48] Carson gives these headlines to chaps 5-10 in his commentary. CARSON, *The Gospel* (1991).

[49] Caiaphas' prophecy of Jesus' death in 11:49-52 is referred to later in the past tense (18:14). Peter's denial is announced in 13:38 and fulfilled in 18:15-18, 25-26 without any explicit reference back to 13:38. The narrator interprets Jesus' arrest and the disciples's freedom in 18:8 as a fulfillment of Jesus' words in 6:39 ("of all that He has given Me I lose nothing").

[50] Salier advises similarly, "While a narrative can be read and re-read in both part and whole, it is suggested that following the linear development of the Gospel narrative is a method that is faithful to the narrative style of the presentation." SALIER, *The Rhetorical Impact*, 15. Reinhartz underlines the importance of a sequential reading when she explains that the "narrative sequence of the gospel, that is, the order in which ideas, events, and metaphors are presented, is important for its interpretation and will be one of the *principal elements* of the narrative used by readers to construct coherent meaning . ." REINHARTZ, *The Word in the World*, 12 (italics added). She qualifies her statement with the idea of a "holistic reading" in which the end of the gospel (20:31) prompts a rereading and re-evaluation of the gospel. Ibid., 12-13. While there may be practical value in doing so, her point is not established with reference to 20:31 (or Mark 16:1-9),

1.2. The Function of the Farewell Discourse for the Passion Narrative

All too often, the interpretation of the Gospel is consumed with excessive attention to exegetical details at the cost of macro-structural observations. Neglecting to discuss the shift between the dominance of the Ἰουδαῖοι in John 1-12 and of κόσμος in John 13-17 is but one example of that.[51] If it is noticed, then mostly without due discussion of its significance. Furthermore, the farewell discourse has often been analyzed as a collection of speeches without considering its connection to and importance for the understanding of the passion narrative.[52] We will address both matters in the following.

1.2.1. The literary gate into the passion account

Despite some retrospective connections between John 13-17 and 1-12,[53] the farewell discourse mainly looks forward to future events, of which some take place just after Jesus finishes his prayer in chapter 17.[54] With regard to the narrated time, some predictions are fulfilled on the same day, such as Judas' betrayal (18:2-3) and Peter's denial (18:15-18, 25-27). Then, "early" (πρωΐ, 18:28) on the "day of preparation for the Passover" (19:14, 31, 42), Jesus is led to Pilate for his trial and crucifixion. Only

---

since Christology and concepts of the end are readily available already at the Gospel's beginning ("Christ" in 1:41, "Son of God" in 1:34, 49; see 2:11 for signs leading to faith).

[51] Beasley-Murray, for example, does not mention the phenomenon among his six points given in the "Introductory Note" to the farewell discourse. BEASLEY-MURRAY, *John*, 222-27.

[52] O'Day's observation deserves full attention, "More than any other discourse block in the gospel, the farewell discourse has been the subject of sustained literary investigation. Jesus' words to his disciples grow so directly out of the setting in which the characters find themselves that it is impossible to interpret the events leading up to Jesus' arrest without giving a central place to the farewell discourse. Yet even here, interpreters do not often pull back to ask larger questions about the discourse – for example, what is the effect of this large block of discourse on the unfolding of the gospel narrative?" O'DAY, "'I have said these things to you . . .'," 145-46. Ashton is one of the few who pull back to ask a larger question such as, "Why in particular, when they [the Jews] play such an important part in the Passion narrative, does Jesus not name them at all in his urgent warnings to his disciples the previous evening? [chaps. 13-17]." ASHTON, "The Identity," 60.

[53] See the origin of Jesus (1:1-14; 13:3; 16:28), Jesus' relationship with the world (1:10-11; 15:18), death and departure (3:13; 6:62; 7:33-34; 13:33; 14:19), individual disciples (Judas: 6:70-71; 13:2; Simon Peter 1:40; 13:6-9; Philip 1:43; 14:8; Thomas: 11:16; 14:5), the sending of the Spirit (1:32-33; 7:37-39; 14:16-23; 16:7); the future destiny of the disciples (9:22, 34-35; 12:42; cf. 16:2). See NEUGEBAUER, *Die eschatologischen Aussagen*, 100-08.

[54] See our table of content for the farewell discourse in chapter 3 (1.2).

three days after the speech, on Sunday, the "first day of the week" (20:1), Jesus rises from the dead, the disciples see him again (John 20-21) as announced before (16:19) and their grief turns into joy (16:20; 20:20).

The connection between John 13-17 and 18-21 as one of prediction and partial fulfillment indicates the purpose of the farewell discourse. It prepares the reader for the passion narrative and announces the events ahead of time, "that when it comes to pass, you may believe" (14:29; cf. 13:19).[55] But besides the point of prophecy fulfilled as another "sign" of Jesus' divine origin and therefore as a reason to believe, the farewell discourse elevates the reader to a divine perspective which serves as a commentary of the following human events. Thus it controls the reader's point of view in at least four ways: (A) The farewell discourse interprets the passion *christocentrically* and *theocentrically*. Jesus goes into the trial and crucifixion as someone who has "authority over all mankind" (17:2; 13:3). He is not pulled out of his life violently but he voluntarily leaves the world and goes back to his Father (13:1; 16:28). While it looks as if soldiers abruptly take his life, God "sent" his son (13:20; 14:24; 15:21; already as early as 4:34) and commanded him to die a death (14:31) that even glorifies his Son (13:31-32; 17:1, 5).[56] All of the following events are under sovereign control even to such an extent that Jesus is able to foreknow and predict the coming of the paraclete after his death, resurrection, and ascension (14:16, 26; 15:26; 16:7)![57] (B) The farewell discourse interprets the passion and the resurrection *eschatologically*. We find language such as Jesus' "going away" and "coming back" that refers to his death and resurrection (14:18-23), to his parousia (13:31-14:5), or to both events at the same time: in 16:16 we read, "A little while, and you will no longer behold me; and again a little while, and you will see

---

[55] In his recent dissertation Weidemann sees in 14:29 a statement that has "programmatischen Charakter für den gesamten zweiten Hauptteil des vierten Evangeliums." WEIDEMANN, *Der Tod Jesu*, 514. The purpose of prediction indicates that the first farewell discourse as a whole functions as a hermeneutical key to John 18-20. For a summary, see 515-26.

[56] Such a view of Jesus' death is prepared already in the first part of the Gospel. See only 3:13-15; 10:17-18; 11:49-50 (and 18:14). And, as many have observed, literally from the beginning to the end the passion account itself contains many apparent clues to the theocentric nature of the event. See our discussion in chapter 3, p. 53.

[57] Eusebius (*Hist. Eccl.* 1.13.15) gives the report about the disciple Thaddeus who went to the king of Edessa. Hearing about the crucifixion of Jesus, the king said that he "wished to take an army and destroy those Jews who crucified him, had I not been deterred from it by reason of the dominion of the Romans." In his response, Thaddeus employs Johannine language and points away from the Jewish antagonists to the theocentric nature of Christ's passion: "Our Lord has fulfilled the will of his Father [e.g., John 4:34; 5:30; 6:39], and having fulfilled it has been taken up to his Father."

(ὄψεσθε) me." The reference to Easter is obvious when we explain the "little while" as the time between the words spoken on Thursday and the resurrection on Sunday. The word ὁράω reappears in the Easter appearances (20:18, 20, 25, 29), and the invitation to pray "in my name" (16:23-24) would be superfluous if it referred to the time after the parousia.[58] But Neugebauer has shown also that the terminology of μικρόν, θεωρεῖν, ἐν ἐκείνῃ τῇ ἡμέρᾳ (v. 23), etc. belongs to the language of parousia.[59] Furthermore, the time of not seeing Jesus is characterized as a time of weeping, lamenting, and grieving (16:20) that will give room to rejoicing over seeing him (16:20). Recognizing the significance of these words for readers who are waiting for Jesus' return, and who are suffering until then, gives credit to the text-pragmatic relevance of the farewell discourse as an address to the second, third and all following generations of believers (see 17:20).[60] Thus, 16:16-24 implies a *double entendre* which aids the reader to understand the disciples' not seeing now and seeing later, and their grieving and rejoicing during Jesus' passion and resurrection, as a paradigmatic experience that applies to them as well as to the first believers.[61] As the disciples are sad because Jesus goes away (16:22),[62] so the readers grieve over Jesus' absence. And as the disciples rejoiced to see the resurrected Lord (20:20), so the readers will rejoice over the return of

---

[58] See DETTWILER, *Die Gegenwart des Erhöhten*, 242.

[59] See Neugebauer's semantic analysis of verbs of seeing (θεωρεῖν, ὁρᾶν, οὐκέτι θεωρεῖν / ὁρᾶν, ἐμφανίζειν), verbs of changing places (ὑπάγειν, πορεύεσθαι, μεταβαίνειν, ἀπέρχεσθαι, ἐξέρχεσθαι, ἔρχεσθαι, ἀφιέναι, ἀκολουθεῖν, παραλαμβάνειν, ἑτοιμάζειν), indications of time (ἐκείνη ἡ ἡμέρα, μικρόν), and expressions of affliction (θλῖψις, λύπη / λυπεῖσθαι). NEUGEBAUER, *Die eschatologischen Aussagen*, 123-34. The problem is that Neugebauer applies the results of his semantic analysis *mechanically* and not *contextually*. Thus he ignores the arguments that point to the Easter-event and interprets 16:16-28 exclusively in terms of the parousia. Schnackenburg makes the opposite mistake when he denies the perspective of the parousia in 16:16. He offers a third interpretation in which 16:16 addresses the church after Easter for whom the promise of seeing Jesus is already fulfilled here and now. SCHNACKENBURG, *Das Johannesevangelium*, 3:175-76. See also his comments to 14:19 on p. 90.

[60] See SCHNELLE, "Ein neuer Blick," 37. Onuki summarizes the evidence by saying with Bultmann that a "'Kombination der auf Ostern und auf die Parusie bezüglichen Terminologie' vorliegt und das Wiedersehen Jesu an Ostern mit seiner Parusie-erscheinung zusammengeschaut wird." ONUKI, *Gemeinde und Welt*, 155, see 152-62. Frey also refers the "not-seeing" to the time of the present readers and the "seeing" to the parousia. FREY, *Die johanneische Eschatologie. Band III*, 207-209.

[61] Dettwiler interprets thus: "Die Ostererfahrung der ersten Jünger wird in dem Sinn enthistorisiert und auf eine Ebene des Theologisch-Grundsätzlichen transponiert, als sie eine *paradigmatische* Erfahrung ist. Was den ersten Jüngern damals zuteil wurde – die Erfahrung des 'Sehens' Jesu -, wird in der gleichen Qualität auch der nachösterlichen joh Gemeinde zuteil." DETTWILER, *Die Gegenwart des Erhöhten*, 242.

[62] Maybe also as Mary wept over the empty tomb (20:11, 13, 15)?

their king. (C) The farewell discourse interprets the passion *universally*. Macrostructurally speaking, the point of view in the Gospel moves from a focus on the world in the prologue (1:1-18) to that of a single nation in the first half of the Gospel (chaps. 2-12), back to a universal perspective in the farewell discourse (chaps. 13-17), and finally again to one people group in the passion narrative (chaps. 18-19).[63] After Jesus experiences hostility in response to his public ministry, he speaks prophetically of rejection by the world in his final address before his passion.[64] As the opening of the Gospel's second part (chaps. 13-20) in which Jesus returns to the Father (cf. 13:1), the chapters 13-17 constitute the literary gate through which the reader enters the passion account. While the narrative about arrest, trial and crucifixion of the Messiah has, by nature of recalling history, a focus on the actual Jewish antagonists,[65] the preceding speech presents the opposition entirely from a universal perspective, as we noticed already above. Not only does the scope of hostility assume worldwide extension, but the disciples are proleptically included into the experience of violent rejection as well (15:18-20; 17:14). By these means the author prepares the reader structurally and conceptually to perceive the Jewish opposition in chapters 18-19 as only one expression of a global violence, and Jesus' story as one of a master whose servants will suffer the same, such as the readers themselves. (D) But the Gospel abstracts even further. The farewell discourse interprets the passion of Christ not just universally but *diabolically*.[66] Judgment is upon this world (12:31) but also on the "ruler of this world" who will be cast out (12:31; 16:11). While the character of Judas has been presented as the special instrument of the devil (see διάβολος in 6:70; 13:2), the "world" as the object of diabolical rule includes the Jews and Pilate as well. There is only an *apparent* dualism between the theocentric and the diabolical aspect of the passion for Jesus insists that the devil "has nothing in me" (14:30).

1.2.2. Pilate as an agent of the world

The responsibility of Pilate and the soldiers in the crucifixion of Jesus within the passion account itself (19:1-3) displays in seminal form that the hostile "world" consists of Jews *and Gentiles*.[67] As previous individuals

---

[63] See the table "Compositional Parallelism (Macrostructure)" on p. 77.

[64] So ASHTON, "The Identity," 66.

[65] The term Ἰουδαῖος occurs 20x in chaps. 18-19, κόσμος only 4x in chap.18 and not at all in chaps. 19-20.

[66] So rightly GRELOT, *Les Juifs*, 185. Weidemann speaks of the "satanologische" preparation of Jesus' passion and resurrection. See WEIDEMANN, *Der Tod Jesu*, 517.

[67] In the Synoptic Gospels Jesus recognizes Pilate and the Roman soldiers explicitly as representatives of the Gentiles when he predicts about being delivered "to the Gentiles

such as Nicodemus and the Samaritan woman represent larger groups, so
Pilate personifies the Roman authority[68] and as such also the non-Jewish
world.[69] Since his question, "What is truth?" (18:38) demonstrates Pilate's

---

(τοῖς ἔθνεσιν)" in order to be mocked, scourged, and crucified (Matt 20:19; cf. Mark
10:33; Luke 18:32). The Fourth Gospel presents individuals in more subtle ways as
representatives of larger groups or people of certain character and attitude. See Collins'
discussion of "Representative Figures" in COLLINS, *These Things Have Been Written*, 1-
45. Also KOESTER, *Symbolism in the Fourth Gospel*, 33-77.

[68] Windisch spoke in his essay from 1923 already about Pilate as "the representative
of the Emperor" and that "Pilate and Christ are representatives of two kingdoms and two
worlds." The author of the Fourth Gospel thus expressed the "Christian antithesis, World
Empire-Kingdom of God, World-ruler-Christ." WINDISCH, "John's Narrative Style," 54.
Schnackenburg speaks of Pilate first as the "Vertreter des römischen Staates" and then as
the "Vertreter irdischer Macht." SCHNACKENBURG, *Das Johannesevangelium*, 3:285, 286.
See also TILBORG, *Reading John*, 52. BARTON, "Christian Community," 294. Keener,
The Gospel of John, 2:1111.

[69] Granskou illustrates that it "is not the Jews alone who are in the darkness" by
pointing, among others, to Pilate who "is a type of witness, but he is not a believer, and
the Roman structure is seen as subservient to the highest authority connections through
Jesus. So Judaism is not set in a rigid darkness-light dichotomy. . . . The fourth
evangelist's theological and symbolic concerns see Jesus totally isolated from everyone
but the Father. He does not place the Jews over against other religious groups; rather,
everything is set against the singular Jesus." GRANSKOU, "Anti-Judaism," 209.
Rensberger understands Pilate as "an agent of 'the world'" who is "undeniably hostile to
'the Jews,' but that does not make him friendly to Jesus, for whose innocence he is not
really concerned. Rather, his aim is to humiliate 'the Jews' and to ridicule their national
hopes by means of Jesus." RENSBERGER, *Johannine Faith*, 92. Markus Barth identifies
Pilate and his soldiers as representatives of "alle Nicht-Juden." BARTH, "Die Juden," 67.
Weidemann explains that Pilate is not just an individual Gentile but a representative of
the pagan Roman empire. As such he demonstrates "daß der Heide wie die 'Juden' zum
κόσμος gehören, daß beide Jesus *gegenüberstehen* und beide ihr *Urteil* empfangen."
WEIDEMANN, *Der Tod Jesu*, 322, also 323, 356. So also Söding who comments "daß die
Entwicklung des ganzen Evangeliums auf den Prozeß zuläuft, den der Vertreter des
römischen Imperiums Jesus macht und den Jesus in Wahrheit dem Vertreter des
römischen Imperiums und damit dem gesamten Kosmos macht." SÖDING, "Die Macht der
Wahrheit," 47, 44. Also SÖDING, "'Was kann aus Nazareth schon Gutes kommen?'," 37.
Phillips calls Pilate "the key Romano-Hellenistic character in the Gospel." PHILLIPS, *The
Prologue*, 208. Here Bultmann makes a distinction that misses the point. He notices on
the one side how Pilate is part of "the world" that is judged by Jesus (18:37; cf. 9:39;
3:19). BULTMANN, *The Gospel of John*, 655. But on the other side the Roman governor
"by no means represents the world in the same way as the Jews and their ruler" whose
"father is the devil, and who therefore are bent on murder and lying (8.44)." Ibid., 647,
656. Bultmann defends his distinction against von Campenhausen who regards the
government, represented by Pilate, as belonging to the world. Ibid., 663 n. 6. Beside the
point that Jesus does *not* call the devil "the father of *the Jews*" but mentions him
elsewhere three times as the "ruler of *the world*" (12:31; 14:30; 16:11; see Matt 4:8-9)

inability "to hear Jesus with understanding and belief and his failure to recognize the truth, Pilate is not of God (see 8:47) and so, like 'the Jews,' he is part of the unbelieving world which rejects Jesus."[70] The Messiah proclaims his mission before Pilate by saying, "I came into the *world*, to testify the truth" (18:37), but Pilate reduces him to the "king of *the Jews*" (18:39), a mere "man" (19:5), thus decreasing the claim while later exaggerating his own power (19:10) before the one who has "authority over all mankind" (ἐξουσίαν πάσης σαρκός, 17:2; 13:2).[71] Therefore, similar to the Jews, the Roman prefect misses seeing and understanding the truth (cf. 14:6), and submitting to the ruling power of the one send by God. Pilate orders the scourging (19:1) and crucifixion of Jesus (19:16), and his soldiers ridicule and wound him with blows and a crown of thorns (19:2) before they crucify him (19:23).[72] Although Jesus tells Pilate that Judas has "greater sin" because of his betrayal (μείζονα ἁμαρτίαν, 19:11),[73] the

---

the usage of the term κόσμος in the Gospel intentionally *blurs* ethnic or racial distinctions and unifies humanity into the same kind of opposition.

[70] BOND, *Pontius Pilate*, 179. Schnackenburg comments that in Pilate's response we find "das gleiche Phänomen wie bei den Juden in Kap. 8, die Jesu Sprache nicht verstehen (8,43). Auch er gehört nicht zu den Menschen, die 'aus der Wahrheit' sind." SCHNACKENBURG, *Das Johannesevangelium*, 3:288, 286. Dunn explains, "Loyalty to Caesar can become an excuse for evading higher obligation to the truth (Jn. 18:38; 19:12-16). Whoever limits his motives and aims to friendship with Caesar shuts himself off from an answer to the question, 'What is truth?' Whoever affirms loyalty only to Caesar is thereby self-condemned (cf. Jn. 16:8-11)." DUNN, "Καῖσαρ," 270.

[71] Weidemann perceives that with the title "King of the Jews" (18:33), Pilate affirms Jesus' kingship (however understood) but wrongly emphasizes its particularity to the exclusion of himself and the Romans. "Pilatus hat also recht, wenn er Jesus als βασιλεύς bezeichnet, aber er irrt, wenn er Jesus als ὁ βασιλεὺς τῶν Ἰουδαίων anspricht, in dem Sinne, dass er als Heide mit dem 'Judenkönig' nichts zu tun hat." WEIDEMANN, *Der Tod Jesu*, 333, also 330.

[72] Because of the use of "the world" in the dialogue with Pilate in 18:31-37, Tilborg concludes that "Jesus' kingship has consequences for the whole of the cosmos. Jesus who as king of the Jews has been rejected by the *cosmos of the Ioudaioi*, posits his kingship before *the cosmos of Pilate*." TILBORG, *Reading John*, 218 (italics his).

[73] For several reasons it seems more likely that Jesus refers the expression "he who delivered me" (19:11) to Judas and not to the Jews (so BULTMANN, *The Gospel of John*, 662 n. 6; SCHNACKENBURG, *Das Johannesevangelium*, 3:302) or to Caiaphas (so BEASLEY-MURRAY, *John*, 340). First, Jesus uses a *singular* "he who delivered Me" (ὁ παραδούς μέ) which does not apply well to the group of "the Jews." Second, the only time that Jesus uses παραδίδωμι before 19:11 is in 13:21 where he speaks about the one individual who is going to betray him. This one is clearly Judas. Third, the word παραδίδωμι occurs fifteen times in John, and ten times it refers to Judas (6:64, 71; 12:4; 13:2, 11, 21; 18:2, 5, 36; 21:20)! It is used for the Jews only in 18:30 and is found once in Pilate's mouth who names "your people and your chief priests" as the deliverers (18:35). Thus, the author prepares the reader from chapter six on to regard Judas as the most important single satanic instrument of betrayal and deliverance into the hands of the

comparison implies indirectly that the governor's involvement in Jesus' trial and crucifixion is nothing less than ἁμαρτία, despite the Roman's efforts to remain uninvolved and neutral (19:4, 6, 8, 12, 14, 15).[74] This pronouncement changes the roles and makes Pilate appear in such a way that he is the accused and Jesus the judge[75] who now convicts the governor in the same way the Paraclete "will convict the world of sin" later (ἐλέγξει τὸν κόσμον περὶ ἁμαρτίας, 16:8; see also 9:39; 3:19).[76] This depiction is far from second-century legends which compare the Roman governor with Abraham, Daniel, and the magi, and make him into an early gentile convert who even tried to evangelize the emperor Tiberius.[77]

Romans. Lastly, the author placed the term Ἰουδαῖοι earlier into the mouth of Jesus (18:20, 36) and he could have done so again in 19:11 if he wanted to compare the guilt of Pilate with that of the Jews. Although Judas is not mentioned when Jesus is handed over from Caiaphas to Pilate (18:28), he is there when Jesus is arrested in the garden (18:3) in the presence of Pilate's "soldiers" (σπεῖρα).

[74] Thus, whatever else the comparison with the greater sin of the one who delivered Jesus means, it expresses at least the audacity of the prisoner to accuse his judge and charge him with injustice. Kysar rightly comments, "The governor's posture throughout the trial is that of neutrality, but John will show that such neutrality is impossible – one is either of the light or of the darkness." KYSAR, *John*, 277. For various interpretations of 19:11 in the sense of exonerating Pilate see WEIDEMANN, *Der Tod Jesu*, 348.

[75] According to Schnackenburg, Pilate "wird zum Unterworfenen." SCHNACKENBURG, *Das Johannesevangelium*, 3:302. See also BULTMANN, *The Gospel of John*, 655. SÖDING, "Die Macht der Wahrheit," 47. WEIDEMANN, *Der Tod Jesu*, 346, 348. A possible interpretation of 19:13 as Jesus sitting on the βῆμα, and not Pilate, fits well with the change of roles in the narrative and is found in the Gospel of Peter (Jesus sits on the 'judgment seat' [καθέδρα κρίσεως, 1:7]; cf. Justin, *1 Apol.* 35,6). De La Potterie argues for this reading on philological grounds by defending the transitive use of καθίζω. DE LA POTTERIE, "Jésus Roi et Juge," 217-47, esp. 221-33. Amedick does not refer to philological reasons but to the "innere Logik des Geschehens" and explains that the "Autor des Petrusevangeliums dürfte darum nur die Vorstellung in Worte gefasst haben, die die Lektüre der anderen Evangelien bei zeitgenössischen Lesern ohnehin evozierte." AMEDICK, "'Iesus Nazarenus Rex Iudaiorum'," 59. There is a parallel for the change of roles in John 3: Nicodemus is the official teacher of Israel (3:10) but in the dialogue he appears as the student and Jesus as the teacher. See KÖSTENBERGER, *John*, 125. The same role reversal happens in John 5:37-47. Jesus is first the accused who then becomes the accuser. HAKOLA, *Identity Matters*, 147.

[76] Schnackenburg sees a trial motive in the Paraclete's convicting of sin, justice and judgment (16:8). SCHNACKENBURG, *Das Johannesevangelium*, 3:146. In Acts 4:25-28, Luke also reads Pilate as a representative for gentile participation in the events of Jesus' arrest, trial and crucifixion (in connection with Psalm 2:1, "Why did the Gentiles rage"; so also Justin, *1 Apol.* 40, who, in this address to the emperor, dares to call Pilate "your procurator" [Πιλάτου τοῦ ὑμετέρου].) and thereby implies imperial responsibility.

[77] Kannaday shows the growing "rise in Pilate's stock" during the second century AD under the pressure of pagan criticism. KANNADAY, *Apologetic Discourse*, 220 (see 216-226). Melito of Sardis (died AD 190) emphasized the *Jewish* responsibility for the death

In sum, the farewell discourse resembles the prologue in at least two points: it serves as a preface and interpretive key to the subsequent narrative (chaps. 18-21), and it broadens the scope of the conflict. This structural arrangement of the global (chaps. 13-17) and local (chaps. 18-19) perspectives on Jesus' suffering and death also answers negatively the question if the passion account heightens the culpability of the Jews.[78] If entered through the literary gate of the prologue and the chapters 13-17, the particular Jewish opposition to Jesus is converted to universal hate against the Savior of the world and his disciples. Thus the reader is guided to perceive the Jewish antagonists in chapters 18-19 as examples which demonstrate *pars pro toto* how the hate of the world (15:18-20) is acted out by failing to comprehend the light of the world (1:5).

1.3. Conclusion

Our discussion of the prologue and the farewell discourse as literary gates into the body of the Gospel in general and chapters 18-21 in particular did not exhaust the contents of 1:1-18 and chapters 13-17 or deny their surplus of theology as literary units in and of themselves.[79] Yet our aim was to show how macro-structural considerations do not merely add *optional* interpretations to an otherwise sufficient and inductive attention to single words, verses, or even chapters. Rather they reveal the narrative's point of view without which the reader focuses on textual fragments that have the potential of conveying the *opposite* of what the author intended. This is the frequent legacy of readings that disregard the compositional parallelism between κόσμος and the Ἰουδαῖοι and contend with an exclusive analysis of "the Jews" as the only adversaries in the story.

---

of Jesus by saying that an "Israelite" killed him (fragment 15 and *Peri Pascha* 96). Justin Martyr (AD 110-165) refers to the *Acts of Pilate* as support for Jesus' miracles (*1 Apol.* 48). And Tertullian (ca. AD 150- 220) said bluntly that Pilate was a Christian (*Apol.* 21). The following centuries continued on this path. Jensen explains that "Augustine hailed Pilate as a convert. Eventually, certain churches, including the Greek Orthodox and Coptic faiths, named Pilate and his wife saints. And when Pilate first shows up in Christian art in the mid-fourth century, he is juxtaposed with Abraham, Daniel and other great believers." JENSEN, "How Pilate Became a Saint," 22 (see 22-31, 47-48). See also EHRMAN, *Lost Christianity*, 20-22.

[78] For literature on the question see SCHOLTISSEK, "Antijudaismus im Johannesevangelium?," 168 n. 81.

[79] The theme of prayer in 14:13-14; 15:16, and 16:23-24, 26 stands independently of chaps. 18-21.

2. The Function of the Narratological Parallelism

Why is it that "the Jews" and "the world" are *so precisely* delegated to different roles (narrator and protagonist) and genres (narrative and speech)?[80] And, asking more broadly, how do narrative and speech relate to each other in the Gospel, especially when both alternate within single pericopes? Scholarship of the past has shown selective interest in some aspects of the speeches such as their poetry[81] and tradition-historical comparison with other literature.[82] While the ἐγώ εἰμι sayings and single speeches such as those in John 10 and 15 together with various aspects of the farewell discourse and the dialogue between Jesus and Pilate have been studied for a long time, Demke has observed recently with regard to German scholarship that other speeches and dialogues are "in der deutschsprachigen wissenschaftlichen Exegese geradezu stiefmütterlich behandelt . . . ."[83] While the situation might be somewhat better in Anglo-Saxon studies, O'Day speaks even here of the "unsettled place of Jesus' discourses."[84]

What is true for the discourses in general applies even more so to the more complex connection between Ἰουδαῖος in the narratives and κόσμος in the speeches, so dominant in John 1-12. Scholars have paid attention to both terms and genre *separately*. Westcott, for example, simply observes without explaining that the expression "the Jews" "occurs rarely in the discourses of the Lord."[85] He fails to mention that κόσμος does occur with

---

[80] Reinhartz, for example, misses this feature and thus fails to see the distinction when she simply equates "the Jews" of the narrative with the second plural "you" of the discourse in 3:11. REINHARTZ, *Befriending the Beloved Disciple*, 69.

[81] Brown discusses the speeches as a whole only with regard to poetic elements such as parallelism, rhyme and especially rhythm. BROWN, *The Gospel*, 1:CXXXII-CXXXV.

[82] Odeberg shows in his monograph the close correspondence between discourses in the first twelve chapters of the Gospel of John and Rabbinic and Mandaean literature. ODEBERG, *The Fourth Gospel* (1968). Schulz's tradition-historical study from 1960 is motivated by new discoveries such as the Dead Sea Scrolls, Oriental texts (Turfan finds), Greek translations of the Old Testament from Qumran-cave 4, the *Nag-Hammadi-*literature found in 1945 and the Palestinian Targum *Neofiti I* discovered in 1956. See SCHULZ, *Komposition und Herkunft*, 3-4.

[83] DEMKE, "Das Evangelium der Dialoge," 164.

[84] O'DAY, "'I have said these things to you ...'," 144. She mentions several factors that lead to this neglect: literary criticism emphasizes "story" which often focuses on narratives and their plot, character, symbols, etc.; common categories such as "narrative" and "discourse" dichotomize the text and prevent the interpretation of both in mutual dependence; and stories are simply more fun to interpret then long speeches. Ibid.

[85] WESTCOTT, *The Gospel*, 1:xvi, n. 1, also 2:284.

unusual frequency in Jesus' speeches.[86] In the volume *Anti-Judaism and the Fourth Gospel* (2001), only Jean Zumstein and Judith Lieu perceive and discuss the omission of the Ἰουδαῖοι from the farewell discourse.[87] Collins' essay, in which he examines the few occurrences of "the Jews" in the speeches of the Gospel, but completely ignores the dominance of the term κόσμος in the same genre, is symptomatic of a concordance-like and thus reductionistic study of the Ἰουδαῖοι.[88] While few have observed the terms' interdependence, fewer have tried to explain it. This neglect is due to the fact that, as O'Day puts it, "Jesus' discourses tend to be handled as a textual phenomenon almost wholly distinct from the 'narrative'."[89]

It will be helpful, therefore, to begin the analysis of the function of Jesus' speeches with general considerations about the relationship between speech and narrative. We will then proceed to observations about specific characteristics of Jesus' discourse and finish with an answer to the question at hand.

2.1. The Large Amount of Dialogue and Direct Speech

As noted above, the categories "speech" and "narrative" often dichotomize a book which was written as a coherent text. But if both belong together, how do they relate to each other? The following discussion tries to answer this question.

The Fourth Gospel has a large amount of direct speech in the form of dialogues and monologues. The table below shows a quantitative comparison between direct speech and narrative in all four Gospels: [90]

---

[86] The same is true with regard to Nothomb. He makes the rare and important observation "que sur 71 mentions des 'Juifs' . . . 60 sont au discours indirect contre 11 seulement au discours direct." NOTHOMB, "Nouveau Regard," But then, without noticing the parallelism to κόσμος in the speeches of Jesus, he categorically rejects to see "the Jews" as only part of "the world" and draws the conclusion that the author uses Ἰουδαῖοι because he wanted to counter proto-Marcionite trends by reminding a Gentile audience of their faith's Jewish roots. Ibid., 68.

[87] ZUMSTEIN, "The Farewell Discourse," 461-78, esp. 463-73. LIEU, "Anti-Judaism," 112-13.

[88] Collins discusses specifically 4:1-42; 13:33; 18:33-38a; 18:38b-40; 19:1-3; 19:19-22. COLLINS, "Speaking of the Jews," 158-75.

[89] O'DAY, "'I have said these things to you …'," 144.

[90] Matthew has a total of 18,278 words of which 12,045 words are direct speech (Jesus: 10,250; others: 1,795) and 6,233 belong to the narrator. Mark has a total of 11,229 words (without 16:9-20) of which 5,156 words are direct speech (Jesus: 3,914; others: 1,242) and 6,073 belong to the narrator. Luke has a total of 19,404 words of which 11,626 words are direct speech (Jesus: 9,197; others: 2,429) and 7,778 belong to the narrator. John has a total of 15,420 words (without 7:53-8:12) of which 8,993 words are direct speech (Jesus: 6,547; others: 2,407) and 6,427 belong to the narrator. The total

	Matthew	Mark	Luke	John
Direct Speech	66 %	46 %	60 %	58 %
Jesus	56 %	35 %	47 %	42 %
Others	10%	11 %	13 %	16 %
Narrator	34 %	54 %	40 %	42 %

In Matthew, Luke and John, direct speech occupies more space than the narrator's contribution (58-66 percent).[91] Among the speakers, the voice of Jesus occupies a place of prominence in all Gospels (35-56 percent). On the other hand, narration plays a subordinate role except in Mark. This is particularly true with regard to the report of actions, in contrast to the narrator's comments, his use of indirect speech, quotations of the Old Testament, etc. The Fourth Gospel includes only a sparse coverage of seven "signs," whereas the other writers describe eighteen to twenty miracles.[92] This scarcity enhances the impact and importance of direct speech in the Gospel of John. Hooker aptly summarizes the evidence:

> For if narrative is typical of Mark, discourse is typical of John. The bulk of the rest of John's gospel – until we come to the passion narrative – is theological discourse, held together by a slight narrative framework: his material is essentially a brief account of certain activities of Jesus, together with lengthy theological comment on the significance of those activities, usually in the mouth of Jesus himself.[93]

Within the context of ancient literature, the historical books of the Old Testament reflect a similar proclivity for direct speech with an average of

---

numbers stem from MORGENTHALER, *Statistik*, 164. All other numbers were counted by hand for this comparison.

[91] Diefenbach's estimate of 65 percent direct speech in the Gospel of John is a little bit too high. DIEFENBACH, *Der Konflikt Jesu*, 56, 57.

[92] For a list and comparison of all miracles in the Gospels, see the chart in HOUSE, *Chronological and Background Charts*, 112-15. The restoring of Malchus' ear (18:10-11), Jesus' resurrection, and the second catch of fish (21:1-14) have to be added to the seven "signs" during Jesus' ministry in John 2-11. Mark records 18 miracles, Matthew and Luke each 20 miracles.

[93] HOOKER, "The Johannine Prologue," 41. Stange spoke in 1915 of the Gospel's "ungewöhnliche Vorliebe für den Dialog." STANGE, *Die Eigenart der johanneischen Produktion*, 28. In his *Vorrede auf das Neue Testament* from 1522, Luther observed, "Weil nun Johannes gar wenig Werk von Christo, aber gar viel seiner Predigt schreibt, wiederum die anderen drei Evangelisten viel seiner Werk, wenig seiner Wort beschreiben, ist Johannis Evangelium das einzige, zarte, rechte Hauptevangelium und den andern dreien weit, weit vorzuziehen und höher zu heben." In *Martin Luther: Ausgewählte Werke*, 6:84.

40 to 50 percent.[94] Thus, Robert Alter can speak of a "Hebrew mode of presentation," that is shaped by a "highly subsidiary role of narration in comparison to direct speech by the characters."[95] But scholars observed parallels with Greco-Roman literature as well. While Greek historians such as Herodotus and Thucydides prefer indirect speech (only 5-27 percent direct speech), other writings such as Homers *Iliad* (67 percent direct speech),[96] Plato's *Dialogues*,[97] Greek drama[98] and Greco-Roman biographies[99] are cited for their inclination for dramatic dialogue similar to the Fourth Gospel.[100]

2.2. The Function of Direct Speech

When Alter speaks not just of the numerical backseat but of the "subsidiary role" of narration, he points already to the superior function of direct speech. According to Polybius, the Greek historian of Rome (ca. 200-118 BC), direct speeches "sum up events and hold the whole history together" (ὡς κεφάλαια τῶν πράξεών ἐστι καὶ συνέχει τὴν ὅλην ἱστορίαν).[101] Thus, although the amount of discourse in ancient Greco-Roman historiography was small, it was deliberately used and placed. Closer analysis shows how, formally, it added variety, immediacy and

---

[94] BAUM, "Zur Funktion," 591. The percentages range from as low as 33 percent in 2 Kings to 91 and 96 percent in Leviticus and Deuteronomy.

[95] ALTER, *The Art of Biblical Narrative*, 64, 65. Reiser explains with regard to the Old Testament in contrast to, for example, Thucydides, "Die Hauptsache der Erzählung steht im Dialog." REISER, "Die Stellung der Evangelien," 18.

[96] BAUM, "Zur Funktion," 592-93. Aune reports a lower number, about "50 percent of the Iliad consists of direct discourse, with 677 examples of direct speech, 88 cases of indirect discourse, rarely longer than two lines, and 39 instances in which a speech act is mentioned but not reported (de Jong 1987, 115)." AUNE, "Direct Discourse," 139. According to Aune, the 861 speeches in Herodotus' work contain 47.5 percent direct discourse which nevertheless "contrasts with the preference for direct discourse in Homer (as in Old Testament narrative)." AUNE, *The New Testament*, 91.

[97] SMART, *The Spiritual Gospel*, 35.

[98] See recent book by BRANT, *Dialogue and Drama* (2004). See also p. 53 n. 200.

[99] Burridge sees the insertion of extensive dialogues and discourses into John's narrative as a feature that is "common in βίοι, especially those of philosophers; much of the *Apollonius of Tyana* is similarly occupied with dialogues and long speeches containing the sage's teaching. The feature of dialogue was also noted in Satyrus' *Euripides*." BURRIDGE, *What Are the Gospels?*, 218, also 220, 225.

[100] According to Dodd, the Johannine dialogues follow "the same general tendency" of those in Plato, Lucian, or Hermetic writings and resemble the traditions of the Synoptic Gospels and of rabbinic teachings as well. But these parallels do not hinder the impression that the Johannine dialogue "is an original literary creation, for which there is no really close parallel." DODD, *The Interpretation*, 445 n. 1.

[101] *Polybius*, 4:369.

emphasis to the narration.[102] With regard to the content, Aune summarizes that in "Greco-Roman historiography, narrative is reserved for describing people's deeds, while speeches provided explanation and analysis."[103] The parallels to the discourses in the Fourth Gospel will become evident in the following.

2.2.1. The speeches interpret the signs

The idea that direct speech serves to "hold the whole history together" describes well the Fourth Gospel's use of discourse and narrative.[104] We have already seen how the prologue is "heading" the narrative and how the farewell discourse precedes and interprets the passion account. Other pairs of narrative and discourse are obvious: Jesus feeds five thousand people (6:1-15) and spiritualizes food in the following speech in which he announces himself as the "bread of life" (6:25-59).[105] The assertion "I am the light of the world" (9:5) is followed by a narrative illustration in which Jesus brings physical light to a man born blind (9:6-7) before final words interpret "seeing" and "blindness" as metaphors for acceptance and belief (9:39). In a similar way, after resurrecting Lazarus to physical life (11:1-44), Jesus uses this event to speak about eternal life (11:25). The character of the miracles as "signs" is thus not fully understood when limited to

---

[102] In order to show the effect of direct speech, Sands puts the dialogue between Jesus and Mary (21:15-17) in indirect speech and concludes that the "vivid drama and beauty have gone out of it." SANDS, *Literary Genius*, 71. Baum explains, "Darüber hinaus erfüllte speziell die direkte (im Unterschied zur indirekten) Redewiedergabe in der antiken Geschichtsschreibung mindestens drei literarische Funktionen. Sie diente dazu, eine Erzählung abwechslungsreich zu gestalten (1), steigerte die Unmittelbarkeit der Personendar-stellung (2) und konnte als Mittel der Betonung eingesetzt werden (3)." BAUM, "Zur Funktion," 594. Baum proceeds to show how the Old Testament as well as Greek literature employ direct speech for these purposes.

[103] AUNE, *The New Testament*, 93. Rebell writes about the "didaktischen Strukturen in den joh Reden und Dialogen." REBELL, *Gemeinde als Gegenwelt*, 17.

[104] Interestingly, Keener wonders about a possible parallel between the Gospel and ancient historiography, "Could these distinctive parts of John's Gospel [Jesus' discourses] function as theological commentary, analogous to the function of speeches in many ancient histories . . . ?" KEENER, *The Gospel of John*, 1:53.

[105] While the speeches exert an *interpretive* influence on the signs, the signs do not merely describe the action but also *illustrate* the meaning of the sayings. Stira, for example, observed with regard to the miracles in John 6: "Die beiden Zeichen, die wunderbare Speisung und der Seewandel Jesu, münden in die Selbstprädikation Jesu in V. 35b ein. Es gibt aber auch eine umgekehrte Wirkung: Die Selbstprädikation Jesu und auch die anderen Aussagen Jesu im hier behandelten Gespräch in Joh 6 helfen die beiden Zeichen tiefer zu verstehen. Das bedeutet, daß die beiden Zeichen und das Gespräch in Joh 6 miteinander verbunden sind, was V. 35b beispielhaft zeigt." STARE, *Durch ihn leben*, 145.

mere proofs for the identity of Jesus as the Son of God. Instead, as the speeches show, the physical actions "signify" spiritual realities that are larger than the light one can see or the mortal life we can live. Dodd describes the connection between speech and narrative as follows:

> The incidents narrated receive an interpretation of their evangelical significance in the discourse; or, to put it otherwise, the truths enunciated in the discourses are given dramatic expression in the actions described. Act and word are one.[106]

Leon Morris links all of the seven signs to a specific discourse.[107]

Signs	Discourses
1. Water into wine (2:1-11)	1. The new birth (3:1-21)
2. Healing the nobleman's son (4:46-54)	2. The water of life (4:1-42)
3. Healing the lame man (5:1-18)	3. The divine son (5:19-47)
4. Feeding the multitude (6:1-15)	4. The bread of life (6:22-65)
5. Walking on the water (6:16-22)	5. The life-giving Spirit (7:1-52)
6. Sight to the man born blind (9:1-41)	6. The light of the world (8:12-59)
7. Raising of Lazarus (11:1-57)	7. The good shepherd (10:1-42)

With Salier, we add an eighth pair. The farewell discourse "prefaces the final and climactic sign of the Gospel, the death and resurrection of Jesus."[108] Sometimes the sign precedes the discourse (1, 3, 4, 5), sometimes the discourse precedes the sign (2, 6, 7, 8). Signs three to six anticipate the theme of the discourse more obviously than the first two. But even if not all pairs are convincing, commentators usually agree that the changing of water into wine has a larger significance than simply providing alcohol for a wedding. If read under the influence of the prologue, the supernatural provisions of wine and health demonstrate Jesus' "glory as of the only begotten from the Father" (1:14).

---

[106] DODD, *The Interpretation*, 384. Bultmann explains, "Originally, their point [of the miracle stories] lay in the miracle they report, but for the evangelist they take on a symbolic or allegorical meaning, and throughout the Gospel he uses them as points of departure for discourses or discussions." BULTMANN, *Theology of the New Testament*, 2:3-4. Van Belle describes the relationship this way, "In the miracle stories, the evangelist narrates Jesus' life-giving power; in the discourses, he explains what can be grasped from seeing a sign." BELLE, *The Signs Source*, 390. Brant writes, "The discourses are the true action of the gospel, just as dialogue is the action of a drama. The Fourth Evangelist presents a limited number of the many signs . . . , selected to anticipate the thematic focus of the discourses. The explicit designation of some actions as semeia (σημεῖα) and repetition render this pattern in the gospel obvious." BRANT, *Dialogue and Drama*, 35; also p. 30 n. 28, 86-87.

[107] MORRIS, *Jesus is the Christ*, 23.

[108] SALIER, *The Rhetorical Impact*, 129. See also CARSON, *The Gospel*, 274.

The Gospel's quantitative dominance of direct speech over narration as well as the interpretive role of direct speech demonstrate that the spoken words function as the main vehicle for communicating the author's point of view. Since Jesus is not only the main protagonist of the story but speaks about three times more than all the other speakers put together, it becomes imperative to ask in the following for the characteristic content and features of his discourses.[109]

2.3. Jesus' Speech Continues the Voice of the Prologue

A first formal observation with regard to Jesus' speeches is that they continue the ideas and language of the prologue in the body of the Gospel.[110] When discussing the prologue's function as a "summary," we noticed eleven key terms in 1:1-18 which are frequently present in the later chapters: ζωή, φῶς, σκοτία, μαρτυρία, μαρτυρέω, πιστεύω, σάρξ, ἀλήθεια, γεννάω, Μωϋσῆς, νόμος. Of these words, φῶς appears after the prologue only in the mouth of Jesus. The same is true for σκοτία when we exclude the literal sense in 6:17 and 20:1.[111] With very few exceptions, it is also only Jesus who employs the terms σάρξ, ἀλήθεια and ζωή.[112] The main protagonist dominates as well the usage of μαρτυρία, μαρτυρέω, πιστεύω, γεννάω, and Μωϋσῆς, each with more than fifty percent of their total occurrence.[113] Thus, what we observed with regard to the usage of κόσμος is part of a larger effort that places loaded language at prominent places such as the prologue and the discourses of the story's hero.

---

[109] Caron chooses John 5 and 8 for analysis because Jesus' point of view, that of the protagonist, as particularly exposed in these chapters through the means of confrontation with the Jews, helps to identify who the Ἰουδαῖοι actually are. He writes, "Comme *Jésus est sans contredit le personnage clé ou le protagoniste* de ce récit tout à fait particulier qu'est l'évangile de Jean, *son 'point de vue'*, ce qu'il pense de ces 'Juifs', comment il les voit, jouera nécessairement un rôle capital dans leur *identification*. Cela est d'autant plus important que le 'point de vue' du Jésus johannique semble reflécter parfaitement celui de l'auteur de l'évangile (Jn 20,31)." CARON, *Qui sont les Juifs*, 54-55 (italics added). In other words, since Jesus is the key-figure in the narrative, his point of view, as expressed among others in the use of κόσμος, also plays a leading role in the interpretation of the Ἰουδαῖοι.

[110] Ruckstuhl comments briefly, "Was der Prolog andeutet, das entrollt sich nachher vor allem in den Reden des Ev." RUCKSTUHL, *Die literarische Einheitlichkeit*, 3; see also 24, 42.

[111] See φῶς in (1:4, 5, 7, 8, 9) 3:19, 20, 21; 5:35; 8:12; 9:5; 11:9,10; 12:35, 36, 46. The metaphorical sense of σκοτία appears in (1:5) 8:12; 12:35, 46.

[112] The exceptions are: for σάρξ see 6:52, for ἀλήθεια see 18:38, and for ζωή see 3:36, 6:68 and 20:31.

[113] An exception is νόμος which, although it appears only in direct speech apart from 1:17, is used by Jesus merely 6 times (42 percent of 14 times total).

Connected with the key-terms is the observation that ten out of the prologue's twelve key concepts that are listed by Robinson appear only in the mouth of Jesus (except 4:44 and 12:41).[114] For example, the notion of the logos' pre-existence (1:1-2) is mentioned merely one more time in Jesus' final prayer (17:5, 24). The expression "in him was life" (ἐν αὐτῷ ζωὴ ἦν, 1:4) finds a similar parallel only in Jesus words, "For just as the Father has life in Himself, even so He gave to the Son also to have life in Himself" (ζωὴν ἔχειν ἐν ἑαυτω, 5:26).[115]

Other similarities between the prologue and the discourses could be mentioned[116] but we want to begin asking why the author has crafted this connection. One historical answer is given by literary critics who refer the phenomenon to a common source.[117] But the idea of dividing the Gospel into large sources of speech and narration fails on stylistic grounds and has found more criticism than support.[118] It is rather the similarity of the

---

[114] See our chart in 1.1.2 (p. 118).

[115] The one walking in darkness does "not have life in himself" (6:53 οὐκ ἔχετε ζωὴν ἐν ἑαυτοῖς) and the believer "has life" only "in his name" (20:31 ζωὴν ἔχητε ἐν τῷ ὀνόματι αὐτοῦ).

[116] Hooker finds a "juxtaposition of historical narrative and theological interpretation" both in prologue and the "rest of the gospel" which consists mostly of "theological discourse, held together by a slight narrative framework." HOOKER, "The Johannine Prologue," 41. Bultmann finds, against Jeremias, rhythmic patterns common to prologue and discourses. BULTMANN, *The Gospel of John*, 15. For a critique see RUCKSTUHL, *Die literarische Einheitlichkeit*, 43-52.

[117] Following Renan, Soltau postulated in 1901 a "Redequelle" because the content of the discourses often appears to be disconnected from the narratives. It consisted of 1:1-18; 3:13-21; 4:10-15; 4:31-38; 5:19-47; 6:32-65; 8:12-19; 8:21-59; 10:1-18; 10:26-42; 14-17, and also 3:31b-36; 12:34-36; 12:44-50; 7:28-36. This "Redequelle" was supplemented by synoptic traditions and the evangelist's own narratives. SOLTAU, "Zum Problem des Johannesevangeliums," 140-42. In another essay, Soltau compares the "Redequelle" with the Letters of Ignatius and concludes that their similarities (see John 16:11 and *Ign. Eph.* 17:1; 19:1; John 15:18 and *Ign. Rom.* 3:3) point to Antioch as the provenance of the discourses. Idem, "Die Reden des vierten Evangeliums," 49-61. See also WELLHAUSEN, *Das Evangelium Johannis*, 102. BULTMANN, *The Gospel of John*, 13 n. 1, 18. After describing Harnack's view that the prologue was composed later than the Gospel, Hofrichter explains, "Andererseits haben aber H. H. Wendt, W. Soltau, R. Bultmann und S. Schulz aus den thematischen Querverbindungen zwischen dem Prolog und den Reden des Evangeliums auf die gemeinsame Zugehörigkeit zu einer Quelle geschlossen, die der Evangelist für seine Arbeit benützt habe." HOFRICHTER, *Im Anfang war der "Johannesprolog"*, 15. More recently, Koester and Ehrman continue to postulate a Signs Source, a Passion Source, and a Discourse Source. KOESTER, *Ancient Christian Gospels*, 256-67. EHRMAN, *The New Testament*, 166-67. See also SCHENKE, "Joh 7-10," 189-90.

[118] See our "Reflections on Method" in chapter 1. Twenty-two of Ruckstuhl's fifty stylistic features appear in the revelatory speeches (OR), but they always have parallels outside of the alleged "source" in narrative parts of the Gospel, including the assumed

genres which mirrors a convention of ancient literature according to which "direct speech uniformly reflects the author's style."[119] Another historical answer suggests that the Gospel of John is related to conventions of Greek drama which knows of a "newly introduced actor" who "delivered not only the prologue but also the subsequent speeches that were interspersed between the odes."[120] Whichever solution is adopted, none of these proposals give a satisfying answer to the question about the purpose of this connection within the Gospel. If the author used different sources, why did he modify them and put them together in this particular way? If conventions of ancient literature and Greek drama inspired him, why did he give them prominence over the synoptic styles, sayings and traditions?

We suggest that the author crafted and placed Jesus' speeches in deliberate relation to the narratives. By extending the voice of the prologue into the words of the main protagonist, the author desires to continue his interpretive influence on the reading of the story. As the prologue imposes the author's point of view on the whole gospel so does the voice of Jesus within the microstructure of the single pericope and before the account about his passion and resurrection (chaps. 13-17). Our previous discussion of the Gospel's universal opening discloses already *what kind* of interpretive influence the author wishes to have. Further analysis of the speeches will strengthen this impression.

2.4. Jesus' Speech Displays a Gnomic Style

When we analyze how Jesus and other speakers use κόσμος we find that the term is often employed to make pithy and memorable remarks about sin (1:29), hate (7:7; 15:18, 19; 17:14), judgment (9:39; 12:31; 16:11),

---

"semeia" tradition (cf. ἐκεῖνος and σκοτία). RUCKSTUHL, *Die literarische Einheitlichkeit*, 213-14.

[119] AUNE, *The New Testament*, 91. Aune refers to examples from the works of Homer and Thucydides. Culpepper explains similarly, "The difference between the idiom of the Johannine Jesus and the synoptic Jesus, on the one hand, and the similarity between this idiom and the language of the Johannine epistles, on the other hand, confirms that when Jesus, the literary character, speaks, he speaks the language of the author and his narrator." CULPEPPER, *Anatomy*, 40-41. Weidemann affirms that "der johanneische Jesus spricht über weite Strecken die Sprache des vierten Evangelisten!" WEIDEMANN, *Der Tod Jesu*, 48. The question of authenticity cannot be addressed here. Meyer insists that the author did not totally blur the "original essential content" of Jesus' speeches with his own point of view, as the absence of the prologue's λόγος in the speeches of Jesus demonstrates. MEYER, *Kritisch-Exegetisches Handbuch*, 32-33. For the view of "historical plausability" despite the imaginative character of direct speech in the Gospels see REISER, "Die Stellung der Evangelien," 9, 19. BAUM, "Zur Funktion," 599-601. AUNE, *The New Testament*, 92.

[120] HARRIS, *Prologue and Gospel*, 13.

darkness (3:19; 8:12), God's love (3:16-17), and Jesus' saving and life-giving mission (4:42; 6:33; 8:12; 11:27; 12:25, 46-47). The statements are often expressed in (or surrounded by) a gnomic style to communicate truths that apply to all people: "men (οἱ ἄνθρωποι) loved the darkness rather than the light" (3:19; see also 5:33; 17:6); "everyone who (πᾶς) believes may in Him have eternal life" (also 3:16 [narrator?]; 4:13; 6:45; 8:34; 11:26; 12:32, 46; etc.); "whoever (ὃς) drinks of the water that I shall give him shall never thirst" (4:14); "No one (οὐδείς) can come to Me, unless the Father who sent Me draws him" (6:44); "This is the bread which comes down out of heaven, so that one (τὶς) may eat of it and not die" (6:46, 51; 10:9; 12:47; 14:23; etc.). Statements with the subject as an articular substantival participle (e.g., 6:47 ὁ πιστεύων, "The one who believes . . . ;" also 6:56, 57; 9:39; 10:1, 2; 11:25; 12:25, 35, 44, 48; 14:12, 21, 24; etc.) as well as the important 'I am' sayings (6:35; 8:12; 10:7, 9, 11, 14; 11:25; 14:6; 15:1, 5) articulate the same inclusiveness. The assertion in 8:12 combines the gnomic element with the term κόσμος: "I am the light of the world (τὸ φῶς τοῦ κόσμου); he who follows Me (ὁ ἀκολουθῶν ἐμοὶ) shall not walk in the darkness, but shall have the light of life."

2.5. *Jesus' Speech Uses the Present Tense*

The gnomic tendency of the speeches is supported by their predominant use of the present tense as opposed to the imperfect, aorist and pluperfect. Frey observes that over 60 percent of the indicative verbs of the speeches in 5:19-47 and 10:1-18 use the present tense, whereas the narrative sections in 6:1-25 and 12:1-11 only come up with 15-23 percent.[121] We have noticed the same difference with regard to the conclusion of the 'Book of Signs' by the narrator (12:37-44) and by Jesus (12:44-50).[122]

While we cannot discuss the shift in verb tenses comprehensively, a special form of the present tense is worth noting, namely the 161 occurrences of the historical present. Steve Booth divided the Gospel into 19 episodes and analyzed the occurrence of the historical present in each episode with regard to three categories: action, speech, and movement.[123] A simple addition of his numbers for each of the nineteen episodes shows that the historical present occurs only 23 times in "action," 123 times in "speech" and 15 times in "movement." Only three of the episodes do not contain any historical present in their speeches (1:1-18; 3:22-36; 10:22-42) while eleven episodes do not use it in the narrative. It is puzzling that

---

[121] FREY, *Die johanneische Eschatologie. Band II*, 32.
[122] See 2.1.12 in chapter 3.
[123] BOOTH, *Selected Peak*, 99.

Booth focuses on the single episodes of the Gospel and seems to overlook the largely differing numbers with regard to the general categories of action and speech. After discussing several theories about the significance of the historical present, he sides with Boos and understands its use as a form of plot development which "is used to highlight those episodes which build suspense toward a climax in the plot structure and directly relate to the author's purpose."[124] Considering the dominance of this tense in the speeches at large, we can broaden his conclusion beyond single episodes to the genre of discourse. The author centered the use of the historical present on the words of the protagonists because it is here where he conveys his purpose most directly.

2.6. Jesus' Speech Displays Simplicity and Lack of Particularity

Another characteristic of the speeches and of the Gospel as a whole is stylistic simplicity. This becomes evident, for example, in a comparison of the total vocabulary used in each of the four Gospels.[125]

Gospel	Text-length	Vocabulary	Words/Vocabulary
Matthew	18,278	1691	10.8
Mark	11,229	1345	8.3
Luke	19,404	2055	9.4
John	15,420	1011	15.2

Although the Gospel of John much longer than the Gospel of Mark (by 4191 words or 35 percent), John's vocabulary is much smaller. While the amplitude between the synoptic relationship of text-length-to-vocabulary ranges from 1.1 (Mark to Luke) to 2.5 (Matthew to Mark), the Fourth Gospel stands out, with the smallest difference being 4.4 (Matthew to

---

[124] Ibid., 100. According to this criteria, the episodes with special prominence are (historical present in the speeches in brackets) 1:19-2:12 (18x), 4:1-42 (12x), 11:1-54 (11x), 13:1-17:26 (17x), 18:1-19:16a (15x), 21:1-25 (17x). Other interpretations of the historical present discussed consider the tense more as a stylistic feature implicating heightened vividness, suddenness / excitement, or imaginative presence. Booth also considers the function of scene introduction (Randy Buth) and cataphoric reference (Stephen Levinson). Ibid., 97-98.

[125] See MORGENTHALER, *Statistik*, 164. The last column (Words/Vocabulary) was added. A computergenerated count with *Bibleworks 7.0* gives a slightly higher number of total words per Gospel in 27th edition of Nestle-Aland: Matthew: 18,346; Mark: 11,304; Luke: 19,482; John: 15,635. These numbers are exactly identical to Davison's computergenerated count from 1984 who used Nestle-Aland's 26th edition. See Kenny, *A Stylometric Study of the New Testament*, 14. For a discussion see KENNY, *A Stylometric Study of the New Testament*, 13-16, who concludes that the different counts "only very rarely" lead to "statistically significant differences." Ibid., 16.

John) and the largest one 6.9 (Mark to John). These numbers explain in statistical terms what is obvious to every reader, namely John's many repetitions. Besides an inclination to a "pointless variety" even with such a limited vocabulary,[126] the author holds on to a word tenaciously once he begins using it.[127] Verbs such as *to be, go/come, do, believe, have, know, give*, and nouns such as *father, world, disciple, Jews, son, life, work, truth, light*, and *water* lead the list of John's "Vorzugswörter."[128] This simplicity of language is especially evident in the speeches in general and in those of Jesus in particular, where most of these words occur. The use of hapax legomena supports this observation. According to Aland's list in his *Vollständige Konkordanz* there are 102 hapax legomena in Matthew, 75 in Mark, 284 in Luke and 84 in John.[129] More specifically, Jesus himself uses 54 of them in Matthew, 21 in Mark, 100 in Luke, but only 14 in John.[130] Thus, while John does use a total amount of hapax legomena that is comparable to Matthew and Mark, the quantity found in the mouth of Jesus is significantly lower. This shows again that there is much less variety and

---

[126] TURNER, *A Grammar of New Testament Greek*, vol. 4, 76. Turner observes, for example, John's frequent use of a "needless synonym; there are two words each for *love, send, heal, ask, speak, do, feed sheep, know* . . . . There is no apparent point in these synonyms beyond the avoiding of monotony, however hard one looks for a subtle distinction." Ibid., 76. Yet Sands finds four verbs for 'see' (βλέπω and ὁράω in 1:29; θεάομαι in 1:32; ἐμπλέπω in 1:36) and observes "different shades of meaning." SANDS, *Literary Genius*, 71. For an impressive collection of variations in Johannine style that often go unnoticed in the English translation (such as παρέλαβον in 1:11 and ἔλαβον in 1:12; ἀποστέλλω and πέμπω in 20:21), see MORRIS, "Variation," 293-319.

[127] Stange speaks of John's "zähe Haften am einmal gefundenen Ausdruck" and that John prefers "das Substantiv zu wiederholen, statt es durch das Pronomen zu ersetzen." He refers to the following nouns and verses as examples: 1:1b (ὁ λόγος); 1:4 (ἡ ζωή); 1:5 (ἡ σκοτία); 3:17 (κόσμος); 2:9 (ὁ ἀρχιτρίκλινος); 3:20 (φῶς); 3:26 (οὗτος); 3:36 (τῷ υἱῷ); 4:1 ('Ιησοῦς beside κύριος); 8:32 (ἀλήθεια); 8:34 (τῆς ἁμαρτίας); 12:1 ('Ιησοῦς); 12:3 (τοὺς πόδας αὐτοῦ); 12:27 (εἰς τὴν ὥραν ταύτην); 12:47 (τὸν κόσμον); 14:21 (ὁ ἀγαπῶν); 15:19 (ἐκ τοῦ κόσμου). STANGE, *Die Eigenart der johanneischen Produktion*, 24. Sands points out that John's "repetition of a noun or phrase is the source of the impressiveness, directness, and vigour of John's style" and illustrates the loss of such vigor by replacing repeated nouns with relative pronouns (e.g., 1:4, 10, 11). SANDS, *Literary Genius*, 52. We agree with the point being made, but the high frequency of κόσμος and 'Ιουδαῖοι is only to a small degree due to the author's habit of repeating a noun instead of replacing it with a pronoun (so, for example, in 3:17; 15:19; 16:28; 17:13-16).

[128] MORGENTHALER, *Statistik*, 182.

[129] See the appendix "Hapaxlegomena des Neuen Testaments, nach Schriften geordnet," in the second volume of ALAND, *Vollständige Konkordanz*, 2:447-60.

[130] They are the following terms: ἁλιεύω, ἀλλαχόθεν, ἀναμάρτητος, δειλιάω, ἐμπόριον, ἐξυπνίζω, καθαίρω, οὐκοῦν, πότερον, προσκυνητής, προσφάγιον, πτέρνα.

more simplicity in Jesus speech compared with the narrator as well as with the Synoptic Jesus.

With this simplicity comes a lack of particularity in the speeches of Jesus. While the narrator carefully locates every event in time and space,[131] Jesus mentions a city only once (Jerusalem in 4:21). His speeches in the Synoptics, on the other side, are replete with names of specific places such as Galilee, Chorazin, Bethsaida, Sidon, Tyre, Capernaum, and Sodom.[132]

Jesus does use particularly Jewish vocabulary such as Law, Moses, Sabbath, and circumcision.[133] As the statistical count above shows, Ἰουδαῖος (46x) dominates chapters 1-12 in comparison with κόσμος (28x). Although Jesus' speeches generalize the content through a gnomic style, they do respond to questions and accusations of *Jewish* interlocutors.

Nevertheless, we noticed in the previous chapter, for example with regard to John 5, that the dialogues focus more on the person of Jesus than on arguing from an inner-Jewish perspective.[134] Furthermore, a comparison with the Synoptics shows the Fourth Gospel's distance from concrete realities.[135] All of the following Jewish groups are mentioned by Jesus in

---

[131] See 2:1, 12-13; 3:23; 4:5-6, 46; 5:1-2; 6:1, 59; 7:2; 8:1-2, 20; 10:22-23; 11:1; 12:1, 12; 13:1; 18:1, 28; 19:14, 31, 42; 20:1. The Gospel of John mentions places that are not found in the Synoptics, such as Bethany beyond the Jordan (1:28), Cana (2:1; 4:46), Aenon near Salim (3:23), Sychar (4:5), "the sheep gate pool which is called in Hebrew Bethzatha" (5:2), Ephraim (11:54), Gabbatha (19:13). The healing of the blind man is the only account of a miracle in the Gospel that begins simply with "As he passed by" (9:1). The reader can assume that Jesus is still in Jerusalem as mentioned before (7:10; 8:1, 20). Every other miracle is located at a place: Cana (2:1), Cana (4:46), Jerusalem (5:1), Sea of Tiberias (6:1), Capernaum (6:17), Bethany (11:1). Sands observes about the Fourth Gospel that the "outstanding feature from a literary point of view is its particularity of detail. It reminds us in this respect of Mark, but with a difference. Mark's account is distinguished by graphic details of action and gesture, especially of Jesus himself. This Gospel gives details rather of time, place, numbers, names of speakers, even where not specially important, and explanatory circumstances." SANDS, *Literary Genius*, 55.

[132] See Galilee (Mark 14:28; 16:7), Chorazin, Bethsaida, Sidon, Tyros (Matt 11:21; Luke 10:13), Capernaum (Matt 11:23; Luke 4:23; 10:15) and Sodom (Matt 10:15; 11:23-24; Luke 10:12; 17:29).

[133] The following Jewish terms can be found in the mouth of Jesus: Ἰσραήλ (3:10), Ἰσραηλίτης (1:47), Ἀβραάμ (8:37, 39, 40, 56, 58), Μωϋσῆς (3:14; 5:45, 46; 6:32; 7:19, 22, 23), νόμος (7:19, 23, 49, 51; 8:5, 17; 10:34), περιτέμνω (7:22), περιτομή (7:22, 23), σάββατον (7:22, 23), ἱερός (18:20), προφήτης (6:45), Ἰουδαῖος (4:22; 13:33; 18:20, 36).

[134] See our discussion in chap. 4 to John 5. Wellhausen commented from this observation that John postulates more than he explains which leads Wellhausen to conclude that the Gospel was written not for outsiders but for Christians. WELLHAUSEN, *Das Evangelium Johannis*, 112, also 122, 125. So also Wellhausen's contemporary William Wrede, as noticed by HAKOLA, *Identity Matters*, 236.

[135] Abbott lists about 350 words in the chapter "Synoptic Words Comparatively Seldom or Never Used by John" in ABBOTT, *Johannine Vocabulary*, 160-87. He

the Synoptics, but never by Jesus in John (though some by the narrator): *high priest, scribes, priests, Levite, teacher of the Law, elders, Sadducees, Pharisees,* and *Herod*.[136] Typical synoptic topics of dispute are absent, such as fasting, purity, divorce, and the election of Gentiles.[137] In addition, the Jesus of the Synoptics speaks explicitly of Old Testament figures such as *Isaac, Jacob, David,* and *Elijah*. While they are not absent from the Fourth Gospel itself (except Isaac), they are never found in the mouth of Jesus.[138] When comparing Matthew/Luke and John, then the omission of the following names in the latter is also noticeable: *Abel, Noah, Lot, Queen*

---

summarizes the results of the comparison as follows: "Generally, we may say that John prefers to pass over local distinctions of sects, classes, and rulers, material distinctions of physical evil, and moral distinctions of various sins, in order to concentrate the mind on the elements of the spiritual world, light and darkness, spiritual life and death, truth and falsehood." Ibid., 157. Abbott's next chapter lists about 200 "Johannine words comparatively seldom or never used by the Synoptists." Ibid., 195-239.

[136] See ἀρχιερεύς (Matt 20:18; Mark 2:26; 10:33; Luke 9:22), γραμματεύς (Matt 5:20; 13:52; 20:18; 23:2, 13, 15, 23, 25, 27, 29, 34; Mark 10:33; Luke 9:22), ἱερεύς (Mark 2:44;), Λευίτης (Luke 10:32), νομικός (Luke 11:46, 52), πρεσβύτερος (Matt 15:2; Luke 9:22), Σαδδουκαῖος (Matt 16:6, 11), Φαρισαῖος (Matt 5:20; 16:6, 11; 23:2, 13, 15, 23, 25, 26, 27, 29; Mark 8:15; Luke 11:39, 42, 43; 12:1; 18:10, 11), Ἡρῴδης (Mark 8:15; see Luke 13:31-32). In the Fourth Gospel, it is the *narrator* who uses ἀρχιερεύς (e.g., 7:32), ἱερεύς (1:19), Λευίτης (1:19), Φαρισαῖος (e.g., 1:24). While πρεσβύτερος and γραμματεύς are used in the pericope of the adulterous woman (John 8:3, 9), text-critical considerations exclude both terms from the list of Johannine vocabulary. Dietzfelbinger explains, "Die Schriftgelehrten fehlen im Johannesevangelium (8,3 gehört nicht zum ursprünglichen Bestand)." DIETZFELBINGER, *Das Evangelium*, 285.

[137] Bultmann observed, "In John, Jesus appears neither as the rabbi arguing about questions of the Law nor as the prophet proclaiming the breaking in of the Reign of God. Rather, he speaks only of his own person as the Revealer whom God has sent. He does not argue about the Sabbath and fasting or purity and divorce but speaks of his coming and his going, of what he is and what he brings the world." BULTMANN, *Theology of the New Testament*, 2:4. Grässer notices the same, "Zwar diskutiert Jesus mit den Juden. Aber die verhandelten Themata sind kaum Fragen des jüdischen Horizontes, also nicht Sabbathgebot (siehe oben S. 80, Anm. 2), nicht Fasten, nicht Reinheit, nicht Ehescheidung, nicht Erwählung Israels und Heidenmission. Dieser israelitische Horizont ist für Joh. versunken. Geblieben ist für ihn allein Jesu Kommen und Gehen und was das an Heil für die *Welt* bedeutet." GRÄSSER, "Die Antijüdische Polemik," 82. See also ONUKI, *Gemeinde und Welt*, 30.

[138] They occur in the mouth of the Synoptic Jesus as follows: Isaac (Matt 8:11; 22:32; Mark 12:26; Luke 13:28; 20:37), Jacob (Matt 8:11; 22:32; Mark 12:26; Luke 13:28; 20:37), David (Matt 12:3; 22:43, 45; Mark 2:25; 12:35-37; Luke 6:3; 20:41-44), Elijah (Matt 11:14; 17:11-12; Mark 9:12-13; Luke 4:25-26). "David" and "Elijah" appear each 2 times in John but much more often in the Synoptics: Matthew uses "David" 17 times, Mark 7 times, Luke 13 times. Matthew uses "Elijah" 9 times, Mark 9 times, Luke 7 times.

of the South, Jonah, Ninevites, Zechariah.[139]

The absence of these Old Testament figures goes together with a very low number of quotations from the Old Testament in the Gospel as a whole and in the mouth of Jesus in particular. Appendix IV ("Loci Citati Vel Allegati") in the 27th edition of Nestle-Aland's *Novum Testamentum Graece* provides a list of quotations and allusions to the Old Testament in the New Testament. A count with regard to the Gospels (without the Apocrypha) reveals the following numbers:[140]

	Matthew	Mark	Luke	John
Quotations	87	46	41	21
in Jesus' speech	59	28	26	7
Allusions	458	152	469	205

Two observations are apparent: first, the Gospel of John uses considerably fewer quotations from the Old Testament than the Synoptics,[141] and, connected with that, the Jesus of John does not quote the Old Testament nearly as much as he does in the other Gospels. The many allusions indicate that the author certainly makes reference to the Old Testament (see 1:45; 4:6; 7:19, 38; 8:58) besides the quotations and he uses explicit (lamb, serpent, manna) as well as implicit (temple, shepherd, vine) typology. Maybe the Jewish festivals have a Christological significance, and Jesus' miracles possibly parallel those of Moses, Elijah and Elisha.[142] All of this sets the Fourth Gospel far apart from Marcion who erased all references to Jewish scriptures out of his version. But most of these

---

[139] See Abel and Zechariah (Matt 23:35; Luke 11:51), Noah (Matt 24:37, 38; Luke 17:26, 28), Lot (Luke 17:28, 29, 32), Queen of the South (Matt 12:42; Luke 11:31), Jonah (Matt 12:39, 40, 41; 16:4; Luke 11:29, 30), Ninivites (Matt 12:41; Luke 11:30).

[140] The numbers do not only include quotations that are introduced with formulas such as "It is written" (e.g., John 2:17; 6:31), "Isaiah the prophet said" (John 1:23; 12:38), or "that the scriptures might be fulfilled" (e.g., John 13:18; 15:25; 19:24, 36), but citations that are quoted without any introduction are listed in the Appendix as well (in the Gospel of John only 1:51 and 12:13, 27). In the margin of the Gospels' text as well as in Appendix IV, Nestle-Aland list the quotations in italics and the allusions in regular print. But sometimes margin and Appendix disagree. A text that is printed in italics in Appendix IV appears in regular print in the Gospel's margin (see Isa 66:14 in John 16:22) or vice versa (Zeph 3:15 in John 12:13; Isa 40:9 in John 12:15; 1 Chr 11:2 in Matt 2:6; Dan 12:11 in Matt 24:15; Ps 22:9 in Matt 27:43). A comparison between the Greek text and the LXX suggests in all cases to agree with the Gospel's margin and count these instances as quotations, not as allusions.

[141] The quotation in 7:38 cannot be identified and is not included in this count. For a similar uncertainty in the Synoptics see Matt 2:23 and Luke 24:46. There are no quotations of the Old Testament in any of the three epistles of John.

[142] See CULPEPPER, "Anti-Judaism," 71.

elements are limited to the narrator's voice in John 1-12 and find parallels in the Synoptics. One cannot avoid the impression that the author crafted the speeches of Jesus with an intentional stylistic uniformity, with distance to particular places and comparatively few explicit quotations of the Old Testament and thus with a lack of concreteness.[143]

Excursus: Interpretations of the Festivals in the Gospel of John

When assessing the meaning and importance of the festivals in the Gospel of John (see 2:13; 5:1; 6:4; 7:1; 13:1; 19:42), three interpretations emerge. (1) When the Gospel is viewed as an evangelistic writing for Jewish adherents, the festivals receive a positive function in the text. Motyer explains it this way: "Raised from the death, Jesus replaces the Temple as the focus of the worship of God's people, so that the *true significance* of the festivals, especially the pilgrim ones, is found in him and not in Jerusalem. . . . After this identification with the Temple, Jesus is presented in turn as the one who incorporates the *real meaning* of the Sabbath (chap. 5), Passover (chap. 6), Tabernacles (chaps. 7-10), and Dedication (chaps. 10-12)."[144] Already Heracleon, the first known interpreter of the Gospel of John from the second century AD, interpreted the reference to the Pascha in John 2:13 as "a model for the suffering of the Savior, when not only was the sheep slain but when eaten it afforded repose and when sacrificed it signified the suffering of the Savior in the world and when eaten it signified the repose in marriage."[145] In 1893, Rabbi Güdemann compared the Jewish festivals in the Gospel with rabbinic literature and concluded that "John" wrote a "pronounced Jewish-Christian Gospel" for readers who are faithful to Judaism.[146] (2) At the opposite end of the spectrum is the view which observes a lack of an *explicit* replacement motif. Lieu assigns much less significance to the festivals than Motyer when she cautions that "although commentators will find numerous links between Jesus' teaching and the details of the festival rituals, John makes no attempt to draw attention to these, or to suggest that Jesus in some way replaces them."[147] Similarly, Fuglseth insists, the "fact that John mentions festivals without any further indication of a theological purpose . . . also suggest that the festival theme in John is not used to introduce an overall re-interpretation of this part of the Jewish traditions."[148] (3) A negative view emerges when the festivals are read within a paradigm of conflict. Hilgenfeld writes an article in response to Güdemann and asks, "Dass der 4. Evangelist schon

---

[143] Stange quoted Haupt who observed already in 1893 against attempts to divide Jesus' speeches into different sources that "*sämtlichen* Reden des 4. Evangeliums diesen Charakter (einer Verblassung des Konkreten) an sich tragen . . . ." STANGE, *Die Eigenart der johanneischen Produktion*, 7 n. 2. So also Broer, "Die Auseinandersetzungen sind viel weniger konkret, . . . Die Fragen des jüdischen Horizonts sind weitgehend versunken, und es geht bei all diesen Gesprächen immer um das Zeugnis von Jesus selbst als dem Gesandten Gottes." BROER, "Die Juden," 337, 338. Güting mentions as well that the author "die historische Konkretion weitgehend reduziert." GÜTING, "Kritik an den Judäern," 178-79.

[144] MOTYER, "The Fourth Gospel," 89 (italics added). See also MENKEN, "Die jüdischen Feste," 269-86.

[145] GRANT, *Second-Century Christianity*, 72.

[146] GÜDEMANN, "Das IV. (Johannes-) Evangelium," 353.

[147] LIEU, "Temple and Synagogue in John," 67.

[148] FUGLSETH, *Johannine Sectarianism*, 251-84, 254.

Rabbinisches berücksichtigt, braucht man nicht zu bestreiten. Aber thut er es, um sich möglichst anzupassen, nicht vielmehr in scharfem Gegensatze?"[149] We recognize the need not just to identify parallels between the Gospel and non-canonical literature, but also to assess the function of the parallels within the larger purpose of the writing. When viewed within the historical context of a conflict with post-70 AD Judaism, the allusions to Jewish festivals acquire a rather inimical sense. Presupposing this conflict, Yee concludes that "the Johannine Jesus now *nullified and replaced* all the Jewish liturgical institutions that the community lost in its divorce from the synagogue: Sabbath, Passover, Tabernacles, and Dedication."[150]

2.7. *Jesus' Speech Translates Particulars into Universals*

When we combine our observations with the details of the speeches as analyzed before (Narratological Parallelism), we gain the impression that, in general, the narrator describes the "Jewishness" of the arising conflict (festivals, Sabbath, law, Moses, etc.) while Jesus points out the "universally applicable characteristics" of the mostly negative response to his message.[151] In other words, the function of the speech is to point "the reader beyond the temporal limits narrated within the story itself"[152] by translating particulars into universals.

For example, the narrator introduces Nicodemus as a Pharisee and leader of the Jews (3:1). And as such he certainly represents, as Collins explains, Jewish leadership (3:1-2) and official Judaism (cf. 3:10).[153] But to stop here means to overlook the scope of Jesus' speech which develops from 3:1-12 to 3:13-21 in such a way that scholars feel the need to assume a change of speakers from Jesus to the narrator or even create

---

[149] HILGENFELD, "Der Antijudaismus," 515.

[150] YEE, *Jewish Feasts and the Gospel of John*, 25-26. See also Brunson who contends that "John's replacement theology is replete throughout the Gospel, and especially evident in the feasts. . . . Thus John portrays Jesus not only as fulfilling but also as replacing holy space, the feasts, and other Jewish institutions." BRUNSON, *Psalm 118 in the Gospel of John*, 147-48. LINCOLN, *The Gospel According to John*, 76-77.

[151] So Culpepper who sees the Jews as "representatives of unbelief." He further explains these universal characteristics of unbelief, "they have never heard or seen the Father (5:37), they do not want to come to Jesus so that they might have life (5:40), they do not have the love of God in themselves (5:42), and they do not receive Jesus (5:43) or seek the glory of God (5:44)." CULPEPPER, *Anatomy*, 129.

[152] O'DAY, "'I have said these things to you ...'," 150.

[153] Motyer thinks that Nicodemus "represents the Jerusalem autorities." MOTYER, *Your Father*, 162. Collins explains Nicodemus as a representative of official Judaism, Jews "who study the Scriptures and know the Mosaic tradition, yet do not come to believe in Jesus, the Messiah and Savior." COLLINS, *These Things Have Been Written*, 14-15. Berger understands Nicodemus even as an "Vertreter christlich gewordener Pharisäer, wie sie Act 15,5 ausdrücklich erwähnt." BERGER, *Im Anfang war Johannes*, 69. But the "we-you" opposition (3:11) as well as the language of condemnation, darkness, and hate (3:18-20) does not suggest that Nicodemus and the group he represents are already Christians.

compositional theories to explain the difference.[154] The content widens in
3:13-21 to universal significance, "God so loved the world . . . " (3:16).
Only here is κόσμος the object of God's love in Johannine literature![155]
Language and thought are very similar to the prologue (see 1:9-10),
especially in 3:19, "And this is the judgment, that the light is come into the
world (τὸ φῶς ἐλήλυθεν εἰς τὸν κόσμον), and men (ἄνθρωποι) loved the
darkness rather than the light; for their deeds were evil." The phrase could
not be more generic since the employment of κόσμος and ἄνθρωποι[156]
interpret Nicodemus' lack of understanding as a universal phenomenon
that transcends particular traits of Jewish people and religion. Hence
Schnackenburg's label "kerygmatische Rede" for 3:13-21 (as well as for
3:31-36).[157] When read in continuity with 3:13-21, Nicodemus stands for
the "entire world as a realm of darkness estranged from God."[158] In this
context, it is significant that the theme of "darkness" is linked to "the
world" and not to "the Jews." The Gospel expresses the dualism between
light and darkness exclusively in connection with Jesus and the world,
never with Jesus and the Jews.[159] An author with anti-Jewish motives
would not have missed the opportunity to use this pictorial and forceful
metaphor and apply it to "the Jews." But the author of the Fourth Gospel

---

[154] BULTMANN, *The Gospel of John*, 153 n. 1. SCHNACKENBURG, *Das Johannes-evangelium* 1:375.

[155] One could point maybe to 1 John 4:10 as a parallel thought, "In this is love, not
that we (ἡμεῖς) loved God, but that He loved us (ἡμᾶς) and sent His Son to be the
propitiation for our sins." And 4:19 "We love, because He first loved us." But while "us"
is clearly opposed to "the world" in 1 John (see 2:15 "Do not love the world") and could
therefore be limited to Christians, κόσμος in John 3:16 does not suggest a numerical
limit. See BROWN, *The Gospel*, 1:133.

[156] The term ἄνθρωπος occurs 59 times in the Gospel of John, and, besides 3:19, it is
used in the sense of "all/any people" also in 1:4, 9; 2:10, 25; 3:4, 27; 5:34, 41; 7:46, 51;
12:43. See also the use of πᾶς to denote "all people" in 2:24, 12:32. Then, ἄνθρωπος is
used 24 times for Jesus (in the title υἱὸς [τοῦ] ἀνθρώπου in 1:51; 3:13, 14; 5:27; 6:27,
53, 62; 8:28; 9:35; 12:23, 34; 13:31; then also 4:29; 5:12; 8:40; 9:16; 10:33; 11:47, 50;
18:14, 29; 19:5), 13 times for specific individuals such as John the Baptist (1:6),
Nicodemus (3:1), etc. (4:28, 50; 5:5, 9, 15; 6:10, 14; 9:1, 11, 24, 30) and 5 times for
undefined individuals (5:7; 7:22, 23; 8:17; 16:21).

[157] SCHNACKENBURG, *Das Johannesevangelium*, 1:375. Opinions vary about the
precise point of transition from personal dialogue to kerygmatic monologue. For
Schnackenburg the kerygmatic speech begins with v. 13. The 27th edition of Nestle-
Aland indicates that the new tone begins with v. 14.

[158] KOESTER, *Symbolism*, 12. Even Schnackenburg, who interprets 3:17 as a rejection
of "unbelieving Judaism," interprets οἱ ἄνθρωποι in 3:19 as unbelievers beyond the Jews
of the time of Jesus. SCHNACKENBURG, *Das Johannesevangelium*, 1:426, 428.

[159] Jesus is "the light of the *world*" (8:12; 9:5; 11:9; 12:46).

had another interest and we see him creating powerful rhetorical monuments which display the universality of sin.

Only in the discourse about the "bread of life" is "the world" the recipient of the "life" (ζωή) that is given (6:33, 51). The author names the benefactors elsewhere with other terms that nevertheless express the same openness to all of humanity, "In him was life and the life was the light of men" (τῶν ἀνθρώπων 1:4). "Everyone who believes" will have "life" (πᾶς ὁ πιστεύων, 3:15, 16; 6:40; also 3:36; 5:24; 6:47; 11:25).[160] The idea in 6:51 of Jesus' sacrificial death, expressed with ὑπέρ (ὑπὲρ τῆς τοῦ κόσμου ζωῆς), also finds parallels in the Gospel: Christ dies for the flock (10:11, 15), for the Jewish nation (11:50-51), for the nations (11:52) and for the disciples (17:19).[161] Thus we can summarize: The bread of God came down from heaven to give life to "the world," which is the flock, the believing disciples of Jesus, consisting of Jews and Gentiles. Although the interlocutors are Jews from Galilee, Jesus' speech points to the benefits of salvation beyond the borders of Israel.[162]

As in 7:7 ("The world cannot hate you; but it hates me"), not "the Jews," but "the world" is the subject of "hate" against Jesus throughout the Gospel (cf. 3:20; 7:7; 15:18, 19, 23, 24, 25). Although we read previously of plots specifically from Jews (5:16, 18), the speeches analyze the specific conflict and interpret it as a universal predicament.

Jesus' self-description as the "light of the world" (φῶς τοῦ κόσμου in 8:12; also 9:5; 11:9; 12:46) evokes Isaianic traditions of universal salvation (Isa 42:6; 49:6; 51:4).[163] The global character of the title corresponds to the inclusive invitation which follows in terms that are open to all: ὁ ἀκολουθῶν ἐμοὶ οὐ μὴ περιπατήσῃ ἐν τῇ σκοτίᾳ, ἀλλ᾽ ἕξει τὸ φῶς τῆς ζωῆς (8:12b). Bultmann explains that, within this dialogue about Jesus' origin (8:14, 23), the connotation of κόσμος is more that of dualism (above versus below) than that of universalism.[164] But, while there might

---

[160] The combination of ζωή and δίδωμι is found only in 6:27, 33; 10:28 (life given to the sheep); and 17:2 (life given to "all that you have given to him").

[161] BEASLEY-MURRAY, *John*, 94. But Schnackenburg doubts that ὑπέρ in these texts carries the sense of "sacrifice" and "atonement" (despite 1:29; 6:51; 17:19) and interprets instead in the sense of "for the sake of" as in 10:11, 15 and 15:13. SCHNACKENBURG, *Das Johannesevangelium*, 2:451.

[162] See SCHNACKENBURG, *Das Johannesevangelium*, 2:56.

[163] SCHNACKENBURG, *Das Johannesevangelium*, 2:241. According to Brown, this proclamation has "been prompted by the ceremonies of the feast of Tabernacles." BROWN, *The Gospel*, 1:343. And Morris understands "light of the world" as a reference to the pillar of fire in the wilderness. MORRIS, *The Gospel*, 437.

[164] So BULTMANN, *The Gospel of John*, 343.

be a shift of nuances throughout the use of κόσμος in the Gospel, both aspects are always present, as is clear already from the prologue.[165]

The words of Jesus in 9:5 and 9:39 frame the healing of the blind as well as the ensuing disputes over breaking the Sabbath, and are somewhat disconnected from the Jewish problem of restoring a man's sight on a holy day.[166] This issue came up before when Jesus healed the invalid (5:1-15), and maybe the author did not see the need to engage Jesus again in an oral defense such as the one in 7:21-24. Instead, while the word of salvation at the beginning (9:5) and that of judgment at the end (9:39) do arise out of the immediate situation, they are not limited to Jesus' own physical conditions of time, place and people. Rather, they stand as paradigms that use the sign's literal level of blindness and darkness, of healing and light to signify Jesus' ongoing mission of salvation and judgment in the lives of the readers. Understood in this way, the nameless blind man who received his sight represents the κόσμος[167] and demonstrates that Jesus is "the light of the world" who came so "that those who do not see may see" (9:39).

The "thieves and robbers" (10:8) in the παροιμία about the Good Shepherd in John 10:1-18 certainly relate to Jesus' conflict with the Pharisees who accuse him of violating the Sabbath. The allegory can also be read as an expression of the conflict between Jews and the church, or as an inner-Christian dispute. Hoskyn goes one step further, "But more is involved even than this, for there is no point in *human history* which lies beyond the horizon of the thieves and robbers of the parable."[168] Although James P. Martin reads the entire Gospel predominantly as a reflection of Jewish opposition against the church after AD 70, John 10 transcends even in his eyes the "original historical situation" and functions "in other

---

[165] Nowhere is the idea of Jesus' vertical descent from above to below and from light to darkness expressed more dramatically than in the prologue where the pre-existent λόγος becomes flesh. Yet, the universal emphasis is equally obvious when we read that John (the Baptist) witnessed so that "all" (πάντες) might believe through him (1:7). And the light that came into "the world" is one that shines on "all people" (πάντα ἄνθρωπον, 1:9).

[166] Schnackenburg points out that the word of salvation in 9:5 does not draw attention to the Sabbath which is introduced only later (9:14) as a reason for the Pharisee's opposition. SCHNACKENBURG, *Das Johannesevangelium*, 2:307. See the comments by Bultmann and Grässer which we quoted in n. 137.

[167] In Koester's words, the blind man "represents humankind." KOESTER, *Symbolism*, 64.

[168] HOSKYN and DAVEY, *The Fourth Gospel*, 368 (italics added). Reinhartz rightly comments that Hoskyn "expands the horizons of the *paroimia* not only to the original Johannine community but to the Christian experience throughout the ages." REINHARTZ, *The Word in the World*, 68.

sociologically similar situations."[169] It is the non-specific language of the παροιμία and Jesus' familiar use of κόσμος (10:36) which supports such an open interpretation. But the inclusion of the non-Jewish world into the allegory is even made explicit when Jesus speaks about "other sheep (ἄλλα πρόβατα) that are not of this sheep pen," and together with the sheep which he already has there will be "one flock and one shepherd" (10:16).[170] Most scholars understand the expression "other sheep" as a reference for the Gentiles, brought in through the mission of the church.[171] The beginning of this harvest might be indicated right after Jesus escapes the subsequent attempt to arrest him and flees to an area "beyond the Jordan" (πέραν τοῦ Ἰορδάνου). The people he finds here believe in him without miracles and simply on account of his verbal witness, just as the Samaritans did (4:39). Their quick approval and response of faith is striking and surprising right after the hostile and lengthy confrontation with the Jews who do not believe although they saw Jesus' mighty miracles.

When the Pharisees resign in frustration because "the world has gone after him" (12:19), the author continues immediately with the statement about the desire of "Greeks" (Ἕλληνές) to see Jesus (12:20). This ordering of statement and narrative makes the Pharisees' word appear like a prophecy come true, and the reader understands that the "world" which went after Jesus is one consisting of Jews and Greeks.[172] The following suggests that these two people-groups function as a merism to describe all nations. After the time of judgment for "the world" (12:31) Jesus says that he will "draw all men to myself" (πάντας, 12:32). Here, the author indicates the universal scope of Jesus' vision not only by the absence of Ἰουδαῖοι and the usage of κόσμος in his speech but also by the inclusive πᾶς which unites all ethnic groups into one object of redemption (see also

---

[169] MARTIN, "John 10:1-10," 171-75. Reinhartz argues as well that this "*paroimia* is by no means exhausted by its parallels to the historical and ecclesiological tales of the gospel narrative." REINHARTZ, *The Word in the World*, 68.

[170] The similarity to Paul's emphasis on the unity between Jews and Gentiles in Eph 2:14-16 is evident. See SCHNACKENBURG, *Das Johannesevangelium*, 3:221.

[171] See BROWN, *The Gospel*, 1:396. SCHNACKENBURG, *Das Johannesevangelium*, 2:376-78. BULTMANN, *The Gospel of John*, 383-84. MORRIS, *The Gospel*, 512. CARSON, *The Gospel*, 388. SCHNELLE, *Das Evangelium*, 180. WILCKENS, *Das Evangelium*, 167.

[172] Bultmann speaks of an "unconscious prophecy" with regard to 12:19. BULTMANN, *The Gospel of John*, 423. So also MOLONEY, "The Function of John 13-17," 47-48. For understanding the Ἕλληνές in 12:20 as "Greeks" and not as "Greek-speaking Jews," see KOSSEN, "Who were the Greeks of John XII 20?," 108. SCHNACKENBURG, *Das Johannesevangelium*, 2:478. BARTON, "Christian Community," 287. Salier reads "the Greeks" as godfearers, proselytes who represent the gentile world. SALIER, *The Rhetorical Impact*, 122.

10:16; 11:52). Judgment and salvation are thus linked not merely to Jewish antagonists but to all of mankind.

Finally, we have seen earlier how the long speech in John 13-17 functions as a literary gate into the passion account and, among other purposes, translates the particulars of opposition against Jesus into universal hate of Jesus' followers. As an agent of the world, Pilate and his soldiers represent Gentile violence against Christians in seminal form. To sum it up in the words of Lieu, while the Jews have "a specific role in the drama being enacted," the "final intentions of the Gospel" emphasize the "'timeless' significance of the rejection of God's revelation."[173]

3. Conclusion

In the last two chapters we have noticed the following: first, the author places the Ἰουδαῖοι in various ways parallel to the κόσμος (compositional, narratological, and conceptual parallelism). Second, it is κόσμος which occurs in places of strategic importance for the interpretation of the text: the prologue serves as a hermeneutical key to the whole Gospel; the farewell discourse is the literary gate into the passion account; and the speeches of Jesus, the hero of the story, operate as a commentary on the narratives. In all three places, the particulars of Jesus' life are translated into universals via the use of κόσμος, a gnomic and repetitive style, and a lack of concreteness. Therefore, third, "the world" emerges as the *Leitwort* with greater importance than "the Jews." When observed within this terminological and structural web of connections, the Ἰουδαῖοι clearly have a subordinate function within the dynamics of the text. The readers' attention is constantly pulled away from the Jewish antagonist and led to perceive "the Jews" as only a part of an opposition that is universal in scope. Given the narrative emphasis of κόσμος, the use of "the Jews" depends on the use of "the world," not vice versa. It is the negative view of "the world" which conditions that of "the Jews."[174] The frequent literalist reading of the Ἰουδαῖοι apart from "the world" distorts the author's point

---

[173] LIEU, "Anti-Judaism," 112.

[174] After observing the connection between Ἰουδαῖοι and κόσμος, Broer rightly concludes that the use of the first depends on that of the latter, ". . . es handelt sich um die Übertragung bzw. Benutzung eines vorgegebenen religiösen Schemas auf Jesus, das die Rolle der Juden mitbedingt. . . . die negative Sicht der Welt, die die negative Sicht der Juden mitbedingt." BROER, "Die Juden," 338. Unfortunately, Broer reverses his observation later when he says that the Jews are the concrete reality behind the world. By choosing Ἰουδαῖοι, the anti-Jewish evangelist went too far in his response to Jewish persecution of the Christian church. Ibid., 339.

of view. We can only agree with Reinhartz who understands "the cosmological tale" as the "meta-tale within the gospel, that is, the overall frame which gives meaning to the narrative, discourse, theology, and metaphors of the gospel."[175]

---

[175] REINHARTZ, *The Word in the World*, 44.

CHAPTER 5

Meaning and Context of "the World"

We have established the functional priority of κόσμος in comparison with
'Ιουδαῖοι. But the question arises why the term receives such a prominent
place in the Gospel. We interpreted the parallelism earlier as a shift from a
local to a universal perspective.[1] As the history of interpretation shows,
this is only one way of understanding the link between both terms which
needs further justification. We will approach the significance of κόσμος
first by asking for its lexical and conceptual meaning. The results will then
be applied to three definitions given to the relationship between 'Ιουδαῖοι
and κόσμος. Lastly, we will venture into the historical context that most
likely caused the author to pen the relationship between "the Jews" and
"the world" the way he did.

1. The Lexical and Conceptual Meaning of κόσμος

1.1. The Meaning of κόσμος outside the New Testament

The term κόσμος is found in Greek literature as early Homer, carrying the
meanings of 'order' (e.g., *Od.* 13.73; *Il.* 12.225) 'ornament' (*Il.* 14.187),
'form,' 'fashion,' 'structure' (*Od.* 8.492), 'honor' or 'credit' (Herodotus
8.60; 8.142) and 'world' / 'universe' as "a special sense of κόσμος among
the philosophers."[2] All of these meanings prevail through the centuries and
are present, for example, in the writings of Dio Chrysostom (AD 40-112),
a Greek orator and philosopher from the first century.[3] The meaning of
'inhabited earth' is "extremely rare in pre-Christian Greek, outside of the
Septuagint."[4] Despite some variations in their cosmologies, the Greek and
Hellenistic philosophers from the Presocratics to Philo used κόσμος in the
sense of 'world' / 'universe' with a *positive* connotation. The term stood

---

[1] See our discussion of the universal content of the prologue and the farewell
discourse in chap. 4.

[2] Our summary of the Greek usage relies on Adams who discusses the use of κόσμος
by Homer, the Presocratics, Plato, Aristotle, Epicureanism, Stoicism, and others. ADAMS,
Constructing the World, 41-77.

[3] For references see ibid., 43 note 11.

[4] Ibid., 43.

for a worldview in which the universe was considered an object of order, unity, beauty and praise that relates to human beings as microcosm to macrocosm.[5]

The Septuagint employs κόσμος mostly in late literature, frequently those writings that were written in Greek to begin with. Occasionally, the term designates 'host' (for צָבָא, e.g., Gen 2;1), 'order' (e.g., *Odes Sol.* 12:2) and 'honor' (e.g., Prov 28:17). But the dominant definition is that of 'ornament' / 'decoration' of women, the city, the temple, etc.[6] and *Wisdom of Solomon* dwells on the meaning of 'world' (e.g., Wis 1:14; 2:24) with the nuance of 'the earth inhabited by people' at some places (Wis 6:24; 10:1; 2 Macc 3:12).

The term κόσμος is found in Philo "far more frequently . . . than in any other ancient writer."[7] In his treatise *De Aeternitate Mundi*, Philo discusses three contemporary definitions of κόσμος as 'universe' (including heaven, stars, earth, animals and plants), 'heaven' (Anaxagoras) and 'time' (Stoics) and chooses to follow the first meaning (*Aet.* 4). While occasionally employing the sense of 'order' (e.g., *Mos.* 2.145; *Spec.* 1.163; *Praem* 76) and 'adornment' / 'beauty' (e.g., *Spec.* 3.187; *Virt.* 21; *Flacc.* 148), Philo usually uses κόσμος in the common philosophical sense of 'world' / universe,' understood as God's creation, made up of four elements (earth, water, air, and fire; *Her.* 281; *Plant.* 120) and divided into heaven (the fixed stars, sun, moon, and other planets [*Congr.* 104; *Aet.* 83]) and earth (land and sea [*Post.* 144], animals and plants [*Spec.* 3.191]). The sense of 'humanity' is only evident when he repeats the Greek view of man as a "small world" (βραχύς κόσμος; see *Post.* 58; *Plant.* 28; *Her.* 155; *Mos.* 2.135).[8]

Josephus uses κόσμος 104 times and mostly in the sense of 'adornment' / 'ornament' for various objects such as women, armor, garments of priests, the temple, the king, or even of speech.[9] In contrast to Philo, the

---

[5] Ibid., 64-69. With regard to the expression μικρὸς κόσμος as a description for the human being "it is usually accepted that Democritus [born ca. 460 BC] coined this phrase [e.g., fr. 34]" Ibid., 46-47.

[6] See the 'ornament of people' (Exod 33:5, 6), of women (2 Sam 1:24; Jdt 10:4; 12:15; Jer 4:30; Ezek 16:11; 23:40), of a city (Jdt 1:14), of the temple (1 Macc 1:22; 2:11), wisdom as the ornament of young people (Prov 20:29; cf. Sir 6:30; 21:21), of the bride (Isa 49:18; 61:10; Jer 2:32), etc.

[7] Ibid., 59. According to *BibleWorks 7.0*, κόσμος occurs 634 times in Philo's writings.

[8] Some prayers in the *Apostolic Constitution* also speak of man as the "(micro)cosm of the cosmos" (3:20; 12:35). See *The Old Testament Pseudepigrapha*, 2:679, 692.

[9] In the sense of 'ornament', Josephus uses κόσμος for women (*A.J.* 1.249, 250, 337; 16.204; 17.68, 81; *B.J.* 4.562), for armor (*A.J.* 3.57; 13.308; *B.J.* 1.76; 4.243), for garments of priests (*A.J.* 3.16, 107, 178; 15.51; 18.90; *B.J.* 2.321), for the temple (*A.J.* 3.126; 8.95, 135; 12.249; 14.107; 15.90; *B.J.* 5.205; 6.241, 391), for the king (*A.J.*

second most frequent usage is that of 'order' in conjunction with political government, sellers on the market, settlement, or military battle ranks.[10] Occasionally we find a spatial meaning of 'world' as creation (e.g., *Ant.* 1.21), habitat (*Ant.* 19.290), or God's temple (*B.J.* 5.548). There is no apparent instance where Josephus uses κόσμος in the sense of 'humanity.'

1.2. The Meaning of κόσμος in the New Testament

The term κόσμος appears a total of 186 times in the New Testament. The Gospel of John uses it 78 times, 1-2 John 24 times, and Revelation 3 times. Together, the Synoptics employ the term only 13 times (without Mark 16:15). Paul uses it 47 times, mostly in 1 Corinthians (21x). The most frequent meaning is that of 'world,' not in Philo's philosophical sense but as the earth (e.g., Matt 25:34; Rom 1:20; Heb 9:26). The term is loaded with a moral qualification as standing in opposition to God and to the church (Gal 4:3; Eph 2:2; James 1:27; 4:4; 2 Peter 1:4). Then, more often and more directly than the Septuagint or any other preceding source, especially Paul emphasizes the sense of κόσμος as 'humanity.' As such, the term stands parallel to 'all men' (πάντας ἀνθρώπους; Rom 5:12) and to 'Gentiles' (ἔθνη; Rom 11:12; 1 Tim 3:16) that 'did not come to know God' (1 Cor 1:21) and therefore are the object of judgment (Rom 3:6; Matt 18:7; 1 Cor 6:2; 11:32) as well as reconciliation (Rom 11:15; 2 Cor 5:19).

1.3. The Meaning of κόσμος in the Johannine Literature

The use of κόσμος in the Johannine literature closely reflects that of other New Testament writers. The meaning of "adornment" does not appear in the 105 occurrences of κόσμος in the Johannine literature,[11] and while the all-encompassing notion of "universe/creation" makes sense in a few places (1:10b parallel to πάντα in 1:3; 17:24; 21:25), the term leans in most cases towards the meaning of "inhabited *world*" and "(fallen) *humanity*"[12] since the author talks about the world of *people* as "the determining feature

---

13.427; 15.5, 104; 17.196; 20.212; *B.J.* 1.358, 451, 590, 671), for the king's palace (*A.J.* 15.306, 318, 324), for speech (*A.J.* 14.2), for a city (15.384; 16.19) and for animals (*B.J.* 7.136).

[10] In the sense of 'order', Josephus uses κόσμος for political government (*A.J.* 1.81, 121; 3.84; 4.184, 193, 312; 5.179; 15.382), for sellers on market (*A.J.* 3.289), for settlement (*A.J.* 4.36, 292), military battle ranks (*A.J.* 4.90; 17.198; *B.J.* 1.673; 2.325; 3.93, 104; 5.50, 79), for 'manner/order of virtue' (κόσμον ἀρετῆς in *A.J.* 18.66) and 'public order' (τοῖς κοινοῖς κόσμου; *A.J.* 19.230).

[11] See the article by SASSE, "κόσμος," 868-95, esp. 883-95.

[12] Sasse categorizes "many passages in John" for the meaning "Humanity, Fallen Creation, the Theatre of Salvation History." Ibid., 890.

of the whole of creation."[13] Sasse is right when he explains that the last two options cannot always be distinguished with precision.[14] See, for example, the statements in 1:10 and 3:17,

> 1:10 He was in the world (ἐν τῷ κόσμῳ ἦν), and the world was made through him, and the world did not know him.

> 3:17 For God did not send the Son into the world (εἰς τὸν κόσμον) to judge the world, but that the world should be saved through him.

At first glance, "in/into the world" carries a spatial sense of "the earth." But both statements speak about κόσμος in the sense of humanity as the agent of rejection (1:10; 7:7; 15:18-19; 1 John 3:1, 13) and as the Son's object of salvation (1:29; 3:17; 1 John 2:2; 4:14). For it is not non-human creation or the earth which does "not know him" or which Jesus "saves" but men and women. The same is true with regard to 9:5, "While I am in the world, I am the light of the world" (see also 1:10). We can say therefore that he who comes "into the world" (1:9; 3:17, 19; 6:14; 9:39; 10:36; 11:27; 12:46; 16:21, 28; 17:18; 18:36; 1 John 4:9) is always the one who accomplishes a mission not aimed at a realm, space, or the universe, but at *humanity*.[15] There are only few texts which suggest an exclusively spatial meaning for κόσμος (see 12:25; 13:1; 17:11, 13; 21:25).

The broad sense of "all human beings" is confirmed by the parallel position not only of Ἰουδαῖοι and κόσμος but also of ἄνθρωπος and κόσμος, such as in 1:9 and 3:19 (italics added),

> 1:9 There was the true light which, coming into the *world*, enlightens *every one*.

> 3:19 And this is the judgment, that the light is come into the *world*, and *people* loved the darkness rather than the light.

---

[13] GUHRT, "κόσμος," 525.

[14] SASSE, "κόσμος," 890. See also GUHRT, "κόσμος," 525.

[15] Guhrt summarizes correctly, "Man belongs so much to the world that *kosmos* in Jn. almost always means the world of men. *Kosmos* in Jn. can certainly be seen under different aspects, . . . Yet it is the world of men that is the determining feature of the whole of creation, notably in those places which speak of sending or coming into the world." GUHRT, "κόσμος," 525. Besides the meanings of "Schöpfung" and "gottfeindliche Welt," Schnackenburg explains that the expression "in die Welt" denotes the "Aufenthalts- und Wohnraum der *Menschen*." SCHNACKENBURG, *Die Johannesbriefe*, 133 (italics his). Although Broer wrongly identifies "the world" only with "the Jews," he rightly emphasizes that κόσμος "nicht als abstrakte Welt gesehen wird." BROER, "Die Juden," 338. Lohse explains, "Aber wenn vom Kosmos gesprochen wird, dann ist vor allem an die Menschen in der Welt gedacht." LOHSE, *Grundriß*, 133.

As we noticed before, so here again: the light that comes into the *world* is one that comes to *people*.[16] Therefore, in the majority of the occurrences, κόσμος assumes the meaning "humanity." This sense is paralleled in the New Testament especially by Paul[17] and elsewhere found occasionally in Hellenistic Jewish writings such as the Septuagint (*Wis* 2:24; 6:24; 10:1; 14:6) and Josephus (*A.J.* 9.242; 10.205; *C. Ap.* 2.138f.). While Greek philosophical literature uses κόσμος mostly to denote 'world' / 'universe,' "human beings are nevertheless related to the κόσμος as microcosm to macrocosm" because they are a part of the whole (e.g., Plato, *Tim.* 30d; 44d-45b).[18]

This lexical conclusion is further confirmed when we consider the conceptual contexts in which the term is used. A brief summary of the Gospel's teaching about "the world" needs to include at least the following elements: (1) Together with all of creation (πάντα, 1:3), humanity is qualified positively as the work of God which was accomplished through the mediation of Christ.[19] (2) Yet, in the present condition, "the world" is marked by "darkness" (1:5) and "sin" (1:29) because it does not "comprehend" the light (1:5) and hates Jesus (7:7; 15:18; also 1:10; 14:17). While the disciples have Jesus as their master (13:16; 15:20), the devil is the "ruler of the world" (12:31; 14:30; 16:11). Jesus does not pray for it (17:9), but the world stands under his judgment instead (16:11; 12:31). (3) Nevertheless, as God's creation it is the object of his love (3:16) and of the Son's mission for salvation (1:29; 3:17; 4:42; 12:47; 6:33, 51; 8:12; 9:5; 14:31; 17:23) that is to be continued by the church (17:18-23; 13:35; 15:27). Thus, the attitude about "the world" fluctuates between positive and negative poles. The affirmative note dominates the first half of the Gospel where the author deals with God's attitude toward the world. The negative aspect appears mostly in John 13-17 and 1 John in which the world's response to God is the main subject.[20]

---

[16] Because of 1:9, Schwankl rightly comments that "die Welt vornehmlich als Menschenwelt gesehen wird." SCHWANKL, *Licht und Finsternis*, 138.

[17] See especially Paul in Rom 3:6, 19; 5:12 (parallel to πάντας ἀνθρώπους); 11:12 (parallel to ἔθνη), 15; 1 Cor 1:20, 21; 3:19; 4:9 (parallel to ἀγγέλοις καὶ ἀνθρώποις); 6:2; 11:32; 2 Cor 5:19; Phil 2:15 (parallel to γενεά); 1 Tim 3:16 (parallel to ἔθνη).

[18] ADAMS, *Constructing the World*, 66.

[19] The divine origin of creation (of "all things," πάντα, 1:3) prohibits assuming a gnostic idea behind "the world" that qualifies all matter as evil and negative. See SCHNACKENBURG, *Das Johannesevangelium*, 3:100, 131, 212. BULTMANN, *The Gospel of John*, 55.

[20] See CASSEM, "A Grammatical and Contextual Inventory," 89. ONUKI, *Gemeinde und Welt*, 50.

Finally, one exceptional sense of κόσμος appears in 1 John 2:15-17,

> Do not love the world, nor the things in the world. If anyone loves the world, the love
> of the Father is not in him. For all that is in the world, the lust (ἐπιθυμία) of the flesh
> and the lust (ἐπιθυμία) of the eyes and the boastful pride of life, is not from the Father,
> but is from the world. And the world is passing away, and also its lusts; but the one
> who does the will of God abides forever.[21]

Here, "the world" describes the realm in which evil desires are at home (2:16). The command not to love "the world" does not refer to humanity but to "the distasteful cosmic trinity"[22] of the lust of the flesh, the lust of the eyes, and the pride of life (see the κοσμικαί ἐπιθυμίαι in Tit 2:12). Greed about material possessions might be the tangible problem behind this description (cf. 3:17).[23] Josephus can speak similarly of the ἡδονή τοῦ κόσμου, part of which was indulgence in the luxuries of Canaan (πλοῦτος, τρυφή), that hindered the Israelites after Joshua's death to obey the law (*Ant.* 5.132).[24] The moral dualism between God and the κόσμος does not deny the world's character as a good creation but recognizes the present condition as one of moral estrangement from God. The world lies "in the power of the evil one" (5:19) and is marked by the "spirit of the antichrist" (4:3). Such an evaluation certainly stands in contrast to the Greek and Hellenistic view of κόσμος as an object of unqualified order, unity, beauty and praise. In contrast to that, Adams understands Paul's use of 'the world' in 1 Corinthians" as "a deliberate challenge to and subversion of this [Greek] world-view."[25] The same ideological shift of semantics can be assumed with regard to the Johannine literature.

---

[21] Schnackenburg says that κόσμος in 1 John 2:15-17 has "eine gewisse Sonderstellung" in the Johannine writings. SCHNACKENBURG *Das Johannesevangelium*, 133. Danker, on the other side, ascribes more occurrences of κόσμος in John to this exceptional meaning of "the system of human existence in its many aspects" (32x) compared with "creation" (3x), "place of inhabitation" (21x), and "humanity in general" (21x). In *BDAG*, 561-63. The reasoning for this decision is not entirely clear, especially since many texts listed under this definition denote a personal agent in the lives of Jesus and the disciples, and not an impersonal "*system* of human existence" (see 1:10c; 7:7; 14:17, 27; 15:18, 19; 16:20; 17:9).

[22] CASSEM, "A Grammatical and Contextual Inventory," 84.

[23] POPKES, *Die Theologie der Liebe Gottes*, 149.

[24] A similar dualism between the pleasures of this world and religious devotion is expressed in 4 Maccabees. The 'tyrant' tests the endurance of Jews by making them choose between either torture or adopting the 'glad life' (ἡδύς βίος) and 'sweet world' (γλυκύς κόσμος) or Greek customs (8:23; see 8:8).

[25] ADAMS, *Constructing the World*, 41.

2. "The World" Symbolizes the Jews

Lexical and conceptual considerations do not automatically answer the question about the identity of the κόσμος in the Gospel of John. Because of the parallelism with the Ἰουδαῖοι, some scholars understand "the world" more narrowly as only a small part of humanity, namely "the world of Judaism." Such a juxtaposition, so it is suggested, interprets a historical conflict between Jews and Christians in terms of a theological-cosmological dualism.

Already in 1834, Friedrich Lücke spoke of the "Jewish κόσμος" in the Gospel of John.[26] When Meeks thinks of "the world," he only considers "the world of Judaism" as the historical opposition of the Johannine community.[27] Thyen notices that Jesus realizes his brothers' request to show himself to "the world" (7:4) by appearing among the Jews into the temple (7:14),[28] and that the hatred of the world towards the disciples (15:18) becomes concrete in the expulsion from the synagogue (ἀποσυνάγωγος in 16:2).[29] Thus, Thyen concludes that the "cosmological dualism" stands in the service of a real conflict, and not vice versa.[30] After showing how "the Jews" and "the world" are used interchangeably in the Gospel (cf. 7:1 and 7:7; 12:9 and 12:12), Klaus Wengst (1990) suggests that the Jews are not representatives of the world, but that the world, which puts pressure on the church, consists specifically of Jews.[31] Adele Reinhartz (2001) similarly observes that "the world is presented in terms

---

[26] LÜCKE, *Commentar*, 1:159. To 6:14 we read, "Alles aber, was den Haß des Jüdischen κόσμος gegen Jesus mehrte, und die letzte große Katastrophe herbeyführen half, verzeichnet Johannes von Kap. 5 an mit großer Sorgfalt." Ibid., 2:79. With regard to 15:20 Lücke writes, "Nahmen die Juden (als Volk, als κόσμος gedacht) die Lehre Jesu an?" Ibid., 2:549.

[27] MEEKS, "Man From Heaven," 69, 71.

[28] THYEN, "'Das Heil kommt von den Juden'," 180. Segovia explains as well: "This 'world' [in 7:4] means the Jews of Judea who are seeking to kill him . . . ." SEGOVIA, "The Love and Hatred," 272.

[29] See earlier Belser with reference to John 16:20, "Hier [chaps.14-16] wird man in dem *ho kosmos* die Hierarchen und Synedristen, die Vertreter des ungläubigen Judentums, erkennen müssen." BELSER, "Der Ausdruck οἱ Ἰουδαῖοι," 220. Against Becker, Dettwiler identifies "the world" in 15:18-19 with the synagogue because of the word ἀποσυνάγωγος in 16:2. DETTWILER, *Die Gegenwart des Erhöhten*, 284-85. So also ONUKI, *Gemeinde und Welt*, 133. MOLONEY, "The Function of John 13-17," 55-56. LINGAD, *The Problems of Jewish Christians*, 123. KEENER, *The Gospel of John*, 1:569 (to 15:18-16:2). WILCKENS, *Das Evangelium*, 12.

[30] THYEN, "'Das Heil kommt von den Juden'," 180.

[31] WENGST, *Bedrängte Gemeinde*, 57.

that strongly resemble the portrayal of the Jews."[32] She then interprets this similarity as an identity in which "the world" is "associated directly with the Jews or their leaders," and therefore leads the compliant reader to flirt with anti-Judaism.[33] Caron (1997) observes that in 8:23 κόσμος is used to define the Ἰουδαῖοι and not the other way round. The Jews are not considered an example of the world, but "the world" is an "attitude" of darkness (σκοτία, 1:4-5) and sin (1:29), a *Jewish* quality and a *Jewish* character trait.[34] In their social-scientific approach to the Gospel, Malina and Rohrbaugh (1998) pursue this path to a radical end. They view κόσμος as a reference mostly to "Israelite society" as part of John's anti-language and exclusive concern with Israel.[35] Consequently, the statement in 3:16, "God so loved the world," means "God so loved the Israelites" because

> the only begotten Son was given to Israel, 'his own,' not to all of humanity. Jesus is Israel's Messiah, for 'messiah' is a social role that occurs only in Israel or on behalf of Israel. Modern readers who assume 'world' refers to all human beings in John are really importing the anachronistic interpretation that comes later in history when Gentile Christians read John in their own ethnocentric perspective. In John's historical circumstances, given John's antagonism to Judeans, 'this world' would then refer to 'this humanity, this people' – that is, Judeans.[36]

---

[32] REINHARTZ, *Befriending the Beloved Disciple*, 36. The "world" in 1:10 is "narrowed to a specific location and community" in 1:11. Since later passages show that "those who reject Jesus are clearly the Jews, the referent for 'world' here can be identified with the Jews." Idem, *The Word in the World*, 38-39. See also PRYOR, "Jesus and Israel," 218. Van den Bussche comments on 1:10-11 that "le monde désigne le monde juif," although he also concedes, "Historiquement la révélation de la Lumière s'adressait à Israël, mais en réalité elle atteint le monde entier." VAN DEN BUSSCHE, *Jean*, 93, 91.

[33] REINHARTZ, *Befriending the Beloved Disciple*, 66. Zumstein stated recently that there "is much at stake in this discussion" about the relationship between 'the Jews' and 'the world.' He continues, if "one could prove that the concepts 'Jews' and 'world' are interchangeable, then it would be necessary to recognize that Christian identity is constructed specifically in the rejection of Jewish identity. We would then be in a constellation marked by the stamp of anti-Judaism. Is this really the case?" ZUMSTEIN, "The Farewell Discourse," 464.

[34] CARON, *Qui sont les Juifs*, 166-67 ("attitude"), 177, 283 ("le 'monde' qui exprime une qualité ou un trait des 'Juifs'"). Idem, "Exploring a religious dimension," 171.

[35] MALINA and ROHRBAUGH, *Social-Science Commentary*, 245-46. There are two other references for κόσμος that occur less frequently: (1) "God's creation" as inert, material (11:9; 17:5, 24; 21:25), (2) "Judeans" (at least in 8:23; 9:39; 12:25, 31; 13:1; 14:30; 16:11; 18:20, 36).

[36] Ibid., 246.

Thus, the use of κόσμος is limited to a *metaphorical* way of speech[37] and belongs to the Gospel's *theological*[38] or *symbolical*[39] language that originates historically in experiences of Jewish violence against Jesus, his disciples, and the Johannine communities. Onuki understands with many others "the world" as part of John's symbolism which carries the sociological function of reinforcing the identity of the Christian communities by interpreting the particular Jewish experience in terms of a transcendent determinism (e.g., 6:44) and dualism (e.g., 8:23-24, 44).[40]

2.1. Criticism

First of all, for the sake of clarity, if κόσμος is a symbol, a metaphor for alienation from God, then "the Jews" are not *representatives* of the world, because a "representative" is someone who speaks or acts on behalf of *others*. Since in this interpretation the meaning of κόσμος tends more towards "realm" and not "humanity," there are no others that could be represented by "the Jews." The Ἰουδαῖοι are therefore not representatives, but the *embodiment* of κόσμος[41] as the realm from below (8:23) that lies in darkness (3:20; 8:12), that is, of the flesh (3:6), and that has the devil as its ruler (12:31; 14:30; 16:11)! In other words, "the Jews are the incarnation of the wicked world,"[42] and κόσμος is part of Gnostic-metaphysical

---

[37] Schnackenburg speaks of a "metaphorische Redeweise von der 'Welt'" as a "Reflexion" about the historical situation of Jesus and his disciples. SCHNACKENBURG, *Das Johannesevangelium*, 3:131. He identifies "das ungläubige Judentum" as the historical referent for "the world." Ibid., 3:132; also 3:106, 3:139, 3:235; 1:147-48.

[38] Wiefel counts κόσμος to the "theologisch gewichtigen Vokabeln." WIEFEL, "Die Scheidung von Gemeinde und Welt," 223.

[39] Rebell speaks throughout his study about the "symbolische Sinnwelt des Joh-Ev," which is evident in the speeches of Jesus (in which κόσμος appears with a high frequency). REBELL, *Gemeinde als Gegenwelt*, 12, 17.

[40] ONUKI, *Gemeinde und Welt*, 34-37, esp. 36. For him, the term κόσμος shifts the historical perspective to a "mehr einheitlich-grundsätzliche Sinnebene ('die Welt'!)." Ibid., 92. He writes with regard to the farewell discourse in chaps. 13-14, "Die zeitgeschichtlich bedingten Einzelheiten wie 'die Juden', 'die Pharisäer' und 'die Synagoge' usw. werden hier auf eine neue, mehr einheitlich-allgemeingültige Sinnebene gehoben. Deshalb werden diese konkreten Begriffe ersetzt durch den Allgemeinbegriff ὁ κόσμος (v. 17.22.27.30)." Ibid., 101. We read with regard to John 15-17, "Er [the author] erklärt Haß und Verfolgung von seiten des Judentums mit Hilfe eines ekklesiologischen Dualismus von 'Gemeinde' und 'Welt'." Ibid., 139. See also BROER, "Die Juden," 338.

[41] Bauer explains that in the Jews "verkörpert sich ihm die gottfeindliche Welt (vgl. 15 18 ff.)." BAUER, *Das Johannesevangelium*, 31.

[42] COLWELL, "The Fourth Gospel," 298. Colwell further, "They [the Jews] are a *racial* group outside the Christian church; Jesus and his disciples are sharply distinguished from them." Ibid., 298 (italics added). Idem, *John Defends the Gospel*, 45. Colwell not only misunderstands (with many others) the parallelism between "the Jews" and "the world"

language which, within the dualistic worldview of the Gospel, aims at *enhancing* the sense of opposition between Judaism and Christianity.[43] With regard to both options which Granskou put before us, the author would then "heighten the anti-Judaism by suggesting that the quintessence of the world's unbelief can be seen in Judaism."[44] Such a definition of the relationship between κόσμος and Ἰουδαῖοι certainly leads to an extremely racial reading of the Gospel which would indeed feed into an anti-Semitic ideology.

The view described above makes the astute observation that κόσμος often serves as the *human* agent in the life of Jesus or as the *human* object of his ministry. But a simple equation of "the world" with "the Jews" boldly overrides the lexical meaning of κόσμος, misinterprets the

---

but he also overlooks the anti-imperial overtones in the Gospel (see more below). When he says that the "cultured pagan who disliked the Jews would have no reason for disliking the Jesus of the Fourth Gospel" (ibid., 47), he is oblivious to the Gospel's exclusivism which aims at *any* centers of worship and rival life-givers other than Jesus.

[43] Baumbach identifies "the world" with "the Jews" and explains, "Johannes hat somit aus 'konfessioneller Rivalität' heraus innerjüdische Gegensätze zwischen dem Juden Jesus und anderen Juden zu prinzipieller Bedeutung mit antijüdischer Spitze erhoben und diesen *Gegensatz* durch Übernahme einer gnostisch-metaphysischen Terminologie metaphysisch *überhöht und gesteigert*." BAUMBACH, "Gemeinde und Welt," 124 (italics added). According to Fischer, "the Jews" in the Gospel of John are a metaphor for disbelievers in general, which is found otherwise only in Gnostic literature. Fischer explains, "Gewiß hat es auch in der werdenden frühkatholischen Kirche eine scharfe Judenpolemik gegeben. Aber daß sie bis zur Metapher 'Juden' für: ungläubige Welt *gesteigert* wurde, ist nur vereinzelt zu finden. Für die Gnosis, sofern sie die *antijüdische* Wendung vollzogen hat, ist die Metapher dagegen selbstverständlich und kann unter der Voraussetzung, daß der Demiurg mit dem Gott der Juden identifiziert wird, sogar im System begründet sein. Der Demiurg ist es, der sich freventlich gegen die obere Welt erhebt mit den Worten: 'Ich bin Gott und außer mir ist keiner'. Dieser Gott wählte sich sein eigenes Volk, das ihm besonders treu ergeben ist: 'Jaldabaoth erwählte Abraham und machte dessen Nachkommen zu Juden' (Iren. *Adv. Haer.* 30.10). Weniger scharf, aber ebenso deutlich heißt es im Philippus-Evangelium: 'Wer den Herrn nicht empfangen hat, ist noch ein Hebräer' (EvPhil 46)." FISCHER, "Der johanneische Christus," 251-52 (italics added). Vollenweider explains, "Die Juden repräsentieren in dieser Hinsicht die gottlose Welt, die unter der Herrschaft Satans steht (12,31; 14,30). Hinter den Juden wird also eine mythische Macht erkennbar, der Teufel oder die Welt, die sich selbst zur Finsternis macht. Das entlastet zwar die Juden von unmittelbarer persönlicher Schuld, führt aber um so schlimmere Assoziationsfelder herauf." VOLLENWEIDER, "Antijudaismus im Neuen Testament," 44. Rensberger sides with Werner Kelber in saying that a symbolic view of the Ἰουδαῖοι "only magnifies the potential or actual anti-Judaism to cosmic proportions. 'The Jews' in John now become a symbol for all human unbelief and opposition to God, the very type of demonization that has led to some of the most violent anti-Semitic outrages of Christian Europe." RENSBERGER, "Anti-Judaism and the Gospel of John," 131. See also REINHARTZ, "'Jews' and Jews in the Fourth Gospel," 214, 225-27.

[44] GRANSKOU, "Anti-Judaism," 204-05.

parallelism between "the Jews" and "the world," and imports questions of historical referent and setting too early.

2.1.1. "The Jews" are a subgroup of "the world."

Some of those scholars who equate the κόσμος with the 'Ιουδαῖοι do so only partially, and thus reveal a problem with their proposal. In his discussion of 3:16, Klaus Wengst speaks several times of the "universal" thrust of the statement.[45] Moloney rightly sees that the Pharisees' complaint "Look, the world has gone after him!" (12:19) is something of a prophecy that is fulfilled in the *Greeks'* coming to Jesus (Ἕλληνές, 12:20). Although for him κόσμος is part of the Gospel's symbolism, Onuki cannot refrain from historizing the term and regarding the Jews as representatives of a larger body of people. In a graphic illustration, he draws "the world" with a circle that is larger than the one for Judaism.[46] Adele Reinhartz reads in 3:19-21 a "universalizing language" that addresses "all readers who have ever lived or who will ever live."[47] The dialogue between Jesus and the Samaritan woman clearly distinguishes both individuals as members of two distinct ethnic groups (4:9). Therefore, when the Samaritans meet Jesus, begin to believe in him, and exclaim that he is "the Savior of the world" (4:42), κόσμος *must* be understood as a reference to a group that is larger than that of ethnic Jews. The Jews are always part of "the world," but "the world" does not refer only to Jews. Not surprisingly, these legitimate and common interpretations of "the world" in 3:16, 12:19-20, 3:19, and 4:42 as "all of humanity," as Jews *and Gentiles*, confirm our lexical analysis and resist therefore a consistent identification of "the world" with Jews.[48]

Do we have to resign with Judith Lieu in saying that "the relationship between 'the world' and 'the Jews' for John is never entirely clear – which determines the boundaries of the other?"[49] The question becomes that as to whether we can limit κόσμος strictly to "the Jews" in some texts while it denotes "Jews and Gentiles" at other places in the same text.[50] We asked a

---

[45] WENGST, *Bedrängte Gemeinde*, 235, 236 ("universalen Heilswillen Gottes"), 239.

[46] ONUKI, *Gemeinde und Welt*, 50, 92-93, 97. The illustration is on p. 82.

[47] REINHARTZ, *Befriending the Beloved Disciple*, 25.

[48] Even texts that suggest a close identification between κόσμος and 'Ιουδαῖοι do not exclude a larger perspective. Schnackenburg, for example, lists the following nuances for κόσμος in 7:4, where the brothers of Jesus tell him to show himself to "to the world," "multitude of people" (12:19), the large world (1 John 4:1), the world in contrast to heaven (cf. 17:15f; 18:36 etc.). SCHNACKENBURG, *Das Johannesevangelium*, 2:194 n. 3.

[49] LIEU, "Temple and Synagogue in John," 55.

[50] Reinhartz explicitly answers this question positively. REINHARTZ, *The Word in the World*, 38.

similar question with regard to another pair of terms and rejected such an option. Although "the Jews" are often interchanged with "the Pharisees" (see 8:12-30; 9:13-23; 9:40 and 10:19), this singular Jewish sect is *only part* of the larger entity called Ἰουδαῖοι (see 11:45-46). Otherwise, given the current inclination to identify the Jews only with religious leaders, we would have to also conclude that, because of the parallelism between Ἰουδαῖοι and κόσμος, "the world" also refers to religious leaders. But this reasoning is absurd and no one suggests that apart, it seems, from Belser in his 1902 article.[51] We have to accept that the author chooses large categories instead of sticking with particular names as the Synoptics do. Thus, as the Pharisees are only a part of the Jews, so the Jews are only a part of the world. Furthermore, identifying "the world" with "the Jews" completely overlooks the dynamics of the compositional and narratological parallelism in the Gospel. The universal prologue serves as a hermeneutical key to the Gospel's narratives about Jewish places and people, not vice versa. And the speeches of Jesus interpret the story and significance of Jewish protagonists and antagonists as part of a universal response of faith and rejection. Therefore, κόσμος is the prominent *Leitwort* in the Gospel and carries the narrative emphasis. The Ἰουδαῖοι serve as a subordinate term with illustrative force. Together with the author's unvaried vocabulary and his lack of concreteness and gnomic style in the speeches, the Gospel reveals the desire to speak in terms that apply to everyone without regard for ethnic origin. Fortna rightly explains that the "opposite of Jew is not Gentile . . . but the exceptional believer in Jesus" and supports his claim with reference to the gnomic tone in 2:23-25 (πᾶς, ἄνθρωπος).[52] The author does not use specific examples of *Gentile* rejection because he employs the life of *Jesus* to make the point, and *his* opponents were *Jews*. Paul illustrates in 1 Thess 2:14-15 how Jesus' suffering by Jewish hands serves to comfort Gentile Christians that suffer 'by their own people' (ὑπὸ τῶν ἰδίων συμφυλετῶν).[53] We thus concur with Brown and others that κόσμος "is a wider concept than 'the Jews'."[54]

---

[51] Although the term "the Jews" does not appear in the farewell discourse, Belser explains that the high priests are present as "die Repräsentanten des ungläubigen κόσμος (15, 18. 21)." BELSER, "Der Ausdruck οἱ Ἰουδαῖοι," 218. Belser holds the same with regard to John 16, "Auch in Kap. 16 kommen die Hierarchen als die Repräsentanten der ungläubigen Welt für den sorgfältig Prüfenden zum Vorschein." Ibid., 219, also p. 220.

[52] FORTNA, "Theological Use of Locale," 92-93. Fortna draws the proper conclusion that the author of the Fourth Gospel "is not in any racial sense anti-Semitic. He does not set Jew and Gentile against each other. Rather he sees two views of salvation . . . in contradiction, and he supposes that this conflict is of universal and eternal significance." Ibid., 94-95.

[53] Segovia maintains against Raymond E. Brown that κόσμος cannot refer to a group larger than the Jews because "the rejection by the Gentiles is hardly mentioned at all in

The ramifications for our question about the use of Ἰουδαῖοι are crucial. If κόσμος is not a term which merely symbolizes the Jews as the only historical referent, but instead "the world" denotes all of humanity as the object of God's love as well as the subject of hate and persecution of Christians, then the Ἰουδαῖοι loose their exclusive role as antagonists! The term "the world" does not only universalize "the specific *temporal* and *spatial* boundaries" of the historical life of Jesus,[55] but because of its parallelism with Ἰουδαῖοι it first of all transcends the *racial* boundaries of Jewish opposition. But we cannot continue this train of thought until we have confronted a major assumption in Johannine scholarship.

2.1.2. Conflict between church and synagogue?

The idea that "the world" means the same thing as "the Jews" does not rest on comprehensive textual analysis, but stems, at least in part, from a theory of conflict between Jews and Jewish-Christians that caused the Gospel's depiction of the opponent as the Ἰουδαῖοι. Though J. Louis Martyn was not the first one to postulate this background, he created a literary monument for this view with his monograph in 1968.[56] His thesis begins with the "key-expression 'to be put out of the synagogue'" (ἀποσυνάγωγος) in John

---

the Gospel." SEGOVIA, "The Love and Hatred," 270 n. 40. He affirms Martyn's thesis about the Gospel's *Sitz im Leben* (Jews persecuting Christians) and maintains that "those who constitute 'the world' [in John 14:17, 19, 22, 27, 30, 31], are the Jews of 13:33." Ibid., 270. But Segovia leaves John 15-17 out of his consideration because it belongs "to one or more later hands on both theological and literary grounds." Ibid., 259. The question is if a *synchronic* interpretation of the Gospel, with chaps. 15-17 included, as well as Segovia's own later reading of the prologue as a voice directed against Judaism *and the Roman empire*, would not provide sufficient evidence of Gentile antagonism in the text.

[54] BROWN, *An Introduction*, 170.

[55] So REINHARTZ, *The Word in the World*, 38 (italics added). In her understanding, the spatial meaning of κόσμος predominates in the Gospel. Ibid., 17, 79.

[56] MARTYN, *History and Theology* (2003). The first edition appeared in 1968, the second in 1979. This view that the writing of the Gospel was motivated by a conflict with Jews, was espoused *before* Martyn, among others, by CARROLL, "The Fourth Gospel," 19-32. PARKES, *The Conflict of the Church*, 83. BROWN, *The Gospel*, 1:LXXIV-LXXV. STRACK and BILLERBECK, *Kommentar zum Neuen Testament*, 4.1:331. GOPPELT, *Christentum und Judentum*, 253. GRÄSSER, "Die Antijüdische Polemik," 86. Schrage speaks of the "exclusion from the national and religious fellowship of the Jews." SCHRAGE, "ἀποσυνάγωγος," 849. See also the scholars mentioned in REBELL, *Gemeinde als Gegenwelt*, 90 n.1. According to Ashton, a version of this thesis was defended as early as 1861 by M. von Aberle who "called the Gospel 'der Absagebrief gegen das restaurierte Judenthum'." ASHTON, "The Identity," 74 n. 74.

9:22; 12:42; 16:2.[57] According to him, it describes a formal decision by Jewish authorities to excommunicate Jewish Christians from the synagogue. Such an action is not conceivable in the lifetime of Jesus and therefore reflects the situation of the post-Easter community. Searching for a "point of correspondence" between John's term and Jewish literature, Martyn finds a close match in the prayer called the "Eighteen Benedictions" (also *Shemoneh Esre* or simply *Amidah*). The prayer appears in the Babylonian Talmud (b.*Berakoth* 28b), but was written earlier, probably between AD 85 and 115 in the rabbinic assembly at Jamnia. The twelfth benediction of this prayer, called the *Birkat HaMinim*, contains this curse, "Let the Nazarenes [Christians] and the Minim [heretics] be destroyed in a moment."[58] Martyn speculates that Jewish authorities used this prayer to detect Jewish Christians in the synagogue for the sake of excommunicating them. The story of the blind man in John 9 is an example of that expulsion projected into the life of Jesus. The traumatic experience of Jewish believers at the end of the first century led to bitterness against official Judaism and motivated the writing of the Gospel in which this opposition appears in form of "the Jews." Thus the text is read as a two-level drama, comprising two perspectives that are not neatly separated, but tightly interwoven: One perspective opens a *window* into the life of Jesus (the "einmalig"level), and the other a *mirror* into the post-Easter Johannine community at the time of the Gospel's composition after AD 70 (the "contemporary" level).[59]

This highly influential thesis summarizes the *opinio communis* in Johannine scholarship and continues to find support with few modifications.[60] At least two points seem uncontested. First, the text as it

---

[57] MARTYN, *History and Theology*, 49. Later he calls ἀποσυνάγωγος "this highly important word." Ibid., 52.

[58] Ibid., 62.

[59] Ibid., 41.

[60] So Onuki, who supports the thesis himself. ONUKI, *Gemeinde und Welt*, 21, 29, 33, 81. Hakola recounts scholars who evaluate Martyn's thesis as "the cornerstone of much current Johannine reasearch" (Rensberger) or as "axiomatic in Johannine studies" (Reinhartz). HAKOLA, *Identity Matters*, 18. A German proponent of the same thesis as Martyn's is WENGST, *Bedrängte Gemeinde* (1981). Idem, "Die Darstellung 'der Juden'," 22-38. See before him already WIEFEL, "Die Scheidung von Gemeinde und Welt," 225-27. Scholars who regard the expulsion from the synagogue, if not the *Birkhat HaMinim*, as the concrete historical context of the Gospel are, among others, SCHNACKENBURG, *Das Johannesevangelium*, 3:235. MEEKS, "Man From Heaven," 55 n. 40. TOWNSEND, "The Gospel of John and the Jews," 83-88. PANCARO, "The Relationship of the Church," 401-402, 404. THYEN, "'Das Heil kommt von den Juden'," 177, 180-82. REBELL, *Gemeinde als Gegenwelt*, 100-12. PRATSCHER, "Die Juden im Johannesevangelium," 181-82. CULPEPPER, "The Gospel of John and the Jews," 281. MANNS, *John and Jamnia*, 29. WAGNER, *Auferstehung und Leben*, 459-61. TROCMÉ, "Les Juifs d'après le Nouveau

stands reflects two levels of experience, that of the historical Jesus (Palestine, Jewish topics of debate, crucifixion) and that of the author and the early church.[61] Luke's division of labor into one account about Jesus in the flesh (Luke) and one about the risen Lord (Acts) are merged into one narrative in the Fourth Gospel.[62] And second, the language of the Gospel is motivated by one or several conflicts.

But the precise location of that conflict in time and space is a matter of dispute. First, the assumed "point of correspondence" with the council of Jamnia is loaded with historical riddles. There are serious doubts about the existence of a "synod" at Jamnia in the modern sense, an official council with the power to decree rules for orthodox liturgy effective for all Jews in all synagogues.[63] When was the prayer "Shemoneh Esre" composed? Were

---

Testament," 20. MATSUNAGA, "Christian self-identification and the twelfth benediction," 355-71. LINK, „*Was redest du mit ihr?*", 326-27. GRELOT, *Les Juifs*, 95-96, 178. ZUMSTEIN, "Zur Geschichte des johanneischen Christentums," 423. FRÜHWALD-KÖNIG, *Tempel und Kult*, 223-24. LABAHN, *Offenbarung in Zeichen und Wort*, 185, 216. SCHAPDICK, *Auf dem Weg in den Konflikt*, 441-57. TOMSON, "'Jews' in the Gospel of John," 195, 197. BURRIDGE, *Four Gospels, One Jesus?*, 153. FUGLSETH, *Johannine Sectarianism in Perspective*, 74-79, 351. PHILLIPS, *The Prologue*, 64, 227. LINCOLN, *The Gospel According to John*, 72 f.

[61] Brown affirms, "All Gospels read the post-resurrectional situation back into the ministry." BROWN, *The Community*, 19. Fuglseth refers to Peter's confession with the plural pronoun (6:68-69), the concern for apostasy (6:60ff), the question of believing without seeing miracles (20:29), the sending of the disciples in 17:18 etc. as "possible references to the later life of a community." FUGLSETH, *Johannine Sectarianism*, 81. German scholars like to speak here with the philosopher Gadamer of "Horizont-verschmelzung," the melting of two perspectives into one. The past of Jesus' life merges together with the presence of the author. See, for example, ONUKI, *Gemeinde und Welt*, 12, 34-37. But beside all recontextualizing and melting of horizons, the author does make a distinction between a pre- and post-Easter perspective and therefore recognizes the chronological priority of Jesus before the church (see 2:22; 7:39; and 12:16).

[62] See BEASLEY-MURRAY, *John*, xlvii-xlviii. SMITH, "John's Quest for Jesus," 236.

[63] Schnelle questions the existence of the alleged Synod, "Es ist unklar, ob es eine 'Synode' von Jamnia überhaupt gegeben hat und welche Beschlüsse dort gefaßt wurden." SCHNELLE, "Die Juden im Johannesevangelium," 224. Boyarin explains, "The only source we have for this 'Yavnean' institution is a Babylonian talmudic story (fourth or fifth century) of Rabban Gamaliel asking Samuel the Small to formulate such a blessing, the latter forgetting it a year later and meditating for two or three hours in order to remember it (b. Ber. 28b-29a). This hardly constitutes reliable evidence, or indeed evidence at all. The aroma of legend hovers over this entire account." BOYARIN, "*Ioudaioi* in John," 220. Aune has shown that the Jewish historian Heinrich Graetz was the author of the Javneh-myth. AUNE, "On the Origins of the 'Council of Javneh' Myth," 491-93. Even if rabbis at a synod of Jamnia, located in the northern part of Judah, ever ordered the cursing of Christians during the daily prayers in the synagogue, it still needs to be shown that such a curse was spoken not only in the land of Israel where the Talmud was composed, but also in the Judaism of the diaspora where the Gospel of John was

Jewish Christians at all the target of the twelfth benediction at the time of its composition?[64] If so, do the ἀποσυνάγωγος-texts in the Gospel of John refer to this formal and large-scale separation of Christianity from Judaism as expressed in the curse, or do they relate more to a local conflict between a synagogue and the Johannine Jewish Christians?[65] Thus, the historical link between the *Birkat HaMinim* and the Gospel of John is rather weak, and its suggestion brings up more questions than it can answer.[66]

Another point of criticism against Martyn is that he has turned *one aspect* of the Gospel into *the key* for its interpretation.[67] Although Martyn

---

most likely written. For the geographical limits of the Talmud's significance, see GOODMAN, "Jews and Judaism," 179; also NICKLAS, *Ablösung und Verstrickung*, 59-60. Motyer explains that "the current consensus seems to be that it was not until after the Bar Kokba revolt that the authority of its successor at Yavneh began to be widely recognized beyond Palestine. In the late first century readers would readily have granted that there was no Jewish 'orthodoxy' in the diaspora, merely a general orthopraxy, and that 'the Jews' of Palestine did not possess authority to regulate what happened elsewhere." MOTYER, *Your Father*, 154.

[64] While the general consensus is that the term "Nazarenes" is a later addition, there is no unanimous interpretation of the identity of the "heretics" (*minim*). Flusser thinks that the *minim* are pre-Christian heretics. Instone-Brewer recently argued that "in Jabneh" is a later addition to the prayer and that the Sadducees are the target of the curse which was written before AD 70. But other scholars contend that the *minim* refer primarily to Jewish Christians (R. E. Brown, Barrett / Thornton, Schiffmann), or include them along with other heretics (Stemberger). Schrage and Barrera conclude that it is not possible to determine who was originally included in the curse. See FLUSSER, "Das Schisma," 230. INSTONE-BREWER, "The Eighteen Benedictions," 25-44, esp. 40-41. BROWN, *The Gospel*, 1:LXXIV. BARRETT and C.-J. THORNTON, eds., *Texte*, 244. SCHIFFMAN, *Texts and Traditions*, 415. SCHRAGE, "ἀποσυνάγωγος," 850. BARRERA, *The Jewish Bible and the Christian Bible*, 166. STEMBERGER, "Die sogenannte 'Synode von Jabne'," 17.

[65] Matsunaga supports Martyn's link between the ἀποσυναγώγος-texts and the *Shemoneh Esreh*. MATSUNAGA, "Christian self-identification," 366. Berger maintains on the other hand, "Die Auseinandersetzung mit den nicht-christlichen Juden im JohEv . . . hat auch mit dem Achtzehnergebet rein gar nichts zu tun." BERGER, *Im Anfang war Johannes*, 83. So also BIERINGER, POLLEYFEYT, and VANDECASTEELE-VANNEUVILLE, "Wrestling with Johannine Anti-Judaism," 11, 12. DE BOER, "The Depiction of 'the Jews'," 146. Frey speaks of the expulsion as a "lokal begrenzten Maßnahme." FREY, "Das Bild 'der Juden'," 45. So also BEASLEY-MURRAY, *John*, 154. SCHMIDL, *Jesus und Nikodemus*, 69-78.

[66] The *Birkat HaMinim* has also been linked to the Gospel of Matthew. For a critical assessment, see RABINOWITZ, "Remnant and Restoration as a Paradigm of Matthew's Theology of Israel," 15-17.

[67] In his preface to the first edition from 1968, Martyn explains that he has "tried to illuminate *one aspect*" of the "setting in which the Fourth Evangelist composed his work." MARTYN, *History and Theology*, x (italics added). But in his introduction to the third edition of Martyn's monograph, Moody Smith says correctly that Martyn viewed "the tension and hostility between 'the Jews' and Jesus as *the key* to the historical life-setting and purpose of the Gospel of John." Ibid., 6 (italics added).

recognizes the "social complexity" of John's communities, he touches only briefly on an inner-Christian conflict with Jewish-Christian members (6:60; 8:31) apart from the church-synagogue dispute.[68] Missing from the picture are controversies with followers of John the Baptist (1:8, 15, 19-24, 30; 3:28-30; 10:41),[69] problems with docetic beliefs (1:14; 19:34-35)[70] and positive relationships between Christians and Jews (1:47-49; 11:31).[71] These manifold and heterogenous problems should warn us against reducing the historical situation to one reason that triggered the writing of the Gospel.[72] The complexity of this historical question about the *Sitz im Leben* is evident when asked with regard to only *one* text. According to Anderson, the bread-of-life discourse in John 6 reflects Johannine Christianity's dialogues and disputes (1) with "mainstream Christianity as represented by all three Synoptic Gospels," (2) with the "local Synagogue," (3) with the "persecution of Christians in Asia Minor (and elsewhere) by Domitian," and (4) with "mainstream churches (esp. Antiochine influence from the mid 80's through the late 90's)."[73] The German proponent of the expulsion-thesis, Klaus Wengst, has acknowledged the overconfidence of his model and modified the subtitle of his book in the third edition accordingly. First he called the theory of a

---

[68] Ibid., 122, 159-63.

[69] Wenham explains that "there is probably controversy with the followers of John the Baptist in the mind of the author. This is suggested by the considerable attention that is given to the question of Jesus and the Baptist in John 1-4, and by the emphasis that the Baptist was not the Messiah, not the light, and that he came to bear witness to Jesus: 'He must increase, but I must decrease' (3:30)." WENHAM, "The Enigma," 172. See also MEEKS, "Man From Heaven," 49. TROCMÉ, "Les Juifs d´après le Nouveau Testament," 19. BURRIDGE, *What Are the Gospels?*, 218.

[70] SCHNELLE, *Antidoketische Christologie* (1987). Also WENHAM, "The Enigma," 173. BURRIDGE, *What Are the Gospels?*, 231.

[71] Jesus was a Jew (4:9), salvation is of the Jews (4:22), and many Jews believe (11:45; 12:11)! Reinhartz argues that the story of the Jews who comfort Mary and Martha (John 11) shows, when read as a two-level story, that there are Christian believers in the Johannine community who are *not* excluded from the synagogue. REINHARTZ, "'Jews' and Jews in the Fourth Gospel," 223.

[72] Schnackenburg cautions as follows, "Bei der faktischen Feststellung aber, welche besonderen, zeitgebundenen Tendenzen der Evangelist verfolgt, muß man sich sicher – das konnte die Untersuchung der Messiasfrage lehren – vor jeder Einseitigkeit hüten." He mentions followers of John the Baptist, Judaism, and Gnostic teachers (1 John) as influences on the writing of the Gospel. SCHNACKENBURG, "Die Messiasfrage," 264. See also ONUKI, *Gemeinde und Welt*, 33.

[73] ANDERSON, "The Sitz im Leben," 27.

Jewish-Christian conflict "the key" to the interpretation of the Gospel of
John, but now it is merely "an attempt."[74]

While Martyn bases his thesis on legendary material, one element
nevertheless stands. Within the complexity of the Gospel, "the Jews" do
occupy a prominent place in the text. The strongest challenge to Martyn's
thesis comes from somewhere else and has to do with his methodological
approach. At least four crucial flaws need to be mentioned.

First, Martyn disconnects words from a coherent system of language by
making the single word ἀποσυνάγωγος (and Ἰουδαῖοι) the key to the
interpretation of the text. For, on the literary level, the expulsion from the
synagogue is connected with "the Jews," which are used in constant
parallel to "the world." But for the most part Martyn completely neglects
the term κόσμος and its interdependence with the Ἰουδαῖοι.[75] When he does
mention "the world," he always equates it with "hostile Judaism."[76] On the
very last page, Martyn bothers to mention the presence of the "Greeks" in
the Gospel (7:35; 12:20), the universal vision (e.g., 4:42), and the Roman
context (Peter's martyrdom in chap. 21). There are many more references
to non-Jews which Martyn neglects, such as the Samaritans (4:1-42), the
"other sheep which are not of this fold" (10:16), the mentioning of the
place "beyond the Jordan" (10:40; cf. Matt 4:15; 8:28) and of "the children
of God who are scattered abroad" (11:52),[77] and Pilate and the Roman
soldiers in the passion narrative. Furthermore, the universal perspective is
expressed in inclusive language such as πάντα (1:3), ἀνθρώπων (1:4),

---

[74] The subtitle of the first edition from 1983 was *Der historische Ort des Johannesevangeliums als Schlüssel zu seiner Interpretation.* The subtitle of the third edition
(1990) changed to: *Ein Versuch über das Johannesevangelium.*

[75] Other scholars, who favor an exclusively Jewish milieu for the Fourth Gospel, are
guilty of the same neglect. The meaning and significance of κόσμος is often completely
absent from their discussion of historical matters. See, for example, BERGER, *Im Anfang
war Johannes*, 64-78. Rebell has determined from the beginning that Jesus' speeches
build up an elaborate world of symbolism. He never examines the use of κόσμος but
always assumes that the term is part of the *textual* "counter-world." He discusses only
two texts, John 2:23-3:21 and 4:1-42, but even here he never analyzes the use of κόσμος
in 3:17, 18, 19 and 4:42. REBELL, *Gemeinde als Gegenwelt*, 134-210. See also TROCMÉ,
"Les Juifs d'après le Nouveau Testament," 19-22.

[76] MARTYN, *History and Theology*, 48, 167.

[77] Geyser tries to limit the meaning of "Children of God" to diaspora Jews without
providing any reasons for his argument. GEYSER, "Israel in the Fourth Gospel," 19. See
also PAINTER, "The Church and Israel," 103, 104, 107. On the other hand, Greek (except
Origen and Cyril of Alexandria), Latin, and many modern commentators refer the
expression exclusively to Gentiles. See PANCARO, "'People of God' in St John's Gospel,"
114 n. 1. Arguments for reading "children of God" as a reference both to Jews and
Gentiles are advanced by SCHNACKENBURG, *Das Johannesevangelium*, 2:451.
CULPEPPER, "The Pivot," 30. GRELOT, *Les Juifs*, 180, 181.

πάντες (1:7), πάντα ἄνθρωπον (1:9), and πάσης σαρκός (17:2).[78] But
Martyn silences this textual voice because it does not fit into the "history
of *Jewish* Christianity" as he reconstructed it beforehand.[79] It is obvious
that, just as the overemphasis on Hellenism as the sole background of the
Gospel led Dodd in the 1950s to disregard the significance of the Ἰουδαῖοι
in his discussion of the Fourth Gospel,[80] so the assumption of an
exclusively Jewish milieu for the Gospel today comes all too often with
blind spots for the data that does not fit into the picture.[81] Thus Brown
rightly complained when he observed Martyn's lack of "sufficient justice
to the presence of Gentiles" in the Johannine communities.[82]

Second, Martyn begins part one of his study in the middle of the
Gospel, namely with an analysis of John 9. Thus, the sequential progress
of thought from the prologue to the Gospel has no chance of influencing
his interpretation of single episodes.

Third, Martyn's historical analysis depends too much on Fortna's form-
critical isolation of a narrative source that underlies the Fourth Gospel.[83]
As a consequence, he creates a dichotomy between narratives and speeches
and fails to consider the latter (because they date late) for the interpretation

---

[78] Not a few scholars also propose that the Greek name "Philip" in 1:44 indicates that
this disciple represents Gentiles. WESTCOTT, *The Gospel*, 1:52. SCHEIN, *Following the
Way*, 24. COLLINS, *These Things*, 25. BRODIE, *The Gospel*, 401. SCHNACKENBURG, *Das
Johannesevangelium*, 2:479. Menken argues in that even the omission of the word σοι in
the quotation of Zech 9:9 in John 12:15 was intended to convey that the king did not
come to Zion only, but to the whole world. "Der vierte Evangelist lenkt wiederholt und in
verschiedenen Formen die Aufmerksamkeit darauf, daß Jesus von Gott her in diese Welt
gekommen ist. . . . Mit σοι würde das Kommen Jesu auf sein Kommen zur 'Tochter
Zion' beschränkt werden." MENKEN, "Die Redaktion," 202. Similarly, Hakola argues
with reference to many other scholars that the quote from Isa 54:13 in John 6:45
intentionally omits Isaiah's words "your sons" [of Israel] inorder to suggest that
"salvation exceeds the borders of Israel." HAKOLA, *Identity Matters*, 234 n. 51.

[79] MARTYN, *History and Theology*, 167.

[80] According to Hakola, Dodd does not offer more than a footnote when discussing
"the Jews" in the second edition of his influential work, *The Interpretation of the Fourth
Gospel* (1963, see p. 242 n. 2). HAKOLA, *Identity Matters*, 22.

[81] For an attempt of a balanced view, see our comments on pp. 60-62, 66-68.

[82] BROWN, "Johannine Ecclesiology," 391. Also HAKOLA, *Identity Matters*, 234 n. 51.

[83] Martyn writes, "It is crucial to note that for the literary analysis pursued at this
juncture . . . *the basic criteria are provided by the discipline of form criticism*." MARTYN,
History and Theology, 35 n. 8 (italics his). He speaks in the following of a "Signs Source
or Signs Gospel" and specifies, "The most significant attempt to recover this hypothetical
document is that of R. T. FORTNA, *The Gospel of Signs: A Reconstruction of the
Narrative Source Underlying the Fourth Gospel* (1970)." Ibid., 69 n. 86. For an early
criticism of Fortna's and Teeple's source criticism see KYSAR, *The Fourth Evangelist*,
33-36; also RUCKSTUHL, *Die literarische Einheitlichkeit*, esp. 310-28. VAN BELLE, *The
Signs Source*, 163-80.

of the signs and for the mentioning of expulsion from the synagogue.[84] The blind man's banishment from the synagogue culminates in the saying, "For judgment I came into this world" (9:39). Jesus' conclusion with reference to the κόσμος (12:46, 47) follows the second reference to ἀποσυνάγωγος in the epilogue of the first half (12:42). And the last occurrence of ἀποσυνάγωγος appears in the farewell discourse which is devoid of the "the Jews" and replete with "the world."

Fourth, many scholars do not choose the narrative in John 9, but the speech in John 15-17, as a window into the social circumstances of the post-Easter communities.[85] The absence of the Ἰουδαῖοι and the opposition of "the world" mentioned therein shifts the focus from a conflict between Jesus and the Jews to one between the church and the larger empire, including Gentiles.

As a result, Martyn is indifferent to "the Jews" as part of a dualism that is universal in scope. He does not exaggerate the element of conflict, but he excludes the hostility of the non-Jewish world from the social setting of the author and his readers. In order to remain true to the lexical meaning of κόσμος and its context in the Gospel, we have to conclude that the ethnic makeup of "the world" consists of Jews and Gentiles. To use the editor's metaphor in the preface: Martyn "gets the credit for a sea change in Johannine studies. Others may have gotten off the ground," while Martyn achieved "sustained flight."[86] But his two-level plane, and that of much of Johannine scholarship, flies too low; it never reaches the third height and thus the heart of the Gospel![87]

---

[84] Moody Smith makes this explicit in his contribution to the third edition when he writes, "While Martyn's thesis does not require Fortna's source-critical results precisely, it does require some cogent explanation of how the content of the Gospel of John, *particularly the narrative content*, is linked to the synagogue controversy. Fortna's work supplies that link, and Martyn has continued to regard it as essentially correct." MARTYN, *History and Theology*, 10-11 (italics added). Also, "Martyn is concerned only with Fortna's Gospel of Signs, the *Grundschrift*, and the subsequent controversy that leads ultimately to its expansion into the Gospel we now know. But Martyn actually deals only with the middle of the spectrum of development as Brown sees it and not at all . . . with any final redaction of the Gospel and the publication of the Letters." Ibid., 13.

[85] See our discussion on pp. 173-75.

[86] MARTYN, *History and Theology*, ix.

[87] For further critical discussion of Martyn's thesis, see MOTYER, *Your Father*, 92-94. NICKLAS, *Ablösung und Verstrickung*, 30-72. HAKOLA, *Identity Matters*, 16-22, 41-86. KYSAR, "The Expulsion from the Synagogue," 237-45. Reinhartz finds three levels of meaning in the Gospel of John (historical, ecclesiological, cosmological) and observes that the third level is often neglected in Johannine scholarship in general, not just by Martyn in particular. REINHARTZ, *The Word in the World*, 6.

3. "The World" Symbolizes Unbelief

While the previous view identified κόσμος with "the Jews," some scholars go to the opposite extreme and understand the term not as a reference to people at all but to a principle, an abstract idea, a system of unbelief instead. Wearing regards "the world" as an element of mystic speculation which uses the visible and temporal only as symbols and types of the "inner" unseen life and eternal reality.[88] Here, κόσμος signifies "the universe built up of *ideas* or personal *attitudes* visited vainly by the revelation of the Logos so miraculously exhibited in the person of Jesus."[89] Grässer uses the heretics in 1 John to define "the world" in the Gospel and interprets the polemic against the Jews as one directed against the "worldliness" of the church itself.[90] Within this language, κόσμος describes the principle of "unbelief" that is embodied in "the Jews." Similarly, Kysar understands κόσμος as "a symbol to represent the realm of unbelief, the realm in which there is total rejection of the truth of God revealed in Christ."[91] Likewise, "the Jews" function as "types of unbelief" and do not refer to empirical people. In his discussion of John 18:20, Hendricks interprets κόσμος as a "state of estrangement and alienation from God," as a "'system' of the central religious institutions of Judaism," and "oppressive system," admitting (with E. M. Sidebottom) that such a view "represents a new trajectory of usage of the term in antiquity."[92]

On the one hand, the definition of κόσμος as an idea, an attitude, a principle, a realm, or a system seems to make sense in a text like the Fourth Gospel which interprets the physical world in metaphysical terms through the use of λόγος, φῶς, σκοτία, ἀλήθεια, ζωή, δόξα, and others. The

---

[88] So WEARING, *The World-View of the Fourth Gospel*, 37-38.

[89] Ibid., 19 (italics added).

[90] Grässer writes, "diese Polemik ist ein Stück johanneischen Dualismus im Dienste praktischer Gemeindeinteressen. Die eigentliche Spitze des Kampfes ist gegen die Verweltlichung des Christentums selber gerichtet! Die Gefahr dazu droht von dem her, was durch die Offenbarung als Krisis auf die Seite der 'Welt', der Lüge, der Finsternis, der 'Juden' verwiesen ist. Sie droht vom Unglauben!" GRÄSSER, "Die Antijüdische Polemik," 90. Goppelt noticed earlier that the "Evangelium kämpft gegen die Verweltlichung des Christentums, die gegen Ende des 1. Jh. in der Gnosis wie im Frühkatholizismus heraufzieht." GOPPELT, *Christentum und Judentum*, 254. Similarly, Schram interprets the "world" language as a criticism of the church, "Their [the Jews'] connection with 'the world' in some sense is clear from the Gospel materials (John 8.23; 18.20), but then 'the world' has yet to be interpreted. And 'the world' can be inside the Church or the individual believer as well." SCHRAM, "The Use of ΙΟΥΔΑΙΟΣ," 160. See also SCHMITHALS, *Johannesevangelium*, 308-10.

[91] KYSAR, *John: The Maverick Gospel*, 50.

[92] HENDRICKS, "A Discourse of Domination," 93-94.

link of κόσμος to the invisible ἄρχων τοῦ κόσμου (12:31; 14:30; 16:11) might strengthen a non-material sense of the word as a symbol. But in the details of the text it does not convince to read 3:16 as "God so loved the realm . . . ." or 15:18 as "If the attitude hates you . . . ." This view relies too heavily on the exceptional and abstract use of κόσμος in 1 John 2:15-17 as "worldliness" and overlooks, on the other hand, the role of "the world" in the Gospel as the *human* subject of hate, killing, and persecution (7:7; 15:18; 16:2). The Gospel's dualism does not only exist in horizontal terms (above-below, e.g., 8:23) but includes the meaning of "the world" as a vertical hostile agent in the lives of Jesus and the church.[93] As such, κόσμος stands in opposition to the disciples and cannot be identified with them, as Grässer likes to do.[94] His position reminds us of de Jonge who regards the Gospel's use of Ἰουδαῖοι as a polemic directed against fellow Christians.[95] Parts of the criticism there applies also here. While Grässer can draw support from the similarities between the Gospel and 1 John, he underemphasizes the differences. The idea of a theological dispute *among believers* appears to be only marginal in the Gospel (6:60-66, 8:31).[96] While 1 John focuses more on "false belief" inside the church (1 John 2:18-19; 4:5), the Gospel's subject centers on "unbelief" outside the group[97] and its burdens for Christians (John 15-17: expulsion from synagogue, persecution of the church). Strange enough, Grässer recognizes this historical context of the evangelist which he describes with Jewish persecution of Christians and expulsion from the synagogue at the time of the Gospel's composition.[98]

This, finally, leads to the last weakness. Despite its inclusive concern, this view sounds similar to the racial reading discussed before. For the question arises why the author chose particularly "the Jews" in order to illustrate the principle of unbelief. While Wearing's mystic author simply

---

[93] Ashton notes that there are two oppositions implied in "the world," a vertical and a horizontal one. ASHTON, *Understanding the Fourth Gospel*, 206-08. Becker distinguishes between a vertical dualism which divides humanity into "the world" and the church ("ekklesiologischen Dualismus Kosmos-Kirche," e.g., John 15:18-25; 16:16-33; chap. 17). BECKER, "Beobachtungen zum Dualismus," 72, 82-85. On the other hand, the Gospel knows of a horizontal dualism which separates heaven from earth and spirit from flesh ("prädestinatianisch-ethischer" dualism, e.g., John 3:1-21). Ibid., 79.

[94] See BAUMBACH, "Gemeinde und Welt," 129. We showed that "the world" refers to humanity and denotes people other than the disciples (section 1.3 in this chapter).

[95] See our discussion in chap. 1 (1.4. Fellow Christians).

[96] This is the criticism of Smith against Käsemann, who assumes an inner-Christian dispute behind the Gospel. SMITH, "John and the Jews," 223.

[97] See SCHMITHALS, *Johannesevangelium*, 204, with reference to Conzelmann.

[98] Grässer even regards the cursing of heretics in the synagogue (Shemoneh Esreh) as part of the author's historical context. GRÄSSER, "Die Antijüdische Polemik," 86.

negates the importance of phenomena in principle,[99] Grässer and Kysar recognize that the immediate problem for the Johannine community had to do with attacks from the Jewish synagogue.[100] But when viewed under these social circumstances and pressures, it is hard to avoid the conclusion drawn earlier that Ἰουδαῖοι is a reference to Jewish enemies outside the church.

4. "The World" Refers to Humanity

If we cannot narrow κόσμος to a symbol for "the Jews" or a mere principle ("worldliness"), then we are required to apply its ordinary lexical meaning. As we noted earlier, in the Gospel, "the world" refers a few times to "creation" as a whole, but mostly to "humanity," describing all people without ethnic distinctions. Such an understanding coheres well with the observation that Jesus' speeches translate the particulars of the narrative about his life into notions of universal applications.[101] When understood this way, we cannot reduce the statement "God so loved the world" merely to God's love towards Israel. The "ruler of this world" (12:31) does not exert his influence just on the life of Jews, but on that of Gentiles as well. The "sin of the world" (1:29; cf. 16:8), which is taken away by the lamb, is

---

[99] Wearing thinks that "racial or political considerations play little or no part whatever" in the Fourth Gospel because the mystic tends "to neglect natural phenomena, human affairs, and social considerations." WEARING, *The World-View of the Fourth Gospel*, 36, 40.

[100] KYSAR, *John: The Maverick Gospel*, 57. He creates the causal connection as tight as can be, "It is the pressure of the concrete situation [conflict with the synagogue] which causes him to make this selection [using Ἰουδαῖοι]." Ibid. For Kysar, the only remaining reason to avoid a racial reading of the text is an assumption about matters behind the text such as the Jewish heritage of the author, "We *may assume* that the writer of the Gospel himself *may have been* of a Jewish heritage, or at least that a large number of those in the local Christian community with him had been Jews. Hence, he is not issuing a judgment upon the Jewish people as a group but communicates to his original readers that the Jewish opponents of the church are a typical kind of human failure to accept Christ." Ibid. (italics added). But if there was an immediate historical conflict with the synagogue, as Kysar presupposes, it is difficult to avoid reading Ἰουδαῖοι as a historical reference to ethnic Jews and not a mere type for human failure.

[101] It is at this point that Wellhausen's proposal fails because he does not consider the universalizing tendency of the speeches. For him, κόσμος refers to Gentiles and the parallelism with Ἰουδαῖοι suggests therefore that Jews are equated with Gentiles in order to deprive them of their status as the chosen people of God: "Das Wichtige ist gerade, daß nicht sie die von der Welt Abgesonderten sind, sondern die Christen, daß sie mit den Heiden völlig zusammen geworfen werden. Darin zeigt sich der tiefe Haß gegen das Volk, das Jesum kreuzigte und seine Jünger verfolgte: es wird verworfen." WELLHAUSEN, *Das Evangelium*, 117.

not a reference to Jewish transgression only, but to that of all human beings. Consequently, the world's hate and rejection of the *logos* (1:10; 15:18, 19; 17:14) does not simply refer to the expulsion of Jewish Christians from the synagogue, but also to hostilities from Gentile opposition. It is the author's intention to say that the kind of opposition which Jesus faced from the Jews is not unique to his experience, but will always happen to all of his followers at any place. Creating this "universal outlook"[102] about Jesus' mission and opposition is the main contribution of the term κόσμος.

4.1. John 15-17 and Gentile Opposition against the Johannine Christians

John 15-17, if not the complete farewell discourse, are the most direct window into the Johannine communities after Easter. These chapters are exclusively addressed to the disciples and not to the public (see 13:1). No references to any time or place are given anywhere between 13:1 and 17:26, which gives the words a tone of timeless relevance. Even though John 13-14 speaks more about the "einmalig level" of the historical Jesus (the betrayal and denial of Judas, death and resurrection, martyrs of the first generation) while chapters 15-17 refer to the "contemporary level" of the Johannine church (expulsion from synagogue, persecution of the church, schism, delay of parousia), the distinction is not absolute.[103] Throughout the chapters, John is concerned with "principles and significance rather than specific events."[104] It is a time of persecution for the church (16:33), weeping and mourning (16:20). Jesus encourages not to fear (14:1, 27) but to abide in him (15:3; 16:1) and to expect suffering as part of following the master who suffered himself (15:20).[105] For our question of anti-Semitism in the Fourth Gospel it is of great importance that, in this mirror of the author's situation, "the world" dominates as the subject of hostility against the church, and not "the Jews." Consequently, several scholars interpret the language as a hint to either local or widespread *gentile* violence against Christians, besides or after the Jewish experience of expulsion from the synagogue. According to Painter, for example, 15:18-25 relates "the theme of Jewish hostility to the later experience of the Johannine community, isolated from the synagogue and

---

[102] FUGLSETH, *Johannine Sectarianism*, 290, also 287-289.

[103] NEUGEBAUER, *Die eschatologischen Aussagen*, 143; see also pp. 111-17, 141-45. See our discussion of Neugebauer's thesis in more detail in chap. 4 (1.2.1. The literary gate into the passion account).

[104] MORRIS, *The Gospel*, 610.

[105] See WENGST, *Bedrängte Gemeinde*, 53-54.

facing a hostile world, perhaps at the time of the third version."[106] Dietzfelbinger, on the other hand, equates "the world" with the synagogue in John 15-16. But he explains that in John 17, the perspective has broadened to a universal scope in which κόσμος stands for the church's opposition from the Hellenistic world.[107] Raymond Brown interprets all of John 14-17 this way:

> The fact that the opposition to 'the Jews' dominates chaps. 5-12 while opposition to the world dominates chaps. 14-17 suggests a chronology in the relationships. . . . The shift in opposition from 'the Jews' to the world may mean that now the Johannine Christians are encountering Gentile disbelief, even as formerly they faced Jewish disbelief.[108]

No matter whether we consider "the world" as hostile Gentiles only in John 17, in the whole farewell discourse, or even in the entire gospel, it is important to recognize that Jews as an ethnic group are *not* singled out as the only unbelievers in humanity. When placed into the macrostructural perspective (prologue, discourse), then *all* occurrences of "the world" function to translate the particular hostilities between Jesus and the Jews to a universal level.

---

[106] PAINTER, "The Farewell Discourses," 534. Unfortunately, Painter does not attempt to identify the "hostile world" any further.

[107] Dietzfelbinger explains with regard to John 17, "Wie weit meint κόσμος (v.6.9.11.13.14.15. 16.18.21.23. 25) überhaupt noch die Synagoge, wie das sonst der Fall ist (15,18ff ist ein besonders handgreifliches Beispiel dafür)? Wird nicht in 17,5.24 der Kosmosbegriff ausgeweitet auf die Menschenwelt überhaupt? Das läßt sich damit erklären, daß die johanneische Gemeinde nach oder neben der Feindschaft der Synagoge in steigendem Maß auch die Feindschaft der hellenistischen Umwelt erfahren hat." DIETZFELBINGER, *Der Abschied des Kommenden*, 342; also p. 350. See also TILBORG, *Reading John*, 218.

[108] BROWN, *The Community*, 63. In other words, "What I would deduce from the Johannine references to the world is that, by the time the Gospel was written, the Johannine community had had sufficient dealings with non-Jews to realize that many of them were no more disposed to accept Jesus than were 'the Jews,' so that a term like 'the world' was convenient to cover all such opposition." Ibid., 65. See also BROWN, *An Introduction*, 170-71. Hengel sees it similarly, "Dem Schicksal, das Jesus von seinem eigenen Volk zuteil wird, entspricht – *vor allem in den Abschiedsreden* – der Hinweis auf den Haß der Welt gegen die Jünger, die mit einem analogen Schicksal rechnen müssen." HENGEL, *Die johanneische Frage*, 297-98 (italics added). Salier explains that κόσμος means "the Jews, in the bulk of the Gospel, and the wider world, especially the Roman government in the trial narratives." SALIER, *The Rhetorical Impact*, 13-14. Our observations of the narratological parallelism between the Ἰουδαῖοι and the κόσμος especially in chaps. 3-12 might caution against Brown's identification of different opponents in chaps. 5-12 and chaps. 14-17.

4.2. Theodicy in the Fourth Gospel: Servants Are Like the Master

More than offering a coherent *theology*, the author offers comfort to a persecuted church with a *theodicy*.[109] In a proverbial statement, Jesus explains twice that his disciples relate to him as servants (δοῦλος) to a master (κύριος): this principle is used positively to encourage the imitation of Jesus' service as exemplified in the foot-washing (13:16), and negatively to prepare the disciples for hate and persecution in the future (15:20; cf. Matt 10:24-25).

The author expresses the parallel between servant and master in many ways throughout the Gospel. Philip imitates Jesus *verbatim* when he extends the invitation to "come and see" to Nathanael (1:46), just as Jesus earlier invited the two disciples of John the Baptist to "come and see" (1:39). Jesus is not of this world (ἐγὼ οὐκ εἰμὶ ἐκ τοῦ κόσμου τούτου, 8:23; cf. 18:36) and the disciples are not of this world either (ἐκ τοῦ κόσμου οὐκ ἐστέ, 15:19). Jesus expresses this point of unity in his prayer (17:14, 16). As he was sent by the father so he sends his disciples (17:18; 20:21). As he was in the father's bosom (εἰς τὸν κόλπον τοῦ πατρὸς, 1:18), so the beloved (ideal) disciple sits just next to Jesus (ἐν τῷ κόλπῳ τοῦ Ἰησοῦ, 13:23).[110] Jesus is the "light" (8:12; 9:5; 11:9; 12:46), and his disciples are called "sons of light" (12:36). The world "hates" Jesus (7:7; 15:18, 24-25) as well as the disciples (15:19; 17:14). Sometimes Jesus does not use the first singular "I" in his speech, but the first plural "we" (3:11; 9:4), thus indicating identity between him and his disciples.

It is this connection of servants to their master which helps the afflicted Christians to understand their suffering, not as a sign of God's absence, but as the necessary mark of true discipleship. The life of the master does not

---

[109] Meeks speaks of the social function of the Gospel which was written "to provide a reinforcement for the community's social identity, which appears to have been largely negative. It provided a symbolic universe which gave religious legitimacy, a theodicy, to the group's actual isolation from the larger society. MEEKS, "The Man from Heaven," 70. Onuki follows Meeks and explains, "Es gilt als gesicherte These der Religionssoziologie, daß jeder religiöse Dualismus im Hinblick auf seine soziale Funktion mehr oder minder Theodizee ist." ONUKI, *Gemeinde und Welt*, 10. Rebell formulates to the point, ". . . die Gemeinde sieht ihr Schicksal mit dem Jesu zusammen und schöpft aus dieser Schicksalsgemeinschaft Kraft, um die Krise zu durchstehen." REBELL, *Gemeinde als Gegenwelt*, 103. Dettwiler explains that the "*theologische Grundproblem* ist dasjenige einer joh Form von *Theodizee*." DETTWILER, *Die Gegenwart des Erhöhten*, 298 (italics his); see also p. 285. While the Gospel puts forth a theodicy for an afflicted church, all four scholars limit the conflict to one with the synagogue because they don't understand κόσμος as a reference which includes non-Jews as well. A theodicy with a broader perspective is offered by POPKES, *Die Theologie der Liebe Gottes*, 322-27.

[110] HOFRICHTER, *Im Anfang war der „Johannesprolog"*, 17. KÄSEMANN, "Aufbau und Anliegen," 2:177.

offer a pool of options and opportunities. As the footwashing is imperative (13:13-17), so persecution is unavoidable. Now the servants suffer from the Gentiles what the master experienced from the Jews.[111] The author's design of corresponding the life of the early church to that of Jesus requires the use of broader terms. Jewish terms for non-Jewish antagonists do not capture clearly enough the violent resistance of Gentiles. Therefore, the author creates the text-internal parallelism between "the Jews" and "the world" for the text-external purpose of addressing readers in a hostile pagan environment.[112] While the Ἰουδαῖοι operate in the life of Jesus, the prologue and the speeches use κόσμος in order to extrapolate the specifically *Jewish* opposition to a level that applies to all of humanity.

5. Reading John in the Roman Empire

A narrative approach that regards the Gospel as a piece of pure literature in which the function of various *dramatis personae* are discovered entirely from within the work itself can finish the inquiry at this point. We can contend with Bultmann's *existential* interpretation according to which the Gospel broadens the historical experience of a Jewish conflict into an opposition by all of humanity against the church.[113] But considering that the Fourth Gospel was written to readers of flesh and blood at the end of

---

[111] Vouga words it well, "On purrait être tenté de conclure de ces quelques pointages que *Jésus a été victime de l'hostilité juive* tandis que *les disciples le sont de la haine du monde*, et que ces deux conceptualités font allusion à des données historiques qui ne se recouvrent pas exactement." VOUGA, *Le cadre historique*, 107 (italics his).

[112] See SCHNELLE, "Die Juden," 228. Idem, *Das Evangelium*, 166.

[113] Bultmann expressed it this way: "Taking the Jewish religion as an example, John makes clear through it how the human will to self-security distorts knowledge of God, makes God's demand and promise into a possession and thereby shuts itself up against God." Because of this abstract understanding of "the Jews," Bultmann writes the expression always in quotation marks! BULTMANN, *Theology of the New Testament*, 2:27. Quiévreux said it to the point, "D'ailleurs, dans tout l'Evangile, ceux qui sont opposés à Jésus et à ses disciples sont non pas les Juifs, mais *le monde*. Le kosmos, chez Jean, n'est pas l'univers, mais l'humanité, c'est-à-dire l'univers conscient. Le monde don't Satan est le chef n'est pas une fraction de l'humanité, mais l'humanité tout entière." QUIÉVREUX, "'Les Juifs'," 257 (italics his). Von Wahlde writes, "Along with Ashton (and Bultmann before him) I would agree that the sense of 'the Jews' is one example of the opposition which is represented more broadly as 'the world' (ὁ κόσμος)." VON WAHLDE, "'The Jews' in the Gospel of John," 53 n. 107. Too cautious in his conclusion, Cook says nevertheless, "insofar as others besides the Jews also fail to believe, the term 'the Jews' lends itself to an expansive application, descriptive of them as well." COOK, "The Gospel of John," 268. He fails to mention the explicit expansion of Jewish unbelief into that of "the world."

the first century AD, we wonder about the *historical* reasons that motivated the penning of the relationship between the Ἰουδαῖοι and the κόσμος the way it is.[114] Reconstructions about a conflict between Synagogue and Christians, so common in Johannine scholarship, limit the setting exclusively to a Jewish context and thus do not capture the universal dimension of the Gospel. From our reading, it seems obvious that current experiences of pagan hostilities motivated the author to use the Jewish opposition against Jesus as an illustration of the world's opposition against the church. In the following, we will attempt to specify the nature of that opposition. We are aware that the element of speculation grows the more we step away from the text and into the world of the first audience. We also do not forget that the Gospel addresses multiple groups with very different problems. Thus, we suggest that the Gospel of John offers various points of contact with the Greco-Roman world that seem pertinent to our subject. But they are understood as elements of a conflict that occurred within a complex web of pressures which together influenced the writing of the text.

5.1. Either Jesus or Caesar (John 19)

Since the Gospel respects the original *Jewish* framework for the life of Jesus, it is not surprising that most chapters do not offer us an *explicit* hint to possible confrontations between the early church and gentile culture. On the other hand, the story culminates in Jesus' trial before the Roman governor in John 19 and points to a conflict between Jesus' claim to kingship and that of the emperor. The absence of a trial before the Jewish Sanhedrin in John's passion account focuses the attention on the Roman trial before Pilate and centers the accusation on Jesus' kingship as the political crime against Rome.[115] The Jews press explicitly for a decision between either Jesus or Caesar. They argue that Pilate is "not a friend of Caesar" (οὐκ εἶ φίλος τοῦ Καίσαρος) when he releases Jesus because "everyone who makes himself out to be a king opposes Caesar" (19:12). And again they reject Jesus with the statement, "We have no king but Caesar" (19:15). The *political* contrast between Jesus and the Caesar might be exaggerated in order to hide mere *religious* charges of blasphemy which would not convince the Roman governor (see 19:7). But in light of 11:45-48 we can also say that the rejection of a Jewish king and affirmation of

---

[114] See Vouga's pointed question, "Pourquoi a-t-il pris la plume?" VOUGA, *Le cadre historique*, 9. See our discussion about "authorial audience" in chapter one (3. Reflections on Method).

[115] See TOWNSEND, "The Gospel of John," 77. According to Morris, "the basic thing is the confrontation of Caesar by Christ, with kingship as the topic for discussion." MORRIS, *The Gospel*, 767.

Caesar's kingship stems from honest concerns about possible Roman retribution against the temple and the Jewish nation as a response to a feared anti-Roman uprising. That fear was based on numerous examples of the recent past. After detailed descriptions of turmoil through rebels such as Judas, Simon and Athronges (Josephus, *A.J.* 12.269-284), Josephus summarizes that during the rule of Herod Archelaus (4 BC – AD 6) "Judaea was filled with brigandage. Anyone might make himself king (βασιλεύς) as the head of a band of rebels" (*A.J.* 12.285).

What about the readers for whom the Gospel was composed and who live *after* the destruction of the temple? Is it possible that the author included the political charges against king Jesus, which challenges imperial sensitivities to non-Roman claims of kingship, into the passion account in order to pick up *ongoing* Roman suspicions about the Christian religion as an attempt to built an alternative kingdom with a ruler other than the emperor?[116] According to the book of Acts, Paul is rejecting such accusations by the Jews in Thessalonica (Acts 17:7) as well as in Caesarea (Acts 25:8) who promoted a false antithesis between Jesus and Caesar (see also Luke 23:2; Matt 22:17). In contrast to Jewish heroes such as Moses, Joshua, David, Esther, Judith, or Judas Maccabeus, Jesus' own behavior and his words (18:36; cf. Justin, *1 Apol.* 11) suggest a pacifist program without weapons and violence. But the author does not encourage Christians to unqualified submission under Caesar. As we will see, the Gospel includes elements of resistance against Rome throughout the account. When Jesus confronts the governor and calls his role as a judge in this unjust trial "sin" (19:11), it becomes clear that "Jesus is not subject to Pilate. The reverse is true."[117] When read through the lenses of the farewell discourse, the passion account is not just a trial in which Jesus is condemned. He has "authority over all mankind" (17:2; cf. 13:3) and no one takes away his life for he himself lays it down (10:17-18). Jesus defends this proposition of power before the representative of the emperor (19:10-11). The passion account itself is a "story of an enthronement in which Jesus is made king by the soldiers, by Pilate, and by the people" so that the text maintains a political statement "against the background of the

---

[116] Keener suggests that the Jews' insistence on having no king but Caesar "may be meant to remind the Johannine community of the claims of the imperial cult." KEENER, *The Gospel of John*, 1:224. Salier explains that the "clearly posed choice offered to the Jews between their 'King' and Caesar underlines the implicit comparison and contrast that has been made throughout the Gospel between the figure of Jesus and the Roman emperor." SALIER, *The Rhetorical Impact*, 164.

[117] TILBORG, *Reading John*, 172. See also our discussion in chapter four (1.2.2. Pilate as an agent of the world).

competition with the Roman emperor."[118] The Jews unite with the Roman under Caesar (19:15) which qualifies even the emperor as an enemy of God.[119]

5.2. Memories of Martyrdom (John 21)

Tacitus (AD 55-117) describes in his *Annals* (15.44) how Nero tried to divert suspicion that he laid fire to Rome by blaming the Christians who then were arrested, convicted of hatred against mankind, mocked and tortured in the most horrendous ways. Peter (and Paul) was among those that died in this persecution around AD 68 (see Eusebius, *Hist. Eccl.* 2.25.5; 3.1.2). The Gospel of John announces his death in 13:38 and foresees it again in 21:18-19. The event was for the readers of the Fourth Gospel already a loss of the past and the prediction therefore a painful reminder of the world's hatred against them.[120] Despite the benefits of the *pax romana* up to this point, Nero's killing of Christians must have brought resentment against the government and a desire for a peace that does not disappear (cf. John 14:27; 16:33).

The death of the apostle was not an isolated expression of Gentile rejection against the Christians. As part of the collective memory in the Christian movement, Johannine believers must have heard, if not experienced themselves, violence from Gentiles *before* the writing of the Gospel of John which might also have influenced the choice of the term κόσμος. Compared with the systematic and universal persecution of Christians in the third and fourth century under the Roman emperors Decius (AD 249-51), Valerian (AD 257-260), and especially Diocletian (AD 303-313), the sporadic and local outbursts of Gentile violence in the

---

[118] TILBORG, *Reading John*, 213. Tilborg spells out this level of meaning on pp. 213-19.

[119] This is the conclusion of Weidemann who follows Neyrey at this point. See WEIDEMANN, *Der Tod Jesu*, 352.

[120] In the following decades, the martyrdom of Peter and Paul served many Christians as examples of encouragement for their own suffering. Around AD 95, at about the same time that the Gospel was written, Clement, bishop of Rome, wrote a letter to the Corinthian church in which he refers to the martyrdom of Peter and Paul as "noble examples of our own generation" after he spoke about the persecutions of Joseph, Moses, David, etc. (1 Clem 5:3-7). Ignatius, bishop of Antioch, who was killed in Rome in AD 107, compares his upcoming death with that of Paul (*Ign. Eph.* 12:2). For a critical discussion of the sources about the martyrdom of Peter and Paul, see SCHMITHALS, "Die Martyrien von Petrus und Paulus," 521-41. What is historically probable, according to Schmithals, is that Peter and Paul were killed in Rome under Nero after the fire in AD 64 as the result of a political intrigue. Their death is different from the martyrs who died due to their confession of Christ, as it happened after the Jewish war when the general persecution of Christians began.

first two centuries seem insignificant.[121] Yet the lesser magnitude might be merely due to the smaller number of Christians, for the expressions of pain and suffering within the life of the early church are many and unmistakable. Clear hints in the New Testament, dating from around AD 50-80, speak explicitly of Gentile opposition against Jesus and the early church. There are many general predictions of suffering and persecution which do not mention the ethnic origin of the antagonist, and thus remain open for fulfillment by opponents from various countries and races (Mark 4:17). "Taking up the cross" becomes the *necessary* condition for an authentic Christian existence (Mark 8:34-35; see 10:29-30; also *Ign. Rom.* 4:1-2; *Ign. Magn.* 5:2). Life under external pressure is so common that we even read in 2 Tim 3:12, "all who desire to live godly in Christ Jesus will be persecuted." Besides the general alarm, voices about pagan rejection are not missing. Jesus predicted with regard to himself that chief priests and scribes "will deliver him to the Gentiles (τοῖς ἔθνεσιν) to mock and scourge and crucify him" (Matt 20:19). The disciples are foretold an exposure to "governors and kings" (ἡγεμόνας δὲ καὶ βασιλεῖς) in the same context (Matt 10:18; Mark 13:9; Luke 21:12; see ἀρχαί and ἐξουσίαι in Luke 12:11). The prediction of future trouble for Christ's sake announces that unspecified enemies "will deliver you to tribulation, and will kill you, and you will be hated by all nations (πάντων τῶν ἐθνῶν) on account of my name" (Matt 24:9; cf. Justin, *1 Apol.* 24).

Strong polemic against pagan life and religion permeates the preaching of the early church[122] and was most likely met with, or even triggered by, angry disapproval. The mentioning of Gentile slander against Christians in 1 Peter 2:12; 3:16 echoes at least a negative *verbal* response (see also *Barn.* 59:3; *Ign. Eph.* 10:1-3; *Ign. Trall.* 8:2).

The detailed records of Paul's work as a missionary among Gentiles testify to tangible hostilities from them on all three mission-journeys between ca. AD 45-60: in Antioch (Acts 13:15), Iconium (14:5) and Lystra (14:19), in Philippi (16:16-24), and in Ephesus (19:23-20:1). While in the first three examples, Gentile citizens in these cities were incited by Jews, the last two texts show an unmediated aggression of Gentiles against Christian preachers who disrupted the tight connection between pagan religions and monetary profits, and thus attacked the foundations of local economies.[123] After all these experiences, we find the apostle reporting to

---

[121] See GONZÁLEZ, *The Story of Christianity*, 1:87.

[122] Matt 5:47; 6:7 [cf. 7:6]; 18:17; cf. 15:24; 1 Cor 1:23; 12:2; Eph 4:17-18; 1 Thess 4:3-5; 1 Pet 2:12; 3:15-17; 4:3; Rev 14:8; 18:23.

[123] Paul exorcized a woman in Philippi who brought in money with her mantic practice (Acts 16). In Ephesus his preaching disturbed the business of the silversmith

Herod Agrippa II. the following words of the Lord which he received years earlier in the vision at Damascus, "(I will deliver) you from the Jewish people *and from the Gentiles*" (Acts 26:17, italics added; cf. 2 Tim 3:11). In another retrospective view, Paul said that he was exposed to "dangers from my countrymen, *dangers from the Gentiles*" (2 Cor 11:26). Finally, Paul explains to the Christians in Thessalonica that they "became imitators of the churches of God in Christ Jesus that are in Judea, for you also endured the *same sufferings* (τὰ αὐτὰ ἐπάθετε) at the hands of your own countrymen (συμφυλετῶν), even as (καθὼς) they did from the Jews" (1 Thess 2:14; cf. Justin, *1 Apol.* 31). Besides general references to "much tribulation" (πολλή θλῖψις, 1:6; 3:3-4; cf. 2 Thess 1:4-6), the letter itself does not specify the kind of suffering these Gentile Christians went through.[124] According to the Book of Acts, Jewish Christians in Jerusalem suffered prison (4:3; 5:17-18), flogging (5:40), stoning (7:54-60), and persecution (8:3) from their own people. If the Christians in Thessalonica endured "the same sufferings" as believers in Judea, then some of these pains must have been part of their experience as well.

We realize that, at least since the middle of the first century, Christians suffered rejection by Jews and Gentiles alike. Both responded with the same intensity of hatred against the same messengers and their message. Although the Gospel of John does not *specify* any Gentile expressions of hostility, the repeated echo about the hatred of the world can easily be understood as a reflection of this opposition (e.g., 15:18, 19; 17:14).

5.3. The Prologue against Pagan Polytheism (John 1)

Polemic against pagan worship and rulers is not saved for the end of the Gospel but starts already on the first page. We noticed earlier with particular attention to the prologue that the Gospel's language displays a complex religion-historical background.[125] Many points of *contact* exist between the Gospel's text and a large variety of literature. But the confession of Jesus as the pre-existent and only-begotten God who became flesh is not simply a synthesis. It includes familiar elements from various

---

Demetrius, who earned a living by selling figurines of the temple dedicated to the goddess Artemis (Acts 19).

[124] The following verses mention the killing of Jesus, the persecution of "us" (Paul, Silas, and Timothy, see 1:1) and their prohibition of speaking the gospel (2:15-16). If Paul lists these sufferings in order to specify the pains of "the churches . . . that are in Judea" (2:14), then they illustrate the tribulations of the believers in Thessalonica as well.

[125] See our discussion in chapter three (1.1.3. The Gospel's *religionsgeschichtliche* complexity).

traditions in such a way that a new and *contrasting* concept emerges.[126] When considering the rhetorical context of the first century, we observe that the prologue entails Jewish and Greco-Roman concepts and worldviews in such a way that it provokes one as much as the other. The presentation of Jesus as a pre-existent deity which became human challenges Jewish monotheism. On the other hand, the claim that Jesus became σάρξ breaks down a barrier between flesh and spirit, mortal and immortal, that colored the Hellenistic worldview.[127] Furthermore, the language about the "only-begotten" (μονογενής) and the notion that no other (οὐδείς) besides Jesus has seen God (1:18) confronts pagan polytheism.[128] Segovia exposes the double-edged offense of the prologue's Christology. As an "ideological construct," the prologue "proves severe for both the Roman Empire and Judaism." While the Jews are challenged by Jesus as a "second divine figure," the overall monotheistic thrust clashes with pagan polytheism and its "entire pantheon of divine figures, both in terms of traditional religion and assimilated cults." Therefore, in any ancient context, "whether that of the Roman Empire or that of Judaism, the implied author declares all beliefs and practices, all institutions and authorities, as 'darkness'."[129]

---

[126] While Dodd affirms the presence of Jewish as well as Greek concepts in the prologue, he nevertheless observes that John creates something new, "John has made out of the two hemispheres of thought and experience, joined in a single term, a new category to comprehend a new and unique fact." DODD, "The Prologue," 12.

[127] PHILLIPS, *The Prologue*, 194, 195. See Origen, *Cels.* 4.14; 5.2; 6.73. Goppelt comments that the statement of Jesus' incarnation opposes also Hellenistic speculations about the Logos and was thus written "in Antithese zu allem, was Juden *und Heiden* über ähnliche Offenbarungsmittler sagen." GOPPELT, *Christentum und Judentum*, 257 n. 4 (italics added). Harris explains, "For on the Greek side the mode of death for gods who took human form was to be whisked away by the intervention of Zeus or some other eternal deity. . . . On the other hand, for the Jews the fact that their God had determined to send a Logos-μονογενὴς as fully human was incredible." HARRIS, *Prologue and Gospel*, 178-79. See also SANDERS and MASTIN, *A Commentary*, 77. PHILLIPS, *The Prologue*, 194, 197, 208. But outside of Hellenistic philosophical circles pagans have no problem of celebrating Paul as a god in human form after he performed miracles in Lystra and Malta (Acts 14:11-13; 28:6).

[128] Celsus calls Christians "a secret and forbidden society" (Origen, *Cels.* 8.17) because they don't "tolerate temples, altars, or images" (*Cels.* 7.62) and refuse to partake in public feasts and idol offerings (*Cels.* 8.21). Lioy points out that God's revelation in the "divine, incarnate Word makes it possible for believing sinners to become genuine members of God's family" and stands "in sharp contrast to pagan notions that humans can somehow acquire the divine essence or become demigods." LIOY, *The Search for Ultimate Reality*, 93.

[129] SEGOVIA, "John 1:1-18," 52, 53-54.

5.4. Provenance, Date, and Audience of the Gospel

Most scholars continue to date the Gospel somewhere between AD 80-100,
which overlaps more or less exactly with the reign of the emperor
Domitian (AD 81-96).[130] We are not interested in trying to pin down the
precise year and exact city of the Gospel's origin. Instead, we content
ourselves with the broadest consensus about these historical questions. The
earliest testimonies about the Gospel's provenance point to Asia Minor in
general, and to Ephesus, the "metropolis of Asia" (πρωτευούση τῆς 'Ασίας,
Josephus *A.J.* 14.224), in particular,[131] places at which the imperial cult
and various mystery religions (see, e.g., Acts 19) were especially
prominent.[132] But taking Ephesus as the provenance for the Gospel does
not reduce the reading of the book to a window into the social situation

---

[130] The following scholars are among those who date the Fourth Gospel between AD
80-100: Godet, Westcott, Brown, Bultmann, Barrett, Borchert, Turner, Mantey, Fuller,
Tasker, Kysar, Bruce, Carson, Beasley-Murray, Köstenberger, Smalley, Moloney,
Witherington, Lightfoot, Dodd, and Martin. See the list in CROTEAU, "An Analysis," 79.
Croteau himself discusses forty-one lines of argument with regard to the dating and
concludes for a timespan of AD 80-100. See also HENGEL, *Die johanneische Frage*, 299.
WILCKENS, *Das Evangelium*, 14. GNILKA, *Johannesevangelium*, 8. KEENER, *The Gospel
of John*, 1:140. TREBILCO, *The Early Christians*, 271-73. KÖSTENBERGER, *John*, 8.

[131] Irenaeus writes, "Then John, the disciple of the Lord, who had even rested on his
breast, himself also gave forth the gospel, while he was living at Ephesus of Asia" (*Haer.*
3.1.1-2 in EUSEBIUS, *Hist. Eccl.* 5.8.4). Eusebius affirms that John died in Ephesus.
(*Eccl. Hist.* 3.1.1). Trebilco discusses and defends the patristic evidence for Ephesus as
the provenance of the Gospel. TREBILCO, *The Early Christians*, 241-63. Vouga lists five
arguments against Egypt or Syria and for Ephesus, or at least Asia Minor: (1) tradition
(Irenaeus); (2) the related book of Revelation (Rev 2-3; cf. Ephesus in 2:1-7); (3) the
prominent role of Thomas, Philip, and Andrew, whose apostolic activity is located in
Asia Minor according to tradition; (4) the criticism of John the Baptist fits the milieu of
Asia Minor (cf. Acts 18:24-25; 19:1-7); (5) the readers of John stem most likely from the
Hellenistic and Roman world. VOUGA, *Le cadre historique*, 10-11. See also HENGEL, *Die
johanneische Frage*, 305. SCHNELLE, *Das Evangelium*, 6. BEASLEY-MURRAY, *John*,
lxxix-lxxx. Other proposals suggest a different provenance mostly because of some
affinities between the Gospel and Philo (Alexandria), Jewish sects and literature
(Palestine), or Ignatius of Antioch (Syria). But this is just another temptation to
emphasize one religious background over the other. If we want to let *all* features of the
Gospel influence our decision, then we can speculate about a journey of pre-literary
traditions from Palestine to Ephesus, where they were united into the written canonical
form. See SCHNACKENBURG, *Das Johannesevangelium*, 1:134. BERGER, *Im Anfang war
Johannes*, 54.

[132] The body of literature about Asia Minor and Ephesus in the first century AD has
grown steadily in the last thirty years. Lüdemann describes and discusses six relevant
monographs (Müller 1976, Trebilco 1991, Thiessen 1995, Günther 1995, Koester 1995,
Strelan 1996). LÜDEMANN, *Primitive Christianity*, 129-36. For a current summary of the
discussion see FIENSY, "The Roman Empire and Asia Minor," 36-56, esp. pp. 52-54 for
"The Emperor Cult in Ephesus."

only of this particular city.[133] As Bauckham has argued, and others before him, the Gospel was most likely written not just for one closed group, but for a "network of communities" that stood "in constant, close communication with each other" through "Christian leaders . . . who traveled widely."[134] If this is true with regard to the Synoptics, it applies all the more to the Gospel of John, with dialogues characterized by a gnomic style and lack of particularity. Explanations for readers unfamiliar with Jewish customs (2:6, 13; 5:1; 6:4; 7:2; 19:31, 40, 42)[135] and translations of very basic Aramaic terms into Greek, such as Ῥαββί (meaning Διδάσκαλε, 1:38) and Μεσσίας (meaning Χριστός, 1:41),[136] strengthen the impression that Gentiles are at least a *part* of the audience.[137] Josephus' *Anitquitates Judaicae* and *Bellum Judaicum*, which were written τοῖς Ἕλλησιν (*A.J.* 1.5; also 1.129; *B.J.* 1.3, 6 [Ἕλληνας . . . καὶ Ῥωμαίων], 16),[138] parallel the Gospel's explanations of Jewish customs

---

[133] Here we agree with TREBILCO, *The Early Christians*, 237-41.

[134] BAUCKHAM, "Introduction," in *The Gospels for All Christians*, 3. In a later essay in the same volume, Bauckham concludes from the parentheses in 3:24 and 11:2 that the readers must have heard already about John the Baptist and Mary from the Gospel of Mark. This indicates that "the Fourth Gospel was written, not for a Johannine community isolated from the rest of the early Christian movement, but for general circulation among the churches in which Mark's Gospel was already being widely read." BAUCKHAM, "John for Readers of Mark," 171. Köstenberger picks up this view in his new commentary when he speaks of a "universal readership." KÖSTENBERGER, *John*, 8. See also NICKLAS, *Ablösung und Verstrickung*, 65-68. See also footnote 149 below.

[135] Culpepper concludes from these texts that a "Jewish audience would not need such explanations." CULPEPPER, *Anatomy*, 220. So also PAINTER, "The Farewell Discourses," 525, 541. HENGEL, *Die johanneische Frage*, 298.

[136] See also Κηφᾶς (meaning Πέτρος, 1:42); Σιλωάμ (meaning Ἀπεσταλμένος, 9:7); Ῥαββουνι (meaning Διδάσκαλε, 20:16). On the other hand, we also find three Greek expressions translated into Aramaic (ἑβραϊστί): προβατικῇ κολυμβήθρα (meaning Βηθζαθά, 5:2); Λιθόστρωτον (meaning Γαββαθα, 19:13); Κρανίου Τόπον (meaning Γολγοθα, 19:17). Josephus himself, who writes to Gentiles, frequently translates terms from Greek to Hebrew as well, maybe explaining terms his readers are familiar with, or at least wanting to deepen his readers' grasp of Jewish language and culture (e.g., *A.J.* 3.134, 144, 151, 157, 237, 252, 291). Harris rightly observes the following, "But when the evangelist finds it necessary to transliterate *messias* in 1.41, or to explain the rite of purification as Jewish in 2.6, it suggests a wider, multi-racial audience of a more universal character." HARRIS, *Prologue and Gospel*, 23. Martyn's and Keener's insistence that the explanations and translations serve diaspora Jews is not convincing. MARTYN, *History and Theology*, 91. KEENER, *The Gospel of John*, 1:155, 157, 496.

[137] See also our discussion of the history-of-religions background in chap. 4, pp. 66-68. See furthermore, BROWN, *The Community*, 55-58. HENGEL, *Die johanneische Frage*, 298. Tomson derives from the explanation of customs that the Gospel was "re-edited in a non-Jewish speech situation." TOMSON, "'Jews' in the Gospel of John," 192.

[138] See MASON, *Josephus*, 94.

such as purification with water (John 2:6; *A.J.* 18.117), the Passover (John 2:13; 6:4; *A.J.* 2.317; 3.248; 10.70), the Jewish Feast of Tabernacles (John 7:2; *A.J.* 13.372), the Sabbath (John 19:31, 42; *A.J.* 3.237), and burial customs (John 19:31, 40; *B.J.* 4.317; *C. Ap.* 2.205) and thus corroborate our view of the Gospel's (at least partially) non-Jewish audience.

The book of Revelation was written to seven churches in Asia Minor (Rev 2-3). Irenaeus mentioned around AD 180 that it dates "towards the end of Domitian's reign," thus ca. AD 95-96 (*Haer.* 5.30.3).[139] Furthermore, Eusebius informs us that John, the apostle and evangelist, wrote Revelation on the island of Patmos at a time when Domitian "was the second [after Nero] to promote persecution [διωγμόν] against us" (*Hist. Eccl.* 3.17-18).[140] The internal witness of Revelation mentions Patmos as the place where the book was composed (1:9). In addition, the book refers to persecution and martyrdom of Christians in the past (e.g., 2:13; 6:9; 16:6; 18:24), the present (e.g., 1:9; 2:9), and the future (e.g., 2:10; 13:10). Considering the external and internal evidence, it is no surprise that there is wide acceptance in scholarship in seeing Rome behind the "great harlot" and "Babylon" in Revelation 17-18 and Domitian's imperial cult and his persecution behind the two beasts from the sea and from the land in Revelation 13.[141] The similarity with the Gospel in provenance and time of composition, and the common origin of both writings in the same Johannine school of thought[142] suggest the possibility that the political pressures which motivated the writing of the Book of Revelation also

---

[139] IRENAEUS, "Against Heresies," *Ante-Nicene Fathers* 1:560.

[140] EUSEBIUS, 1:235.

[141] OSBORNE, *Revelation*, 8-9, 497. BEALE, *The Book of Revelation*, 5-9. Kraybill speculates that the "appearance of seven stars on some Domitian coins could have motivated John to answer with his own image of Jesus, world conqueror, holding seven stars in his right hand (Rev. 1.16). . . . it is possible the huge statue of Domitian found at Ephesus is the very 'image of the beast' condemned by John of Patmos (Rev. 13.13-15)." KRAYBILL, *Imperial Cult and Commerce*, 64. A more cautious conclusion suggests that the author of Revelation is not struggling against a "'hard' form of the imperial cult" but against "the 'soft' imperial cult, understood as an especially prominent example of pagan religious praxis in general." KLAUCK, *The Religious Context*, 330.

[142] In his extensive study about the relationship between Revelation and the other Johannine compositions, Frey dates all five writings of the Corpus Johanneum to the last decade of the first century AD and concludes that Revelation clearly belongs in the vicinity of the Johannine school ("eindeutig zum Umkreis dieser johanneischen Schule"). FREY, "Erwägungen," 415. The differences in vocabulary, syntax, and style between Revelation and the Gospel are not genre-related, and therefore point to a different author. But similar phrases (esp. Rev 1-3 and the Gospel), motives, and theology reveal the close relationship between both writings. Frey thinks, with Strecker (and against Taeger), that the Gospel was written after Revelation. Ibid., 394-415. For the same conclusion, see also TREBILCO, *The Early Christians*, 615.

exerted their influence on the composition of the Fourth Gospel.[143] Could it be that the imperial worship posed a threat large enough for the Johannine communities to require clarification and encouragement through the writing of the Fourth Gospel?[144]

Excursus: Knowledge of the Old Testament in the Greco-Roman World

The Jewishness of the Gospel of John, or of any of the Synoptics, does not necessarily deny the presence of Gentiles among the authorial audience. For one thing, not every element in a Gospel has to be equally relevant for every listener.[145] One could speculate that Jewish elements are included for Jewish readers without excluding Gentiles from the audience. But beyond this neat division, we have to take into account that the spreading of diaspora Judaism made Gentiles *somewhat* familiar with Jewish heros, old traditions and current customs. Seneca (ca. 4 BC – AD 65) and Horace (65-8 BC) mention that the Sabbath was kept by a large part of the non-Jewish population, though often without knowing.[146] Juvenal (ca. AD 55-128) describes a Roman father who keeps the Sabbath, worships one God, and refrains from eating pork. His son goes even further and gets circumcised and becomes a proselyte (*Sat.* 14.96-106).[147] In order to prove the antiquity of the Jews, Josephus lists in his book *Contra Apion* twenty-four Egyptian, Chaldean, Phoenician and Greek historians who all mention the Jews in their sources (1.73-320).[148]

---

[143] This would even be true if the Gospel was written during Domitian's reign and Revelation later during Trajan's reign. See FREY, "Erwägungen," 427. Both emperors persecuted Christians and caused the same suffering at different times.

[144] According to Quimby, John 15:18-16:3 not only warns Christians about "the hostilities of the Jews, but it forewarns of the yet harsher threats of the Roman authorities" who, in the days of emperor worship, put "deadly pressures upon all Christians to conform to Caesar's decrees." QUIMBY, *John*, 43. Quimby derives support for his thesis from "the contemporary book of Revelation" which "bears lurid witness" to the "blood, sweat, tears and death" of Christians. Ibid., 43. Goppelt observes close parallels between the Fourth Gospel and Revelation with regard to the Johannine connection of Judaism and the world. Jerusalem is a symbol of the world which is, like Egypt and Sodom, hardened in sin and kills the witnesses of Christ (11:7-8). Jerusalem is called "the great city" (τῆς πόλεως τῆς μεγάλης, 11:8) as is Babylon (ἡ πόλις ἡ μεγάλη, 17:18; 18:10). The war against Christ and his church (Rev 12:17), which the Jews began (Rev 2:9; 3:9), will be completed by the world. GOPPELT, *Christentum und Judentum*, 260-61.

[145] See BAUCKHAM, "For Whom Were the Gospels Written?" 24. GAGER, *Moses in Greco-Roman Paganism* (1972).

[146] See Seneca, *Lucil.* 95.47 and Horace, *Sat.* I 9.71-72.

[147] See SÄNGER, "Heiden – Juden – Christen," 160-61.

[148] In his fascinating monograph, *The Interpretation of the Old Testament in Greco-Roman Paganism* (2004), Cook begins with a review of twenty-one pagan historians from the pre-Christian era who show familiarity with the Old Testament. COOK, *The Interpretation*, 4-54. Unfortunately, the works of many of these ancient historians are not preserved and the reference to them in some remaining sources is all we have. Mendels offers nine factors that contributed to the loss of ancient historical works among which are physical reasons (wars, fires, earthquakes and floods), the banning of books by

He quotes extensively from some of their works and it is evident that at least educated kings, soldiers, historians and philosophers, including (according to Josephus) prominence such as Aristotle (1.176-183) and Pythagoras (1.162-176), knew, for example, of Abraham (*A.J.* 14.255; also 1.240-241), Noah and the flood (*C. Ap.* 1.130-132), Moses (1.290, 309) and Solomon (1.114). There was familiarity among Gentiles with Jewish purity laws (1.164), dietary laws (1.182), circumcision (1.169), the exact size and interiors of the temple in Jerusalem (1.132, 198-199), specific high priests (1.187), tithes (1.188), and the Sabbath (1.209). Philo points out that Jewish houses of prayer have spread "in every part of the habitable world (οἰκουμένη)" (*Flacc.* 49; see also Acts 2:5). He not only explains about Moses' Torah, certainly with exaggeration, that "the fame of his laws has spread throughout the world and reached the ends of the earth (διὰ πάσης τῆς οἰκουμένης)" (*Mos.* 1.2) but that the Torah had *influenced the behavior* of the whole world, as their resting on the seventh day, their fasting, and king Ptolemie's desire for the translation of the Hebrew Scriptures demonstrate (*Mos.* 2.20-44). Clement of Alexandria calls the philosophers of the Greeks "thieves" because they took teachings from Moses and the prophets without giving credit to their source (*Stromata* V.1; see also Justin, *1 Apol.* 44, 59-60; Origen, *Cels.* 4.11).

Christian missionaries also spread the knowledge of the Jewish Scriptures among Gentiles. Paul quotes the Old Testament extensively in Romans, Galatians, and 1-2 Corinthians. Mark, probably recording Peter's preaching to gentiles in Rome (Eusebius, *Hist. eccl.* 2.15; 6.14), quotes the Old Testament twice as much (46x) than John (21x). And Luke tells his gentile readers (see Luke 1:1; Eusebius, *Hist. eccl.* 6.25) of Jewish expectations about the Messiah (e.g., Luke 1:32-33; 2:11; 24:25-26, 44-46). Cook devotes ca. 300 pages to discuss the detailed use of the OT in the works of Celsus, Porphyry and Julian, all pagan writings composed between the 2nd and 4th century AD. He demonstrates that "it was the advent of Christianity that seems to have finally generated a *close* reading of the OT on the part of pagan intellectuals."[149] We realize that quick conclusions from Jewish elements of a text to an exclusively Jewish context and Jewish readers deserve cautious evaluation. We suggest that the Gospel of John is better understood when read as a book written for Jews *and Gentiles.*[150]

5.5. Anti-Imperial Christology

The emperor worship, which developed out of the Hellenistic cult of rulers that goes back to the fourth century BC, consisted of everything that makes up a religion. There were emperor temples with temple taxes, high priests,

---

authorities, their heavy use by later sources ("cannibalization"), etc. MENDELS, "The Formation of an Historical Canon of the Greco-Roman Period," 3-19, esp. 5-6.

[149] COOK, *The Interpretation*, 1 (italics added).

[150] Hengel said with reference to John 21:24, "Mit dem Hinweis auf den Verfasser ist nicht mehr nur die johanneische Schule, sondern *die ganze Kirche angesprochen.* Auch die Aufgabe des Petrus 21,15-17 und der Hinweis auf sein Martyrium 21,18f. zeigt *die ökumenische Weite des (bzw. der?) Herausgeber.*" HENGEL, *Die Evangelienüberschriften,* 32 n. 72 (italics added). See also now HENGEL, *The Four Gospels,* 106-108. Schnackenburg maintained as well, "denn im letzten spricht er [the author] nicht einzelne Gruppen an, seien es Juden- oder Heidenchristen, Palästinenser oder Menschen in der Diaspora, Samariter, Griechen oder andere Hellenisten, sondern alle Glaubenden als solche, alle 'Kinder Gottes' (vgl. 1,12)." SCHNACKENBURG, "Die Messiasfrage," 262.

processions, feasts, sacrifices, games, hymns and confessions.[151] The general Roman policy of tolerance for other cults did not only include occasional lapses such as Caligula's, who "deified" himself (ἐξεθείαζέν, Josephus, *A.J.* 19.4) and demanded to worship his statue in Jerusalem's temple (*A.J.* 18.257-309; cf. also 19.300), but by the time of Trajan (AD 98-117) it had gradually developed to the point where participation in the cultic rituals became a test for piety and loyalty to the ruler. While forms and diffusion of the cult varied throughout the first century, its presence is visibly evident at least since the reign of Tiberius (AD 14-37). Temples dedicated to him with priest and cult are known from eleven cities in Asia Minor, and at least some of them go back to his lifetime.[152] An honorific inscription for Tiberius from Lycia reads as follows: "The people of Myra (honour) the emperor Tiberius, the exalted god, son of exalted gods, lord of land and sea, the benefactor and savior of the entire world."[153] What does such a context contribute to the understanding of the Gospel of John?

In his classic, *Light from the Ancient East*, written in 1908, Adolf Deissmann observes striking parallels in the usage of Christological and Greco-Roman terminology in general and imperial titles in particular.[154] The evidence discussed above leads Deissmann to the conclusion:

> Thus there arises a polemical parallelism between the cult of the emperor and the cult of Christ, which makes itself felt where ancient words derived by Christianity from the treasury of the Septuagint and the Gospels happen to coincide with solemn concepts of the Imperial cult which sounded the same or similar.[155]

Many of Deissmann's observations stood the test of time and continue to find support in the latest research about the general Greco-Roman context of Christianity.[156] Since the early 1990s, the imperial cult as the political

---

[151] For an introduction to the imperial cult, see KLAUCK, *The Religious Context*, 250-330. TILBORG, *Reading John*, 174-212. The studies by Price and Friesen are classics in the field: PRICE, *Rituals and Power* (1984). FRIESEN, *Twice Neokoros* (1993). See now also FRIESEN, *Imperial Cults and the Apocalypse of John*, 5-131. TREBILCO, *The Early Christians*, 11-52.

[152] KLAUCK, *The Religious Context*, 302. At the end of the first century, by "the time John wrote Revelation at least thirty-five cities in Asia Minor carried the title of 'temple warden' (νεωκόρος) for the divine Caesars." KRAYBILL, *Imperial Cult*, 60. In an appendix, Price offers a list of 156 imperial temples and shrines in Asia Minor from the first and second century AD. PRICE, *Rituals and Power*, 249-74; see also the maps on pp. xxii-xxv.

[153] KLAUCK, *The Religious Context*, 302.

[154] DEISSMANN, *Light from the Ancient East* (1927).

[155] Ibid., 342.

[156] See KLAUCK, *The Religious Context* (2003). Klauck affirms Deissmann's work as a "pioneering work of great value" and confirms the parallels between the Greco-Roman

and religious context of Paul's letters[157] as well as that of the Gospels[158] receives more attention than ever in Biblical studies.[159] The Gospel of John is not excluded from this endeavor. Tilborg has attempted the most comprehensive comparison between the Gospel of John and the many inscriptions from Ephesus. He not only finds that titles for Jewish leaders

---

culture and christological titles (σωτήρ, "son of [a] god," κύριος, θεός), and the concept of εὐαγγέλιον. Ibid., 328-29.

[157] For a survey, see CARTER, "Vulnerable Power," 453-88. Saunders briefly discusses Mark 12:1-17, 10:42, Jas 4:4, 1 Pet 2:13-17, Rom 13:1-7, 1 Cor 6:1-8, 1 Cor 8:4-6, and Col 1:15 in the context of the imperial cult. SAUNDERS, "Paul and the Imperial Cult," 227-38. Horsley is a pioneer in this field of research. See *Paul and Empire*, ed. HORSLEY (1997). The first half of this volume provides important essays by historians and archaeologists about the imperial cult in the first century AD. Elliott recently described the trends in Pauline scholarship this way, "Roman imperial ritual and propaganda filled the environment in which the apostle Paul worked. In convergent ways, recent studies of the imperial cult, on the one hand, *and* of Paul's 'theology,' on the other, are moving away from the individualistic, cognitivist concerns of classical Christian theology, and toward an understanding of the meaning of symbols and the function of rituals in representing relationships of power." ELLIOTT, "The Apostle Paul's Self-Presentation as anti-Imperial Performance," 67. And Maier, who has worked at the intersection of Roman empire, iconography, and New Testament, speaks of the "recent return to imperial motifs" as a "recovery of an approach much explored at the start of the twentieth century of which A. Deissmann . . . is representative." MAIER, "Barbarians, Scythians and Imperial Iconography in the Epistle to the Colossians," 387 n. 6. In the following, he mentions the works of P. Oakes (2001), D. Seeley (1994), K. Wengst (1987), D. Georgi (1991), N. Elliot (1994), R. Horsley (1998, 2000, 2004), M. Tellbe (2001), and E. Faust (1993). Bryan, who recently traced the relationship between the Roman empire and Israel, Jesus, Luke-Acts, 1 Peter, and Revelation, refered the raising of the matter since the last decade of the twentieth century to the rise of "the kind of thinking and critique that we have come to call 'postcolonial.'" BRYAN, *Render to Caesar*, 5. See also CROSSAN and REED, *In Search of Paul: How Jesus's Apostle Opposed Rome's Empire with God's Kingdom* (2004).

[158] A few of the more recent proposals to read the Gospels as counter-narratives to the Roman Empire are coming from the following scholars. With regard to Matthew, see SIM, *Apocalyptic Eschatology* (1996). Carter argues that "Matthew's Gospel contests and resists the Roman Empire's claims to sovereignty over the world." CARTER, *Matthew and Empire*, 1. *The Gospel of Matthew in its Roman Imperial Context*, ed. RICHES and SIM, (2005). The first four essays in this volume are relevant beyond the Gospel of Matthew. With regard to Mark, see VAN-IERSEL, *Mark* (1998). INCIGNERI, *The Gospel to the Romans* (2003). ROSKAM, *The Purpose of the Gospel of Mark* (2004). With regard to Luke-Acts, see BRENT, "Luke-Acts and the Imperial Cult in Asia Minor," 411-28.

[159] Haaland observes the same with regard to scholarship on Josephus: "The focus on Josephus' Roman context has been one of the most significant traits of recent research on Josephus." HAALAND, "Josephus and the Philosophers of Rome," 297. Mason confirms in the preface to the second edition of his *Josephus and the New Testament* (2003) that "Josephus's environment in Rome and the importance of that context for his first audiences is a new emphasis in general." MASON, *Josephus*, x.

and for Jesus in the Gospel match terms used for pagan (religious) leaders, institutions, emperors and the goddess Artemis in Asia's metropolis,[160] but also that characteristics of Jerusalem can be found in Ephesus, such as the location close to a sea with a mountain, city gates, a bathhouse, a stoa, a river, several gardens, special buildings, a temple, free men and slaves, etc. Thus, when the Gospel is read within the social context of Ephesus or any other major Hellenistic city, the semantic parallels evoke a political message, "not the emperor(s) but Jesus alone can lay claim to these titles [e.g., son of God, God], because he alone has proved in word and deed that he is from God."[161] It is worth discussing a few parallels that seem especially pertinent for our understanding of the hostile "world" in the Gospel of John.

5.5.1. Lord

Besides using κύριος for God (12:13 [Psa 118:25]; 12:38 [Isa 53:1]) and once for Philip (12:21), this word is employed mostly with reference to Jesus. The NIV, TNIV, and NRSV translate it always as "Sir" when used as an address for Jesus by someone who is not a disciple (4:11, 15, 19, 49; 5:7; 6:34; 8:11; 9:36). Jesus' own use is rendered, "(Teacher and) Lord" or "master" (13:13, 14, 16; 15:15, 20) and when the narrator or the disciples choose κύριος for Jesus, the three translations always render as "Lord."[162] The background of the LXX is evident in the quotation by John the Baptist of Isaiah 40:3 in John 1:23. But the title also resonates strongly in a non-

---

[160] Inscriptions in Ephesus contain terms for leaders (ἄρχων, ἀρχιερεύς, βασιλεύς, γραμματεύς), an institution (συνέδριον), emperors (υἱὸς τοῦ θεοῦ, θεός, κύριος, σωτήρ), and the goddess Artemis (ἡ θεός, ἡ θέα, κυρία, σώτειρα) which interfere with the text of the Gospel of John. TILBORG, *Reading John*, 25-51.

[161] Ibid., 53. Tilborg states that this message was "not originally foreseen" by the Gospel because it was composed in response to Jewish partners and Jewish traditions. Ibid., also p. 97. On the other hand, he insists that the Gospel "cannot be imagined without the influence of Hellenistic thoughts and customs and that it is unintelligible without knowledge of Hellenistic philosophy, religion, and culture." Ibid., 3. And at the end he reads John's passion account as a story of enthronement on the "background" of Jesus' competition with the emperor. Ibid., 213-19. Furthermore, Tilborg reads the κόσμος-language in John 17 and 18:31-37 in a broad sense and regards the title "my Lord and my God" in 20:28 as a *direct reference* to all imperial cults which use these divine titles" (italics added). Ibid., 218. Thus, his answer to the question about authorial intent remains somewhat ambiguous.

[162] See the narrator (6:23; 11:2; 20:20; 21:7, 12), John the Baptist (1:23 [Isa 40:3]), Peter (6:68; 13:6, 9, 36, 37; 21:15, 16, 17, 20, 21), the blind man (9:38), Mary and Martha (11:3, 34), Martha (11:21, 27, 39), Mary (11:32), the disciples (11:12; 20:25), the beloved disciple (13:25; 21:7), Thomas (14:5; 20:28), Philip (14:8), Judas (14:22), Mary Magdalene (20:2, 13, 18).

Jewish setting. In the Gentile context of Corinth, where there are many "so-called gods" (λεγόμενοι θεοί), "many gods and many lords" (θεοὶ πολλοὶ καὶ κύριοι πολλοί), Paul insists that there is "one God" (εἷς θεὸς) and "one Lord Jesus Christ" (εἷς κύριος Ἰησοῦς Χριστὸς) by whom are all things, and we exist through Him" (1 Cor 8:5-6).[163] Deissmann observes the significance of this title for Jesus in the pagan world when he explains that "at the time when Christianity originated 'Lord' was a divine predicate intelligible to the whole Eastern world. St. Paul's confession of 'Our Lord Jesus Christ' was his cosmopolitan expansion of a local Aramaic cult-title, *Marana*."[164] What does it mean in the cultural context of the Roman empire to give Jesus a divine predicate that resonates with a wide variety of readers? Klappert explains that the "effect of the confession *kyrios Iēsous*, used by the Christians in proclaiming Jesus as the Lord, was to destroy this vital ideology of the Roman *imperium*, and the reaction it called forth was the persecution of Christians during the first three centuries."[165] And Köstenberger comments with regard to 15:20 ("A slave is not greater than his master"), "The claim of Christians that Jesus – and he alone – is Lord (*kurios*), pitted them against Roman imperial religion, which attributed that title to the emperor."[166] It is important to understand that we do not try to trace the religious-historical *origin* of the confession, "Jesus is Lord." The Gospel of John does not provide evidence for such analysis because of its late date. Rather, we attempt to understand the *rhetorical effect* of Christian preaching within a cosmopolitan setting of the Roman empire where an overlap of terms and concepts suggests a comparison that is obvious.

5.5.2. Savior of the world

In John 4, the reader's understanding of Jesus grows gradually through the questions and statements made by the Samaritan woman. Her own view of Jesus progresses from that of a patriarch (4:12) to a prophet (4:19) and finally a Messiah (4:25). This development culminates when the Samaritans call Jesus the "Savior of the world" (4:42). Deissmann observes that the title σωτὴρ τοῦ κόσμου "was bestowed with sundry

---

[163] In his argument against the pagan critic Celsus, Origen quotes Paul's words from 1 Cor 8:5-6 and states Jesus' "superiority to all rulers" (*Cels.* 8.4), elaborating that Christians "should not worship any ruler among Persians, or Greeks, or Egyptians, or of any nation whatever" (*Cels.* 8.6).

[164] DEISSMANN, *Light from the Ancient East*, 350.

[165] KLAPPERT, "King, Kingdom," 2:373.

[166] KÖSTENBERGER, *John*, 465. According to Celsus, Christians speak the "language of sedition" when they say that it is impossible to serve many masters (Matt 6:24). Origen, *Cels.*, 8.2 (see 2-8).

variations in the Greek expression on Julius Caesar, Augustus, Claudius, Vespasian, Titus, Trajan, Hadrian, and other Emperors in inscriptions of the Hellenistic East."[167] In a much cited article, Craig H. Koester shows how Jesus' welcome by the Samaritans in 4:40 has a striking resemblance to the way visiting rulers were invited to a town.[168] Furthermore, while the title σωτήρ was used for gods in Greco-Roman sources and for God (e.g., Isa 45:15) and human deliverers (Othniel and Ehud, Judg 3:9, 15) in the LXX, the closest resemblance to the *whole* acclamation σωτὴρ τοῦ κόσμου in 4:42 comes from inscriptions in which emperors from Julius Caesar until Hadrian are hailed similarly![169] These and other features of the story suggest "that the passage was intended to evoke imperial associations."[170]

Franz Jung challenges this connection in his elaborate study about the use of σωτήρ as a Hellenistic title of honor in the New Testament.[171] Jung's main thesis is that the confession to Jesus as "savior" in the New Testament is not a Christian attack against rival claims in the context of the early church. Rather, it is an expression of deep gratitude for God's revelation in his son.[172] Jung observes with regard to John 4:42 that the concept of "Savior" for Jesus and for emperors in pagan sources do not overlap since Jesus does not obtain public honor and respect and he does not want to create distance between him and the saved ones as it is typical for a ruler.[173] But Jung's case is overstated and his focus is too narrow. He acknowledges that the title "Savior of the world" used for Jesus suggests at least a "superficial" comparison with the emperors.[174] The context of the dialogue with the Samaritan woman presents this Savior of the world in

---

[167] DEISSMANN, *Light from the Ancient East*, 364.

[168] Koester refers to Vespasian, about whom Josephus writes, "The population [of Sennabris, near Tiberias] opened their gates to him and went out to meet him, hailing him as savior and benefactor" (σωτῆρα καὶ εὐεργέτην, *B.J.* 3.459). KOESTER, "'The Savior of the World'," 666. Similarly, when Titus approached Antioch, many men and women with their children met him as far as four miles outside of the city limits, "stretched out their right hands, greeting him, and making all sorts of acclamations to him" (*B.J.* 7.102).

[169] Koester mentions titles such as σωτὴρ τῆς οἰκουμένης (Julius Caesar, Claudius, Hadrian), σωτὴρ τῶν Ἑλλήνων τε καὶ τῆς οἰκουμένης πάσης (Augustus), εὐεργέτης καὶ σωτὴρ τοῦ σύμπαντος κόσμου (Augustus, Tiberius), etc. Ibid., 667.

[170] Ibid. Schnackenburg explains, "Aber der Titel 'Heiland der Welt' spielt auch im hellenistischen Bereich eine nicht geringe Rolle, und der Evangelist wird ihn bewußt als 'Verkündigungswort' aufgenommen haben." SCHNACKENBURG, *Das Johannesevangelium*, 1:491. Also CARSON, *The Gospel*, 232. KEENER, *The Gospel of John*, 1:627-28. KÖSTENBERGER, *John*, 164-65. SALIER, *The Rhetorical Impact*, 74.

[171] JUNG, *ΣΩΤΗΡ: Studien zur Rezeption eines Hellenistischen Ehrentitels im Neuen Testament* (2002).

[172] Ibid., III.

[173] Ibid., 301.

[174] Ibid., 299.

radical contrast to rival forms of Gentile worship. Thus, the Samaritans are not just grateful for God's revelation in his Son, but their confession also shows that they have turned away from their idolatry. Furthermore, by limiting his study to one acclamation, Jung overlooks that this title "Savior of the world" appears in a Gospel which contains other titles with similar associations to the imperial cult, such as 'Lord,' 'God,' 'Son of God' (see below). Finally, Jung's conceptual perspective neglects to consider the cultural context within which the reader approaches this text. The Roman Empire in general and Domitian in particular did not offer Christians the freedom to worship Jesus without challenging them to honor other gods at the same time. Within that context, the evangelist needed to *communicate* Jesus' exclusivity without *copying* an exact imperial notion of salvation which would have blurred the differences to Jesus' mission (see 14:27; 18:36).[175]

5.5.3. My Lord and my God

After Jesus' resurrection and before the important purpose statement in 20:30-31, Thomas is led in a dramatic way to confess Jesus as "my Lord and my God" (20:28). The title θεός for Jesus frames the Gospel (1:1, 18; 20:28) and thus indicates the Christological emphasis. Deissmann cites evidence from Mediterranean cults as early as 24 BC which use the title κύριος καὶ θεός. Domitian was the first Caesar who was addressed this way.[176]

Mastin investigates the ascription of the title κύριός μου καὶ ὁ θεός μου to Jesus in John 20:28 and of ὁ κύριος καὶ ὁ θεὸς ἡμῶν in Rev 4:11 to God.[177] The LXX is not the only source which provides parallels for the combination κύριος καὶ θεός (Ps 85:15; 87:2), but Suetonius records of the emperor Domitian (AD 81-96):

> With no less arrogance he began as follows in issuing a circular letter in the name of his procurators, "Our Master and our God (*Dominus et deus noster*) bids that this be done." And so the custom arose of henceforth addressing him in no other way even in writing or in conversation (*Dom.*, 13.2).[178]

Mastin argues that, since the Book of Revelation as well as the Gospel of John are commonly dated at the end of the first century and located in Asia Minor and Ephesus where the imperial cult was especially developed (see

---

[175] Link's rejection of an anti-imperial connotation in John 4:42 suffers from the same weaknesses just mentioned with regard to Jung. LINK, „*Was redest du mit ihr?*," 361-64.

[176] DEISSMANN, *Light from the Ancient East*, 361-62.

[177] MASTIN, "Imperial Cult," 352-65.

[178] Ibid., 354.

Dio Cassius, LI. 20. 6-8), it is "not impossible that John XX. 28 was composed at this time, and that it was a considered rebuttal of the claims made on behalf of the Emperor by the Imperial cult."[179]

A difficulty with this point of contact might be that the Latin *Dominus et deus noster* in the traditions from Suetonius and Martial is translated in the Greek texts of Dio Chrysostom and Dio Cassius with δεσποτής καὶ θεός and not with ὁ κύριος καὶ ὁ θεός.[180] But given the increased use of κύριος for emperors in the papyri, the different wording does not seriously challenge Mastin's conclusion.[181] In the acclamation of a deity, the difference between κύριος and δεσποτής might not be that large after all. In the First letter of Clement, written around AD 95 and thus contemporary to the Gospel of John, God is named with all three titles: θεὸς καὶ δεσπότης τῶν πνευμάτων καὶ κύριος (1 Cl 64:1).

By discussing the imperial connotations of Christological titles such as 'Lord,' 'Savior of the world,' and 'My Lord and my God' we have only started to understand the rhetorical effect of the Gospel in the Roman context of the first century. Different scholars offer many more observations in the same vein about single statements,[182] other titles for Jesus[183] or even miracles.[184] Criticism against or silence about some

---

[179] Ibid., 364. See also SANDERS and MASTIN, *A Commentary*, 437-38. KÖSTENBERGER, *John*, 579-80. The same imperial pressures were exerted on the Jewish community as well. After Masada fell to the Romans around AD 74, the Sicarii fled to Alexandria in Egypt and persuaded many Jews there "to esteem the Romans to be no better than themselves, and to look upon God as their only Lord and Master" (θεὸν δὲ μόνον ἡγεῖσθαι δεσπότην, *B.J.* 7.410).

[180] See TILBORG, *Reading John*, 56.

[181] Tilborg explains that "from Nero on, the title κύριος is used increasingly (Nero 43 times; Vespasian 58 times; Domitian 115 times; Trajan 280 times; Hadrian 492 times). Therefore, a (negative) reference of Jn 20:28 to Domitian's κύριος καὶ θεός is more than probable, although the ambiguity of the reference cannot be proved." Ibid., 56.

[182] Köstenberger comments on 14:27, "The *pax Romana* ('Roman peace'), secured by the first Roman emperor, Augustus (30 BC-AD 14), had obtained and was maintained by military might. The famous *Ara Pacis* ('altar of peace'), erected by Augustus to celebrate his inauguration of the age of peace, still stands in Rome as a testimony to the world's empty messianic pretensions (Beasley-Murray 1999:262). The peace given by Jesus, on the other hand, was not afflicted with the burden of having been achieved by violence (cf. 18:11)." KÖSTENBERGER, *John*, 443-44. Josephus quotes a decree which testifies to the Roman desire to establish "happiness" (εὐδαιμονία) and "firm peace" (βεβαία εἰρήνη) in their empire (*A.J.* 14.248). Standing before Gaius, Philo praises Augustus Gaius as an emperor who "diffused peace (εἰρήνην) in every direction over earth and sea, to the very furthest extremities of the world" (*Legat.* 309).

[183] According to Brown, the title 'Son of God' (in 1:34, 49; 3:18; 5:25; 10:36; 11:4, 27; 19:7; 20:31) "would appeal to a gentile religious background where the gods are sons." BROWN, *The Gospel*, 1:LXXVII. Although he specifically focuses on the wording θεοῦ υἱός that is unique to Matthew (with the prepositive genitive only in Matt 14:33;

connection to the imperial cult is mostly limited to those scholars who contend with a purely narrative approach to the Gospel. Moloney argues that the confession "My Lord and my God" is not uttered "*against* something [Domitian] but *for* Christ."[185] But Moloney rejects two aspects that appear to be different sides of the same coin. His sole focus on "literary features found in the narrative of the fourth Gospel" seems to exclude the historical context *a priori*.[186]

5.5.4. The fourth gospel and the mystery cults

In his assessment of Deissmann's work, Klauck adds that the imperial cult "is only one partial aspect of a much larger complex of ideas" and that it "does not appear in isolation, but as part of the entire polytheistic system."[187] González explains, "In order to achieve greater unity, imperial policy sought religious uniformity by following two routes: religious syncretism – the indiscriminate mixing of elements from various religions – and emperor worship."[188] In Ephesus alone, the citizens worshiped a

---

27:43, 54), Mowery's article might have implications for reading the Gospel of John in an imperial context as well. MOWERY, "Son of God in Roman Imperial Titles," 100-10.

[184] Jesus' walk on water (6:16-21) could have reminded the authorial audience of the emperor Caligula (12-41 A.D) who, after having build a long bridge, rode over it and called himself "lord of the sea" (δεσπότης τῆς θαλάσσης; Josephus, *A.J.* 19.6). Suetonius finds Caligula's motive for this spectacular extravagance in the words of astrologers to Tiberius according to which Caligula "had no more chance of becoming an emperor than of riding about over the gulf of Baiae with horses" (Suetonius, *Cal.* 4.19.3). Cotter comments that this "remembrance of Suetonius shows us that in the administration of Tiberius, which was the time of Jesus himself, the image of a man riding over the waves was already used as a metaphor for what is impossible for a human being." W. COTTER, *Miracles in Greco-Roman Antiquity*, 159. Labahn considers an intentional analogy to Caligula and explains: "Der im Seewandel mit der Machfülle Jahwes für die Seinen epiphane Jesus ist gegen alle antike Herrscherideologie und Selbstanmaßung der wahre *Basileus* des himmlischen Königreichs seines Vaters." LABAHN, *Jesus als Lebensspender*, 288-89. Labahn also considers anti-imperial implications for the healing of the βασιλικός (Ibid, 205). Nevertheless, his form-critical study searches more for pre-literary influences behind the Gospel than for the rhetorical function of the miracles for the reader before the text. And in a later monograph, Labahn regards a conflict of Jewish Christians with the synagogue about Jesus' messianic claims as the more probable social context and reason for the inclusion of Jesus' walk on water into the Gospel. See LABAHN, *Offenbarung in Zeichen und Wort*, 216, also 185.

[185] MOLONEY, *The Gospel of John*, 539-40. Although Bonney says he attempts not to "read the text as if it floats in a vacuum detached from its history of interpretation," his narrative analysis of the Thomas story does not relate the confession "my Lord and my God" to the Greco-Roman world. BONNEY, *Caused to Believe*, 7.

[186] MOLONEY, *The Gospel of John*, 15.

[187] KLAUCK, *The Religious Context*, 328.

[188] GONZÁLEZ, *The Story of Christianity*, 1:14.

multitude of gods, "including Aphrodite, Apollos, Asclepius, Athena, Cabiri, Demeter, Dionysus, Egyptian Cults, Ge, God Most High, Hecate, Hephaestus, Hercules, Hestia, the Mother goddess, Pluton, Poseidon, Zeus and other minor deities,"[189] and above all stood Artemis as the most powerful deity of the city. The imperial cult coexisted and interrelated in various ways with the worship of gods and goddesses and both are often literally two sides of the same coin. Ephesians called themselves guardians of the cults of Artemis and of the emperors ("twice neokoros").[190] Not surprisingly, comparisons with the Fourth Gospel's high Christology and ancient mystery cults suggest allusions to this polytheistic system as well. In his recent study, Willis H. Salier is able to link all eight "signs" in the Gospel of John (including Jesus' resurrection) to parallels with Greco-Roman gods, goddesses, and emperors.[191] He does not use the parallels in order to postulate the religious-historical origin of the Gospel traditions, but to consider the text's impact on a broad and diverse audience that includes Gentiles.[192] Salier frequently insists that there is not just a movement from the text to the reader (narrative analysis), but also from the reader to the text (rhetorical analysis). His thesis is that "each narrative [about a sign] portrays Jesus as a life-giver in ways that would be intelligible to a variety of readers in the ancient world."[193] While Salier regards a Jewish framework and the Hebrew Scriptures as the primary background to interpret the signs, he insists that "at the same time rival life-givers from the contemporary culture are compared and found wanting through the activity of Jesus."[194] The merit of his study is not only that he brings together single observations that were made many times before, but

---

[189] TREBILCO, *The Early Christians*, 19 n. 47.

[190] Ibid., 29. Tilborg mentions, for example, that a "coin of Domitian has been preserved on which, on the obverse, Domitian's head can be seen together with his name, and on the reverse there is an image of Zeus Olympios with in his right hand the statue of Artemis . . . ." TILBORG, *Reading John*, 178, also 199. Dedications of buildings to the emperor "are linked with dedications to other divinities: to Dionysus, Demeter, Asklepios, Hera, and in Ephesus especially and rather exclusively to Artemis." Ibid., 189. Tilborg explains that in Ephesus, Artemis is the "primary deity" and the emperor supervises the activities in the temple of Artemis as the goddesses' σύνθρονος. Ibid., 190-91, also p. 176. The relation is so close that the emperors were venerated "in the cult-places of other gods such as Demeter, Dionysus, Asklepios." Ibid., 195.

[191] SALIER, *The Rhetorical Impact* (2004). See also part 3 ("Hellenistic Stories") in MARTIN, *Narrative Parallels to the New Testament* (1988) and part 1 ("Gods and heroes who heal") in COTTER, *Miracles in Greco-Roman Antiquity* (1999).

[192] SALIER, *The Rhetorical Impact*, 68, 110. For his study about the audience, see especially pp. 10-15.

[193] Ibid., 17.

[194] Ibid., 118.

that he connects them within a paradigm that is large enough to fit Jewish and Gentile readers alike. Some examples suffice to make the point.

The "I am" statements of Jesus remind some scholars not only of previous biblical traditions, but of self-declarations of the Egyptian goddess Isis[195] who was worshiped under different names all over the world in the Hellenistic-Roman age as the "supreme universal deity."[196] The miraculous change from water to wine (John 2) shows Jesus' "superiority to the wine god, Dionysus"[197] for whom there was a temple right across the Jordan in Scythopolis and whose worship was concentrated in Minor Asia.[198] If the title "savior of the world" in 4:42 carries imperial connotations, then the subsequent healing of the official's son also includes a "possible nuance" of "implicit polemic against other gods and

---

[195] Consider, for example, the "Hymn of Isis," a text from the 1 or 2 century AD found in Asia Minor, "I am Isis. . . . I am the eldest daughter of Kronos. I am wife and sister of King Osiris. I am she who findeth fruit for men. I am mother of King Horus. I am she that riseth in the dog star. I am she that is called goddess by women. . . . I am the Queen of war. I am the Queen of the thunderbolt. . . . I am the rays of the sun. . . . I am called the Lawgiver. . . . I am Lord (κύριος, masculine form) of rainstorms. . . . " Quoted in *Hellenistic Commentary*, 272-73. See also MACRAE, "The Fourth Gospel," 23-24. VOUGA, *Le cadre historique*, 13. HARRIS, *Prologue and Gospel*, 137-39, 141, 192.

[196] TRIPOLITIS, *Religions of the Hellenistic Roman Age*, 27. For the different names given to Isis, see Apuleius, *Metamorphoses*, 11.

[197] SCHEIN, *Following the Way*, 42, 31. Second Maccabees (6:7-9) already records the forced partaking of Judean Jews in sacrifices and processions during the feast of Dionysus during the reign of Antiochus Epiphanes (175-163 BC). Justin Martyr makes the parallels between Jesus and Dionysus *explicit* in the second century (see *Dial.* 69:2; *Apol.* I.37, 62). In modern scholarship, Julius Grill interpreted Jesus already in 1923 as an antitype to Dionysus. See FREY, "Auf der Suche," 16. Pilhofer draws attention not only to John 2, but also to food and meals in the Synoptics as parallels to Dionysus. PILHOFER, "Dionysos und Christus," 73-91, esp. 83-84. See also BACON, *The Gospel of the Hellenists*, 162-64. BAUER, *Das Johannesevangelium*, 47. LINNEMANN, "Die Hochzeit zu Kana und Dionysos," 417. SLOYAN, *John*, 36. *Hellenistic Commentary*, 249. SALIER, *The Rhetorical Impact*, 64-70. KOESTER, *Symbolism*, 85. Broer responds in detail to John P. Meier's rejection of a connection between John 2 and the Dionysus-cult. BROER, "Das Weinwunder zu Kana," 291-308. Wick even argued recently that the whole Gospel of John was written to reject the cult of Dionysus in an implicit way. WICK, "Jesus gegen Dionysos?," 179-98.

[198] So NOETZEL, *Christus und Dionysos*, 17. Noetzel rightly criticizes Bultmann's use of Dionysus-legends as the literary *source* for John 2 (genealogy). But he wrongly rejects the idea that John 2 was written in *response* to the Dionysus cult (analogy). See the discussion in LABAHN, *Jesus als Lebensspender*, 146-56, who himself does not see a direct polemic in John 2 against the Dionysus cult but a tradition-historical borrowing of motifs for explaining the Christian faith (ibid., 155).

emperors."[199] By healing the lame man at the pool (John 5), Jesus fulfills expectation otherwise ascribed to the god Asclepius who possibly had a shrine at Bethesda.[200] The feeding of the multitude in John 6 resembles the "action of a generous and wealthy benefactor, if not a god" and includes a "subtle polemic" against the popular goddess Demeter who was responsible for the provision of grain.[201]

Many of these associations were not only available to merely some readers at few limited localities, but all over the Roman empire, since the gods of Asclepius and Dionysus were "publicly promoted by kings and emperors" and, as popular cults, revered everywhere.[202] The monotheistic faith of Jews and Christians clashed head on with this polytheism. Paul's preaching against the Artemis cult in Ephesus ("gods made with hands are no gods at all," Acts 19:26) as well as Jesus' dialogue with the Samaritan woman (esp. John 4:21-24) did not leave any room for Rome's syncretism. While Paul barely escaped death in the theater, Timothy, according to his Vita, was killed in Ephesus during the time of Domitian "because he resisted against the feast of Dionysus."[203]

5.6. Attempts about a Likely Scenario

What was the situation of the authorial audience that required the writing of the Gospel with its narrative emphasis on the κόσμος and all the explicit (chap. 19, 21) and implicit polemic against the emperor and pagan

---

[199] SALIER, *The Rhetorical Impact*, 74. Labahn also understands the healing in 4:46-54 as an "Aktualisierung" or "Illustration" of the σωτήρ-title in 4:42 with possible critcism of imperial claims implied. LABAHN, *Jesus als Lebensspender*, 204-05.

[200] A "large clay vessel with many snakes on it" was found "in a cistern near Bethseda [*sic*] in the late nineteenth century" which "increases the possibility that a shrine to Asclepius . . . existed at Bethesda." See CHARLESWORTH, "Jesus Research," 50. Justin Martyr recognizes the similarity between Jesus and Asclepius due to their healing activities (*Apol.* I.22). See also *Hellenistic Commentary*, 267. SCHEIN, *Following the Way*, 84, 88, 93. ROUSSEAU and ARAV, *Jesus & His World*, 157. SALIER, *The Rhetorical Impact*, 100-02. Labahn does not seem to know of this probable material association of Bethesda with the Asclepius-cult and (therefore) allows a contrast with other places of healing merely as a side-effect of John 5 but not as a direct polemic. LABAHN, *Jesus als Lebensspender*, 225-26.

[201] SALIER, *The Rhetorical Impact*, 106-07.

[202] TRIPOLITIS, *Religions*, 23. Labahn also points out that "der Dionysuskult in der alten Welt geradezu 'allgegenwärtig' war und seine Einflüsse bis in den syropalästinischen Raum sich hinein verfolgen lassen." LABAHN, *Jesus als Lebensspender*, 155, esp. n. 186.

[203] TILBORG, *Reading John*, 129, also pp. 95, 127. Justin Martyr recounts how Christians have formerly worshiped Dionysus, Asclepius and other gods but now "despise [κατεφρονήσαμεν] them, though threatened with death for it" (*Apol.* I.25).

polytheism? Besides the previous comments on single links between the Gospel of John and the Greco-Roman world, a variety of scholars have attempted to reconstruct a more precise *Sitz im Leben* for the Johannine communities in a predominantly Gentile world. According to Vouga (1977), the expulsion from the synagogue (not before AD 85-90) led to the Christians' loss of the Jews' privileged protection (*religio licita*) and thus "provoqué les sanctions romaines."[204] The demands of the imperial cult as well as the dominance of syncretism in Asia Minor challenged the exclusive worship of Jesus Christ and exposed Christians to the Roman charge of political insurrection.[205] Within this political development, John 15-17 point to persecutions under the emperor Domitian after AD 93 in Asia Minor.[206] The announcement in John 16:2 captures this situation when Jesus first speaks of the disciples' expulsion from the synagogue after which they are killed by those that render their death as a service to god (λατρείαν προσφέρειν τῷ θεῷ).[207]

In his short book *John's Gospel in New Perspective. Christology and the Realities of Roman Power* (1992), Richard Cassidy lays out his attempt to read the Gospel as an encouragement to Christians who suffer violence from the hand of the Roman emperor. Cassidy mentions two motives for the persecution: first, the Jewish tax (*Fiscus Judaicus*), which Domitian "vigorously" (*acerbissime*) enforced to fill up his depleted treasuries (Suetonius, *Dom.* 12.2) in the name of the Roman god Jupiter Capitolinus, led to an increased scrutiny of groups such as Jewish Christians who might claim not to be Jews in order to avoid the payment.[208] Second, the cult of

---

[204] VOUGA, *Le cadre historique*, 104.

[205] Ibid., 11-12; see also pp. 97-111.

[206] Ibid., 10. See also BRUMLIK, "Johannes: Das judenfeindliche Evangelium," *Kul* 4 (1989): 107. But Brumlik fails to apply this scenario to the question of anti-Semitism in the Fourth Gospel. Although Schmidl dismisses the idea as "spekulativ" because of the lack of sources and the locally limited scope of the conflict, he admits the possibility of Roman persecution, "Denkbar ist, daß durch die Abgrenzung vom Judentum die johanneische Gemeinde den Schutz einer *religio licita* verlor und somit der Verfolgung durch die Römer ausgesetzt war." SCHMIDL, *Jesus und Nikodemus*, 78. Bultmann explains with regard to 16:2-4 that the exclusion from the synagogue led to the Christian loss of protection as a *religio licita*. But he does not unpack the implication of this loss and limits the murderers, mentioned in John 16:2b, to Jews only. BULTMANN, *Das Evangelium*, 428. See also LINGAD, *The Problems of Jewish Christians*, 109-10, who follows R. E. Brown.

[207] Vouga thus makes clear, "c'est donc à des persécutions romaines que Jn 16/2 fait allusion. Si les Juifs n'en pas été les responsables directs, ils ont encouragé ces procédures contre les chrétiens." VOUGA, *Le cadre historique*, 104.

[208] Cassidy writes that, because of this tax system, two groups "came under increased scrutiny for payment of the tax. One group consisted of those who lived as Jews without publicly acknowledging that they were Jews. The other group consisted of born Jews

Rome's emperor demanded religious loyalty and worship which Christians were not willing to give except to Jesus Christ. Greek writings and inscriptions show that titles for Jesus such as 'Lord' (e.g., 1:23; 11:2), 'my Lord and my God' (20:28), and 'Savior of the world' (4:42) were also given to Roman emperors.[209] Cassidy asks if the author of the Gospel attached those titles to Jesus in order to "preclude that an emperor such as Nero or a pagan god of healing might also appropriately be given such acclaim."[210] Cassidy points to key concepts in the farewell discourse that reflect a situation of persecution and apostasy, such as "persecute you" (15:20), "abide in me" (15:4), "let not your hearts be troubled" (14:1-3), and "keep them from the evil one" (17:15). Jesus' own trial before Pilate encourages the disciples to "resist Roman intimidation and seek to bear witness to the truth."[211] Thomas' confession "my Lord and my God" (20:28) challenges the readers "to speak the same words publicly."[212] The depictions of Peter and the beloved disciple in chapter 21 display "two distinct forms of discipleship" within the context of external pressure, of which the first leads to martyrdom and the second to faithful witness.[213] Thus, Cassidy shows how the author reveals consciousness of Roman realities and provides support for Christians under Roman rule.

Finally, Jörg Frey recently pointed to the *fiscus Iudaicus* as the cause for significant legal insecurity of Christians in the Roman empire during Domitian's reign.[214] Implemented after the destruction of the temple in AD 70, the forced payment of those who were Jews or who lived according to the Jews also affected Gentiles who became Christians, since the new religion was perceived as a part of Judaism. Gentile Christians could attempt to avoid the payment, but then they were vulnerable to being denounced by Jews and challenged by Romans to sacrifice before the

---

who claimed not to be Jewish." CASSIDY, *John's Gospel*, 9. See also VOUGA, *Le cadre historique*, 109. On the other hand, Downing cautions against a connection between Christian persecution (as indicated in Revelation) and the exaction of Jewish tax under Domitian because, as he says, "There is no Roman evidence to suggest that action to obtain payment resulted in people being put to death." And in note 33, "None seems forthcoming; Suetonius's *Domitian* 12.2 does not suggest the abused old man was on trial for his life." DOWNING, "Pliny's Prosecutions of Christians," 247.

[209] With regard to the title "lord and god," Cassidy observes that the "focus narrows to the rule of just one emperor, Domitian," who demanded to be addressed with this title. CASSIDY, *John's Gospel*, 14. He refers to the following evidence: Suetonius, *Dom.* 13.2; Martial, *Epigrams* 10.72.1-3; Dio Chrysostom, *Discourses* 45,1.

[210] CASSIDY, *John's Gospel*, 35.

[211] Ibid., 56.

[212] Ibid., 76.

[213] Ibid., 79.

[214] FREY, "Das Bild 'der Juden'," 33-53, esp. 47-48.

image of the emperor. Any attempt to pay the *fiscus Iudaicus* would have been met with opposition from Jews who did not want to be associated with the *superstitio* and extend the legal protection of Judaism to Christians. Jewish Christians enjoyed exemption from the emperor cult, but only as long as they were not expulsed from the synagogue. In such a case, they found themselves in the same precarious situation as their fellow Gentile believers. According to Frey, the "hate" of the world in 15:18-19 refers to Gentile sentiments, and 16:2 alludes to the Roman power as the main enemy who kills Christians after they were expulsed from the synagogue as an act of religious devotion.[215] The conflict with the Jews happened a while ago, and the negative use of Ἰουδαῖοι mostly in John 5-12 reveals that the author considers "the Jews" as a dramatic means.[216]

The explanations of Vouga, Cassidy and Frey incorporate the best observations about the Gospel into a socio-political model of conflict that operates with the most common assumptions about the text's historical origin (date and provenance), and with contextual information from sources that date from the same or a slightly later period. So far, the model received only little attention and recognition, despite its explanatory power.[217] Some scholars reject Vouga's thesis because it does not seem to fit into the dominant paradigm of conflict between the synagogue and the church.[218] Beasley-Murray commends Cassidy's work for drawing "attention to the role of the Roman power in the persecution of the Church in the early period of its existence."[219] Yet he also criticizes Cassidy for neglecting the insights of Leonhard L. Thompson and his study *The Book of Revelation: Apocalypse and Empire* (1990). Thompson has challenged the importance of conflict with the emperor cult for the Book of

---

[215] Ibid., 49. Less explicit, but nevertheless pointing to the openness of the language in 16:2, Ashton remarks, "'They' of course are the Jews, but their role has already been usurped by ὁ κόσμος – the world; and though they are not far away (who else had the power to expel people from the synagogue?), they are not named." ASHTON, "The Identity," 66. Blasi explains with reference to 16:2 that the "third Johannine layer" of composition shows Christians who feared persecution "at the hands of both Jews and Gentiles." BLASI, *A Sociology of Johannine Christianity*, 195.

[216] FREY, "Das Bild 'der Juden'," 40, 42, 45, 49.

[217] Anderson discusses and affirms Cassidy's thesis, which "offers very convincing evidence that, based on Pliny's Letter to Trajan (X.96) and Trajan's Rescript (X.97), Christians were being persecuted, sometimes simply for bearing the name 'Christian'." ANDERSON, "The Sitz im Leben," 63 n. 51, also pp. 42-46. Stegemann affirms Vouga's connection of Jewish expulsion and Roman persecution in John 16:2 and with it the fear about Roman authorities among Johannine Christians. STEGEMANN, "Die Tragödie der Nähe," 116, 117, 122 n. 13.

[218] See WENGST, *Bedrängte Gemeinde*, 51 n. 127. REBELL, *Gemeinde als Gegenwelt*, 93.

[219] BEASLEY-MURRAY, *John*, cxiv.

Revelation. In his eyes, the sources of authors such as Pliny the Younger, Suetonius, Tacitus, and Dio Cassius describe Domitian with a strong negative bias while the friendly picture by writers contemporary to the emperor (Statius and Quintilian) are much more credible. We have no room to discuss Thompson's thesis in any detail. But even if some of the ancient historians painted Domitian's portrait too dark, it hardly justifies to dismiss their descriptions altogether. According to Klauck's recent evaluation of the discussion, it is indisputable that Domitian did use the expression *Dominus et deus noster* in his letters and edicts.[220] The first imperial temple in Ephesus was erected during *his* lifetime and it was also during *his* reign that the religious epithet φιλοσέβαστος, "pious and loyal to the emperor," became a desired claim with which people and institutions honored themselves.[221] After secular games in AD 88, Domitian ordered the minting of coins which depict him as a larger-than-life figure in or outside a temple, and before him kneel three figures with outstretched arms "in supplication before the Emperor. . . . It is likely that the Emperor in this image is dictating prayers rather than receiving veneration himself, but such a distinction may have been lost on people who knew the Emperor sometimes was worshipped."[222] It seems that even if we agree with Thompson's interpretation of ancient texts, there still remains plenty of *material* evidence which depicts Domitian's zeal for religious attention. Fiensy compares Thompson's thesis with the archeological research of Price and Friesen and concludes, "It is hard to deny . . . that the establishment of the new emperor cult in Ephesus in 89-90 C.E. lay behind the Book of Revelation."[223]

5.7. Illustration from Pliny the Younger

In this context of cult and worship, the titles mentioned above are not mere kerygmatic means, and they do not only imply a battle of ideas. Rather,

---

[220] KLAUCK, *The Religious Context*, 310. Also BEALE, *The Book of Revelation*, 9-12.

[221] TILBORG, *Reading John*, 197-98.

[222] KRAYBILL, *Imperial Cult*, 62.

[223] FIENSY, "The Roman Empire and Asia Minor," 53. With Thompson, Trebilco rejects an allusion in Revelation to the persecution of Christians under Domitian. TREBILCO, *The Early Christians in Ephesus*, 343-44. On the other hand, Friesen recently argued in detail that only an understanding of the imperial cult allows us to make sense of John's radical criticism of the society's values. He criticizes Thompson's approach by saying that his "book worked from the text of Revelation toward social setting and relied heavily on Lévi-Strauss for his understanding of the function of myth. I have worked from material related to social setting toward the text of Revelation and have relied heavily on Sullivan and the Eliade tradition regarding the function of myth." FRIESEN, *Imperial Cults and the Apocalypse of John*, 165.

they provoked Christians to dishonor pagan gods and disconnect in practice from idolatry. As an association distinct from the synagogue (cf. ἀποσυνάγωγος in 9:22; 12:42; 16:2), the Johannine communities did not enjoy the right of being a *religio licita* and were thus not exempted from participation in the imperial cult. The earliest and most elaborate witness outside the New Testament about the resulting conflict between Christians and the Roman government is found in the correspondence between Pliny the Younger, governor of Bithynia since AD 110, and the emperor Trajan (AD 98-117). In one letter, Pliny asks how to prosecute Christians whom he challenged in the past with the following three tests:

> An anonymous pamphlet has been circulated which contains the names of a number of accused persons. Among these I considered that I should dismiss any who denied that they were or ever had been Christians when they had repeated after me a formula of invocation to the gods and had made offerings of wine and incense to your statue (which I had ordered to be brought into court for this purpose along with the images of the gods), and furthermore had reviled the name of Christ: none of which things, I understand, any genuine Christians can be induced to do.[224]

(1) Invoking the gods, (2) offering prayer with incense to the emperor's image, and (3) cursing Christ were drastic religious measures used by Pliny to evaluate in a "ceremonial test of devotion" the political loyalties of Christians.[225] Pliny felt forced to take this course of action because "this superstition" had spread to cities and villages. He reports the following success as a result:

> I think though that it is still possible for it to be checked and directed to better ends, for there is no doubt that people have begun to throng the temples which had been almost entirely deserted for a long time; the sacred rites which had been allowed to lapse are being performed again, and flesh of sacrificial victims is on sale everywhere, though up till recently scarcely anyone could be found to buy it.[226]

It becomes clear that, with the refusal to participate in the imperial cult, Christians visibly and practically withdrew from pagan temples, religious

---

[224] Pliny the Younger, *Letters*, X.96, 5. *Pliny*, 2:287, 289.

[225] SCHOWALTER, *The Emperor and the Gods*, 5. Schowalter attempts a more precise analysis of the relationship between the emperor Trajan and the gods. For that purpose, he investigates especially Pliny's writing *Panegyricus* from around AD 100 which addresses the emperor in Rome and was written with the hope that "those who had been pressured to give divine honors to Domitian could revert to praising the emperor as a human being." Ibid., 73 (cf. *Pan.* 2.3-4). Schowalter's textual analysis does not consider the imperial cult in general nor the situation of Asia Minor in particular and has to be read with these limits in mind.

[226] Pliny the Younger, *Letters*, x.96, 10. *Pliny*, 291.

rites and the purchase of sacrificial meat, and thus threatened the balance of power in which religion, politics, and economy were closely tied together.[227] Within a situation somewhat similar like this the Christology of John seems to encourage unbending faithfulness to Jesus and complete rejection of any form of syncretism.[228]

5.8. Examples of resistance

Given the prevalence of the imperial cult in the Roman empire, Pliny's problem with Christians is hardly unique to Bithynia.[229] The life of Ignatius, bishop of Antioch in Syria, presents us not only with an individual example of Pliny's scenario but also with the strongest indirect confirmation for our reading of κόσμος as the Roman empire. Eusebius mentions "that Ignatius was sent from Syria to Rome and became food for wild animals because of his testimony to Christ" (Eus., *Eccl. His.* 3.36; cf. *Ign. Eph.* 1.2). This happened in Rome's Colisseum between AD 110-117, during the reign of the emperor Trajan. Before his death, Ignatius wrote seven letters to churches in Asia Minor and beyond. In the one addressed to the Christians who live in Rome, the city of his death, Ignatius does not know a better way to encourage the readers than with the language of the Gospel of John, "Christianity is not a matter of persuasion, but is greatest

---

[227] For a helpful summary of the scholarly dispute between Sherwin-White and Ste. Croix in the 1950s and 1960s (and later T. D. Barnes in the 1990s) about the reasons why Christians were persecuted in the Roman empire, see KANNADAY, *Apologetic Discourse*, 200-06. Kannaday concludes that all three scholars, despite their differences, understand that "beneath Pliny's swift execution of Roman justice lies some unwritten but preconceived notion that persons unwilling to deny their Christianity deserve to die." Ibid., 206. Kannaday offers further details about pagan perceptions of Christians in the second century AD in chap. 1, where he outlines the "Pagan Opposition to Christianity and Christian Apologetic" by summarizing the works of pagan critics on the one hand (Pliny, Tacitus, Suetonius, Lucian, Apuleius, Marcus Cornelius Fronto, Celsus, Porphyry), and those of early Christian apologists on the other (e.g., Quadratus, Aristides, Justin Martyr, Tatian, Athenagoras, Theophilus, Melito, Clement of Alexandria, Origen, Tertullian, and Minucius Felix). For further description and discussion, see WILKEN, *The Christians as the Romans Saw Them* (1984). COOK, *The Interpretation of the New Testament in Greco-Roman Paganism* (2002).

[228] While Schnackenburg (*Das Johannesevangelium*, 3:139) connects 16:2 with Justin's reference to Jews killing Christians, probably during the war of Bar-Cocheba in AD 132-135 (*Dialogue with Trypho* 133.6), Brown connects John 16:2 with Pliny's persecution which is much closer in time to the composition of the Gospel. BROWN, *An Introduction*, 169. See also HALDIMANN, *Rekonstruktion und Entfaltung*, 274 n. 199. In Downing's view, Revelation and 1 Peter address "the same situation" as Pliny's description of official judicial action against Christians on a large scale. DOWNING, "Pliny's Prosecutions of Christians," 233.

[229] See FREY, "Das Bild 'der Juden'," 48.

when it is hated by the world" (μισῆται ὑπὸ κόσμου, *Ign. Rom.* 3.3; cf. John 15:18). "Do not give to the world (κόσμῳ) the man who wants to belong to God" (*Ign. Rom.* 6.2). "The ruler of this world ('Ο ἄρχων τοῦ αἰῶνος τούτου) wants to take me captive and destroy my purpose toward God" (*Ign. Rom.* 7.1; cf. John 12:31; 14:30; 16:11).[230] Maybe Ignatius uses Johannine terminology in order to evoke the Gospel's larger concept of theodicy: dying for his witness to Christ is not a shameful disaster. The bishop is merely the servant who imitates the master's life and death. What is apparent is that John's use of κόσμος suited Ignatius well to describe *gentile* hostilities.[231]

Similarly, the Epistle to Diognetus from the second century AD, written by an unknown author, picks up John 15:18 when mentioning that "the world hates Christians" (μισεῖ καὶ Χριστιανοὺς ὁ κόσμος, Diogn. 6:5). More specifically, Christians are pressured to "deny God" (ἀρνήσασθαι θεὸν, *Diogn.* 10:7) and face persecution by the Greeks (διώκονται, 5:17), punishment (κολαζόμενοι, 6:9; 10:7) and death by fire

---

[230] The term κόσμος appears in Ignatius' letters as follows: *Ign. Magn.* 5.2; *Ign. Rom.* 2.2; 3.2, 3; 4:2; 6.1, 2. While John uses ὁ ἄρχων τοῦ κόσμου, Ignatius employs the expression ὁ ἄρχων τοῦ αἰῶνος τούτου with the same meaning in *Ign. Eph.* 17.1; 19.1; *Ign. Magn.* 1.2; *Ign. Trall.* 4.2; *Ign. Rom.* 7.1; *Ign. Phil.* 6.2. The terms κόσμος and αἰών can be synonymous, as a comparison with 1 Cor 3:19 (σοφίαν τοῦ κόσμου τούτου) and 2:6 (σοφίαν . . . τοῦ αἰῶνος τούτου) shows. See also Sasse, "κόσμος," 885. Barnabas speaks of the devil as the "evil ruler" (ὁ πονηρὸς ἄρχων, *Barn.* 4:13), and Didache mentions him as the "world-deceiver" (ὁ κοσμοπλανής, *Did.* 16:4).

[231] In his first *Apology*, written ca. AD 150-155 (see *Apol.* I.46) and addressed to the emperor Antonius Pius [AD 138-161], Justin Martyr fights the accusation of "atheism," leading even to punishments without a trial (*Apol.* I.5), and emphasizes that in the context of emperor worship (*Apol.* I.21) "we worship God only, but in other things we gladly serve you" (*Apol.* I.27). In AD 156, Polycarp, the "teacher of Asia" and "father of the Christians" (*Mart. Pol.* 12.2), was killed through fire in Smyrna because Gentiles and Jews of the city accused Christians of being "atheists" (ἄθεοι, *Mart. Pol.* 3:2; 9:2). Polycarp in particular was accused as a "destroyer of our gods, who teaches many people not to sacrifice or worship" (ὁ τῶν ἡμετέρων θεῶν καθαιρέτης, ὁ πολλοὺς διδάσκων μὴ θύειν μηδὲ προσκυεῖν, *Mart. Pol.* 12:2). The chief of police tried to convince Polycarp, "But what harm is it to say 'Lord Caesar' [κύριος Καῖσαρ], and to offer sacrifice [καὶ θῦσαι], and to be saved? [from martyrdom]?" (*Mart. Pol.* 8:2; Euseb., *Hist. Eccl.*, 4.15). The opposite example of Polycarp is Quintus who "took the oath and sacrificed" (ὁμόσαι καὶ ἐπιθῦσαι) after the governor persuaded him (*Mart. Pol.* 4.2). Probably at the end of the 2nd century AD, Celsus gathers his arguments against Christianity in his book *On the True Doctrine* and accuses Christians of meeting in secret in order to avoid the death penalty. In his response to Celsus, Origin .explains that "the Roman Senate, and the princes of the time, and the soldiery, and the people . . . made war upon their doctrine, and would have prevented (its progress) . . . had it not, by the help of God, escaped the danger, and risen above it, so as (finally) to defeat the whole world in its conspiracy against it" (Origen, *Cels.*, 1.3).

(τὸ πῦρ τὸ πρόσκαιρον, 10:8) if they refuse to do so. While loving those who hate them (6:6; also *2 Clement* 13:4; *Did.* 1:3; 2:7), Christians, on the other side, "despise the world" (κόσμος), meaning they "disregard those whom the *Greeks* (τῶν Ἑλλήνων) consider gods, and do not observe the superstition of the *Jews*" (Ἰουδαίων, Diogn. 1, italics added). The extended polemic against pagan idolatry in chapter 2 is a famous literary monument in early patristic literature. Again, as in Ignatius' letters, κόσμος, a term borrowed apparently from John's Gospel, is understood to consist of Jews *and Greeks* and carries connotations of religious systems opposite to the Christian faith.

A conflict between Rome and non-Roman religions is neither unique to Christians, nor only a phenomenon of the late first century AD. While Romans were able to tolerate temples from foreign nations in their city, this liberal attitude changed when ancient Roman values and virtues were thought to be compromised. Tiberius ordered the destruction of the temple of the Egyptian goddess Isis and the crucifixion of her priests in AD 19 after Paulina, a noble Roman woman, was deceived and sexually dishonored in Isis's temple (Josephus, *A.J.* 18:65-80). Some vicious Jews convinced a wealthy Roman woman to send gold to the temple in Jerusalem. When Tiberius learned that they had misused the gifts for their own greed, the emperor expulsed all Jews from Rome in AD 14 and send four thousand of them to the island Sardinia (Josephus, *A.J.* 18:81-84; Tacitus, *Ann.* 2.85).[232] The Jews were forced out of Rome again in AD 41 under Claudius (cf. Acts 18:1-2). Levinskaya explains that Romans were concerned "with the preservation of traditional Roman virtues and beliefs and took measures to protect Roman society from the unwanted influence of oriental cults."[233]

According to Josephus, the Jews of Antioch were challenged in AD 66-67 to "sacrifice after the manner of the Greeks" (τὸ ἐπιθύειν ὥσπερ νόμος ἐστὶ τοῖς Ἕλλησιν) in order to discover who was part of an alleged plot against the city (Josephus, *B.J.* 7.50-51). Most Jews did not comply and were "massacred" (ἀνῃρέθησαν). While the occasion for the massacre relates to a unique combination of circumstances, the kind of test used to identify political loyalties was certainly applied in other cities at different times as well.

---

[232] See MOEHRING, "The Persecution of the Jews and the Adherents of the Isis Cult at Rome A.D. 19," 293-04.

[233] LEVINSKAYA, *The Book of Acts*, 31. With regard to the concrete clashes between Roman culture and Jewish religion see MASON, *Josephus*, 59. Among the other despised religions was also the Egyptian religion which, as Tacitus states, worships "many animals and images of monstrous form" (*Hist.* 5.5). The 2nd century Christian apologists Aristides later joins in this polemic (*Apology*, 12).

Tacitus, a friend of Pliny the Younger, delivers an anti-Semitic tirade against the Jewish religion in Book 5 of his *Historia* (5.1-13), written probably between AD 100-110.[234] According to him, Jews have "a novel form of worship, opposed to all that is practiced by other men" (5.4). They "despise all gods" (5.5), have a mere "mental conception of Deity" and "call those profane who make representations of God in human shape out of perishable materials" (5.5). When the Jews "were ordered by Caligula to set up his statue in the temple, they preferred the alternative of war" (5.9). Thus, the Jews are a "race detested by the gods" (5.3) and "the most degraded out of other races" (5.5). Tacitus gives many more reasons and myths to support his sentiment. While some criticism is unique to the Jews (circumcision, temple, emphasis on racial separation), Christians share many of the faults as well (monotheism, no images, against syncretism). It is thus only a small step to project the anger, expressed here against the Jews, on Christians. And it does not come as a surprise when Tacitus labels both religions as "superstitious" (*Hist.* 5.8; *Ann.* 15.44) and infected with the "hatred of mankind" (*Hist.* 5.5; *Ann.* 15.44).

Romans viewed Greek philosophers with ambivalence if not with as much suspicion as Egyptian cults or the Jewish and Christian religion. Stoic philosophers emphasized quiet contemplation versus action in public life and were thus open for the Roman charge of treason, for 'what one avoids, one condemns' (Seneca, *Ep.* 14.8). Tacitus, Pliny, Suetonius and Dio Cassius relate how the Senate's Stoic oppositionists such as Thrasea Paetus in the 60s, Helvidius Priscus in the 70s, and Herennius Senecio in the 90s were expelled from Rome and even executed by Vespasian and Domitian.[235] The Pythagorean philosopher Apollonius of Tyana was tried before Domitian because he was "accused of receiving obeisance like a god."[236] As a close contemporary to the Gospel of John at the end of the first century, he shows how even claims of divinity *simpler* than those of Jesus quickly led to confrontation with this emperor.[237]

---

[234] TACITUS, *The Annals*, 294-98.

[235] Tacitus, *Ann.* 16.34-35; Suetonius, *Vesp.* 15; *Dom.* 10. Dio Cassius 62.15; 66-67. See HAALAND, "Josephus and the Philosophers of Rome," 297-316, esp. 300-06.

[236] *Life of Apollonius* 7.20; 7.21 (274.6; 275.21-23). See JONES, "Apollonius of Tyana," 79.

[237] For a review of Rome's opponents, including philosophers, magicians, astrologers, diviners, and prophets, see MACMULLEN, *Enemies of the Roman Order* (1966). CARTER, "Vulnerable Power," 466-70.

6. Conclusion

Granskou asked the question whether the use of κόσμος dilutes the Gospel's anti-Judaism or heightens it. We are now in the position to respond. In the context of the Gospel, κόσμος means "humanity" with few exceptions. Scholars who regard the term "the world" as a symbol or metaphor for the Jews within the Gospel's cosmological dualism deprive the term of its lexical and conceptual content. We suppose that this view bases its conclusion less on comprehensive analysis of the text than on a paradigm of conflict between synagogue and church (Martyn) that needs revision. Neither does "the world" simply denote a principle of unbelief, since the term is mostly used for a *personal* agent throughout the Gospel. When understood with its usual lexical meaning, within the context of the Gospel (parallel to Ἰουδαῖοι), and within the socio-political cotext at the end of the first century AD, the term κόσμος is part of a theodicy which aims to encourage readers who suffer under *Roman* persecution. We contend, therefore, that the Gospel does not focus its polemic on the Jews as a race but situates the opposition of the historical Jesus in a post-Easter context of universal hate and persecution.

CHAPTER 6

Summary and Conclusion

1. Summary

In the post-holocaust context, the question about the meaning of "the Jews" ('Ιουδαῖοι) in the Gospel of John drew more critical and scholarly attention than any other text and tradition of early Christianity (chap. 1). We observed that past and current discussions suffer too often from reductionist studies that focus on a single term ('Ιουδαῖοι) with a narrow meaning ("authorities" or "Judeans"), on a single text (chap. 5, chap. 8, chaps. 18-19, etc.), a single genre (narratives vs. speeches), or a single context (conflict with Judaism; chap. 2). Even more recent synchronic approaches centered only on certain *parts* of the Gospel and failed to remedy the situation (e.g., Caron, Nicklas, Diefenbach, Hakola). We therefore suggest a reinvestigation that considers the whole text as the proper context, and a sequential reading as the proper method for the understanding of "the Jews."

When analyzed synchronically, 'Ιουδαῖοι does not only appear with neutral (e.g., 2:6, 13; 19:40, 42), negative (e.g., 5:16; 10:31) and positive (e.g., 4:9, 22; 11:45; 18:33) nuances (chap. 3), but we also find the term in parallel position to κόσμος throughout the Gospel (chap. 4). More specifically, and on a macrostructural level (compositional parallelism), the prologue (1:1-18) and the farewell discourse (chaps. 13-17) use κόσμος while 'Ιουδαῖοι dominates the "book of signs" (chaps. 1b-12) and the passion account (chaps. 18-19). From a microstructural perspective (narratological parallelism), our analysis of single episodes revealed that, with few exceptions, the author concentrates the use of κόσμος on the discourses of the speakers and reserves 'Ιουδαῖοι mostly for the voice of the narrator (see Appendix 2).

This *specific* design of the parallelism led to the question how the terms' location in the text influences the function of their relationship (chap. 5). The diffusion of the terminology shows that the author placed κόσμος in places of strategic importance. The prologue and farewell discourse are literary gates and thus hermeneutical keys for the narratives that follow. Jesus´ speech interprets the narratives and gives them meaning beyond the obvious appearance. This means for the parallelism between

Ἰουδαῖοι and κόσμος that "the world" carries the narrative emphasis and either heightens the Gospel's anti-Judaism or dilutes it (Granskou).

In order to answer that question, we turned to the study of the meaning and context of κόσμος (chap. 6). Of all the lexical possibilities ("adornment," "creation," "inhabited world," "humanity"), the author uses κόσμος mostly in the broad sense of "humanity." This meaning is not only supported by the parallel term ἄνθρωπος (e.g., 1:9; 3:19), but also by statements in which κόσμος appears as the subject of actions (such as "knowing" in 1:9; "hating" in 7:7; 15:18; 17:14, or "going" in 12:19) and the object of God's love (3:16), of Jesus' ministry (e.g., 1:29; 8:26; 18:20), and of the Paraclete's influence (16:8).

Scholars who regard κόσμος as a symbol for Ἰουδαῖοι place the parallelism into the service of a cosmic dualism which functions to point out the Jews as a race that live under the special influence of the devil. Not only does this reading contain racist implications that few interpreters are willing to spell out, but it also violates the lexical and conceptual meaning of the term. We suggest that the purpose of the parallelism is often tilted in favor of this view, because Martyn's assumption about a conflict between the synagogue and a Christian community as the *Sitz im Leben* of the Gospel dominates current Johannine scholarship. While Martyn rightly grasps the significance of a historical opposition for the narrative makeup of the Gospel, he unjustly excludes Gentiles from the group of antagonists because he limits his focus on the narrative genre with its heavy concentration on the Ἰουδαῖοι.

Despite the importance of Martyn's paradigm, the same authors who interpret the parallelism as a cosmic dualism concede the universal import in texts such as 3:16, 19; 4:42; and 12:19-20 and reveal therefore their inconsistent understanding of κόσμος in the Gospel of John. Instead of depriving the term of its usual lexical content, we suggest that the author chose κόσμος in order to describe the universal scope of the church's mission (4:42; 12:19-20; 13:35; 17:18-23) as well as its opposition (1:10; 15:18-19). The structural rhythm, according to which κόσμος appears in the literary gates of the Gospel's two main parts (prologue; farewell discourse) as well as in the interpretive speeches in contrast to the narratives, reveals the author's intent to translate the particulars of Jesus' life *throughout* the text into universal notions that apply to Jews and Gentiles alike. This effort is supported with a gnomic style and a lack of concreteness in Jesus' speeches. The logical bridge between the world of Jesus and that of the post-Easter church is built explicitly with the proverbial statement of the servant who is not greater than the master (John 13:16; 15:20). While this connection underlies various concepts in the Gospel (e.g., 1:39 and 1:46; 17:14, 16), Jesus uses it directly to prepare his disciples for the inevitable experience of hate and persecution. A theodicy emerges in which the rejection and death of the master by Jews serves to explain the same experience of his servants through Gentiles.

We propose at this point that, against Bultmann and others, the *literary* relationship between "the Jews" and "the world" as one between a part and the whole (synecdoche) does not exclude an *empirical* element in the usage of the term Ἰουδαῖοι (see 4:9, 22; 2:6; 8:33, 37). Ethnic-religious connotations are not compromised by the examples of Jewish drop outs such as Christians who left the synagogue, voluntarily or involuntarily (cf. ἀποσυνάγωγος, 9:22; 12:42; 16:2). If Gentiles can become "Jews" by joining the religious community (cf. ἰουδαΐζω in Esth 8:17; Gal 2:14; Josephus *B.J.* 2.454; Ignatius *Magn.* 10.3; Ἰουδαῖοι in Bel 28; 2 Macc 9:17), then Jews can become non-Jews by exiting the religious community.[1] Memories of Jesus' Jewishness (4:9) reveal the ongoing awareness about the historical origin (also 4:22), probably with regret about the parting of the ways.

The Gospel's probable provenance and date suggest considering the socio-political circumstances at the end of the first century in Asia Minor, if not the whole Roman empire, as the historical context of the author and his readers. The Gospel's reference to rivalry between Jesus and Caesar in the passion account (John 19) as well as to Peter's martyrdom under Nero (chap. 21) reflect the ideological tension between the Johannine communities and the emperor and exemplify Christian suffering inflicted by Roman hands. The Gospel's Christology as well as Jesus' miracles challenge not only the religious titles claimed by the emperor (see "Lord," "Savior of the World," "My Lord and my God") but confront the whole polytheistic system of the empire (including Isis, Dionysus, Asclepius) with an alternative form of worship that resists any syncretistic compromise. Attempts about a likely scenario behind the Gospel point out how the emperor cult became a deadly challenge for Christians who lost the privileged protection of the Jews (*religio licita*) once they stepped out of the social and religious boundaries of the synagogue (see Vouga, Cassidy, Frey). The *fiscus Iudaicus*, introduced after the destruction of the temple in AD 70 and reinforced by Domitian, possibly catalyzed the problem for Gentile and Jewish Christians. The correspondence between Pliny the Younger and the emperor Trajan illustrates how the Roman empire confronted the Christian faith with tests of Roman piety once the government's suspicion arose (invoking gods, praying to the emperor's

---

[1] Barrett speculates about the author of the Gospel that he "may also have ceased to be a Jew in that he became ἀποσυνάγωγος (9:22; 16.2) – not by his own desire, but by command of the synagogue." BARRETT, *The Gospel of John and Judaism*, 70.

image, cursing Christ). Ignatius' letter to the Romans shows how John's use of κόσμος provided a helpful category to describe *Roman* hostilities against Christians not too long after the composition of the Gospel.

An illustration may aid in understanding the Gospel's dynamics between the Ἰουδαῖοι and the κόσμος. Imagine that someone videotapes a choir. There are about twenty members divided into different subgroups, such as tenor, soprano, bass. Each subgroup numbers three to four singers. Sometimes the camera zooms so close to a singer that only her face fills the picture. In this moment, only one person is visible on the screen, but the ear hears the song of a whole group. Next, the camera zooms to the subgroup of the sopranos and captures the picture of three or four individuals, singing the same part. Here again, the screen displays only a part of the whole. When the focus captures the complete choir, audible and visible impressions cohere and make sense. In the same way, when John looks at the historical particulars, when he zooms really close to the life of Jesus, he sees certain Jewish names and precise locations in Judea and Galilee. But, from his point of view *after Easter*, the Jews are only a subgroup of the "choir," there must be more to explain this song of rejection and hate now experienced also outside of Palestine in a pagan context. So he zooms further away from the particulars and uses the prologue, a farewell discourse, and the speeches to point to a global principle of human response to divine revelation. Theology does not part with history; the author does not create a cosmological "tale" or fiction. Both perspectives are true to reality and were tangibly experienced. The author uses the story of the master to explain the storm of the servants. The past of the leader becomes the prologue for the life of his followers.

2. Conclusion

Our synchronic and historical analysis demands the conclusion that, contrary to a literalist reading and in contrast to the charges of anti-Semitism, the Gospel of John cannot legitimately be employed for a special fingerpointing to the Jews as the perpetrators of Jesus' death. Most current translations of the text and contributions to the debate affirm our result, but they do so by trying to *narrow* the referent for the Ἰουδαῖοι to religious leaders or Judeans. On the contrary, we suggest that the Gospel's answer lies in the *broadening* of the term to a universal scope via the use of κόσμος. By these means, the specific circumstances fade into the background, and the (gentile) world becomes part of the drama. The author insists that the opposition against Jesus continues in the opposition against the church. In this "relecture," the author's conditions are not projected

Chapter 6

retrospectively into the time of Jesus so as to deliver an anachronistic account, but past history is actualized for present purposes.[2] The particular opposition (by the Jews) in a particular place (Judea) is explicitly, frequently and clearly converted into a theme of universal conflict between Jesus and the Roman empire (historical), if not between Jesus and humanity in general (existential). Thus, modern Jews and Gentiles alike only understand this Gospel when they finish it with the confession "mea culpa" on their lips.[3]

When understood within the universal dualism of the Gospel, even an ethnic-religious meaning for Ἰουδαῖοι cannot serve racial theories of gentile superiority. Bold voices have maintained this in a time where it was tempting to adopt a racist reading of the text. Francis Evelyn upheld in 1938 that the writer of the Gospel disproves "the very theory for which the Nazis claim his patronage" because it is a "supra-racial" account which defies all "rivalries of race or class."[4] And while Bultmann's commentary on John, published in 1941, shocked the world *after* the holocaust mostly because of the theory of dislocation, it must have been a provocation if not

---

[2] Grelot formulates this way with regard to the confrontation between Christians and Jews at the end of the first century AD. GRELOT, *Les Juifs*, 39, 50. Borowitz thinks that because of "Berkouwer's *biblicism*, we might expect him to be the most explicit anti-Semite of the group studied here. In fact, however, Berkouwer seems almost devoid of anti-Jewish sentiment. Rather he systematically applies a *universalizing hermeneutics* to passages that speak of the Jews as opponents of the Christ or the Church. He applies them to humanity as a whole, omitting significant reference to the Jews of Jesus' time or since." BOROWITZ, *Contemporary Christologies*, 179 (italics added). Borowitz creates a false dichotomy between 'biblicism' and 'universalizing hermeneutics' because the author of the Fourth Gospel himself envisions already the opposition of humanity.

[3] See BARTH, "Die Juden," 92. Similarly Carson, who writes that peace "was secured by an innocent man who suffered and died at the hands of the Romans, of the Jews, and of all of us." CARSON, *The Gospel*, 506. Against Rubli-Guthauser and Stegemann, Sänger affirms the Jewish role in the crucifixion of Jesus. But with Stegemann he distinguishes between responsibility and guilt and explains that the latter can only correctly be expressed in words such as these by Paul Gerhard, "'Ich, ich und meine Sünden, die sich wie Körnlein finden des Sandes an dem Meer, die haben dir erreget das Elend, das dich schläget, und deiner schweren Martern Heer'." SÄNGER, "'Auf Betreiben der Vornehmsten'," 25.

[4] EVELYN, "The Supra-Racial Gospel," 420-21. A few pages before this article, an anonymous author published his report about a recent visit to Germany. Under the headline "The Fight for Christianity in Germany" (*ExpTim* 49 [1938]: 408-11), he notices the difference between the Confessional Church and the 'German Christians' who are "compromise people, endeavouring to combine Christianity and National Socialism." Ibid., 409. The author also speaks about the "'Nazification' of the church." The Christian faith stands in radical contrast to the ideology of National Socialisms which owes its ideas to Alfred Rosenberg's *The Myth of the Twentieth Century* with its 'Blood and Soil' ideology and its "gospel of the superiority of German blood." Ibid., 408.

an insult to Nazi supporters *during* WW II because the *existential* interpretation was a slap in the face of moral distinctions along *racial* lines.[5] This conclusion stands independent of apologetic interests. In 1894, Claude Goldsmith Montefiore (1858-1938), the Jewish scholar who studied the New Testament more intensively than any other Jew before him, wrote a long article in order to ask the question specifically about the Gospel of John: "What is its religious value to the average modern Jew?"[6] What might be surprising to hear in our post-Holocaust context is that he does not lament or even mention the Gospel's use of the Ἰουδαῖοι on any of the fifty pages of his essay. We find him instead praising the use of the double meanings in the Gospel which "cannot fail to cause pleasure and profit." He applauds the author's "beautiful use of the ideas of love and sacrifice," its "elaborate simplicity of art," and the universalism which is "one of the best features in the Gospel."[7] The tone starts to change after eight pages when he discusses the Gospel's dualism that divides humanity into elected believers that are saved by faith in Christ and the nonbelievers who will be judged. It contradicts Montefiore's universalist ideal and provokes his protest when the "glad communion with God . . . is asserted to be the patent and prerogative of one religion only and of a single book."[8] This study concurs that the real stumbling block of the Fourth Gospel for a Christian dialogue not just with Jews but with believers of any non-Christian religion is not a dualism of race but one of religion.

---

[5] Bultmann stated his political views elsewhere more explicitly. In an essay from 1933, he wrote in response to a pro-Nazi demonstration in Marburg, that "*as a Christian, I must deplore the injustice that is also being done precisely to German Jews*" (italics added). Quoted in BOROWITZ, *Contemporary Christologies*, 185. In contrast to his friend and colleague at Marburg, Martin Heidegger, Bultmann did not join the Nationalist Socialist party but the Confessing Church. See KELLEY, *Racializing Jesus*, 132 (pp. 129-64). Meeks notices that, in contrast to Kittel, Bultmann "stood resolutely against the antisemitic measure [of removing Jewish scholars from the university], while Kittel published a pamphlet supporting it." MEEKS, "A Nazi New Testament Professor Reads His Bible," 541-42. See also FORSTMAN, *Christian Faith in Dark Times*, 222-42. DE VALERIO, *Altes Testament und Judentum im Frühwerk Rudolf Bultmanns* (1994).

[6] MONTEFIORE, "Notes on the Religious Value," 26.

[7] Ibid., 30, 31, 45.

[8] Ibid., 67.

Table 1. Different English Translations of Ἰουδαῖος in the Gospel of John

Translations		Jews	Jewish (man / people)	Judea(ns)	Jewish Authorities / Leaders	Leaders	Om. / subst. w. crowd / people
1611	KJV	70		1			
1982	NKJV	70		1			
1994	KJ 21	70		1			
1901	ASV	70		1			
1963	NASV	68	2	1			
1952	RSV	68	2	1			
1990	NRSV	66	4	1			
2001	ESV	68	2	1			
1958	AB	63	5	1	2		
1966	JB	60	9	1			1
1985	NJB	60	9	1			1
1972	JBP	60	7	1			3
1978	NIV	62	8	1			
2002	TNIV	38	9	1	13	1	9
1976	GNT	13	3	3	19		33
1995	CEV	10	8	1	6	11	35
1989	JNT	11	1	59			
1993	TM	58	6	1	3		3
1996	NLT	11	4	1	26		29
2000	HCSB	62	8	1			
2000	NET	16	9	10	32		4

Table 2. Different German Translations of Ἰουδαῖος in the Gospel of John

Translations	*Juden*	*Jüdisch*	*Judäa, Judäer*	*Jüdische Führer*	*Führer*	*Om. / subst. with Menschen etc.*
1951 Schlachter	70	1	1			
1980 EinheitsÜS	69	1	1			
1984 rev. Luther	69	1	1			
1993 rev. Elberfelder	70		1			
1996 Hoffnung für Alle	49		2		10	10
1997 Gute Nachricht	25		1	17		28
1998 Münchener NT			71 (*Judaier*)			
2002 Neues Leben	32		1	11		27
2005 Herder	70		1			

Table 3. The Distribution of κόσμος and Ἰουδαῖος in the Gospel of John

Chs.	κόσμος (78x)				Ἰουδαῖος (71x)			
	Narra-tor	Jesus	Jew	Gentile	Narra-tor	Jesus	Jew	Gentile
1	9, 10 (3x)		29		19			
2					6, 13, 18, 20			
3		16, 17 (3x), 19			1, 22, 25			
4				42	9	22		9
5					1, 10, 15, 16, 18			
6		33, 51	14		4, 41, 52			
7		7	4		1, 2, 11, 13, 15, 35			
8		12, 23 (2x), 26			22, 31, 48, 52, 57			
9		5 (2x), 39			18, 22 (2x)			
10		36			19, 24, 31, 33			
11		9	27		19, 31, 33, 36, 45, 54, 55		8	
12		25, 31 (2x), 46, 47 (2x)	19		9, 11			

Chs.	κόσμος (78x)				Ἰουδαῖος (71x)			
	Narra-tor	Jesus	Jew	Gentile	Narra-tor	Jesus	Jew	Gentile
13	1 (2x)					33		
14		17, 19, 27, 30, 31	22					
15		18, 19 (5x)						
16		8, 11, 20, 21, 28 (2x), 33 (2x)						
17		5, 6, 9, 11 (2x), 13, 14 (3x), 15, 16 (2x), 18 (2x), 21, 23, 24, 25						
18		20, 36 (2x), 37			12, 14, 31, 38	20, 36		33, 35, 39
19					7, 12, 14, 19, 20, 21, 31, 38, 40, 42		21 (2x)	3
20					19			
21	25							
Tot.	7x	64x	6x	1x	59x	4x	3x	5x

Bibliography

Ancient Sources

The Annals and the Histories by P. Cornelius Tacitus. Transl. by A. J. Church and W. J. Brodribb. Chicago: William Benton, 1952.

The Anti-Nicene Fathers. Translation of the Writings of the Fathers down to A.D. 325. Vols. 1-10. Ed. A. Roberts, J. Donaldson. Grand Rapids: Eerdmans, 1969-73.

Eusebius. *The Ecclesiastical History*. Transl. by Kirsopp Lake. Volume 1. Reprint. LCL 153. Cambridge, MA: Harvard, 1980.

Irenaeus. "Against Heresies." In *Ante-Nicene Fathers: Translations of the Writings of the Fathers down to A.D. 325*, ed. A. Roberts and J. Donaldson, 1:308-567. New York: Charles Scribner's Sons, 1899.

Josephus: With an English Translation by H. St. J. Thackeray. 9 vols. LCL. Cambridge, MA: Harvard, 1979.

Origen. "Against Celsus." In *Ante-Nicene Fathers: Translations of the Writings of the Fathers down to A.D. 325*, ed. A. Roberts and J. Donaldson, 4:395-669. Grand Rapids: Eerdmans, 1972.

Pliny: Letters and Panegyricus. 2 vols. Transl. by Betty Radice. LCL 59. Cambridge, MA: Harvard University Press, 1975.

Polybius: The Histories. Transl. by W. R. Paton. LCL 159. Cambridge, MA: Harvard, 1976.

Pseudo-Gregory of Nyssa: Testimonies against the Jews. Transl. with an Introduction and Notes by Martin C. Albl. Writings from the Greco-Roman World 5. Atlanta: Society of Biblical Literature, 2004.

SEG: Supplementum Epigraphicum Graecum. Vol. L 2000. Ed. by A. Chaniotis, R. S. Stroud, and J. H. M. Strubbe. Amsterdam: J. C. Gieben, 2003.

St. Justin Martyr: The First and Second Apologies. Transl. by Leslie W. Barnard. ACW 56. New York: Paulist Press, 1997.

Suetonius: With an English Translation by J. C. Rolfe. 2 vols. LCL. Cambridge, MA: Harvard University Press, 1935.

Tertullian. *Adversus Marcionem. Books 4 and 5*. Ed. and transl. by Ernest Evans. OECT. Oxford: Clarendon Press, 1972.

The Old Testament Pseudepigrapha. Vols. 1-2. Ed. by James H. Charlesworth. New York: Doubleday, 1983-1985.

Wise, M., M. Abegg Jr., and E. Cook. *The Dead Sea Scrolls – A New Translation*. New York: HarperCollins, 1996.

Commentaries

Bacon, Benjamin W. *The Gospel of the Hellenists*. New York: Henry Holt and Company, 1933.

Barrett, C. K. *The Gospel According to St. John*. London: SPCK, 1958.

Bauer, Walter. *Das Johannesevangelium*. 3rd ed. HNT 6. Tübingen: Mohr Siebeck, 1933.

Beale, G. K. *The Book of Revelation*. NIGTC. Grand Rapids: Eerdmans, 1999.

Beasley-Murray, George. *John*. 2nd ed. WBC 36. Nashville: Thomas Nelson Publishers, 1999.

Becker, Jürgen. *Das Evangelium nach Johannes*. 3rd ed. ÖTK 4.1. Gütersloh: Gütersloher Verlagshaus, 1991.

Borowitz, Eugene B. *Contemporary Christologies: A Jewish Response*. New York: Paulist Press, 1980.

Brodie, Thomas L. *The Gospel According to John: A Literary and Theological Commentary*. New York: Oxford University Press, 1993.

Brown, Raymond E. *The Gospel According to John*. AB 29-30. Garden City, NY: Doubleday & Company, 1966-1970.

–. *An Introduction to the Gospel of John*. Ed., updated, introduced, and concluded by Francis J. Moloney. New York: Doubleday, 2003.

Bultmann, Rudolf. *Das Evangelium des Johannes*. 2 vols. 21nd ed. KEK. Göttingen: Vandenhoeck & Ruprecht, 1986.

–. *The Gospel of John: A Commentary*. Transl. by G. R. Beasley-Murray, R. W. N. Hoare, and J. K. Riches. Philadelphia: The Westminster Press, 1971.

Busse, Ulrich. *Das Johannesevangelium: Bildlichkeit, Diskurs und Ritual. Mit einer Bibliographie über den Zeitraum 1986-1998*. BETL 162. Leuven: University Press, 2002.

Carson, D. A. *The Farewell Discourse and Final Prayer of Jesus: An Exposition of John 14-17*. Grand Rapids: Baker, 1980.

–. *The Gospel According to John*. Leicester: IVP, 1991.

Colwell, Ernest C. *John Defends the Gospel*. Chicago: Willett, Clark & Company, 1936.

Dietzfelbinger, Christian. *Das Evangelium nach Johannes*. 2 vols. ZBK. Zürich: Theologischer Verlag, 2001.

Gnilka, Joachim. *Johannesevangelium*. 5th ed. NEchtB 4. Würzburg: Echter Verlag, 1999.

Hellenistic Commentary to the New Testament. Ed. by E. M. Boring, K. Berger, and C. Colpe. Nashville: Abingdon Press, 1995.

Holtzmann, H. J. *Evangelium, Briefe und Offenbarung des Johannes*. Hand-Commentar zum Neuen Testament. Tübingen: Mohr Siebeck, 1908.

Hoskyns, Edwyn Clement. *The Fourth Gospel*. Ed. by F. N. Davey. London: Faber and Faber, 1947.

Keener, Craig S. *The Gospel of John: A Commentary*. 2 vols. Peabody, MA: Hendrickson, 2003.

Keil, Carl Friedrich. *Commentar über das Evangelium des Johannes*. Leipzig: Dörffling und Franke, 1881.

Köstenberger, Andreas J. *Encountering John: The Gospel in Historical, Literary, and Theological Perspective*. Grand Rapids: Baker, 1999.

–. "John." In: *New Dictionary of Biblical Theology*. Ed. by T. Desmond Alexander, Brian S. Rosner, D.A. Carson, and Graeme Goldsworthy. Downers Grove, IL: IVP, 2000.

–. "John." In: *Zondervan Illustrated Bible Background Commentary: New Testament*. Ed. by C. E. Arnold. Grand Rapids: Zondervan, 2002.

–. *John*. BECNT. Grand Rapids: Baker, 2004.

Kysar, Robert. *John: The Maverick Gospel*. Atlanta: John Knox Press, 1976.

–. *John*. ACNT. Minneapolis, MN: Augsburg Publishing House, 1986.

LaVerdiere, Eugene. *Luke*. Wilmington, DE: Michael Glazier, 1988.

Lindars, Barnabas. *The Gospel of John*. New Century Bible. London: Marshall, Morgan & Scott, 1972.

Lücke, Friedrich. *Commentar über das Evangelium des Johannes*. 2 vols. 2nd ed. Bonn: Eduard Weber, 1833-1834.

Malina, Bruce, and Richard L. Rohrbaugh. *Social-Science Commentary on the Gospel of John*. Minneapolis: Fortress, 1998.

Meyer, Heinrich August Wilhelm. *Kritisch-Exegetisches Handbuch über das Evangelium des Johannes*. 5th ed. Göttingen: Vandenhoeck & Ruprecht, 1869.

Moloney, Francis J. *The Gospel of John*. Sacra Pagina 4. Collegeville, MN: The Liturgical Press, 1998.

Morris, Leon. *The Gospel According to John*. NICNT. Grand Rapids: Eerdmans, 1989.

Osborne, Grant R. *Revelation*. BECNT. Grand Rapids: Baker, 2002.

Plummer, A. *The Gospel According to S. John*. CGTSC. Cambridge: Cambridge Univ. Press, 1882.

Ridderbos, Herman. *The Gospel of John: A Theological Commentary*. Transl. by John Vriend. Grand Rapids: Eerdmans, 1997.

Robertson, Archibald T. *Word Pictures in the Greek New Testament*. Vol. 5. Nasville: Broadman Press, 1932.

Sanders, J. N., and B. A. Mastin. *A Commentary on the Gospel According to St. John*. HNTC. Peabody, MA: Hendrickson, 1988.

Schenke, Ludger. *Johannes*. Kommentare zu den Evangelien. Düsseldorf: Patmos Verlag, 1998.

–. *Das Johannesevangelium: Einführung – Text – dramatische Gestalt. Übersetzung aus dem Griechischen von Ludger Schenke, Rainer Feige und Johannes Neugebauer*. Stuttgart: Kohlhammer, 1992.

Schlatter, Adolf. *Der Evangelist Johannes: Wie er spricht, denkt und glaubt*. 3rd ed. Stuttgart: Calwer Verlag, 1960.

Schnackenburg, Rudolf. *Das Johannesevangelium*. HTKNT. Freiburg: Herder, 1965–1984.

–. *Die Johannesbriefe*. 5th ed. HTKNT 13. Freiburg: Herder, 1975.

Schnelle, Udo. *Das Evangelium nach Johannes*. THKNT 4. Leipzig: Evangelische Verlagsanstalt, 1998.

Sloyan, Gerard. *John*. Interpretation. Atlanta: John Knox Press, 1988.

Smart, W. A. *The Spiritual Gospel: The Quillian Lectures Emory University*. NewYork: Abingdon-Cokesbury Press, 1945.

Strack, Hermann L., and Paul Billerbeck. *Kommentar zum Neuen Testament aus Talmud und Midrasch*. Vols. 1-4. München: C. H. Becksche Verlagsbuchhandlung, 1922-1928.

Tholuck, A. *Commentar zum Evangelio Johannis*. 5th ed. Hamburg: Friedrich Perthes, 1837.

Thompson, Marianne M. "John, Gospel of." In: *Dictionary of Jesus and the Gospels*. Ed. by Joel B. Green and Scot McKnight. Downers Grove, IL: InterVarsity Press, 1992.

Tillmann, Fritz. *Das Johannesevangelium*. 4th ed. Bonn: Peter Hanstein, 1931.

Van den Bussche, Henri. *Jean: Commentaire de l'évangile spirituel*. Paris–Bruges: Desclée de Brouwer 1967.

Wellhausen, Julius. *Das Evangelium Johannis.* Berlin: Georg Reimer, 1908.
Westcott, Brooke Foss. *The Gospel Acording to St. John.* 2 vols. London: John Murray, 1908.
Wilckens, Ulrich. *Das Evangelium nach Johannes.* NTD 4. Göttingen: Vandenhoeck & Ruprecht, 1998.

Monographs and Articles

Abbott, Edwin A. *Johannine Vocabulary: A Comparison of the Words of the Fourth Gospelwith those of the Three.* London: Adam and Charles Black, 1905.
Adams, Edward. *Constructing the World: A Study in Paul's Cosmological Language.* Studies of the New Testament and Its World. Edinburgh: T&T Clark, 2000.
Aland, Kurt. *Vollständige Konkordanz zum Griechischen Neuen Testament. Band II: Spezialübersichten.* Berlin: de Gruyter, 1978.
Allen, E. L. "The Jewish Christian Church in the Fourth Gospel." *Journal of Biblical Literature* 74 (1955): 88-92.
Alter, Robert. *The Art of Biblical Narrative.* New York: Basic Books, 1981.
Amedick, Rita. "'Iesus Nazarenus Rex Iudaiorum.' Hellenistische Königsikonographie und das Neue Testament." In: *Picturing the New Testament,* ed. A. Weissenrieder, F. Wendt and P. von Gemünden, 53-66. WUNT II/193. Tübingen: Mohr Siebeck, 2005.
Anderson, Paul N. "The Sitz im Leben of the Johannine Bread of Life Discourse and Its Evolving Context." In: *Critical Readings of John 6,* ed. by R. Alan Culpepper, 1-59. Leiden: Brill, 1997.
Anti-Judaism and the Fourth Gospel: Papers of the Leuven Colloquium, 2000. Ed. by R. Bieringer, D. Pollefeyt, F. Vandecasteele-Vanneuville. Jewish and Christian Heritage Series, vol. 1. Assen: Royal Van Gorcum, 2001.
Anti-Judaism and the Fourth Gospel. Ed. by R. Bieringer, D.Pollefeyt, and F. Vandecasteele-Vanneuville. Louisville: Westminster John Knox, 2001.
Arnold, Bill T., David B. Weisberg. "Babel und Bibel und Bias." *Bible Review* 18 (2002): 32-40, 47.
Ashton, John. "The Identity and Function of the ΙΟΥΔΑΙΟΙ in the Fourth Gospel." *Novum Testamentum* 27 (1985): 40-75.
–. *Understanding the Fourth Gospel.* Oxford: Clarendon Press, 1991.
Aune, David E. *The New Testament in Its Literary Environment.* Philadelphia: The Westminster Press, 1987.
–. "On the Origins of the 'Council of Javneh' Myth." *Journal of Biblical Literature* 110 (1991): 491-93.
–. *The Westminster Dictionary of New Testament and Early Christian Literature and Rhetoric.* Louisville: Westminster John Knox Press, 2003.
Aviam, Mordechai. "First century Jewish Galilee: An Archaeological Perspective." In *Religion and Society in Roman Palestine: Old Questions, New Approaches,* ed. Douglas R. Edwards, 7-27. New York: Routledge, 2004.
Balfour, Glenn. "Is John's Gospel Anti-Semitic? With Special Reference to its Use of the Old Testament." Ph.D. diss., University of Nottingham, 1995.
–. "Is John's Gospel Anti-Semitic?" *Tyndale Bulletin* 48 (1997): 369-72.
Balz, Horst, and Gerhard Schneider, eds. *Exegetical Dictionary of the New Testament.* 3 vols.Grand Rapids: Eerdmans, 1993.

Barr, James. *The Concept of Biblical Theology: And Old Testament Perspective.* Minneapolis: Fortress, 1999.

Barrett, Charles K. "John and Judaism." In: *Anti-Judaism and the Fourth Gospel,* ed. R. Bieringer, D. Pollefeyt, and F. Vandecasteele-Vanneuville, 231-46. Louisville: Westminster John Knox, 2001.

Barrett, Charles K. *The Gospel of John and Judaism.* Philadelphia: Fortress Press, 1970.

Barrett, Charles K., and Claus-Jürgen Thornton, eds. *Texte zur Umwelt des Neuen Testaments.* 2nd ed. UTB, vol. 1591. Tübingen: Mohr Siebeck, 1991.

Barth, Markus. "Die Juden im Johannes-Evangelium. Wiedererwägungen zum Sitz im Leben, Datum und angeblichen Anti-Judaismus des Johannes-Evangeliums." In: *Teufelskinder oder Heilsbringer – Die Juden im Johannes-Evangelium,* ed. Dietrich Neuhaus, 39-94.Arnoldshainer Texte 64. Frankfurt: Haag und Herchen, 1990.

Barton, Stephen C. "Christian Community in the Light of the Gospel of John." In: *Christology, Controversy and Community: New Testament Essays in Honour of David R. Catchpole,* ed. D. G. Horrell and C. M. Tuckett, 279-301. Leiden: Brill, 2000.

Bauckham, Richard. "For Whom Were the Gospels Written?" In: *The Gospels for All Christians,* ed. Richard Bauckham, 9-48. Grand Rapids: Eerdmans, 1998.

–. "John for Readers of Mark." In: *The Gospels for All Christians,* ed. Richard Bauckham, 147-71. Grand Rapids: Eerdmans, 1998.

Bauer, Walter. *A Greek-English Lexicon of the New Testament and Other Early Christian Literature.* 2nd ed. Transl. by W. F. Arndt and F. W. Gingrich. Chicago: The University of Chicago Press, 1979.

Baum, Armin. "Zur Funktion und Authentizitätsanspruch der oratio recta. Hebräische undgriechische Geschichtsschreibung im Vergleich." *Zeitschrift für die alttestamentliche Wissenschaft* 115 (2003): 586-607.

Baum, Gregory. *Is the New Testament Anti-Semitic? A Re-examination of the New Testament.* Glen Rock, NJ: Paulist Press, 1965.

–. *The Jews and the Gospel: A Re-examination of the New Testament.* Westminster, MD: Newman, 1961.

Baumbach, Günther. "Gemeinde und Welt im Johannes-Evangelium." *Kairos* 14 (1972): 121-36.

Beck, Norman. *Mature Christianity in the 21st Century: The Recognition and Repudiation of the Anti-Jewish Polemic of the New Testament.* 2nd rev. ed. The American Interfaith Institute. New York: Crossroad, 1994.

–. *Mündiges Christentum im 21. Jahrhundert: Die antijüdische Polemik des Neuen Testaments und ihre Überwindung.* Transl. by Christoph Kock, Thomas Krapf, and Christoph Münz. Veröffentlichungen aus dem Institut Kirche und Judentum, vol. 26. Berlin: Institut Kirche und Judentum, 1998.

Becker, Jürgen. "Beobachtungen zum Dualismus im Johannesevangelium." *Zeitschrift für die neutestamentliche Wissenschaft* 65 (1974): 71-86.

Bell, Richard H. *The Irrevocable Call of God.* WUNT 184. Tübingen: Mohr Siebeck, 2005.

Belser, J. "Der Ausdruck οἱ Ἰουδαῖοι im Johannesevangelium." *Theologische Quartalschrift* 84 (1902): 168-222.

Berger, Klaus. *Bibelkunde des Alten und Neuen Testaments. Zweiter Teil: Neues Testament.*4th ed. UTB 972. Heidelberg: Quelle & Meyer, 1991.

–. *Im Anfang war Johannes: Datierung und Theologie des vierten Evangeliums.* Stuttgart: Quell, 1997.

Besier, Gerhard. *Die Kirchen und das Dritte Reich. Bd. 3: Spaltungen und Abwehrkämpfe 1934-1937.* Berlin: Propyläen, 2001.

Betz, Hans Dieter. "Jesus and the Cynics: Survey and Analysis of a Hypothesis." In: *Antike und Christentum. Gesammelte Aufsätze IV*, 32-56. Tübingen: Mohr Siebeck, 1998.

Beulter, Johannes. "Response from a European Perspective." *Semeia* 53 (1991): 191-202.

Blasi, Anthony J. *A Sociology of Johannine Christianity*. Texts and Studies in Religion 69.Lewiston, NY: The Edwin Mellen Press, 1996.

Bock, Darrell L., Gregory J. Herrick. *Jesus in Context: Background Readings for Gospel Study*. Grand Rapids: Baker, 2005.

Bockmuehl, Markus. *This Jesus. Martyr, Lord, Messiah*. Downers Grove: IVP, 1994.

Bond, Helen K. *Pontius Pilate in history and interpretation*. SNTSMS 100. Cambridge: Cambridge University, 1998.

Bonney, William. *Caused to Believe: The Doubting Thomas Story at the Climax of John's Christological Narrative*. BIS 62. Leiden: Brill, 2002.

Booth, Steve. *Selected Peak Marking Features in the Gospel of John*. American University Studies 7.178. New York: Peter Lang, 1996.

Borgen, Peder. "Observations on the Targumic Character of the Prologue of John." *New Testament Studies* 16 (1969): 288-95.

Borowsky, Irvin J. "The Language of Religion: A Force for Asserting Life; A Force for Degradation." In: *Removing Anti-Judaism from the Pulpit*, ed. Howard C. Kee, and Irvin J. Borowsky, 7-10. New York: Continuum, 1996.

Böttrich, Christfried. "Judas Iskarioth zwischen Historie und Legende." In: *Gedenkt an das Wort: Festschrift für Werner Vogler zum 65. Geburtstag*, ed. C. Kähler, M. Böhm, and C. Böttrich, 34-55. Leipzig: Evangelische Verlagsanstalt, 1999.

Bowen, Clayton R. "The Fourth Gospel as Dramatic Material." *Journal of Biblical Literature* 49 (1930): 292-305.

Bowman, John. *The Fourth Gospel and the Jews: A Study in R. Akiba, Esther and the Gospel of John*. PTMS 8. Pittsburgh: Pickwick, 1975.

Boyarin, Daniel. "The Gospel of the Memra: Jewish Binitarianism and the Prologue to John." *Harvard Theological Review* 94 (2001): 243-84.

–. *"Ioudaioi* in John and the prehistory of 'Judaism'." In: *Pauline Conversation in Context: Essays in Honor of Calvin J. Roetzel*, ed. J. C. Anderson, P. Sellew, and C. Setzer, 216-39. JSNT Supp, vol. 221. Sheffield: Sheffield Academic Press, 2002.

Boys, Mary C., and Barbara Veale Smith. "A Select, Annotated Bibliography on Jewish-Christian Relations." *Religious Education* 91 (1996): 600-20.

Brant, Jo-Ann. *Dialogue and Drama: Elements of Greek Tragedy in the Fourth Gospel*. Peabody, MA: Hendrickson, 2004.

Bratcher, Robert G. "'The Jews' in the Gospel of John." *The Bible Translator* 26 (1975): 401-09.

Brent, Allen. "Luke-Acts and the Imperial Cult in Asia Minor." *Journal of Theological Studies* 48 (1997): 411-28.

Brodie, Thomas L. *The Quest for the Origin of John's Gospel: A Source-Oriented Approach*. New York: Oxford University Press, 1993.

Broer, Ingo."Die Juden im Johannesevangelium. Ein beispielhafter und folgenreicher Konflikt." *Diakonia* 14 (1983): 332-41.

–. "Das Weinwunder zu Kana (Joh 2,1-11) und die Weinwunder der Antike." In: *Das Urchristentum in seiner literarischen Geschichte: Festschrift für Jürgen Becker*, ed. U. Mell and U. B. Müller, 291-308. BZNW 100. Berlin: de Gruyter, 1999.

Brouwer, Wayne. *The Literary Development of John 13-17: A Chiastic Reading*. DS 182. Atlanta: Society of Biblical Literature, 2000.

Brown, Raymond E. *The Community of the Beloved Disciple*. New York: Paulist Press, 1979.

–. "Johannine Ecclesiology – The Community's Origins." *Interpretation* 31 (1977): 379-93.

Brueggemann, Walter. *Theology of the Old Testament: Testimony, Dispute, Advocacy.* Minneapolis: Fortress Press, 1997.

Brumlik, Michael. *Der Anti-Alt: Wider die furchtbare Friedfertigkeit.* Frankfurt: Eichborn, 1990.

–. "Johannes: Das judenfeindliche Evangelium." *Kirche und Israel* 4 (1989): 102-13.

–. "Johannes: Das judenfeindliche Evangelium." In: *Teufelskinder oder Heilsbringer – Die Juden im Johannes-Evangelium,* ed. Dietrich Neuhaus, 6-21. Arnoldshainer Texte 64. Frankfurt: Haag und Herchen, 1990.

Brunson, Andrew C. *Psalm 118 in the Gospel of John. An Intertextual Study on the New Exodus Pattern in the Theology of John.* WUNT II/158. Tübingen: Mohr Siebeck, 2003.

Bryan, Christopher. *Render to Caesar: Jesus, the Early Church and the Roman Superpower.* Oxford: Oxford University Press, 2005.

Bultmann, Rudolf. *Theology of the New Testament.* 2 vols. Transl. by Kendrick Grobel. New York: Charles Scribner's Sons, 1955.

Burridge, Richard A. *What Are the Gospels? A Comparison with Graeco–Roman Biography.* 2nd ed. Biblical Resource Series. Grand Rapids: Eerdmans, 2004.

–. *Four Gospels, One Jesus? A Symbolic Reading.* 2nd ed. Grand Rapids: Eerdmans, 2005.

Caron, Gérald. "Exploring a Religious Dimension: The Johannine Jews." *Studies in Religion* 24 (1995): 159-71.

–. *Qui sont les Juifs de l'Évangile de Jean?* Recherches 35. Quebec: Bellarmin, 1997.

Carroll, James. *Constantine's Sword: The Church and the Jews. A History.* New York: Houghton Mifflin, 2001.

Carter, Warren. *Matthew and Empire: Initial Explorations.* Harrisburg, PA: Trinity Press, 2001.

–. "The Prologue and John's Gospel: Function, Symbol and the Definitive Word." *Journal for the Study of the New Testament* 39 (1990): 35-58.

–. "Vulnerable Power: The Roman Empire Challenged by the Early Christians." In: *Handbook of Early Christianity: Social Science Approaches,* ed. A. J. Blasi, J. Duhaime, and P–A Turcotte, 453-88. New York: Altamira Press, 2002.

Carter, Warren, and John Paul Heil. *Matthew's Parables: Audience-Oriented Perspectives.*CBQMS 30. Washington, DC: Catholic Biblical Association of America, 1998.

Cassem, N. H. "A Grammatical And Contextual Inventory of the Use of κόσμος in the Johannine Corpus with some Implications for a Johannine Cosmic Theology." *New Testament Studies* 19 (1972-73): 81-91.

Cassidy, Richard J. *John's Gospel in New Perspective: Christology and the Realities of Roman Power.* Maryknoll, NY: Orbis Books, 1992.

Chancey, Mark A. *The Myth of a Gentile Galilee.* SNTSMS 118. New York: Cambridge University, 2002.

–. *Greco-Roman Culture and the Galilee of Jesus.* SNTSMS 134. Cambridge: Cambridge University Press, 2005.

Charlesworth, James H., ed. *Jews and Christians: Exploring the Past, Present, and Future.* New York: Crossroad, 1990.

Charlesworth, James H., ed. *The Old Testament Pseudepigrapha.* 2 vols. Garden City, NY: Doubleday, 1983-1985.

Charlesworth, James H. "The Gospel of John: Exclusivism Caused by a Social Setting Different from That of Jesus (John 11:54 and 14:6)." In: *Anti-Judaism and the FourthGospel*, ed. R. Bieringer, D. Pollefeyt, and F. Vandecasteele-Vanneuville, 247-78. Louisville: Westminster John Knox, 2001.

–. "Jesus Research and Near Eastern Archaeology: Reflections on Recent Developments." In: *Neotestamentica et Philonica: Studies in Honor of Peder Borgen*, ed. D. E. Aune, T. Seland, and J. H. Ulrichsen, 37-70. NovTSup 151. Leiden: Brill, 2003.

Chilton, Bruce. *Rabbi Jesus: An Intimate Biography*. New York: Doubleday, 2000.

Classen, Carl Joachim. *Rhetorical Criticism of the New Testament*. Leiden: Brill, 2002.

Cohen, Shaye D. "Ἰουδαῖος τὸ γένος and Related Expressions in Josephus." In: *Josephus and the History of the Greco–Roman Period*, ed. F. Pavente and J. Sievers, 22-38. Leiden: Brill, 1994.

–. "*Ioudaios*: 'Judean' and 'Jew' in Susanna, First Maccabees and Second Maccabees." In: *Geschichte – Tradition – Reflexion: Festschrift für Martin Hengel zum 70 Geburtstag*, ed. H. Cancik, H. Lichtenberger, and P. Schäfer, 1:211-20. Tübingen: Mohr Siebeck, 1996.

Cohn-Sherbock, Dan. *The Crucified Jew: Twenty Centuries of Christian Anti-Semitism*. Grand Rapids: Eerdmans, 1997.

Collins, Raymond F. "Speaking of the Jews: 'Jews' in the Discourse Material of the Fourth Gospel." In: *Anti-Judaism and the Fourth Gospel*, ed. R. Bieringer, D. Pollefeyt, and F. Vandecasteele-Vanneuville, 158-75. Louisville: Westminster John Knox, 2001.

–. *These Things Have Been Written: Studies on the Fourth Gospel*. Grand Rapids: Eerdmans, 1990.

Colwell, Ernest C. "The Fourth Gospel and the Struggle for Respectability." *Journal of Religion* 14 (1934): 286-305.

–. *John Defends the Gospel*. Chicago: Willett, Clark & Company, 1936.

Cook, John G. *The Interpretation of the New Testament in Greco–Roman Paganism*. Peabody, MA: Hendrickson, 2002.

–. *The Interpretation of the Old Testament in Greco-Roman Paganism*. Studien und Texte zu Antike und Christentum 23. Tübingen: Mohr Siebeck, 2004.

Cook, Michael James. "The Gospel of John and the Jews." *Review and Expositor* 84 (1987): 259-71.

Cotter, Wendy. *Miracles in Greco-Roman Antiquity: A Sourcebook*. New York: Routledge, 1999.

Crossan, John D. *The Roots of Anti-Semitism in the Gospel Story of the Death of Jesus*. San Francisco: Harper Publishers, 1995.

–. *Who Killed Jesus? Exposing the Roots of Anti-Semitism in the Gospel Story of the Death of Jesus*. San Francisco: Harper Publishers, 1995.

–. "The Passion after the Holocaust." In: *A Shadow of Glory: Reading the New Testament after the Holocaust*, ed. Tod Linafelt, 171-84. New York: Routledge, 2002.

Crossan, John D., and Jonathan L. Reed. *In Search of Paul: How Jesus's Apostle Opposed Rome's Empire with God's Kingdom*. San Francisco: Harper, 2004.

Croteau, David A. "An Analysis of the Arguments for the Dating of the Fourth Gospel." *Faith & Mission* 20 (2003): 47-80.

Culpepper, R. Alan. *Anatomy of the Fourth Gospel: A Study in Literary Design*. Philadelphia: Fortress Press, 1983.

–. "Anti-Judaism in the Fourth Gospel as a Theological Problem for Christian Interpreters."In: *Anti-Judaism and the Fourth Gospel*, ed. R. Bieringer, D.Pollefeyt, and F. Vandecasteele-Vanneuville, 61-82. Louisville: Westminster John Knox, 2001.

–. "The Gospel of John and the Jews." *Review and Expositor* 84 (1987): 273-88.

–. "The Gospel of John as a Threat to Jewish-Christian Relations." In: *Overcoming Fear between Jews and Christians*, ed. J. H. Charlesworth, 21-43. The American Interfaith Institute. New York: Crossroad, 1993.

–. "The Pivot of John's Prologue." *New Testament Studies* 27 (1980-81): 1-31.

Cuming, G. J. "The Jews in the Fourth Gospel." *Expository Times* 60 (1948–1949): 290-92.

Dahl, Nils Alstrup. "The Johannine Church and History." In: *The Interpretation of John*, ed. J. Ashton, 147-67. Edinburgh: T&T Clark, 1997.

Danker, Frederick William, rev. and ed. *A Greek-English Lexicon of the NewTestament and other Early Christian Literature*. 3rd ed. Chicago: University of Chicago Press, 2000.

Davies, Alan T. "The Aryan Christ: A Motif in Christian Anti-Semitism." *Journal of Ecumenical Studies* 12 (1975): 569-79.

Davies, Margaret. *Rhetoric and Reference in the Fourth Gospel*. JSNTSup 69. Sheffield: Sheffield Academic Press, 1992.

De Boer, Martinus C. "The Depiction of 'the Jews' in John's Gospel: Matters of Behavior and Identity." In: *Anti-Judaism and the Fourth Gospel*, ed. R. Bieringer, D. Pollefeyt, and F. Vandecasteele-Vanneuville, 141-57. Louisville: Westminster John Knox, 2001.

De Jonge, Henk Jan. "Jewish Arguments Against Jesus At the End of the First Century C.E. According to the Gospel of John." In: *Aspects of Religious Contact and Conflict in the Ancient World*, ed. Pieter Willem Van der Horst, 45-55. Utrechtse Theologische Reeks 31. Utrecht: Theologische Faculteit, 1995.

–. "'The Jews' in the Gospel of John." In: *Anti-Judaism and the Fourth Gospel*, ed. R. Bieringer, D. Pollefeyt, and F. Vandecasteele-Vanneuville, 121-40. Louisville: Westminster John Knox, 2001.

De La Potterie, I. "Jésus Roi et Juge d'après Jn 19,13." *Biblica* 41 (1960): 217-47.

De Valerio, Karolina. *Altes Testament und Judentum im Frühwerk Rudolf Bultmanns*. BZNW 71. Berlin: Walter de Gruyter, 1994.

Deines, Roland. *Die Pharisäer: Ihr Verständnis im Spiegel der christlichen und jüdischen Forschung seit Wellhausen und Graetz*. WUNT 101. Tübingen: Mohr Siebeck, 1997.

Deissmann, Adolf. *Light From the Ancient East: The New Testament Illustrated by Recently Discovered Texts of the Graeco–Roman World*. Transl. by Lionel R. M. Strachan. 4th ed. New York: George H. Doran Company, 1927.

Demke, Christoph. "Das Evangelium der Dialoge. Hermeneutische und methodologische Beobachtungen zur Interpretation des Johannesevangeliums." *Zeitschrift für Theologie und Kirche* 97 (2000): 16-82.

Deschner, Karlheinz. "Die unheilvollen Auswirkungen des Christentums." In: *Religionskritik. Arbeitstexte für den Unterricht*. Stuttgart: Reclam, 1984.

Dettwiler, Andreas. *Die Gegenwart des Erhöhten: Eine exegetische Studie zu den johanneischen Abschiedsreden (Joh 13,31-16,33) unter besondererBerücksichtigung ihres Relecture-Charakters*. FRLANT 169. Göttingen: Vandenhoeck & Ruprecht, 1995.

Diefenbach, Manfred. *Der Konflikt Jesu mit den 'Juden': Ein Versuch zur Lösung der johanneischen Antjudaismus-Diskussion mit Hilfe des antiken Handlungsverständnisses.* NA 41. Münster: Aschendorff Verlag, 2002.

Dietzfelbinger, Christian. *Der Abschied des Kommenden: Eine Auslegung der johanneischen Abschiedsreden.* WUNT 95. Tübingen: Mohr Siebeck, 1997.

Dodd, C. H. *The Interpretation of the Fourth Gospel.* Cambridge: Cambridge University, 1954.

–. "The Prologue to the Fourth Gospel and Christian Worship." In: *Studies in the Fourth Gospel,* ed. F. L. Cross, 9-22. London: A. R. Mowbray & Co, 1957.

Downing, F. Gerald. "Pliny's Prosecutions of Christians: Revelation and 1 Peter." In: *The Johannine Writings,* ed. S. E.Porter and C. A. Evans, 232-49. The Biblical Seminar 32. Sheffield: Sheffield Academic Press, 1995.

–. "The Jewish Cynic Jesus." In: *Jesus, Mark and Q: The Teaching of Jesus and its Earliest Records.* Ed. by M. Labahn, A. Schmidt, 184-214. JSNTSupp. 214. Sheffield: Sheffield Academic Press, 2001.

Dunn, James D. G. "Καῖσαρ." In: *The New International Dictionary of New Testament Theology,* ed. by Colin Brown, 1:269-270. Grand Rapids: Zondervan, 1979.

–. "The Embarrassment of History: Reflections on the Problem of 'Anti-Judaism' in the Fourth Gospel." In: *Anti-Judaism and the Fourth Gospel,* ed. R. Bieringer, D. Pollefeyt, and F. Vandecasteele-Vanneuville, 41-60. Louisville: Westminster John Knox, 2001.

Ebrard, J. H. A. *Wissenschaftliche Kritik der evangelischen Geschichte. Ein Kompendium für Geistliche und Studirende.* 2nd ed. Erlangen: Verlag von Heyder & Zimmer, 1850.

Ehrman, Bart D. *Lost Christianity: The Battles for Scripture and the Faiths We Never Knew.* Oxford: Oxford University Press, 2003.

–. *The New Testament: A Historical Introduction to the Early Christian Writings.* New York: Oxford University Press, 2004.

Elliott, Neil. "The Apostle Paul's Self-Presentation as anti-Imperial Performance." In: *Paul and the Imperial Roman Order,* ed. Richard A. Horsley, 67-88. Harrisburg, PA: Trinity Press International, 2004.

Epp, Eldon J. "Anti-Semitism and the Popularity of the Fourth Gospel." *Central Conference American Rabbis Journal* 22 (1975): 35-57.

Ericksen, Robert P. *Theologians under Hitler: Gerhard Kittel, Paul Althaus and Emanuel Hirsch.* New Haven: Yale University Press, 1985.

Evans, Craig A. *Ancient Texts for New Testament Studies: A Guide to Background Literature.* Peabody, MA: Hendrickson, 2005.

Evans, Craig A., and Donald A. Hagner, eds. *Anti-Semitism and Early Christianity: Issues of Polemic and Faith.* Minneapolis: Augsburg-Fortress, 1993.

Evelyn, Francis A. "The Supra-Racial Gospel." *Expository Times* 49 (1938): 419-21.

Falk, Gerhard. *The Jew in Christian Theology. Martin Luther's Anti-Jewish Vom Schem Hamphoras, Previously Unpublished in English, and Other Milestones in Church Doctrine Concerning Judaism.* Jefferson, NC: McFarland & Company, 1992.

Farmer, William R., ed. *Anti-Judaism and the Gospels.* Harrisburg, PA: Trinity Press International, 1999.

Feine, Paul, and Johannes Behm. *Introduction to the New Testament.* Ed. by Werner G. Kümmel. Transl. by A. J. Mattill Jr. 14th rev. ed. Nashville: Abingdon Press, 1966.

Fenske, Wolfgang. *Wie Jesus zum "Arier" wurde: Auswirkungen der Entjudaisierung Christi im 19. und zu Beginn des 20. Jahrhunderts.* Darmstadt: Wissenschaftliche Buchgesellschaft, 2005.

Fischel, Jack R., and Susan M. Ortmann. *The Holocaust and Its Religious Impact: A Critical Assessment and Annotated Bibliography*. Bibliographies and Indexes in Religious Studies54. Westport, CT: Praeger Publishers, 2004.

Fischer, Diac. "Ueber den Ausdruck: οἱ Ἰουδαῖοι im Evangelium Johannis. Ein Beitrag zur Charakteristik desselben." *Tübinger Zeitschrift für Theologie* 2 (1840): 96-135.

Fischer, Karl Martin. "Der johanneische Christus und der gnostische Erlöser." In: *Gnosis und Neues Testament: Studien aus Religionswissenschaft und Theologie*, ed. Karl-Wolfgang Tröger, 245-66. Gütersloh: Gütersloher Verlagshaus, 1973.

Fitzmyer, Joseph A. "Qumran Literature and the Johannine Writings." In: *Life in Abundance: Studies of John's Gospel in Tribute to Raymond E. Brown*, ed. John R. Donahue, 117-33. Collegeville, MN: Liturgical Press, 2005.

Flannery, Edward H. *The Anguish of the Jews: Twenty-Three Centuries of Antisemitism*. New York: Macmillan, 1964.

Flusser, David. "Das Schisma zwischen Judentum und Christentum." *Evangelische Theologie* 40 (1980): 214-39.

Forstman, Jack. *Christian Faith in Dark Times: Theological Conflicts in the Shadow of Hitler*. Louisville: Westminster / John Knox Press, 1992.

Fortna, Robert T. "Theological Use of Locale in the Fourth Gospel." *Anglican Theological Review* 3 (1974): 58-95.

Fredriksen, Paula. *Jesus of Nazareth, King of the Jews: A Jewish Life and the Emergence of Christianity*. New York: Knopf, 1999.

Freeman, Clarence Hal. "The Function of Polemic in John 7 and 8." Ph.D. diss., Southern Baptist Theological Seminary, 1991.

Frey, Jörg. "Auf der Suche nach dem Kontext des vierten Evangeliums. Eine forschungsgeschichtliche Einführung." In: *Kontexte des Johannesevangeliums: Das vierte Evangelium in religions- und traditionsgeschichtlicher Perspektive*, ed. Jörg Frey and Udo Schnelle, 3-44. Tübingen: Mohr Siebeck, 2004.

–. "Das Bild 'der Juden' im Johannesevangelium und die Geschichte der johanneischen Gemeinde." In: *Israel und seine Heilstraditionen im Johannesevangelium: Festgabe für Johannes Beutler SJ zum 70. Geburtstag*, ed. M. Labahn, K. Scholtissek, and A. Strotmann, 33-53. Paderborn: Schöningh, 2004.

–. *Die johanneische Eschatologie. Band I: Ihre Probleme im Spiegel der Forschung seit Reimarus*. WUNT 96. Tübingen: Mohr Siebeck, 1997.

–. *Die johanneische Eschatologie. Band II: Das johanneische Zeitverständnis*. WUNT 110. Tübingen: Mohr Siebeck, 1998.

–. *Die johanneische Eschatologie. Band III: Die eschatologische Verkündigung den johanneischen Texten*. WUNT 117. Tübingen: Mohr Siebeck, 2000.

–. "Erwägungen zum Verhältnis der Johannesapokalypse zu den übrigen Schriften des Corpus Johanneum." In: Martin Hengel, *Die johanneische Frage: Ein Lösungsversuch*, 326-429. WUNT 67. Tübingen: Mohr Siebeck, 1993.

–. "Heiden – Griechen – Gotteskinder. Zu Gestalt und Funktion der Rede von den Heiden im 4. Evangelium." In: *Die Heiden: Juden, Christen und das Problem des Fremden*, ed. R. Feldmeier and U. Heckel, 228-68. Tübingen: Mohr Siebeck, 1994.

Freyne, Sean. "Behind the Names: Galileans, Samaritans, Ioudaioi." In: *Galilee and Gospel: Collected Essays*, 114-31. WUNT 125. Tübingen: Mohr Siebeck, 2000.

–. "Galilee and Judea. The Social World of Jesus." In: *The Face of New Testament Studies: A Survey of Recent Research*, ed. Scott McKnight and Grant R. Osborne, 21-35. Grand Rapids: Baker, 2004.

Friesen, Steven J. *Imperial Cults and the Apocalypse of John: Reading Revelation in the Ruins*. Oxford: Oxford University Press, 2001.

–. *Twice Neokoros: Ephesus, Asia and the Cult of the Flavian Imperial Family*. Leiden: Brill, 1993.

Frühwald-König, Johannes. *Tempel und Kult: Ein Beitrag zur Christologie des Johannesevangeliums*. BU 27. Regensburg: Verlag Friedrich Pustet, 1998.

Fuglseth, Kåre Sigvald. *Johannine Sectarianism in Perspective: A Sociological, Historical, and Comparative Analysis of Temple and Social Relationships in the Gospel of John, Philo, and Qumran*. NovTSup 119. Leiden: Brill, 2005.

Fuller, Roy Dale. "Contemporary Judaic Perceptions of Jesus: Implications for Jewish-Christian Dialogue." Ph.D. diss., The Southern Baptist Theological Seminary, 1992.

Gager, J. G. *Moses in Greco-Roman Paganism*. JBL Monograph Series 16. Nashville: Abingdon Press, 1972.

Gager, John. *The Origins of Antisemitism: Attitudes Towards Judaism in Pagan and Christian Antiquity*. Oxford: Oxford University Press, 1985.

Gellately, Robert, and Ben Kierman, eds. *The Scepter of Genocide: Mass Murder in Historical Perspective*. Cambridge: Cambridge University Press, 2003.

Geyser, A. S. "Israel in the Fourth Gospel." *Neotestamentica* 20 (1986): 13-20.

Gibbs, J. M. "Mark 1, 1-15, Matthew 1, 1-4, 16, Luke 1, 1-4, 30, John 1, 1-51: The Gospel Prologues and their Function." In: *Studia Evangelica*, ed. E. A. Livingstone, 154-88. TU 112. Berlin: Akademie-Verlag, 1973.

Goldhagen, Daniel. *A Moral Reckoning: The Role of the Catholic Church in the Holocaust and its Unfulfilled Duty to Repair*. New York: Alfred A. Knopf, 2002.

González, Justo L. *The Story of Christianity*, vol. 1, *The Early Church to theDawn of the Reformation*. Vol. 1. New York: HarperCollins Publisher, 1984.

Goodman, Martin. "Jews and Judaism in the Mediterranean Diaspora in the Late-Roman Period: The Limitations of Evidence." In: *Ancient Judaism in its Hellenistic Context*, ed. Carol Bakhos, 177-203. JSJSup 95. Brill: Leiden, 2005.

Goppelt, Leonhard. *Christentum und Judentum im ersten und zweiten Jahrhundert: Ein Aufriß der Urgeschichte der Kirche*. BFCT 55. Gütersloh: C. Bertelsmann Verlag, 1954.

The Gospel of Matthew in its Roman Imperial Context. Ed. by J. Riches and D. C. Sim. JSNTSup 276. London: T&T Clark International, 2005.

Graf Reventlow, Henning. *Hauptprobleme der Biblischen Theologie im 20. Jahrhundert*. EF 203. Darmstadt: Wissenschaftliche Buchgesellschaft, 1983.

Granskou, David. "Anti-Judaism in the Passion Accounts of the Fourth Gospel." In: *Anti-Judaism in Early Christianity*. Vol 1, *Paul and the Gospels*, ed. Peter Richardson, 201-16. Studies in Christianity and Judaism 2. Waterloo, Canada: Wilfrid Laurier University Press, 1986.

Grant, Frederick C. *An Introduction to New Testament Thought*. New York:Abingdon-Cokesbury, 1950.

Grant, Robert M. *Second-Century Christianity: A Collection of Fragments*. 2nd ed. Louisville: Westminster John Knox Press, 2003.

Grässer, Erich. "Die Antijüdische Polemik im Johannesevangelium." *New Testament Studies* 10 (1964-65): 74-90.

–. "Die Juden als Teufelssöhne in Johannes 8.37-47." In: *Antijudaismus im Neuen Testament?*, ed. W. P. Eckert, N. P. Levenson, and M. Stöhr, 157-70. München: Kaiser, 1967.

Grelot, Pierre. *Les Juifs dans l'évangile selon Jean: Enquête historique et réflexion théologique*. CahRB 34. Paris: Gabalda, 1995.

Grohmann, Marianne. "Judentum und Christentum: Verhältnisbestimmungen am Ende des 20. Jahrhunderts." *Theologische Rundschau* 69 (2004): 151-81.

Grundmann, Walter. *Jesus der Galiläer und das Judentum.* 2nd ed. Leipzig: G. Wigand, 1941.

Güdemann, M. "Das IV. (Johannes-) Evangelium und der Rabbinismus." *Monatsschrift für Geschichte und Wissenschaft des Judentums* 37 (1893): 249-57, 297-303, 345-56.

Guhrt, J. "κόσμος." In: *The New International Dictionary of New Testament Theology*, ed. by Colin Brown, 1:521-526. Grand Rapids: Zondervan, 1975.

Gundry, Robert H. "How the Word in John's Prologue Pervades the Rest of the Fourth Gospel." In: *The Old is Better: New Testament Essays in Support of Traditional Interpretations*, 324-59. WUNT 178. Tübingen: Mohr Siebeck, 2005.

Gutbrod, W., G. von Rad, K. G. Kuhn. "'Ισραήλ,'Ισραηλίτης, 'Ιουδαῖος, etc." In: *Theological Dictionary of the New Testament*, ed. by G. Friedrich, transl. by G. W. Bromiley, 3:356-391. Grand Rapids: Eerdmans, 1965.

Güting, Eberhard. "Kritik an den Judäern in Jerusalem. Literarkritische Beiträge zu einem unabgeschlossenen Gespräch über den Evangelisten Johannes." In: *Israel als Gegenüber: Vom Alten Orient bis in die Gegenwart. Studien zur Geschichte eines wechselvollen Zusammenlebens. Festschrift zum 50. Jahrestag der Instituts-Neugründung in Münster*, ed. Folker Siegert, 158-201. Schriften des Institutum Judaicum Delitzschianum 6. Göttingen: Vandenhoeck & Ruprecht, 2000.

Haaland, Gunnar. "Josephus and the Philosophers of Rome: Does *Contra Apionem* Mirror Domitian's Crushing of the 'Stoic Opposition'?" In: *Josephus and Jewish History in Flavian Rome and Beyond*, ed. Joseph Sievers, Gaia Lembi, 297-316. JSJSupp 104. Leiden: Brill, 2005.

Haenchen, Ernst. "Probleme des Johanneischen 'Prologs'." In: *Gott und Mensch: Gesammelte Aufsätze von Ernst Haenchen*, 114-43. Tübingen: Mohr Siebeck, 1965.

Haacker, Klaus. "Gottesdienst ohne Gotteserkenntnis: Joh 4,22 vor dem Hintergrund der jüdisch-samaritischen Auseinandersetzung." In: *Wort und Wirklichkeit. Studien zur Afrikanistik und Orientalistik. Teil 1: Geschichte und Religionswissenschaft – Bibliographie. Festschrift für Eugen Ludwig Rapp*, ed. B. Benzing, O. Böcher, G. Mayer, 110-26. Meisenheim: Verlag Anton Hain, 1976.

–. "Die neutestamentliche Wissenschaft und die Erneuerung des Verhältnisses zwischen Christen und Juden." In: *Biblische Theologie als engagierte Exegese: Theologische Grundfragen und thematische Studien*, 76-89. TVG. Wuppertal: Brockhaus, 1993.

Hahn, Ferdinand. "'Das Heil kommt von den Juden.' Erwägungen zu Joh4,22b." In: *Wort und Wirklichkeit: Studien zur Afrikanistik und Orientalistik. Teil I: Geschichte und Religionswissenschaft – Bibliographie. Festschrift für Eugen Ludwig Rapp*, ed. B. Benzing, O. Böcher, G. Mayer, 67-84. Meisenheim: Verlag Anton Hain, 1976.

–. "'Die Juden' im Johannesevangelium." In: *Kontinuität und Einheit: Festschrift für Franz Mußner*, ed. P. G. Müller and W. Stenger, 430-38. Freiburg: Herder, 1981.

Hakola, Raimo. *Identity Matters: John, the Jews and Jewishness.* NovTSup 118. Leiden: Brill, 2005.

Haldimann, Konrad. *Rekonstruktion und Entfaltung: Exegetische Untersuchungen zu Joh 15 und 16.* BZNW 104. Berlin-New York: de Gruyter, 2000.

Haldimann, Konrad, and Hans Weder. "Aus der Literatur zum Johannesevangelium 1985–1994. Zweiter Teil: Synchrone Analysen." *Theologische Rundschau* 69 (2004): 75-115.

Hallbäck, Geert. "The Gospel of John as Literature: Literary Readings of the Fourth Gospel." In: *New Readings in John: Literary and Theological Perspectives. Essays from the Scandinavian Conference on the Fourth Gospel Århus 1997*, ed. J. Nissen and S. Pedersen, 31-46. JSNTSup 182. Sheffield: Sheffield Academic Press, 1999.

Halpern, Baruch. *The First Historians: The Hebrew Bible and History.* University Park, PA: The Pennsylvania State University Press, 1996.

Harrington, Daniel J. "Response to Joseph A. Fitzmyer, S.J. 'Qumran Literature and the Johannine Writings'." In: *Life in Abundance: Studies of John's Gospel in Tribute to Raymond E. Brown*, ed. John R. Donahue, 134-37. Collegeville, MN: Liturgical Press, 2005.

Harris, Elizabeth. *Prologue and Gospel: The Theology of the Fourth Evangelist.*

Hasitschka, Martin. "Joh 8,44 im Kontext des Gesprächsverlaufes von Joh 8,21-59." In: *Theology and Christology in the Fourth Gospel: Essays by the members of the SNTS Johannine Writings Seminar*, ed. G. Van Belle, J. G. Van der Watt and P. Maritz, 109-116. BETL 184. Leuven: University Press, 2005.

Haufe, Günter. "Israel-Polemik in Q." In: *Gedenkt an das Wort: Festschrift für Werner Vogler zum 65. Geburtstag*, ed. C. Kähler, M. Böhm, and C. Böttrich, 56-67. Leipzig: Evangelische Verlagsanstalt, 1999.

Hendricks, Obery M. "A Discourse of Domination: A Socio-Rhetorical Study of the Use of IOUDAIOS in the Fourth Gospel." Ph.D. diss., Princeton University, 1995.

Hengel, Martin. *Die Evangelienüberschriften.* Heidelberg: Carl Winter Universitätsverlag, 1984.

–. *Die johanneische Frage: Ein Lösungsversuch.* WUNT 67. Tübingen: Mohr Siebeck, 1993.

–. "Die Schriftauslegung des 4. Evangeliums auf dem Hintergrund der urchristlichen Exegese." *Jahrbuch für biblische Theologie* 4 (1989): 249-88.

–. *The Four Gospels and the One Gospel of Jesus Christ. An Investigation of the Collection and Origin of the Canonical Gospels.* Harrisburg, PA: TrinityPress International, 2000.

–. "The Geography of Palestine in Acts." In *The Book of Acts in Its Palestinian Setting.* Ed. by R. Bauckham, 27-78. Grand Rapids: Eerdmans, 1995.

–. *The Son of God: The Origin of Christology and the History of Jewish-Hellenistic Religion.*Philadelphia: Fortress Press, 1976.

–. "Judaism and Hellenism Revisited." In: *Hellenism in the Land of Israel*, ed. by J.J. Collins, G.E. Sterling, 6-37. Christianity and Judaism in Antiquity 13. Notre Dame: University of Notre Dame Press, 2001.

Heschel, Susannah. "Reading Jesus as a Nazi." In: *A Shadow of Glory: Reading the New Testament after the Holocaust*, ed. Tod Linafelt, 27-41. New York: Routledge, 2002.

Hilgenfeld, A. "Der Antijudaismus des Johannes-Evangeliums." *Zeitschrift für wissenschaftliche Theologie* 36 (1893): 507-17.

Hirsch, Emanuel. *Studien zum vierten Evangelium: Text, Literarkritik, Entstehungsgeschichte.* Tübingen: J. C. B. Mohr (Paul Siebeck), 1936.

Hoegen-Rohls, Christina. *Der nachösterliche Johannes: Die Abschiedsreden als hermeneutischer Schlüssel zum vierten Evangelium.* WUNT II/84. Tübingen: Mohr Siebeck, 1996.

Hofrichter, Peter. *Im Anfang war der „Johannesprolog": Das urchristliche Logosbekenntnis – die Basis neutestamentlicher und gnostischer Theologie.* BU 17. Regensburg: Pustet, 1986.

Holmén, Tom. "The Jewishness of Jesus in the 'Third Quest'." In: *Jesus, Mark and Q: The Teaching of Jesus and its Earliest Records.* Ed. by M. Labahn, A. Schmidt, 143-62. JSNTSupp. 214. Sheffield: Sheffield Academic Press, 2001.

Hooker, Morna D. "The Johannine Prologue and the Messianic Secret." *New Testament Studies* 21 (1974): 40-58.

Horsley, Richard. *Galilee: History, Politics, People.* Valley Forge, PA: Trinity Press International, 1995.

House, Wayne H. *Chronological and Background Charts of the New Testament.* Grand Rapids: Zondervan, 1981.

Hughes, Leslie G. "A Literary Analysis of the Role of the Jewish Leadership in the Fourth Gospel." Ph.D. diss., New Orleans Baptist Theological Seminary, 1994.

Incigneri, Brian. *The Gospel to the Romans: The Setting and Rhetoric of Mark's Gospel.*Leiden: Brill, 2003.

Instone-Brewer, David. "The Eighteen Benedictions and the *Minim* Before 70 CE." *Journal of Theological Studies* 54 (2003): 25-44.

–. *Traditions of the Rabbis in the Era of the New Testament.* Vol. 1. Grand Rapids: Eerdmans, 2004.

Isaac, Jules. *Jesus and Israel.* Transl. by Sally Gran. New York: Holt, Rinehart and Winston, 1971.

Jensen, Robin M. "How Pilate Became a Saint." *Bible Review* 19 (2003): 22-31, 47-48.

Jewish Identity in the Greco-Roman World, ed. J. Frey, D. R. Schwartz. AGAJU. Leiden: Brill, 2007.

Johnson, Luke Timothy. "Reading after the Holocaust. A New Testament Scholar Responds to Emil Fackenheim." In: *A Shadow of Glory: Reading the New Testament after the Holocaust,* ed. Tod Linafelt, 216-31. New York: Routledge, 2002.

Jones, Christopher. "Apollonius of Tyana, Hero and Holy Man." In: *Philostratus's Heroikos: Religion and Cultural Identity in the Third Century C.E,* ed. E. B. Aitken and J. K. Berenson Maclean, 75-84. Writings from the Greco-Roman World 6. Atlanta: Society of Biblical Literature, 2004.

Journet, Charles. *The Church of the Word Incarnate.* London: Sheed and Ward, 1955.

Jung, Franz. *ΣΩΤΗΡ: Studien zur Rezeption eines Hellenistischen Ehrentitels im Neuen Testament.* NA 39. Münster: Aschendorff Verlag, 2002.

Kannaday, Wayne C. *Apologetic Discourse and the Scribal Tradition: Evidence of the Influence of Apologetic Interests on the Text of the Canonical Gospel.* SBLTC 5. Atlanta: Society of Biblical Literature,2004.

Käsemann, E. "Aufbau und Anliegen des johanneischen Prologs." In: *Exegetische Versuche und Besinnungen,* 2:155-80. Göttingen: Vandenhoeck & Ruprecht, 1964.

Kaufman, Philip S. *The Beloved Disciple: Witness against Anti-Semitism.* Collegeville, MN: The Liturgical Press, 1991.

Keith, Graham. *Hated Without a Cause? A Survey of Anti-Semitism.* Carlisle: Paternoster, 1997.

Kelley, Shawn. *Racializing Jesus: Race, ideology and the formation of modern biblical scholarship.* London: Routledge, 2002.

Kellum, L. Scott. *The Unity of the Farewell Discourse: The Literary Integrity of John 13.31-16.33.* JSNTSup 256. London: T&T Clark International, 2004.

Kemper, Friedmar. "Zur literarischen Gestalt des Johannesevangeliums." *Theologische Zeitschrift* 43 (1987): 247-64.

Kenny, Anthony. *A Stylometric Study of the New Testament.* Oxford: Clarendon Press, 1986.

Klappert, B. "King, Kingdom." In: *The New International Dictionary of New Testament Theology,* ed. by Colin Brown, 2:372-389. Grand Rapids: Zondervan, 1979.

Klassen, William. *Judas: Betrayer or Friend of Jesus?* Minneapolis: Fortress, 1996.

Klauck, Hans-Josef. *The Religious Context of Early Christianity: A Guide to Graeco-Roman Religions.* Transl. by Brian McNeil. Minneapolis: Fortress Press, 2003.

Klein, Charlotte. *Theologie und Anti-Judaismus.* München: Kaiser, 1975.

Klinghoffer, David. *Why the Jews Rejected Jesus: The Turning Point in Western History.* New York: Doubleday, 2005.

Koch, Stefan. *Rechtliche Regelung von Konflikten im frühen Christentum.* WUNT II/174. Tübingen: Mohr Siebeck, 2004.

Koester, Craig R. "Jesus as the Way to the Father in Johannine Theology (John 14,6)." In: *Theology and Christology in the Fourth Gospel: Essays by the members of the SNTS Johannine Writings Seminar,* ed. G. Van Belle, J. G. Van der Watt, and P. Maritz, 117-33. BETL 184. Leuven: University Press, 2005.

–. "'The Savior of the World' (John 4:42)." *Journal of Biblical Literature* 109 (1990): 665-80.

–. *Symbolism in the Fourth Gospel: Meaning, Mystery, Community.* 2nd ed. Minneapolis: Fortress Press, 2003.

Koester, Helmut. *Ancient Christian Gospels: Their History and Development.* London: SCM Press, 1990.

Kohler, Kaufmann. "New Testament." In: *The Jewish Encyclopedia.* Ed. by Isidore Singer. New York: Funk and Wagnalls Company, 1905.

Kossen, H. B. "Who were the Greeks of John XII 20?" In: *Studies in John. Presented to Professor Dr. J. N. Sevenster on the Occasion of His Seventieth Birthday,* 97-110. NovTSup 24. Leiden: Brill, 1970.

Köstenberger, Andreas J. "'What is Truth?' Pilate's Question in Its Johannine and Larger Biblical Context." *Journal of the Evangelical Theological Society* 48 (2005): 33-62.

Krause, Deborah, Timothy K. Beal. "Higher Critics on Late Texts. Reading Biblical Scholarship after the Holocaust." In: *A Shadow of Glory. Reading the New Testament after the Holocaust,* ed. Tod Linafelt, 18-26. New York: Routledge, 2002.

Kraybill, J. Nelson. *Imperial Cult and Commerce in John's Apocalypse.* JSNTSup 132. Sheffield: Sheffield Academic Press, 1996.

Kvalbein, Hans. "The Kingdom of God and the Kingship of Christ in the Fourth Gospel." In: *Neotestamentica et Philonica: Studies in Honor of Peder Borgen,* ed. D. E. Aune, T. Seland, and J. H. Ulrichsen, 215-32. NovTSup 151. Leiden: Brill, 2003.

Kysar, Robert. "Anti-Semitism and the Gospel of John." In: *Anti-Semitism and Early Christianity: Issues of Polemic and Faith,* ed. Craig A. Evans and Donald A. Hagner, 113-27. Minneapolis: Fortress, 1993.

–. *The Fourth Evangelist and His Gospel: An Examination of Contemporary Scholarship.* Minneapolis: Augsburg Publishing House, 1975.

–. "The Expulsion from the Synagogue: The Tale of a Theory." In *Voyages with John: Charting the Fourth Gospel,* 237-45. Waco, TX: Baylor University Press, 2005.

Labahn, Michael. *Jesus als Lebensspender. Untersuchungen zu einer Geschichte der johanneischen Tradition anhand ihrer Wundergeschichten.* BZNW 98. Berlin: de Gruyter, 1999.

–. *Offenbarung in Zeichen und Wort. Untersuchungen zur Vorgeschichte von Joh 6,1-25 a und seiner Rezeption in der Brotrede.* WUNT II/117. Tübingen: Mohr Siebeck, 2000.

Lamarche, Paul. "Le Prologue de Jean." *Recherches de science religieuse* 52 (1964): 497-537.

Leibig, Janis E. "John and 'the Jews': Theological Anti-Semitism in the Fourth Gospel." *Journal of Ecumenical Studies* 20 (1983): 209-34.

Leistner, Reinhold. *Antijudaismus im Johannesevangelium? Darstellung des Problems in derneueren Auslegungsgeschichte und Untersuchung der Leidensgeschichte.* Frankfurt: Lang, 1974.

Léon-Dufour, Xavier. *Dictionary of the New Testament.* Transl. by Terrence Prendergast. San Francisco: Harper & Row, 1980.

Levinskaya, Irina. *The Book of Acts in Its Diaspora Setting.* The Book of Acts in Its First Century Setting, vol. 5. Grand Rapids: Eerdmans, 1996.

Lieu, Judith. "Anti-Judaism in the Fourth Gospel: Explanation and Hermeneutics." In: *Anti-Judaism and the Fourth Gospel,* ed. R. Bieringer, D. Pollefeyt, and F. Vandecasteele-Vanneuville, 101-17. Louisville: Westminster John Knox, 2001.

–. "Temple and Synagogue in John." *New Testament Studies* 45 (1999): 51-69.

Limbeck, M. "Das Judasbild im Neuen Testament." In: *Heilvoller Verrat? Judas im Neuen Testament,* ed. H. L. Goldschmidt and M. Limbeck, 37-101. Stuttgart: Katholisches Bibelwerk, 1976.

Lincoln, Andrew T. *The Gospel According to Saint John.* Black's New Testament. Commentaries. Peabody, MA: Hendrickson, 2005.

Lindemann, Andreas. "Moses und Jesus Christus. Zum Verständnis des Gesetzes im Johannesevangelium." In *Das Urchristentum in seiner literarischen Geschichte. FS Jürgen Becker,* ed. U. Mell, U. B. Müller, 309-334. Berlin: Walter de Gruyter, 1999.

Lingad, Jr., Celestino G. *The Problems of Jewish Christians in the Johannine Community.* Tesi Gregoriana Serie Teologia 73. Rome: Editrice Pontificia Università Gregoriana, 2001.

Link, Andrea. *„Was redest du mit ihr?" Eine Studie zur Exegese-, Redaktions- und Theologiegeschichte von Joh 4,1-42.* BU 24. Regensburg: Verlag Friedrich Pustet, 1992.

Linnemann, Eta L. "Die Hochzeit zu Kana und Dionysos." *New Testament Studies* 20 (1974): 408-18.

Lioy, Dan. *The Search for Ultimate Reality: Intertextuality Between the Genesis and Johannine Prologues.* Studies in Biblical Literature 93. New York: Peter Lang, 2005.

Loader, William. "Jesus and the Law in Joh." In: *Theology and Christology in the Fourth Gospel: Essays by the members of the SNTS Johannine Writings Seminar,* ed. G. Van Belle, J. G. Van der Watt, and P. Maritz, 135-54. BETL 184. Leuven: University Press, 2005.

Lohse, Eduard. *Grundriß der neutestamentlichen Theologie.* 2nd ed. Stuttgart: Kohlhammer, 1974.

Long, V. Philips. *The Art of Biblical History.* Grand Rapids: Zondervan, 1994.

Longenecker, Richard. *The Christology of Early Jewish Christianity.* SBT 2/17. London: SCM Press, 1970.

Löw, Konrad. *Die Schuld: Christen und Juden im Urteil der Nationalsozialisten und der Gegenwart.* Gräfelfing: Resch Verlag, 2002.

Lowe, Malcolm "Who were the *IOYΔAIOI?*" *Novum Testamentum* 18 (1976):101-30.

Lüdemann, Gerd. *Primitive Christianity: A Survey of Recent Studies and Some New Proposals.* Transl. by John Bowden. London: T & T Clark, 2003.

Lütgert, Wilhelm. "Die Juden im Johannesevangelium." In: *Neutestamentliche Studien: Georg Heinrici zu seinem 70. Geburtstag dargebracht von Fachgenossen, Freunden und Schülern,* 147-54. Leipzig: Hinrichs'sche Buchhandlung, 1914.

Luther, Martin. *Ausgewählte Werke.* Ed. by H. H. Borcherdt and Georg Merz, 3rd ed. Vols. 1-6. München: Chr. Kaiser Verlag, 1951-1958.

MacMullen, Ramsay. *Enemies of the Roman Order: Treason, Unrest, and Alienation in the Empire.* Cambridge, MA: Harvard University, 1966.

Maher, Michael. "Knowing the Tree by its Roots: Jewish Context of the Early Christian Movement." In: *Christian Origins: Worship, Belief and Society*, ed. Kieran J. O'Mahony, 1-28. JSNTSup 241. Sheffield: Sheffield Academic Press, 2003.

Maier, Harry O. "Barbarians, Scythians and Imperial Iconography in the Epistle to the Colossians." In: *Picturing the New Testament: Studies in Ancient Visual Images*, ed. A. Weissenrieder, F. Wendt, P. von Gemünden, 385-406. WUNT II/193. Tübingen: Mohr Siebeck, 2005.

Manns, Fréderic. *John and Jamnia: How the Break Occurred Between Jewsand Christians c. 80-100 A.D.* Jerusalem: Franciscan Printing Press, 1988.

Marchione, Margeritha. *Consensus and Controversy: Defending Pope Pius XII.* New York : Paulist, 2002.

–. *Pope Pius XII: Architect for Peace.* New York: Paulist, 2000.

Marrow, Stanley B. "Κόσμος in John." *Catholic Biblical Quarterly* 64 (2002): 90-102.

Martin, Francis. *Narrative Parallels to the New Testament.* Atlanta: Scholars Press, 1988.

Martin, James P. "John 10:1-10." *Interpretation* 32 (1978): 171-75.

Martyn, J. Louis. *History and Theology in the Fourth Gospel.* 3rd ed. Louisville: Westminster John Knox, 2003.

März, Claus-Peter. "Die theologische Interpretation der Jesus-Gestalt bei Lukas." In: *Gedenkt an das Wort: Festschrift für Werner Vogler zum 65. Geburtstag*, ed. C. Kähler, M. Böhm, and C. Böttrich, 134-49. Leipzig: Evangelische Verlagsanstalt, 1999.

Mastin, B. A. "Imperial Cult and the Ascription of the Title θεός to Jesus (John XX.28)." In: *Studia Evangelica*, ed. E. A. Livingstone, 352-65. TU 112. Berlin: Akademie-Verlag, 1973.

Matsunaga, Kikuo. "Christian self-identification and the twelfth benediction." In: *Eusebius, Christianity, and Judaism*, ed. H. W. Attridge and G. Hata, 355-371. Leiden: Brill, 1992.

Mason, Steve. *Josephus and the New Testament.* 2nd ed. Peabody, MA: Hendrickson, 2003.

Mayer, Reinhold. "'Ich bin der Weg, die Wahrheit und das Leben.' Ein Versuch über das Johannes-Evangelium aus Anlass der neu erwachten Debatte zur Judenmission." In: *Johannes aenigmaticus: Studien zum Johannesevangelium für Herbert Leroy*, ed. Stefan Schreiber and Alois Schimpfle, 183-95. BU 29. Regensburg: Verlag Friedrich Pustet, 2000.

Meeks, Wayne A. "Am I a Jew? Johannine Christianity and Judaism." In: *Christianity, Judaism and Other Graeco-Roman Cults*, ed. Jacob Neusner, 163-86. Leiden: Brill, 1975.

–. "A Nazi New Testament Professor Reads His Bible: The Strange Case of Gerhard Kittel." In: *The Idea of Biblical Interpretation: Essays in Honor of James L. Kugel*, ed. Hindy Najman and Judith H. Newman, 513-44. Leiden: Brill, 2004.

–. "Man From Heaven in Johannine Sectarianism." *Journal of Biblical Literature* 91 (1972): 44-72.

Meier, John P. *A Marginal Jew: Rethinking the Historical Jesus.* Vol. 1. New York: Doubleday, 1991.

Mendels, Doron. "The Formation of an Historical Canon of the Greco-Roman Period: From the Beginnings to Josephus." In: *Josephus and Jewish History in Flavian Rome and Beyond*, ed. Joseph Sievers, Gaia Lembi, 3-19. JSJSupp 104. Leiden: Brill, 2005.

Menken, Maarten J. J. "Die jüdischen Feste im Johannesevangelium." In: *Israel und seine Heilstraditionen im Johannesevangelium: Festgabe für Johannes Beutler SJ zum*

70. Geburtstag, ed. M. Labahn, K. Scholtissek, and A. Strotmann, 269-86. Paderborn: Schöningh, 2004.

–. "Die Redaktion des Zitates aus Sach 9,9 in Joh 12,15." *Zeitschrift für die neutestamentliche Wissenschaft* 80 (1989): 193-209.

–. "Observations on the Significance of the Old Testament in the Fourth Gospel." In: *Theology and Christology in the Fourth Gospel: Essays by the members of the SNTS Johannine Writings Seminar*, ed. G. Van Belle, J. G. Van der Watt, and P. Maritz, 155-75. BETL 184. Leuven: University Press, 2005.

Miller, Ed. L. *Salvation-History in the Prologue of John: The Significance of John 1:3/4.* NovTSup 60. Leiden: Brill, 1989.

Minear, Paul S. "The Disciples and the Crowds in the Gospel of Matthew." *Anglican Theological Review* 3 (1974): 28-44.

Miranda, Elena. "La Comunità Giudaica Di Hierapolis Di Frigia." *Epigraphica Anatolica* 31 (1999): 109-55.

Moehring, Horst R. "The Persecution of the Jews and the Adherents of the Isis Cult at Rome A.D. 19." *Novum Testamentum* 3 (1959): 293-304.

Moloney, Francis J. "The Function of John 13-17 within the Johannine Narrative." In: *"What is John?"* Vol. 2, *Literary and Social Readings of the Fourth Gospel*, ed. Fernando F. Segovia, 43-65. SBLSymS 7. Atlanta: Scholars Press, 1998.

–. *The Gospel of John: Text and Context.* BIS 72. Leiden: Brill, 2005.

Montefiore, C. G. "Notes on the Religious Value of the Fourth Gospel." *Jewish Quarterly Review* 7 (1894): 24-74.

Moreland, Milton. "The Galilean response to earliest Christianity: A Cross-Cultural Study of the Subsistence Ethic." In: *Religion and Society in Roman Palestine: Old Questions, New Approaches*, ed. Douglas R. Edwards, 37-48. New York: Routledge, 2004.

Morgenthaler, Robert. *Statistik des neutestamentlichen Wortschatzes.* Zürich: Gotthelf-Verlag, 1958.

Morris, Leon. *Jesus is the Christ: Studies in the Theology of John.* Grand Rapids: Eerdmans, 1989.

–. "Variation – A Feature of the Johannine Style." In: *Studies in the FourthGospel*, 293-319. Grand Rapids: Eerdmans, 1969.

Motyer, Stephen. "The Fourth Gospel and the Salvation of Israel: An Appeal for a New Start." In: *Anti-Judaism and the Fourth Gospel*, ed. R. Bieringer, D. Pollefeyt, and F. Vandecasteele-Vanneuville, 83-100. Louisville: Westminster John Knox, 2001.

–. *Your Father the Devil? A New Approach to John and "the Jews."* Paternoster Biblical and Theological Monographs. Carlisle: Paternoster Press, 1997.

Mowery, Robert L. "Son of God in Roman Imperial Titles and Matthew." *Biblica* 83 (2002): 100-10.

Neuer Wettstein: Texte zum Neuen Testament aus Griechentum und Hellenismus. Band I/2: Texte zum Johannesevangelium. Ed. by U. Schnelle. Berlin: de Gruyter, 2001.

Neugebauer, Johannes. *Die eschatologischen Aussagen in den johanneischen Abschieds-reden: Eine Untersuchung zu Johannes 13 – 17.* BWANT 140. Stuttgart: Kohlhammer, 1995.

Neuhaus, Dietrich, ed. *Teufelskinder oder Heilsbringer – Die Juden im Johannes-Evangelium.* Arnoldshainer Texte, vol. 64. Frankfurt: Haag und Herchen, 1990.

The New International Dictionary of New Testament Theology. Ed. by Colin Brown. 4 vols. Grand Rapids: Zondervan, 1986.

Nicklas, Tobias. *Ablösung und Verstrickung: "Juden" und Jüngergestalten als Charaktere der erzählten Welt des Johannesevangeliums und ihre Wirkung auf den impliziten Leser.* RST 60. Frankfurt: Lang, 2001.

–. "'153 große Fische' (Joh 21,11). Erzählerische Ökonomie und 'johanneischer Überstieg'." *Biblica* 84 (2003): 366-87.

–. "Literarkritik und Leserrezeption. Ein Beitrag zur Methodendiskussion am Beispiel Joh 3,22-4,3." *Biblica* 83 (2002): 175-92.

Nineham, D. E. "The Genealogy in St. Matthew's Gospel and Its Significance for the Study of the Gospels." *Bulletin of the John Rylands University Library of Manchester* 58 (1975–76): 421-44.

Noetzel, Heintz. *Christus und Dionysos. Bemerkungen zum religions-geschichtlichen Hintergrund zu Johannes 2,1-11.* Stuttgart: Calwer, 1960.

Nothomb, Paul. "Nouveau Regard sur 'les Juifs' de Jean." *Foi et Vie* 71 (1972): 65-69.

Novakovic, Lidija. *Messiah, the Healer of the Sick.* WUNT II/170. Tübingen: Mohr Siebeck, 2003.

Oberman, Heiko A. *The Roots of Anti-Semitism in the Age of Renaissance and Reformation.* Transl. by James I. Porter. Philadelphia: Fortress Press, 1984.

O'Neill, J. C. "The Jews in the Fourth Gospel." *Irish Biblical Studies* 18 (1996): 58-74.

O'Day, Gail R. "'I have said these things to you …' The Unsettled Place of Jesus' Discourses in Literary Approaches to the Fourth Gospel." In: *Word, Theology and Community in John*, ed. J. Painter, R. Alan Culpepper, and Fernando F. Segovia, 143-54. St. Louis: Chalice Press, 2002.

Oesterreicher, John. *The New Encounter Between Christians and Jews.* New York: Philosophical Library, 1986.

Onuki, Takashi. *Gemeinde und Welt im Johannesevangelium: Ein Beitrag zur Frage nach der theologischen und pragmatischen Funktion des johanneischen 'Dualismus.'* WMANT 56. Neukirchen-Vluyn: Neukirchener Verlag, 1984.

Painter, John. "The Church and Israel in the Gospel of John: A Response." *New Testament Studies* 25 (1978–1979): 103-12.

–. "The Farewell Discourses and the History of Johannine Christianity." *New Testament Studies* 27 (1981): 525-43.

Pancaro, Severino. "'People of God' in St John's Gospel." *New Testament Studies* 16 (1969–70), 114-129.

–. "The Relationship of the Church to Israel in the Gospel of John." *New Testament Studies* 21 (1974–1975): 396-405.

Parsenios, George L. *Departure and Consolation: The Johannine Farewell Discourses in Light of Greco-Roman Literature.* NovTSup 117. Leiden: Brill, 2005.

Patterson, Stephen J. "The Prologue to the Fourth Gospel." In: *Jesus in the Johannine Tradition,* ed. R. T. Fortna and T. Thatcher, 325-32. Louisville: Westminster John Knox, 2001.

Paul and Empire: Religion and Power in Roman Imperial Society. Ed. by Richard A. Horsley. Harrisburg, PA: Trinity Press International, 1997.

Paul and the Imperial Roman Order. Ed. by Richard A. Horsley. Harrisburg, PA: Trinity Press International, 2004.

Pawlikowski, John T. "Accomplishments and Challenges in the Contemporary Jewish-Christian Encounter." In: *Removing Anti-Judaism from the Pulpit,* ed. Howard C. Kee and Irvin J. Borowsky, 29-35. New York: Continuum, 1996.

Pedersen, Sigfred. "Anti-Judaism in John's Gospel: John 8." In: *New Readings in John: Literary and Theological Perspectives. Essays from the Scandinavian Conference on the Fourth Gospel in Århus 1997*, ed. J. Nissen and S. Pedersen, 172-93. Sheffield: Sheffield Academic Press, 1999.

Petersen, Birte. *Theologie nach Auschwitz? Jüdische und christliche Versuche einer Antwort*. 3rd ed. Veröffentlichungen aus dem Institut Kirche und Judentum, vol. 24. Berlin: Institut Kirche und Judentum, 2004.

Phillips, Peter M. *The Prologue of the Fourth Gospel: A Sequential Reading*. Library of New Testament Studies 294. London: T&T Clark, 2006.

Pietrantonio, Ricardo. "Los Ἰουδαῖοι en el Evangelio de Juan." *Revista Biblica* 47 (1985): 27-41.

Pilhofer, Peter. "Dionysos und Christus. Zwei Erlöser im Vergleich." In: *Die frühen Christen und ihre Welt: Greifswalder Aufsätze 1996-2001*, 73-91. WUNT 145. Tübingen: Mohr Siebeck, 2002.

Pippin, Tina. "'For Fear of the Jews': Lying and Truth-Telling in Translating the Gospel of John." *Semeia* 76 (1996): 81-97.

Popkes, Enno Edzard. *Die Theologie der Liebe Gottes in den johanneischen Schriften. Zur Semantik der Liebe und zum Motivkreis des Dualismus*. WUNT 2/197. Tübingen: Mohr Siebeck, 2005.

Porsch, Felix. "'Ihr habt den Teufel zum Vater' (Joh 8,44). Antijudaismus im Johannesevangelium?" *Bibel und Kirche* 44 (1989): 50-57.

Pratscher, Wilhelm. "Die Juden im Johannesevangelium." *Bibel und Liturgie* 59 (1986): 177-85.

–. "Tiefenpsychologische Erwägungen zur negativen Rede von 'den Juden' im Johannesevangelium." In: *Theology and Christology in the Fourth Gospel: Essays by the members of the SNTS Johannine Writings Seminar*, ed. G. Van Belle, J. G. Van der Watt, and P. Maritz, 277-90. BETL 184. Leuven: University Press, 2005.

Price, S. R. F. *Rituals and Power: The Roman Imperial Cult in Asia Minor*. Cambridge: Cambridge University Press, 1984.

Pryor, John W. "Jesus and Israel in the Fourth Gospel – John 1:11." *Novum Testamentum* 32 (1990): 201-18.

–. *John: Evangelist of the Covenant People. The Narrative & Themes of the Fourth Gospel*. Downers Grove, IL: InverVarsity Press, 1992.

Quiévreux, François. "'Les Juifs' dans le quatrième Evangile." *Foi et Vie* 57 (1958): 249-61.

Rabinowitz, Noel Scott. "Remnant and Restoration as a Paradigm of Matthew's Theology of Israel." Ph.D. diss., The Southern Baptist Theological Seminary, 2004.

Rebell, Walter. *Gemeinde als Gegenwelt: Zur soziologischen und didaktischen Funktion des Johannesevangeliums*. BBET 20. Frankfurt: Lang, 1987.

Reed, David A. "How Semitic Was John? Rethinking the Hellenistic Background to John 1:1." *Anglican Theological Review* 85 (2003): 709-26.

Reed, Jonathan L. "Galilean Archaeology and the Historical Jesus." In: *Jesus Then & Now: Images of Jesus in History and Theology*, ed. Marvin Meyer, Charles Hughes, 113-29. Harrisburg, PA: Trinity Press International, 2001.

Reim, Günter. "Joh 8,44 – Gotteskinder / Teufelskinder. Wie antijudaistisch ist 'Die wohl antijudaistischste Äußerung des Neuen Testaments'?" *New Testament Studies* 30 (1984): 619-24.

Reinhartz, Adele. *Befriending the Beloved Disciple: A Jewish Reading of the Gospel of John*. New York: Continuum, 2001.

–. "'Jews' and Jews in the Fourth Gospel." In: *Anti-Judaism and the Fourth Gospel*, ed. R. Bieringer, D. Pollefeyt, and F. Vandecasteele-Vanneuville, 213-27. Louisville: Westminster John Knox, 2001.

–. "John 8:31-59 from a Jewish Perspective." In: *Anti-Judaism and the Fourth Gospel*, ed. R. Bieringer, D. Pollefeyt, and F. Vandecasteele-Vanneuville, 213-27. Louisville: John Knox, 2001.

–. *The Word in the World: The Cosmological Tale in the Fourth Gospel*. SBLMS 45. Atlanta: Scholars Press, 1992.

Reiser, Marius. "Die Stellung der Evangelien in der antiken Literaturgeschichte." *Zeitschrift für die neutestamentliche Wissenschaft* 90 (1999): 1-27.

Rendtorff, Rolf. "Did Christianity Die in Auschwitz?" In: *A Shadow of Glory: Reading the New Testament after the Holocaust*, ed. Tod Linafelt, 155-68. New York: Routledge, 2002.

Rensberger, David. "Anti-Judaism and the Gospel of John." In: *Anti-Judaism and the Gospels,* ed. William R. Farmer, 120-57. Harrisburg, PA: Trinity Press International, 1999.

–. *Johannine Faith and Liberating Community*. Philadelphia: The Westminster Press, 1988.

–. "The Politics of John: The Trial of Jesus in the Fourth Gospel." *Journal of Biblical Literature* 103 (1984): 395-411.

Richardson, Peter, and David Granskou, eds. *Anti-Judaism in Early Christianity*. Vol. 1, *Paul and the Gospels*. Waterloo, Canada: Wilfried Laurier University Press, 1986.

Richter, Georg. *Studien zum Johannesevangelium*. Ed. by J. Hainz. BU 13. Regensburg: Verlag Friedrich Pustet, 1977.

Rissi, Mathias. "Die 'Juden' im Johannesevangelium." In: *Aufstieg und Niedergang der römischen Welt: Geschichte und Kultur Roms im Spiegel der neueren Forschung*, vol. II 26.3., ed. Wolfgang Haase, 2099-2141. Berlin: de Gruyter, 1996.

Rittner, R., S. D. Smith, and I. Steinfeld, eds. *The Holocaust and the Christian World: Reflections on the Past, Challenges for the Future*. New York: Continuum, 2000.

Robinson, J. A. T. "The Relation of the Prologue to the Gospel of St. John." *New Testament Studies* 9 (1962-63): 120-29.

Roskam, H. N. *The Purpose of the Gospel of Mark in its Historical and Social Context*. NovTSup 114. Leiden: Brill, 2004.

Roth, John K. "What does the Holocaust have to do with Christianity?" In: *The Holocaust and the Christian World: Reflections on the Past, Challenges for the Future*, ed. C. Rittner, S. D. Smith, and I. Steinfeld, 5-10. New York: Continuum, 2000.

Rousseau, John J., and Rami Arav. *Jesus & His World: An Archaeological and Cultural Dictionary*. Minneapolis: Fortress Press, 1995.

Ruckstuhl, E. *Die literarische Einheitlichkeit des Johannesevangeliums: Der gegenwärtige Stand der einschlägigen Forschung*. NTOA 5. Göttingen: Vandenhoeck & Ruprecht, 1987.

Ruckstuhl, E., and P. Dschulnigg. *Stilkritik und Verfasserfrage im Johannesevangelium*. Göttingen: Vandenhoeck & Ruprecht, 1991.

Ruether, Rosemary R. *Faith and Fratricide: The Theological Roots of Antisemitism*. Minneapolis: Seabury, 1974.

Salier, Willis Hedley. *The Rhetorical Impact of the Sēmeia in the Gospel of John*. WUNTII/186. Tübingen: Mohr Siebeck, 2004.

Sanders, Ed Parish. *The Historical Figure of Jesus*. New York: Penguin Books, 1993.

Sands, P. C. *Literary Genius of the New Testament*. Westport, CT: Greenwood Press, 1970.

Sänger, Dieter. "'Auf Betreiben der Vornehmsten unseres Volkes' (Iosephus ant. Iud. XVIII 64). Zur Frage einer jüdischen Beteiligung an der Kreuzigung Jesu." In: *Das*

Urchristentum in seiner literarischen Geschichte: Festschrift für Jürgen Becker, ed. U. Mell and U. B. Müller, 1-25. BZNW 100. Berlin: de Gruyter, 1999.

–. "Heiden – Juden – Christen. Erwägungen zu einem Aspekt frühchristlicher Missionsgeschichte." *Zeitschrift für die neutestamentliche Wissenschaft* 89 (1998): 145-72.

Sasse, H. "κοσμέω, κόσμος, κόσμιος, κοσμικός." In: *Theological Dictionary of the New Testament*, ed. by G. Friedrich, transl. by G. W. Bromiley, 3:868-898. Grand Rapids: Eerdmans, 1965.

Saunders, Ross. "Paul and the Imperial Cult." In: *Paul and His Opponents*, ed. Stanley E. Porter, 227-38. Pauline Studies 2. Leiden: Brill, 2005.

Schapdick, Stefan. *Auf dem Weg in den Konflikt: Exegetische Studien zum theologischen Profil der Erzählung vom Aufenthalt Jesu in Samarien (Joh 4,1-42) im Kontext des Johannesevangeliums*. BBB 126. Berlin: Philo, 2000.

Schein, Bruce E. *Following the Way: The Setting of John's Gospel*. Minneapolis: Augsburg Publishing House, 1980.

Schenke, Ludger. "Der 'Dialog Jesu mit den Juden' im Johannesevangelium: Ein Rekonstruktionsversuch." *New Testament Studies* 34 (1988): 573-603.

–. "Joh 7-10: Eine dramatische Szene." *Zeitschrift für die neutestamentliche Wissenschaft* 80 (1989): 172-92.

Schiffman, Lawrence H. *Texts and Traditions: A Source Reader for the Study of Second Temple and Rabbinic Judaism*. Hoboken, NJ: Ktav Publishing House, 1998.

Schmidl, Martin. *Jesus und Nikodemus: Gespräch zur johanneischen Christologie. Joh 3 in schichtenspezifischer Sicht*. BU 28. Regensburg: Verlag Friedrich Pustet, 1998.

Schmithals, Walter. *Johannesevangelium und Johannesbriefe: Forschungsgeschichte und Analyse*. BZNW 64. Berlin: de Gruyter, 1992.

–. "Die Martyrien von Petrus und Paulus." In: *Paulus, die Evangelien und das Urchristentum: Beiträge von und zu Walter Schmithals zu seinem 80. Geburtstag herausgegeben*, ed. Cilliers Breytenbach, 521-41. Leiden: Brill, 2004.

Schnackenburg, Rudolf. "Die Messiasfrage im Johannesevangelium." In: *Neutestamentliche Aufsätze: Festschrift für Josef Schmid*, ed. J. Blinzler, O. Kuss, and F. Mussner, 240-64. Regensburg: Pustet, 1963.

Schnelle, Udo. *Antidoketische Christologie im Johannesevangelium: Eine Untersuchung zur Stellung des vierten Evangeliums in der johanneischen Schule*. FRLANT 144. Göttingen: Vandenhoeck & Ruprecht, 1987.

–. "Ein neuer Blick. Tendenzen gegenwärtiger Johannesforschung." *Berliner Theologische Zeitschrift* 1 (1999): 21-40.

–. "Die Juden im Johannesevangelium." In: *Gedenkt an das Wort: Festschrift für Werner Vogler zum 65. Geburtstag*, ed. C. Kähler, M. Böhm, and C. Böttrich, 217-30. Leipzig: Evangelische Verlagsanstalt, 1999.

Scholder, Klaus. *Die Kirchen und das Dritte Reich. Bd. 1: Vorgeschichte und Zeit der Illusionen 1918-1934. Bd. 2: Das Jahr der Ernüchterung 1934*. Frankfurt: Ullstein, 1977.

Scholtissek, Klaus. "Antijudaismus im Johannesevangelium? Ein Gesprächsbeitrag." In: *„Nun steht aber die Sache im Evangelium ..." Zur Frage nach den Anfängen des christlichen Antijudaismus*, ed. R. Kampling, 151-81. 2nd ed. Paderborn: Ferdinand Schöningh, 1999.

–. "Relecture und réécriture: Neue Paradigmen zu Methode und Inhalt der Johannesauslegung aufgewiesen am Prolog 1,1-18 und der ersten Abschiedsrede 13,31-14,31." *Theologie und Philosophie* 75 (2000): 1-29.

Schowalter, Daniel N. *The Emperor and the Gods: Images from the Time of Trajan*. HDR 28. Minneapolis: Fortress Press, 1993.

Schrage, W. "ἀποσυνάγωγος." In: *Theological Dictionary of the New Testament*, ed. by G. Friedrich, transl. by G. W. Bromiley, 7:848-852. Grand Rapids: Eerdmans, 1971.

Schram, Terry L. "The Use of ΙΟΥΔΑΙΟΣ in the Fourth Gospel: An Application of some Linguistic Insights to a New Testament Problem." D.Th. diss., State University of Utrecht, 1974.

Schreckenberg, Heinz. *Die christlichen Adversus-Judaeos-Texte und ihr literarisches und historisches Umfeld: Bd. 1 (1-11 Jh.)*. 4th ed. Frankfurt: Lang, 1999.

Schulz, Siegfried. *Komposition und Herkunft der Johanneischen Reden*. BWANT 81. Stuttgart: Kohlhammer, 1960.

Schweitzer, Albert. *Von Reimarus zu Wrede: Eine Geschichte der Leben-Jesu-Forschung*. Tübingen: J. C. B. Mohr, 1906.

Scott, Bernard Brandon. "The Birth of the Reader." *Semeia* 52 (1991): 83-102.

Segovia, Fernando F. "John 1:1-18 as Entrée into Johannine Reality. Representation and Ramifications." In: *Word, Theology and Community in John*, ed. J. Painter, R. Alan Culpepper, and Fernando F. Segovia, 33-64. St. Louis: Chalice Press, 2002.

–. "The Love and Hatred of Jesus and Johannine Sectarianism." *Catholic Biblical Quarterly* 43 (1981): 258-72.

Shaked, Idan, and Dina Avshalom-Gorni. "Jewish Settlement in the Southeastern Hula Valley in the First Century CE." In: *Religion and Society in Roman Palestine: Old Questions, New Approaches*, ed. Douglas R. Edwards, 28-36. New York: Routledge, 2004.

Shepherd, Massey H. "The Jews in the Gospel of John: Another Level of Meaning." *Anglican Theological Review* 56 (1974): 95-112.

Siegert, Folker. "Vermeintlicher Antijudaismus und Polemik gegen Judenchristen im Neuen Testament." In: *The Image of the Judaeo-Christians in Ancient Jewish and Christian Literature*, ed. Peter J. Tomson and Doris Lambers-Petry, 74-105. WUNT 58. Tübingen: Mohr Siebeck, 2003.

Sikes, Walter W. "The Anti-Semitism of the Fourth Gospel." *Journal of Religion* 21 (1941): 23-30.

Sim, David C. *Apocalyptic Eschatology in the Gospel of Matthew*. SNTSMS 88. Cambridge: Cambridge University, 1996.

Simon, Marcel. *Verus Israel: Étude sur les relations entre chrétiens et juifs dans l'empire romain (135-425)*. Paris: E. de Boccard, 1948.

–. *Verus Israel: A Study of the Relations Between Christians and Jews in the Roman Empire (135-425)*. Transl. by H. McKeating. Oxford: Oxford University Press, 1986.

Smiga, George M. *Pain and Polemic: Anti-Judaism in the Gospels*. New York: Paulist, 1992.

Smith II, Carl B. *No Longer Jews. The Search for Gnostic Origins*. Peabody, MA:Hendrickson Publishers, 2004.

Smith, Dennis E. "Narrative Beginnings in Ancient Literature and Theory." *Semeia* 52 (1991): 1-9.

Smith, D. Moody. "John and the Jews." *Interpretation* 23 (1969): 220-23.

–. "John's Quest for Jesus." In: *Neotestamentica et Philonica: Studies in Honor of Peder Borgen*, ed. D. E. Aune, T. Seland, and J. H. Ulrichsen, 233-53. NovTSup 151. Leiden: Brill, 2003.

–. "Judaism and the Gospel of John." In: *Jews and Christians: Exploring the Past, Present, and Future*, ed. J. H. Charlesworth, 76-96. New York: Crossroad, 1990.

Smith, Roger W. "American Self-Interest and the Response to Genocide." *The Chronicle of Higher Education* July 30 (2004): B6-9.

Söding, Thomas. "Die Macht der Wahrheit und das Reich der Freiheit. Zur johanneischen Deutung des Pilatus-Prozesses (Joh 18,28-19,16)." *Zeitschrift für Theologie und Kirche* 93 (1996): 35-58.

–. "'Was kann aus Nazareth schon Gutes kommen?' (Joh 1.46). Die Bedeutung des Judeseins Jesu im Johannesevangelium." *New Testament Studies* 46 (2000): 21-41.

Soltau, Wilhelm. "Die Reden des vierten Evangeliums." *Zeitschrift für die neutestamentliche Wissenschaft* 17 (1916): 49-61.

–. "Zum Problem des Johannesevangeliums." *Zeitschrift für neutestamentliche Wissenschaft* 2 (1901): 140-49.

Späth, Andreas. *Luther und die Juden*. Bonn: Verlag für Kultur und Wissenschaft, 2001.

Staley, Jeff. *The Print's First Kiss: A Rhetorical Investigation of the Implied Reader in the Fourth Gospel*. SBLDS 82. Atlanta: Scholars Press, 1988.

Stange, Erich. *Die Eigenart der johanneischen Produktion: Ein Beitrag zur Kritik der neueren Quellenscheidungshypothesen und zur Charakteristik der johanneischen Psyche*. Dresden: C. Ludwig Ungelenk, 1915.

Stare, Mira. *Durch ihn leben: Die Lebensthematik in Joh 6*. NA 49. Münster: Aschendorff, 2004.

Stegemann, Wolfgang. "Gab es eine jüdische Beteiligung an der Kreuzigung Jesu?" *Kirche und Israel* 13 (1998): 3-24.

Stegemann, Ekkehard. "Die Tragödie der Nähe. Zu den judenfeindlichen Aussagen des Johannesevangeliums." *Kirche und Israel* 4 (1989): 114-22.

Stegemann, Ekkehard, and Wolfgang Stegemann. "König Israels, nicht König der Juden?" Jesus als König Israels im Johannesevangelium." In: *Messias-Vorstellungen bei Juden und Christen*, ed. Ekkehard Stegemann, 41-56. Stuttgart: Verlag W. Kohlhammer, 1993.

Stemberger, Günther. "Die sogenannte 'Synode von Jabne' und das frühe Christentum." *Kairos* 19 (1977): 14-21.

Stern, David H. *Jewish New Testament Commentary*. Clarksville, MD: Jewish New Testament Publications, 1994.

Stibbe, Mark W. G. *John as Storyteller: Narrative Criticism and the Fourth Gospel*. Cambridge: Cambridge University Press, 1994.

Suhl, Alfred. "Beobachtungen zu den Passionsgeschichten der synoptischen Evangelien." In: *Von Jesus zum Christus: Christologische Studien. Festgabe für Paul Hoffmann zum 65. Geburtstag*, ed. Rudolf Hoppe and Ulrich Busse, 321-77. Berlin: de Gruyter, 1998.

Synan, Edward A. *The Popes and the Jews in the Middle Ages*. New York: Macmillan Company, 1965.

Tanzer, Sarah J. "Salvation Is *for* the Jews: Secret Christian Jews in the Gospel of John." In: *The Future of Early Christianity: Essays in Honor of Helmut Koester*, ed. Birger A. Pearson, 285-300. Minneapolis: Fortress Press, 1991.

Theobald, Michael. *Die Fleischwerdung des Logos: Studien zum Verhältnis des Johannesprologs zum Corpus des Evangeliums und zu 1 Joh*. NA 20. Münster: Aschendorffsche Verlagsbuchhandlung, 1988.

Theological Dictionary of the New Testament. Ed. by G. Friedrich. Transl. by G. W. Bromiley. 10 vols. Grand Rapids: Eerdmans, 1964–1976.

Thompson, M. M. "John, Gospel of." In: *Dictionary of Jesus and the Gospels*, ed. Joel B. Green, Scot McKnight, 368-383. Downers Grove, IL: IVP, 1992.

Thyen, Hartwig. "Aus der Literatur zum Johannesevangelium." *Theologische Rundschau* (1975): 222-52.

–. "'Das Heil kommt von den Juden'." In: *Kirche: Festschrift für Günther Bornkamm zum 75. Geburtstag*, ed. D. Lührmann and G. Strecker, 163-84. Tübingen: Mohr Siebeck, 1980.

–. "Das Johannes-Evangelium als Literarisches Werk." In: *Teufelskinder oder Heilsbringer – Die Juden im Johannes-Evangelium*, ed. Dietrich Neuhaus, 112-32. Arnoldshainer Texte, vol. 64. Frankfurt: Haag und Herchen, 1990.

Tilborg, Sjef Van. *Reading John in Ephesus*. NovTSup 83. Leiden: Brill, 1996.

Tolmie, Francois D. "The ΊΟΥΔΑΙΟΙ in the Fourth Gospel: A Narratological Perspective." In: *Theology and Christology in the Fourth Gospel: Essays by the members of the SNTS Johannine Writings Seminar*, ed. G. Van Belle, J. G. Van der Watt, and P. Maritz, 377-97. BETL 184. Leuven: University Press, 2005.

–. *Jesus' Farewell to the Disciples: John 13:1-17:26 in Narratological Perspective*. BIS 12. Leiden: Brill, 1995.

Tomson, Peter J. *'If this be from Heaven ...': Jesus and the New Testament Authors in their Relationship to Judaism*. Transl. by J. Dyk. Sheffield: Sheffield Academic Press, 2001.

–. "'Jews' in the Gospel of John as Compared with the Palestinian Talmud, the Synoptics, and Some New Testament Apocrypha." In: *Anti-Judaism and the Fourth Gospel*, ed. R. Bieringer, D. Pollefeyt, and F. Vandecasteele-Vanneuville, 176-212. Louisville: Westminster John Knox, 2001.

–. *Presumed Guilty: How the Jews Were Blamed for the Death of Jesus*. Minneapolis: Fortress Press, 2005.

Townsend, John T. "The Gospel of John and the Jews: The Story of a Religious Divorce." In *Antisemitism and the Foundations of Christianity*, ed. A. Davies, 72-97. New York: Paulist, 1979.

Trebilco, Paul. *The Early Christians in Ephesus from Paul to Ignatius*. WUNT 166. Tübingen: Mohr Siebeck, 2004.

Tripolitis, Antonía. *Religions of the Hellenistic Roman Age*. Grand Rapids: Eerdmans, 2002.

Trocmé, Étienne. "Les Juifs d'après le Nouveau Testament." *Foi et Vie* 90 (1991): 3-22.

Tsuchido, Kiyoshi. "Is There Anti-Semitism in the Fourth Gospel? An Exegetical Study of John 11:45-54." *Annual of the Japanese Biblical Institute* 21 (1995): 57-72.

Turner, Nigel. *A Grammar of New Testament Greek*. Vol. 4, *Style*. Edinburgh: T.&.T. Clark, 1976.

Van Belle, Gilbert. *The Signs Source in the Fourth Gospel: Historical Survey and Critical Evaluation of the Semeia Hypothesis*. BETL 116. Leuven: University Press, 1994.

–. "'Salvation is from the Jews': The Parenthesis in John 4:22b." In: *Anti-Judaism and the Fourth Gospel: Papers of the Leuven Colloquium, 2000*. Ed. by R. Bieringer, D. Pollefeyt, F. Vandecasteele-Vanneuville, 370-400. Jewish and Christian. Heritage Series 1. Assen: Royal Van Gorcum, 2001.

Van der Watt, Jan G. *Family of the King: Dynamics of Metaphor in the Gospel According to John*. Biblical Interpretation Series 47. Leiden: Brill, 2000.

Van-Iersel, Bas M. F. *Mark: A Reader-Response Commentary*. JSNTSup 164. Sheffield: Sheffield Academic Press, 1998.

Vatican Council II: The Conciliar and Post Conciliar Documents. Ed. by Austin Flannery. Collegeville, MN: The Liturgical Press, 1975.

Vermes, Geza. *The Changing Faces of Jesus*. New York: Penguin Compass, 2000.

Visotzky, Rabbi Burton L. "Methodological Considerations in the Study of John's Interaction with First-Century Judaism." In: *Life in Abundance: Studies of John's*

Gospel in Tribute to Raymond E. Brown, ed. John R. Donahue, 91-107. Collegeville, MN: Liturgical Press, 2005.

Vollenweider, Samuel. "Antijudaismus im Neuen Testament. Der Anfang einer unseligen Tradition." In: *Antijudaismus – Christliche Erblast*, ed. W. Dietrich, G. Martin, and U. Luz, 40-55. Stuttgart: Kohlhammer, 1999.

Von Harnack, Adolf. "Über das Verhältnis des Prologs des vierten Evangeliums zum ganzen Werk." *Zeitschrift für Theologie und Kirche* 2 (1892): 189-231.

Voorwinde, Stephen. *Jesus' Emotions in the Fourth Gospel. Human or Divine?* Library of New Testament Studies 284. London: T&T Clark International, 2005.

Vouga, François. *Le cadre historique et l'intention théologique de Jean*. Paris: Beauchesne, 1977.

Waetjen, H. C. "The Genealogy as the Key to the Gospel according to Matthew." *Journal of Biblical Literature* 95 (1976): 205-30.

Wagner, Josef. *Auferstehung und Leben: Joh 11,1-12,19 als Spiegel johanneischer Redaktions- und Theologiegeschichte*. BU 19. Regensburg: Verlag Friedrich Pustet, 1988.

Wahlde, Urban C. von. "'The Jews' in the Gospel of John: Fifteen Years of Research (1983–1998)." *Ephemerides Theologicae Lovanienses* 76 (2000): 30-55.

–. "The Johannine 'Jews': A Critical Survey." *New Testament Studies* 28 (1982): 33-60.

Watson, Alan. *Jesus and the Jews: The Pharisaic Tradition in John*. Athens: University of Georgia, 1995.

Waubke, Hans-Günther. *Die Pharisäer in der protestantischen Bibelwissenschaft des 19. Jahrhunderts*. BHT 107. Tübingen: Mohr Siebeck, 1998.

Wearing, Thomas. *The World-View of the Fourth Gospel: A Genetic Study*. Chicago: The University of Chicago, 1918.

Weatherly, Jon A. *Jewish Responsibility for the Death of Jesus in Luke-Acts*. JSNTSup 106. Sheffield: Sheffield Academic Press, 1994.

Wehrmann, Jürgen. "Der Weg und die Wiege. Bruce E. Scheins Entdeckung der Landschaften und Orte als Schlüssel zum Verständnis des Johannes-Evangeliums." In: *Teufelskinder oder Heilsbringer – Die Juden im Johannes-Evangelium*, ed. Dietrich Neuhaus, 95-111. Arnoldshainer Texte 64. Frankfurt: Haag und Herchen, 1990.

Weidemann, Hans-Ulrich. *Der Tod Jesu im Johannesevangelium: Die erste Abschiedsrede als Schlüsseltext für den Passions und Osterbericht*. BZNW 122. Berlin: de Gruyter, 2004.

Wengst, Klaus. *Bedrängte Gemeinde und verherrlichter Christus: Der historische Ort des Johannesevangeliums als Schlüssel zu seiner Interpretation*. Biblisch-theologische Studien 5. Neukirchen-Vluyn: Neukirchener Verlag, 1981.

–. *Bedrängte Gemeinde und verherrlichter Christus. Ein Versuch über das Johannesevangelium*. 3rd ed. München: Chr. Kaiser Verlag, 1990.

–. "Die Darstellung 'der Juden' im Johannes-Evangelium als Reflex jüdisch-judenchristlicher Kontroverse." In: *Teufelskinder oder Heilsbringer – die Juden im Johannes-Evangelium*, ed. Dietrich Neuhaus, 22-38. Arnoldshainer Texte 64. Frankfurt: Haag und Herchen, 1990.

Wenham, David. "The Enigma of the Fourth Gospel: Another Look." *Tyndale Bulletin* 48 (1997): 149-78.

White, Martin C. "The Identity and Function of Jews and Related Terms in the Fourth Gospel." Ph.D. diss., Emory University, 1972.

Wick, Peter. "Jesus gegen Dionysos? Ein Beitrag zur Kontextualisierung des Johannesevangeliums." *Biblica* 85 (2004): 179-98.

Wiefel, Wolfgang. "Die Scheidung von Gemeinde und Welt im Johannesevangelium auf dem Hintergrund der Trennung von Kirche und Synagogue." *Theologische Zeitschrift* 35 (1979): 213-27.

Wilken, Robert L. *The Christians as the Romans Saw Them.* New Haven: Yale University, 1984.

Williams, A. Lukyn. *Adversus Judaeos.* Cambridge: Cambridge University Press, 1935.

Williams, Margaret H. "The Meaning and Function of Ἰουδαῖος in Greco-Roman Inscriptions." *Zeitschrift für Papyrologie und Epigraphic* 116 (1997): 249-62.

Williamson, Clark M. *A Guest in the House of Israel: Post-Holocaust Church Theology.* Louisville: Westminster John Knox, 1993.

Williamson, Clark M., and Ronald J. Allen. "Interpreting Difficult Texts." In: *Removing Anti-Judaism from the Pulpit,* ed. Howard C. Kee, and Irvin J. Borowsky, 36-42. New York: Continuum, 1996.

Windisch, Hans."Das johanneische Christentum und sein Verhältnis zum Judentum und zu Paulus." *Die Christliche Welt* 47 (1933): 98-107, 147-54.

–. "John's Narrative Style." In: *The Gospel of John as Literature: An Anthology of Twentieth-Century Perspectives,* ed. Mark W. G. Stibbe, 25-64. NTTS 17. Leiden: Brill, 1993.

Winter, Martin. *Das Vermächtnis Jesu und die Abschiedsreden der Väter: Gattungsgeschichtliche Untersuchung der Vermächtnisrede im Blick auf Joh. 13-17.* FRLANT 161. Göttingen: Vandenhoeck & Ruprecht, 1994.

Woodbridge, Paul. "'The World' in the Fourth Gospel." In: *Witness to the World: Papers from the Second Oak Hill College Annual School of Theology,* ed. David Peterson, 1-31. Carlisle: Paternoster Press, 1999.

Word, Theology and Community in John. Ed. by J. Painter, R. Alan Culpepper, and Fernando F. Segovia. St. Louis: Chalice Press, 2002.

Yee, Gale. *Jewish Feasts and the Gospel of John.* Zacchaeus Studies: New Testament. Wilmington, DE: Michael Glazier, 1989.

Zenger, Erich. "Exegese des Alten Testaments im Spannungsfeld von Judentum und Christentum." *Theologische Revue* 98 (2002): 357-58.

Ziffer, Walter. "Two Epithets for Jesus of Nazareth in Talmud and Midrash." *Journal of Biblical Literature* 85 (1966): 356-57.

Zumstein, Jean. "Zur Geschichte des johanneischen Christentums." *Theologische Literaturzeitung* 122 (1997): 417-28.

–. "Crise du Savoir et Conflit des Interprétations Selon Jean 9: Un Exemple du Travail de L'école Johannique." In *Early Christian Voices: In Texts, Traditions, and Symbols. Essays in Honor of Francois Bovon,* ed. David H. Warren, Ann G. Brock, David W. Pao, 167-78. Brill Academic Publishers, 2003.

–. "Die Abschiedsreden (Johannes 13,31–16,33) und das Problem des Antijudaismus." In *Kreative Erinnerung: Relecture und Auslegung im Johannesevangelium,* 189-205. Abhandlungen zur Theologie des Alten und Neuen Testaments, vol. 84. Zürich: Theologischer Verlag Zürich, 2004.

–. "The Farewell Discourse (John 13:31-16:33) and the Problem of Anti-Judaism." In *Anti-Judaism and the Fourth Gospel: Papers of the Leuven Colloquium, 2000,* ed. R. Bieringer, D. Pollefeyt, F. VAndecasteele-Vanneuville, 461-78. Jewish and Christian Heritage Series, vol. 1. Assen: Royal Van Gorcum, 2001.

Index of References

1. Hebrew Bible / Old Testament

2. New Testament

	99	7:19-24	30
6:42	44	7:19	10, 144, 146
6:44	140, 163	7:20	10, 16
6:45	64, 140, 144, 173	7:21-24	98, 149
6:46	118, 140	7:22	144, 149
6:47	104, 140, 150	7:23	100, 123, 144, 149
6:49	99	7:25	10, 18
6:51	55, 99, 119, 140, 149,	7:26-27	84
	150, 159	7:27	30
6:52	27, 119, 137	7:28	107
6:53	99, 104, 119, 138, 149	7:30	112
6:56	119, 140	7:31	30, 74
6:57	140	7:32	10, 101, 145
6:58	99	7:33f.	124
6:59	107, 143	7:34	118
6:60-66	28, 29, 30, 169, 176	7:35-36	121
6:60	168, 171	7:35	9, 17, 41, 63, 70, 100,
6:62	118, 124, 149		172
6:64	129	7:37f.	124
6:68	137, 169, 195	7:38	64, 146
6:69	84, 168	7:39	169
6:70-71	124, 127, 129	7:40-44	17
7:1-24	99–100	7:41-42	30
7:1	9, 10, 16, 20, 21, 27,	7:42	70
	100, 147, 161	7:43	30
7:2	9, 21, 23, 25, 26, 53, 63,	7:45	10, 101
	101, 143, 189	7:46	15, 149
7:3-5	29	7:47f.	10, 44
7:3	21, 42	7:48-49	15
7:4	161, 163	7:49	42, 99, 143
7:5	45	7:50	123
7:7	16, 100, 108, 118, 140,	7:51	143, 149
	150, 159, 161, 176, 180,	7:52	42
	215	8:1f.	143, 144
7:10	144	8:2	107
7:11	9, 100	8:3	17, 145
7:12	17	8:5	143
7:13	9, 10, 27, 100	8:9	17, 145
7:14	42, 107, 161	8:11	195
7:15	9, 17, 42, 63, 94, 100	8:12-59	100-102
7:16	118	8:12	55, 56, 83, 88, 101, 118,
7:17	84, 118		138, 140, 149, 150, 159,

3. Old Testament Apocrypha

4. Old Testament Pseudepigrapha

5. Dead Sea Scrolls

6. Philo

7. Josephus

8. Mishnah, Talmud

9. Early Christian Literature

10. Greco-Roman Literature

Index of Modern Authors

Index of Subjects and Key Terms

Wissenschaftliche Untersuchungen zum Neuen Testament

Alphabetical Index of the First and Second Series

Böhlig, Alexander: Gnosis und Synkretismus. Vol. 1 1989. *Vol. 47* – Vol. 2 1989. *Vol. 48.*

Böhm, Martina: Samarien und die Samaritai bei Lukas. 1999. *Vol. II/111.*

Böttrich, Christfried: Weltweisheit – Menschheitsethik – Urkult. 1992. *Vol. II/50.*

Bolyki, János: Jesu Tischgemeinschaften. 1997. *Vol. II/96.*

Bosman, Philip: Conscience in Philo and Paul. 2003. *Vol. II/166.*

Bovon, François: Studies in Early Christianity. 2003. *Vol. 161.*

Brocke, Christoph vom: Thessaloniki – Stadt des Kassander und Gemeinde des Paulus. 2001. *Vol. II/125.*

Brunson, Andrew: Psalm 118 in the Gospel of John. 2003. *Vol. II/158.*

Büchli, Jörg: Der Poimandres – ein paganisiertes Evangelium. 1987. *Vol. II/27.*

Bühner, Jan A.: Der Gesandte und sein Weg im 4. Evangelium. 1977. *Vol. II/2.*

Burchard, Christoph: Untersuchungen zu Joseph und Aseneth. 1965. *Vol. 8.*

– Studien zur Theologie, Sprache und Umwelt des Neuen Testaments. Ed. by D. Sänger. 1998. *Vol. 107.*

Burnett, Richard: Karl Barth's Theological Exegesis. 2001. *Vol. II/145.*

Byron, John: Slavery Metaphors in Early Judaism and Pauline Christianity. 2003. *Vol. II/162.*

Byrskog, Samuel: Story as History – History as Story. 2000. *Vol. 123.*

Cancik, Hubert (Ed.): Markus-Philologie. 1984. *Vol. 33.*

Capes, David B.: Old Testament Yaweh Texts in Paul's Christology. 1992. *Vol. II/47.*

Caragounis, Chrys C.: The Development of Greek and the New Testament. 2004. *Vol. 167.*

– The Son of Man. 1986. *Vol. 38.*

– see *Fridrichsen, Anton.*

Carleton Paget, James: The Epistle of Barnabas. 1994. *Vol. II/64.*

Carson, D.A., O'Brien, Peter T. and *Mark Seifrid* (Ed.): Justification and Variegated Nomism.
Vol. 1: The Complexities of Second Temple Judaism. 2001. *Vol. II/140.*
Vol. 2: The Paradoxes of Paul. 2004. *Vol. II/181.*

Chae, Young Sam: Jesus as the Eschatological Davidic Shepherd. 2006. *Vol. II/216.*

Ciampa, Roy E.: The Presence and Function of Scripture in Galatians 1 and 2. 1998. *Vol. II/102.*

Classen, Carl Joachim: Rhetorical Criticsm of the New Testament. 2000. *Vol. 128.*

Colpe, Carsten: Iranier – Aramäer – Hebräer – Hellenen. 2003. *Vol. 154.*

Crump, David: Jesus the Intercessor. 1992. *Vol. II/49.*

Dahl, Nils Alstrup: Studies in Ephesians. 2000. *Vol. 131.*

Deines, Roland: Die Gerechtigkeit der Tora im Reich des Messias. 2004. *Vol. 177.*

– Jüdische Steingefäße und pharisäische Frömmigkeit. 1993. *Vol. II/52.*

– Die Pharisäer. 1997. *Vol. 101.*

Deines, Roland and *Karl-Wilhelm Niebuhr* (Ed.): Philo und das Neue Testament. 2004. *Vol. 172.*

Dennis, John A.: Jesus' Death and the Gathering of True Israel. 2006. *Vol. 217.*

Dettwiler, Andreas and *Jean Zumstein* (Ed.): Kreuzestheologie im Neuen Testament. 2002. *Vol. 151.*

Dickson, John P.: Mission-Commitment in Ancient Judaism and in the Pauline Communities. 2003. *Vol. II/159.*

Dietzfelbinger, Christian: Der Abschied des Kommenden. 1997. *Vol. 95.*

Dimitrov, Ivan Z., James D.G. Dunn, Ulrich Luz and *Karl-Wilhelm Niebuhr* (Ed.): Das Alte Testament als christliche Bibel in orthodoxer und westlicher Sicht. 2004. *Vol. 174.*

Dobbeler, Axel von: Glaube als Teilhabe. 1987. *Vol. II/22.*

Dryden, J. de Waal: Theology and Ethics in 1 Peter. 2006. *Vol. II/209.*

Du Toit, David S.: Theios Anthropos. 1997. *Vol. II/91.*

Dübbers, Michael: Christologie und Existenz im Kolosserbrief. 2005. *Vol. II/191.*

Dunn, James D.G.: The New Perspective on Paul. 2005. *Vol. 185.*

Dunn , James D.G. (Ed.): Jews and Christians. 1992. *Vol. 66.*

– Paul and the Mosaic Law. 1996. *Vol. 89.*

– see *Dimitrov, Ivan Z.*

–, *Hans Klein, Ulrich Luz* and *Vasile Mihoc* (Ed.): Auslegung der Bibel in orthodoxer und westlicher Perspektive. 2000. *Vol. 130.*

Ebel, Eva: Die Attraktivität früher christlicher Gemeinden. 2004. *Vol. II/178.*

Ebertz, Michael N.: Das Charisma des Gekreuzigten. 1987. *Vol. 45.*

Eckstein, Hans-Joachim: Der Begriff Syneidesis bei Paulus. 1983. *Vol. II/10.*

– Verheißung und Gesetz. 1996. *Vol. 86.*

Ego, Beate: Im Himmel wie auf Erden. 1989. *Vol. II/34.*

Ego, Beate, Armin Lange and *Peter Pilhofer* (Ed.): Gemeinde ohne Tempel – Community without Temple. 1999. *Vol. 118.*

– and *Helmut Merkel* (Ed.): Religiöses Lernen in der biblischen, frühjüdischen und frühchristlichen Überlieferung. 2005. *Vol. 180.*

Hartog, Paul: Polycarp and the New Testament. 2001. *Vol. II/134.*

Heckel, Theo K.: Der Innere Mensch. 1993. *Vol. II/53.*

– Vom Evangelium des Markus zum viergestaltigen Evangelium. 1999. *Vol. 120.*

Heckel, Ulrich: Kraft in Schwachheit. 1993. *Vol. II/56.*

– Der Segen im Neuen Testament. 2002. *Vol. 150.*

– see *Feldmeier, Reinhard.*

– see *Hengel, Martin.*

Heiligenthal, Roman: Werke als Zeichen. 1983. *Vol. II/9.*

Hellholm, D.: see *Hartman, Lars.*

Hemer, Colin J.: The Book of Acts in the Setting of Hellenistic History. 1989. *Vol. 49.*

Hengel, Martin: Judentum und Hellenismus. 1969, ³1988. *Vol. 10.*

– Die johanneische Frage. 1993. *Vol. 67.*

– Judaica et Hellenistica. Kleine Schriften I. 1996. *Vol. 90.*

– Judaica, Hellenistica et Christiana. Kleine Schriften II. 1999. *Vol. 109.*

– Paulus und Jakobus. Kleine Schriften III. 2002. *Vol. 141.*

– and *Anna Maria Schwemer:* Paulus zwischen Damaskus und Antiochien. 1998. *Vol. 108.*

– Der messianische Anspruch Jesu und die Anfänge der Christologie. 2001. *Vol. 138.*

Hengel, Martin and *Ulrich Heckel* (Ed.): Paulus und das antike Judentum. 1991. *Vol. 58.*

– and *Hermut Löhr* (Ed.): Schriftauslegung im antiken Judentum und im Urchristentum. 1994. *Vol. 73.*

– and *Anna Maria Schwemer* (Ed.): Königsherrschaft Gottes und himm-lischer Kult. 1991. *Vol. 55.*

– Die Septuaginta. 1994. *Vol. 72.*

–, *Siegfried Mittmann* and *Anna Maria Schwemer* (Ed.): La Cité de Dieu / Die Stadt Gottes. 2000. *Vol. 129.*

Hernández Jr., Juan: Scribal Habits and Theological Influence in the Apocalypse. 2006. *Vol. II/218.*

Herrenbrück, Fritz: Jesus und die Zöllner. 1990. *Vol. II/41.*

Herzer, Jens: Paulus oder Petrus? 1998. *Vol. 103.*

Hill, Charles E.: From the Lost Teaching of Polycarp. 2005. *Vol. 186.*

Hoegen-Rohls, Christina: Der nachösterliche Johannes. 1996. *Vol. II/84.*

Hoffmann, Matthias Reinhard: The Destroyer and the Lamb. 2005. *Vol. II/203.*

Hofius, Otfried: Katapausis. 1970. *Vol. 11.*

– Der Vorhang vor dem Thron Gottes. 1972. *Vol. 14.*

– Der Christushymnus Philipper 2,6-11. 1976, ²1991. *Vol. 17.*

– Paulusstudien. 1989, ²1994. *Vol. 51.*

– Neutestamentliche Studien. 2000. *Vol. 132.*

– Paulusstudien II. 2002. *Vol. 143.*

– and *Hans-Christian Kammler:* Johannesstudien. 1996. *Vol. 88.*

Holtz, Traugott: Geschichte und Theologie des Urchristentums. 1991. *Vol. 57.*

Hommel, Hildebrecht: Sebasmata. Vol. 1 1983. *Vol. 31.* Vol. 2 1984. *Vol. 32.*

Horbury, William: Herodian Judaism and New Testament Study. 2006. *Vol. 193.*

Horst, Pieter W. van der: Jews and Christians in Their Graeco-Roman Context. 2006. *Vol. 196.*

Hvalvik, Reidar: The Struggle for Scripture and Covenant. 1996. *Vol. II/82.*

Jauhiainen, Marko: The Use of Zechariah in Revelation. 2005. *Vol. II/199.*

Jensen, Morten H.: Herod Antipas in Galilee. 2006. *Vol. II/215.*

Johns, Loren L.: The Lamb Christology of the Apocalypse of John. 2003. *Vol. II/167.*

Jossa, Giorgio: Jews or Christians? 2006. *Vol. 202.*

Joubert, Stephan: Paul as Benefactor. 2000. *Vol. II/124.*

Jungbauer, Harry: „Ehre Vater und Mutter". 2002. *Vol. II/146.*

Kähler, Christoph: Jesu Gleichnisse als Poesie und Therapie. 1995. *Vol. 78.*

Kamlah, Ehrhard: Die Form der katalogischen Paränese im Neuen Testament. 1964. *Vol. 7.*

Kammler, Hans-Christian: Christologie und Eschatologie. 2000. *Vol. 126.*

– Kreuz und Weisheit. 2003. *Vol. 159.*

– see *Hofius, Otfried.*

Kelhoffer, James A.: The Diet of John the Baptist. 2005. *Vol. 176.*

– Miracle and Mission. 1999. *Vol. II/112.*

Kelley, Nicole: Knowledge and Religious Authority in the Pseudo-Clementines. 2006. *Vol. II/213.*

Kieffer, René and *Jan Bergman (Ed.):* La Main de Dieu / Die Hand Gottes. 1997. *Vol. 94.*

Kierspel, Lars: The Jews and the World in the Fourth Gospel. 2006. *Vol. 220.*

Kim, Seyoon: The Origin of Paul's Gospel. 1981, ²1984. *Vol. II/4.*

– Paul and the New Perspective. 2002. *Vol. 140.*

– "The 'Son of Man'" as the Son of God. 1983. *Vol. 30.*

Klauck, Hans-Josef: Religion und Gesellschaft im frühen Christentum. 2003. *Vol. 152.*

Klein, Hans: see *Dunn, James D.G.*

Kleinknecht, Karl Th.: Der leidende Gerecht-fertigte. 1984, ²1988. *Vol. II/13.*

Klinghardt, Matthias: Gesetz und Volk Gottes. 1988. *Vol. II/32.*

Kloppenborg, John S.: The Tenants in the Vineyard. 2006. *Vol. 195.*

Koch, Michael: Drachenkampf und Sonnen-frau. 2004. *Vol. II/184.*

Koch, Stefan: Rechtliche Regelung von Kon-flikten im frühen Christentum. 2004. *Vol. II/174.*

Köhler, Wolf-Dietrich: Rezeption des Matthäusevangeliums in der Zeit vor Irenäus. 1987. *Vol. II/24.*

Köhn, Andreas: Der Neutestamentler Ernst Lohmeyer. 2004. *Vol. II/180.*

Kooten, George H. van: Cosmic Christology in Paul and the Pauline School. 2003. *Vol. II/171.*

Korn, Manfred: Die Geschichte Jesu in verän-derter Zeit. 1993. *Vol. II/51.*

Koskenniemi, Erkki: Apollonios von Tyana in der neutestamentlichen Exegese. 1994. *Vol. II/61.*

– The Old Testament Miracle-Workers in Early Judaism. 2005. *Vol. II/206.*

Kraus, Thomas J.: Sprache, Stil und histori-scher Ort des zweiten Petrusbriefes. 2001. *Vol. II/136.*

Kraus, Wolfgang: Das Volk Gottes. 1996. *Vol. 85.*

Kraus, Wolfgang and *Karl-Wilhelm Niebuhr* (Ed.): Frühjudentum und Neues Testament im Horizont Biblischer Theologie. 2003. *Vol. 162.*

– see *Walter, Nikolaus.*

Kreplin, Matthias: Das Selbstverständnis Jesu. 2001. *Vol. II/141.*

Kuhn, Karl G.: Achtzehngebet und Vaterunser und der Reim. 1950. *Vol. 1.*

Kvalbein, Hans: see *Ådna, Jostein.*

Kwon, Yon-Gyong: Eschatology in Galatians. 2004. *Vol. II/183.*

Laansma, Jon: I Will Give You Rest. 1997. *Vol. II/98.*

Labahn, Michael: Offenbarung in Zeichen und Wort. 2000. *Vol. II/117.*

Lambers-Petry, Doris: see *Tomson, Peter J.*

Lange, Armin: see *Ego, Beate.*

Lampe, Peter: Die stadtrömischen Christen in den ersten beiden Jahrhunderten. 1987, ²1989. *Vol. II/18.*

Landmesser, Christof: Wahrheit als Grundbe-griff neutestamentlicher Wissenschaft. 1999. *Vol. 113.*

– Jüngerberufung und Zuwendung zu Gott. 2000. *Vol. 133.*

Lau, Andrew: Manifest in Flesh. 1996. *Vol. II/86.*

Lawrence, Louise: An Ethnography of the Gospel of Matthew. 2003. *Vol. II/165.*

Lee, Aquila H.I.: From Messiah to Preexistent Son. 2005. *Vol. II/192.*

Lee, Pilchan: The New Jerusalem in the Book of Relevation. 2000. *Vol. II/129.*

Lichtenberger, Hermann: Das Ich Adams und das Ich der Menschheit. 2004. *Vol. 164.*

– see *Avemarie, Friedrich.*

Lierman, John: The New Testament Moses. 2004. *Vol. II/173.*

– (Ed.): Challenging Perspectives on the Gospel of John. 2006. *Vol. II/219.*

Lieu, Samuel N.C.: Manichaeism in the Later Roman Empire and Medieval China. ²1992. *Vol. 63.*

Lindgård, Fredrik: Paul's Line of Thought in 2 Corinthians 4:16-5:10. 2004. *Vol. II/189.*

Loader, William R.G.: Jesus' Attitude Towards the Law. 1997. *Vol. II/97.*

Löhr, Gebhard: Verherrlichung Gottes durch Philosophie. 1997. *Vol. 97.*

Löhr, Hermut: Studien zum frühchristlichen und frühjüdischen Gebet. 2003. *Vol. 160.*

– see *Hengel, Martin.*

Löhr, Winrich Alfried: Basilides und seine Schu-le. 1995. *Vol. 83.*

Luomanen, Petri: Entering the Kingdom of Heaven. 1998. *Vol. II/101.*

Luz, Ulrich: see *Dunn, James D.G.*

Mackay, Ian D.: John's Raltionship with Mark. 2004. *Vol. II/182.*

Maier, Gerhard: Mensch und freier Wille. 1971. *Vol. 12.*

– Die Johannesoffenbarung und die Kirche. 1981. *Vol. 25.*

Markschies, Christoph: Valentinus Gnosticus? 1992. *Vol. 65.*

Marshall, Peter: Enmity in Corinth: Social Conventions in Paul's Relations with the Corinthians. 1987. *Vol. II/23.*

Mayer, Annemarie: Sprache der Einheit im Epheserbrief und in der Ökumene. 2002. *Vol. II/150.*

Mayordomo, Moisés: Argumentiert Paulus logisch? 2005. *Vol. 188.*

McDonough, Sean M.: YHWH at Patmos: Rev. 1:4 in its Hellenistic and Early Jewish Setting. 1999. *Vol. II/107.*

McDowell, Markus: Prayers of Jewish Women. 2006. *Vol. II/211.*

McGlynn, Moyna: Divine Judgement and Divine Benevolence in the Book of Wisdom. 2001. *Vol. II/139.*

Meade, David G.: Pseudonymity and Canon. 1986. *Vol. 39.*

Meadors, Edward P.: Jesus the Messianic Herald of Salvation. 1995. *Vol. II/72.*

Meißner, Stefan: Die Heimholung des Ketzers. 1996. *Vol. II/87.*

Mell, Ulrich: Die „anderen" Winzer. 1994. *Vol. 77.*

– see *Sänger, Dieter.*
Mengel, Berthold: Studien zum Philipperbrief. 1982. *Vol. II/8.*
Merkel, Helmut: Die Widersprüche zwischen den Evangelien. 1971. *Vol. 13.*
– see *Ego, Beate.*
Merklein, Helmut: Studien zu Jesus und Paulus. Vol. 1 1987. *Vol. 43.* – Vol. 2 1998. *Vol. 105.*
Metzdorf, Christina: Die Tempelaktion Jesu. 2003. *Vol. II/168.*
Metzler, Karin: Der griechische Begriff des Verzeihens. 1991. *Vol. II/44.*
Metzner, Rainer: Die Rezeption des Matthäusevangeliums im 1. Petrusbrief. 1995. *Vol. II/74.*
– Das Verständnis der Sünde im Johannesevangelium. 2000. *Vol. 122.*
Mihoc, Vasile: see *Dunn, James D.G..*
Mineshige, Kiyoshi: Besitzverzicht und Almosen bei Lukas. 2003. *Vol. II/163.*
Mittmann, Siegfried: see *Hengel, Martin.*
Mittmann-Richert, Ulrike: Magnifikat und Benediktus. *1996. Vol. II/90.*
Mournet, Terence C.: Oral Tradition and Literary Dependency. 2005. *Vol. II/195.*
Mußner, Franz: Jesus von Nazareth im Umfeld Israels und der Urkirche. Ed. von M. Theobald. 1998. *Vol. 111.*
Mutschler, Bernhard: Das Corpus Johanneum bei Irenäus von Lyon. 2005. *Vol. 189.*
Niebuhr, Karl-Wilhelm: Gesetz und Paränese. 1987. *Vol. II/28.*
– Heidenapostel aus Israel. 1992. *Vol. 62.*
– see *Deines, Roland*
– see *Dimitrov, Ivan Z.*
– see *Kraus, Wolfgang*
Nielsen, Anders E.: "Until it is Fullfilled". 2000. *Vol. II/126.*
Nissen, Andreas: Gott und der Nächste im antiken Judentum. 1974. *Vol. 15.*
Noack, Christian: Gottesbewußtsein. 2000. *Vol. II/116.*
Noormann, Rolf: Irenäus als Paulusinterpret. 1994. *Vol. II/66.*
Novakovic, Lidija: Messiah, the Healer of the Sick. 2003. *Vol. II/170.*
Obermann, Andreas: Die christologische Erfüllung der Schrift im Johannesevangelium. 1996. *Vol. II/83.*
Öhler, Markus: Barnabas. 2003. *Vol. 156.*
– see *Becker, Michael*
Okure, Teresa: The Johannine Approach to Mission. 1988. *Vol. II/31.*
Onuki, Takashi: Heil und Erlösung. 2004. *Vol. 165.*
Oropeza, B. J.: Paul and Apostasy. 2000. *Vol. II/115.*
Ostmeyer, Karl-Heinrich: Kommunikation mit Gott und Christus. 2006. *Vol. 197.*
– Taufe und Typos. 2000. *Vol. II/118.*

Paulsen, Henning: Studien zur Literatur und Geschichte des frühen Christentums. Ed. von Ute E. Eisen. 1997. *Vol. 99.*
Pao, David W.: Acts and the Isaianic New Exodus. 2000. *Vol. II/130.*
Park, Eung Chun: The Mission Discourse in Matthew's Interpretation. 1995. *Vol. II/81.*
Park, Joseph S.: Conceptions of Afterlife in Jewish Insriptions. 2000. *Vol. II/121.*
Pate, C. Marvin: The Reverse of the Curse. 2000. *Vol. II/114.*
Peres, Imre: Griechische Grabinschriften und neutestamentliche Eschatologie. 2003. *Vol. 157.*
Philip, Finny: The Origins of Pauline Pneumatology. 2005. *Vol. II/194.*
Philonenko, Marc (Ed.): Le Trône de Dieu. 1993. *Vol. 69.*
Pilhofer, Peter: Presbyteron Kreitton. 1990. *Vol. II/39.*
– Philippi. Vol. 1 1995. *Vol. 87.* – Vol. 2 2000. *Vol. 119.*
– Die frühen Christen und ihre Welt. 2002. *Vol. 145.*
– see *Becker, Eve-Marie.*
– see *Ego, Beate.*
Pitre, Brant: Jesus, the Tribulation, and the End of the Exile. 2005. *Vol. II/204.*
Plümacher, Eckhard: Geschichte und Geschichten. 2004. *Vol. 170.*
Pöhlmann, Wolfgang: Der Verlorene Sohn und das Haus. 1993. *Vol. 68.*
Pokorný, Petr and *Josef B. Souček:* Bibelauslegung als Theologie. 1997. *Vol. 100.*
Pokorný, Petr and *Jan Roskovec* (Ed.): Philosophical Hermeneutics and Biblical Exegesis. 2002. *Vol. 153.*
Popkes, Enno Edzard: Die Theologie der Liebe Gottes in den johanneischen Schriften. 2005. *Vol. II/197.*
Porter, Stanley E.: The Paul of Acts. 1999. *Vol. 115.*
Prieur, Alexander: Die Verkündigung der Gottesherrschaft. 1996. *Vol. II/89.*
Probst, Hermann: Paulus und der Brief. 1991. *Vol. II/45.*
Räisänen, Heikki: Paul and the Law. 1983, ²1987. *Vol. 29.*
Rehkopf, Friedrich: Die lukanische Sonderquelle. 1959. *Vol. 5.*
Rein, Matthias: Die Heilung des Blindgeborenen (Joh 9). 1995. *Vol. II/73.*
Reinmuth, Eckart: Pseudo-Philo und Lukas. 1994. *Vol. 74.*
Reiser, Marius: Syntax und Stil des Markusevangeliums. 1984. *Vol. II/11.*
Rhodes, James N.: The Epistle of Barnabas and the Deuteronomic Tradition. 2004. *Vol. II/188.*

Richards, E. Randolph: The Secretary in the Letters of Paul. 1991. *Vol. II/42.*

Riesner, Rainer: Jesus als Lehrer. 1981, ³1988. *Vol. II/7.*

– Die Frühzeit des Apostels Paulus. 1994. *Vol. 71.*

Rissi, Mathias: Die Theologie des Hebräerbriefs. 1987. *Vol. 41.*

Roskovec, Jan: see *Pokorný, Petr.*

Röhser, Günter: Metaphorik und Personifikation der Sünde. 1987. *Vol. II/25.*

Rose, Christian: Die Wolke der Zeugen. 1994. *Vol. II/60.*

Rothschild, Clare K.: Baptist Traditions and Q. 2005. *Vol. 190.*

– Luke Acts and the Rhetoric of History. 2004. *Vol. II/175.*

Rüegger, Hans-Ulrich: Verstehen, was Markus erzählt. 2002. *Vol. II/155.*

Rüger, Hans Peter: Die Weisheitsschrift aus der Kairoer Geniza. 1991. *Vol. 53.*

Sänger, Dieter: Antikes Judentum und die Mysterien. 1980. *Vol. II/5.*

– Die Verkündigung des Gekreuzigten und Israel. 1994. *Vol. 75.*

– see *Burchard, Christoph*

– and *Ulrich Mell* (Hrsg.): Paulus und Johannes. 2006. *Vol. 198.*

Salier, Willis Hedley: The Rhetorical Impact of the Semeia in the Gospel of John. 2004. *Vol. II/186.*

Salzmann, Jorg Christian: Lehren und Ermahnen. 1994. *Vol. II/59.*

Sandnes, Karl Olav: Paul – One of the Prophets? 1991. *Vol. II/43.*

Sato, Migaku: Q und Prophetie. 1988. *Vol. II/29.*

Schäfer, Ruth: Paulus bis zum Apostelkonzil. 2004. *Vol. II/179.*

Schaper, Joachim: Eschatology in the Greek Psalter. 1995. *Vol. II/76.*

Schimanowski, Gottfried: Die himmlische Liturgie in der Apokalypse des Johannes. 2002. *Vol. II/154.*

– Weisheit und Messias. 1985. *Vol. II/17.*

Schlichting, Günter: Ein jüdisches Leben Jesu. 1982. *Vol. 24.*

Schnabel, Eckhard J.: Law and Wisdom from Ben Sira to Paul. 1985. *Vol. II/16.*

Schnelle, Udo: see *Frey, Jörg.*

Schröter, Jens: see *Frey, Jörg.*

Schutter, William L.: Hermeneutic and Composition in I Peter. 1989. *Vol. II/30.*

Schwartz, Daniel R.: Studies in the Jewish Background of Christianity. 1992. *Vol. 60.*

Schwemer, Anna Maria: see *Hengel, Martin*

Scott, Ian W.: Implicit Epistemology in the Letters of Paul. 2005. *Vol. II/205.*

Scott, James M.: Adoption as Sons of God. 1992. *Vol. II/48.*

– Paul and the Nations. 1995. *Vol. 84.*

Shum, Shiu-Lun: Paul's Use of Isaiah in Romans. 2002. *Vol. II/156.*

Siegert, Folker: Drei hellenistisch-jüdische Predigten. Teil I 1980. *Vol. 20* – Teil II 1992. *Vol. 61.*

– Nag-Hammadi-Register. 1982. *Vol. 26.*

– Argumentation bei Paulus. 1985. *Vol. 34.*

– Philon von Alexandrien. 1988. *Vol. 46.*

Simon, Marcel: Le christianisme antique et son contexte religieux I/II. 1981. *Vol. 23.*

Snodgrass, Klyne: The Parable of the Wicked Tenants. 1983. *Vol. 27.*

Söding, Thomas: Das Wort vom Kreuz. 1997. *Vol. 93.*

– see *Thüsing, Wilhelm.*

Sommer, Urs: Die Passionsgeschichte des Markusevangeliums. 1993. *Vol. II/58.*

Souèek, Josef B.: see *Pokorný, Petr.*

Spangenberg, Volker: Herrlichkeit des Neuen Bundes. 1993. *Vol. II/55.*

Spanje, T.E. van: Inconsistency in Paul? 1999. *Vol. II/110.*

Speyer, Wolfgang: Frühes Christentum im antiken Strahlungsfeld. Vol. I: 1989. *Vol. 50.*

– Vol. II: 1999. *Vol. 116.*

Stadelmann, Helge: Ben Sira als Schriftgelehrter. 1980. *Vol. II/6.*

Stenschke, Christoph W.: Luke's Portrait of Gentiles Prior to Their Coming to Faith. *Vol. II/108.*

Sterck-Degueldre, Jean-Pierre: Eine Frau namens Lydia. 2004. *Vol. II/176.*

Stettler, Christian: Der Kolosserhymnus. 2000. *Vol. II/131.*

Stettler, Hanna: Die Christologie der Pastoralbriefe. 1998. *Vol. II/105.*

Stökl Ben Ezra, Daniel: The Impact of Yom Kippur on Early Christianity. 2003. *Vol. 163.*

Strobel, August: Die Stunde der Wahrheit. 1980. *Vol. 21.*

Stroumsa, Guy G.: Barbarian Philosophy. 1999. *Vol. 112.*

Stuckenbruck, Loren T.: Angel Veneration and Christology. 1995. *Vol. II/70.*

Stuhlmacher, Peter (Ed.): Das Evangelium und die Evangelien. 1983. *Vol. 28.*

– Biblische Theologie und Evangelium. 2002. *Vol. 146.*

Sung, Chong-Hyon: Vergebung der Sünden. 1993. *Vol. II/57.*

Tajra, Harry W.: The Trial of St. Paul. 1989. *Vol. II/35.*

– The Martyrdom of St. Paul. 1994. *Vol. II/67.*

Theißen, Gerd: Studien zur Soziologie des Urchristentums. 1979, ³1989. *Vol. 19.*

Theobald, Michael: Studien zum Römerbrief. 2001. *Vol. 136.*

Theobald, Michael: see *Mußner, Franz.*

Thornton, Claus-Jürgen: Der Zeuge des Zeugen. 1991. *Vol. 56.*
Thüsing, Wilhelm: Studien zur neutestamentlichen Theologie. Ed. von Thomas Söding. 1995. *Vol. 82.*
Thurén, Lauri: Derhethorizing Paul. 2000. *Vol. 124.*
Tolmie, D. Francois: Persuading the Galatians. 2005. *Vol. II/190.*
Tomson, Peter J. and *Doris Lambers-Petry* (Ed.): The Image of the Judaeo-Christians in Ancient Jewish and Christian Literature. 2003. *Vol. 158.*
Trebilco, Paul: The Early Christians in Ephesus from Paul to Ignatius. 2004. *Vol. 166.*
Treloar, Geoffrey R.: Lightfoot the Historian. 1998. *Vol. II/103.*
Tsuji, Manabu: Glaube zwischen Vollkommenheit und Verweltlichung. 1997. *Vol. II/93.*
Twelftree, Graham H.: Jesus the Exorcist. 1993. *Vol. II/54.*
Urban, Christina: Das Menschenbild nach dem Johannesevangelium. 2001. *Vol. II/137.*
Visotzky, Burton L.: Fathers of the World. 1995. *Vol. 80.*
Vollenweider, Samuel: Horizonte neutestamentlicher Christologie. 2002. *Vol. 144.*
Vos, Johan S.: Die Kunst der Argumentation bei Paulus. 2002. *Vol. 149.*
Wagener, Ulrike: Die Ordnung des „Hauses Gottes". 1994. *Vol. II/65.*
Wahlen, Clinton: Jesus and the Impurity of Spirits in the Synoptic Gospels. 2004. *Vol. II/185.*
Walker, Donald D.: Paul's Offer of Leniency (2 Cor 10:1). 2002. *Vol. II/152.*
Walter, Nikolaus: Praeparatio Evangelica. Ed. von Wolfgang Kraus und Florian Wilk. 1997. *Vol. 98.*
Wander, Bernd: Gottesfürchtige und Sympathisanten. 1998. *Vol. 104.*
Watt, Jan G. van der: see *Frey, Jörg*
Watts, Rikki: Isaiah's New Exodus and Mark. 1997. *Vol. II/88.*
Wedderburn, A.J.M.: Baptism and Resurrection. 1987. *Vol. 44.*

Wegner, Uwe: Der Hauptmann von Kafarnaum. 1985. *Vol. II/14.*
Weissenrieder, Annette: Images of Illness in the Gospel of Luke. 2003. Vol. II/164.
–, *Friederike Wendt* and *Petra von Gemünden* (Ed.): Picturing the New Testament. 2005. *Vol. II/193.*
Welck, Christian: Erzählte ‚Zeichen'. 1994. *Vol. II/69.*
Wendt, Friederike (Ed.): see *Weissenrieder, Annette.*
Wiarda, Timothy: Peter in the Gospels. 2000. *Vol. II/127.*
Wifstrand, Albert: Epochs and Styles. 2005. *Vol. 179.*
Wilk, Florian: see *Walter, Nikolaus.*
Williams, Catrin H.: I am He. 2000. *Vol. II/113.*
Wilson, Walter T.: Love without Pretense. 1991. *Vol. II/46.*
Wischmeyer, Oda: Von Ben Sira zu Paulus. 2004. *Vol. 173.*
Wisdom, Jeffrey: Blessing for the Nations and the Curse of the Law. 2001. *Vol. II/133.*
Wold, Benjamin G.: Women, Men, and Angels. 2005. *Vol. II/2001.*
Wright, Archie T.: The Origin of Evil Spirits. 2005. *Vol. II/198.*
Wucherpfennig, Ansgar: Heracleon Philologus. 2002. *Vol. 142.*
Yeung, Maureen: Faith in Jesus and Paul. 2002. *Vol. II/147.*
Zimmermann, Alfred E.: Die urchristlichen Lehrer. 1984, ²1988. *Vol. II/12.*
Zimmermann, Johannes: Messianische Texte aus Qumran. 1998. *Vol. II/104.*
Zimmermann, Ruben: Christologie der Bilder im Johannesevangelium. 2004. *Vol. 171.*
– Geschlechtermetaphorik und Gottesverhältnis. 2001. *Vol. II/122.*
– see *Frey, Jörg*
Zumstein, Jean: see *Dettwiler, Andreas*
Zwiep, Arie W.: Judas and the Choice of Matthias. 2004. *Vol. II/187.*

For a complete catalogue please write to the publisher
Mohr Siebeck • P.O. Box 2030 • D–72010 Tübingen/Germany
Up-to-date information on the internet at www.mohr.de

2016.01.04   90.00